BRANDING YOURSELF

How to Use Social Media to Invent or
Reinvent Yourself

Third Edition

ERIK DECKERS
KYLE LACY

Branding Yourself, Third Edition

ISBN-13: 978-0-7897-5901-6

ISBN-10: 0-7897-5901-2

Library of Congress Control Number: 2017953923

Printed in the United States of America

1   17

Trademarks

Editor-in-Chief
Greg Wiegand

Senior Acquisitions Editor
Laura Norman

Managing Editor
Sandra Schroeder

Development Editor
Leslie O'Neill

Project Editor
Lori Lyons

Copy Editor
Larry Sulky

Project Manager
Dhayanidhi Karunanidhi

Cover Designer
Chuti Prasertsith

CONTENTS AT A GLANCE

I Why Should I Care About Self-Promotion?   1

   1   Welcome to the Party..3
   2   How Do You Fit in the Mix?...21

II Your Network Is Your Castle—Build It   41

   3   Blogging: Telling Your Story..43
   4   LinkedIn: Networking on Steroids.......................................75
   5   Twitter: Sharing in the Conversation..................................95
   6   Facebook: Developing a Community of Friends....................119
   7   Say Cheese: Sharing Photos and Videos.............................141
   8   Other Social Networking Tools...169
   9   Googling Yourself: Finding Yourself on Search Engines........183
  10   Bringing It All Together: Launching Your Brand..................205
  11   Measuring Success: You Like Me, You Really Like Me!..........225

III Promoting Your Brand in the Real World   247

  12   How to Network: "Hello, My Name Is..."............................249
  13   Public Speaking: We Promise You Won't Die.....................283
  14   Getting Published: "I'm an Author!".................................311
  15   Personal Branding: Using What You've Learned to
       Land Your Dream Job...335

       Index..361

TABLE OF CONTENTS

I   WHY SHOULD I CARE ABOUT SELF-PROMOTION? 1

1   Welcome to the Party   **3**

What Is Self-Promotion? 4

Why Is Self-Promotion Important? 5

What Self-Promotion Is Not 5

What Can Self-Promotion Do for You and
Your Career? 5

Personal Branding 6

What Is Personal Branding? 7

Go Brand Yourself 7

How to Build Your Brand 8

Personal Branding Case Study: Mignon Fogarty,
Grammar Girl 8

The Five Universal Objectives of Personal Branding 11

1. Discover Your Passion 11

2. Be Bold 12

3. Tell Your Story 14

4. Create Relationships 15

5. Take Action 16

Who Needs Self-Promotion? 17

Meet Our Heroes 19

2   How Do You Fit in the Mix?   **21**

The Basics of Building Your Personal Brand Story 22

Writing Your Personal Brand Story 23

Prioritize Accomplishments 23

Writing Your Personal Brand Biography 24

How Do Our Heroes Use the Personal
Brand Biography? 27

Personal Branding Case Study: Park Howell 29

Telling Your Complete Brand Story 31

The Law of Anecdotal Value 33

Surround Yourself with Passionate People 34

Sharing Memories and Stories 34

Ten Do's and Don'ts of Telling Your Story 35

  1. Don't Post Pictures that Would Shock
    Your Mother 36

  2. Don't View Your Personal Brand Story as a
    Sales Pitch 36

  3. Don't Post Something You'll Regret 36

  4. Don't Ask for Things First; Ask for
    Things Second 37

  5. Don't Get Distracted 37

  6. Don't Underestimate the Power of Your Network 38

  7. Do Invest in Yourself 38

  8. Do Invest in Other People 38

  9. Do Be Visible and Active 38

  10. Do Take Some Time for Yourself 39

II YOUR NETWORK IS YOUR CASTLE—BUILD IT 41

3 Blogging: Telling Your Story   43

What Is Blogging? 44

  A Clarification of Terms 46

  Why Should You Blog? 46

Personal Branding Case Study: Jonathan Thomas,
Anglotopia.com 49

Choose Your Blogging Platforms 50

  Blogspot.com/Blogger.com 51

  WordPress.com and WordPress.org 52

  Other Blogging Platforms 53

  Which Platform Is Right for You? 56

Setting Up a Blog 56

  Purchasing and Hosting a Domain Name 57

Getting Inspired 58

  What Should You Write About? 59

  Finding Subject Matter 61

  How to Write a Blog Post 62

Writing for Readers vs. Writing for Search Engines 64

  It's About the Quality of the Writing 64

  Google Expects You to Write Good Stuff 64

How Often Should You Post? 66

How Long Should Your Posts Be? 66
But My Posts Are Too Long! 68
SEO Through Blogging 69
How Does This Apply to Our Four Heroes? 70
The Do's and Don'ts of Blogging 71
Do's 72
Don'ts 73
A Final Note on the Rules of Blogging 74

4 LinkedIn: Networking on Steroids   75

The Basics of LinkedIn 76
What Are Degrees of Connectedness? 77
What's in a LinkedIn Profile? 77
Cool LinkedIn Features for Personal Branding 82
Making Contacts on LinkedIn 83
Transforming Your Contacts into Connections 86
The Importance of Recommendations 87
Personal Branding Case Study: Anthony Juliano 89
Ten Do's and Don'ts of LinkedIn 91
1. Do Upload a Professional Picture 91
2. Do Connect to Your Real Friends and Contacts 92
3. Do Keep Your Profile Current 92
4. Do Delete People Who Spam You 93
5. Do Make Your Summary Look Its Best 93
6. Don't Use LinkedIn Like Facebook and Twitter 93
7. Don't Sync LinkedIn with Twitter 93
8. Don't Decline Invitations—Archive Them 94
9. Don't Ask Everyone for Recommendations 94
10. Don't Forget to Use Spelling and
Grammar Check 94

5 Twitter: Sharing in the Conversation   95

Why Should You Use Twitter? 96
What Can Twitter Do for You? 97
Personal Branding Case Study: @HaggardHawks 99
How Do You Use Twitter? 103
Creating a Twitter Profile 103
Finding Followers 104

Sending Out Tweets 105

Retweeting Content 106

Applications for Twitter Domination 107

What Should You Tweet (and Not Tweet)? 111

Personal Branding Case Study: @MuslimIQ 113

Seven Do's and Don'ts While Using Twitter 115

Twitter Tips in 140 Characters or Less 116

How Should Our Four Heroes Use Twitter? 117

6   Facebook: Developing a Community of Friends   119

Why Should You Use Facebook? 120

What Can Facebook Do for You? 122

Reconnect with Old Classmates and Coworkers 122

Professionally Brand Yourself 122

Be Philanthropic 123

Find Local Events 123

What You Should Know About Facebook 124

Professional Page vs. Personal Profile 124

The Basics: Creating a Personal Profile 126

Stay in Control of Your Profile 127

Your Personal Page Privacy Settings 127

Setting Up Your Privacy Settings for Your
Personal Account 128

Working with Your Customized URL 130

Using a Professional Page for Personal Branding 131

Using Insights to Track Your Content Growth 133

Setting Up Your Professional Page 134

Top Four Tips for Using Facebook 135

Ten Do's and Don'ts of Facebook 136

Facebook Tips in 140 Characters or Less 139

7   Say Cheese: Sharing Photos and Videos   141

Why Video 142

Where to Put Your Videos 144

Shooting Video With Regular Digital Cameras 148

Recording Screen Capture Videos 149

Personal Branding Case Study: Lynn Ferguson &
Mark Tweddle 149

What Should I Make Videos Of? 151

Why Post Photos? 152

Where to Post Your Photos 152

Copyright: Understanding Creative Commons 156

Creative Commons 157

Embedding Videos and Photos in Your Blog 158

Adding Photos 158

Adding Videos 161

SEO for Videos and Photos 162

YouTube SEO 162

Photo SEO 164

The Video Résumé 165

A Cautionary Note About Video Résumés 167

Photos and Video Tips in 140 Characters 168

8   Other Social Networking Tools   169

Google+ 170

Quora 171

Meetup.com 173

Email Newsletters 175

Podcasts 176

Listen to Podcasts 176

Why Podcast? 176

What Do You Need? 177

What Should Your Podcast be About? 177

Producing the Podcast 178

Personal Branding Case Study: John J. Wall, Marketing
Over Coffee Podcast 179

How Does This Apply to Our Four Heroes? 180

**9   Googling Yourself: Finding Yourself on
Search Engines   183**

Have You Ever Googled Yourself? 184

What Do You Want Others to Find? 185

Search Engine Optimization 187

What SEO Used To Be 187

What SEO Looks Like Now 189

How Can You Influence These Factors? 191

Add Video 194

Reverse Search Engine Optimization 195

What if You Share a Common Name? 196

Search Engine Tools 198

Google Alerts 198

TalkWalker.com 198

Google Image Search 199

Bing 199

Yahoo! 200

The Value of Reputation Management 200

Reputation Management Tools 201

How Do Our Heroes Use SEO? 202

Reputation Management Tips in 140 Characters 203

10   Bringing It All Together: Launching Your Brand   205

What Is a Personal Brand Campaign? 206

How Do Our Heroes Build Their P&T Statements? 208

Why Is a Personal Brand Campaign Important? 211

Personal Branding Case Study: Sheryl Brown 212

Building Your Personal Brand Campaign 214

Developing Your Personal Brand Campaign 214

Implementing Your Personal Brand Campaign 215

Automating Your Personal Brand Campaign 217

Unique Ways to Launch Your Branding Campaign 218

How Should Our Heroes Launch Their Brands? 221

Do's and Don'ts of Launching Your Personal Brand 221

**11   Measuring Success: You Like Me,
You Really Like Me!   225**

Why Should You Measure? 226

What Should You Measure? 227

Reach 227

Engagement 227

Quality versus Quantity 228

Visibility 229

Influence 229

How Should You Measure? 231

Measuring Your Blogging Effectiveness 231

Using Google Analytics for Your Blog 232

Setting Up a Google Analytics Account 233

Installing Google Analytics 234

Getting an Overview of Your Website Performance 235

Measuring Your Twitter Effectiveness 237

Measuring Your Facebook Effectiveness 239

Measuring Your LinkedIn Effectiveness 239

Measuring Your YouTube Effectiveness 240

Four More Measurement Tools 242

Effectively Measuring Your Personal Brand 243

How Can Our Heroes Use Analytics and
Measurement? 244

Do's and Don'ts for Analytics and
Measurement 245

Analytics Tips in 140 Characters 245

III　PROMOTING YOUR BRAND IN THE REAL WORLD......247

12　How to Network: "Hello, My Name Is..."　　249

Why Should I Bother Networking? 250

Personal Branding Case Study: Starla West 251

The Rules of Networking 252

It's Not About You 252

Giver's Gain Is Not Quid Pro Quo 254

Be Honest Online and Offline 256

You're Just as Good as Everyone Else 257

Avoid Selfish People 258

Network with Your Competition 258

Personal Branding Case Study: Hazel Walker 260

Three Types of Networking 261

Networking Groups 261

Meeting New People 262

The Networking Dance 262

What Should You Say? 263

Networking Faux Pas 264

    Don't Deal Your Own Cards 264

    Don't Use Clever Elevator Pitches 265

    Don't Sign People Up for Your
    Newsletter 266

After the Meeting 266

One-on-One Networking 267

    How to Set Up the One-On-One
    Networking Meeting 267

    What to Talk About 268

    No One Wants a Sales Pitch 270

    The "Pick-Your-Brain" Meeting 270

How to Make an Email Introduction 272

The Follow-Up 274

    Forwarding Articles and Links 274

    Sharing Opportunities 275

    Making Connections 275

But I Just Don't Want to Meet the Other Person ... 276

    Be Honest 276

    What if the Other Person Isn't Honest? 277

Personal Branding Case Study: Dave Delaney 278

Network While You Still Have a Job 279

Don't Discount Serendipity 279

Do's and Don'ts of Networking 280

    Do 280

    Don't 281

How Would Our Heroes Network? 281

13   Public Speaking: We Promise You Won't Die   283

Should You Speak in Public? 284

    No, Seriously 284

    But You Hate Speaking in Public 284

Overcoming Your Fear of Public Speaking 285

    Toastmasters 285

    Classes at Your Local College or University ... 286

    Seminars and Courses 286

    Speakers Associations 287

    Private or Executive Coaches 287

Personal Branding Case Study: Lorraine Ball 287

Finding Your Speaking Niche 289

How to Launch Your Speaking Career 291

    Identify Speaking Opportunities 292

    Industry Groups 293

    Civic Groups 295

    Conferences, Trade Shows, and Expos 295

    Introducing Yourself 297

    Promoting Your Talk 298

Personal Branding Case Study: Crystal Washington 300

Giving Your Talk 301

Important Technology Tips for Presenters 303

How Does Public Speaking Apply to
Our Four Heroes? 307

Speaking Tips in 140 Characters 308

14 Getting Published: "I'm an Author!"   311

Why Should I Become a Published Writer? 313

Personal Branding Case Study: Jackie Bledsoe 314

Finding Publishing Opportunities 316

    Local Newspapers 317

    Business Newspapers 318

    Specialty Magazines and Newspapers 319

    Hobby Publications 320

    Major Mainstream Magazines 321

    Go Horizontal Instead of Vertical 321

Build Your Personal Brand with Your Writing 322

Publication Rights 324

Create Your Own Articles' Niche 325

Getting Started 326

Getting Paid 328

    Paying Your Dues 329

    The Myth of Exposure 329

The Do's and Don'ts of Writing for Publication 330

How Can Our Heroes Turn to Writing for
Publication? 332

15   Personal Branding: Using What You've Learned to Land Your Dream Job   335

Using Your Network to Find a Job 337

Twitter: Connections in 140 Characters 338

LinkedIn: Professional Connections 338

Creating a Résumé 342

Should I Write a Paper Résumé? 342

How Does Social Media Fit in Your Résumé? 343

Six Tips for Listing Social Media on Your Résumé 344

Personal Branding Case Study: Jason Falls 345

Do's and Don'ts of Résumé Building 346

Don't Rely on the Job Boards 350

Try the Company Job Boards 351

Use LinkedIn to Bypass Job Boards 352

Skip HR Altogether—Work Your Network 352

Tell Your Friends 353

The Informational Interview 354

Start Your Own Company 356

How Can Our Heroes Find a Job
Through Networking? 357

Job Searching Tips in 140 Characters 358

Index 361

About the Authors

Erik Deckers is the owner and president of Pro Blog Service, a ghost blogging and content marketing agency. He has been blogging since 1997 and speaks widely on social media topics. He is also a newspaper humor columnist and award-winning playwright. Erik coauthored *No Bullshit Social Media: The All-Business, No-Hype Guide to Social Media Marketing* with Jason Falls. He was the Kerouac House Writer-In-Residence in Spring 2016. Find him at ErikDeckers.com.

Kyle Lacy is the Vice President of Marketing at Lessonly, a leading online training provider. He has an in-depth understanding of the application of social and interactive media for both small and large businesses and regularly speaks on topics ranging from social media adoption to interactive marketing trends across email, mobile, and social media. Kyle has been recognized as one of Indiana's 40-under-40 by the *Indianapolis Business Journal*, Anderson University's Young Alumni of the Year, and TechPoint's Young Professional of the Year. Learn more about Kyle at KyleLacy.com.

Deckers and Lacy coauthored the first edition of *Branding Yourself.*

Dedication

Erik
To Toni, Maddie, Emma, and Ben.

Kyle
To Rachel and Caden.

Acknowledgments

We often say that social media is a community, and this book is no different. We couldn't have done it without some very special people.

The words "thank you" don't do justice to our appreciation for your help. First, thank you to Katherine Bull, for taking a chance on us *twice*, and Laura Norman for gambling on us for a third. Thanks also to Lori Lyons, Leslie O'Neill, Dhayanidhi Karunanidhi, and Larry Sulky.

We also want to thank the people in our lives and our community who helped us gain the knowledge, experience, and insights to produce this book. We appreciate everything you have ever done for us. So thank you, in no particular order: Paul Lorinczi, Brandon Coon, the wonderful people who make up Lessonly— Lorraine Ball, Hazel Walker, Douglas Karr, Jason Falls, Tony Scelzo, Noah Coffey, and Shawn Plew— and the whole Lacy clan of Dan, Rainy, Kayla, Zach and Kelly, Lindsay Manfredi, Jay Baer, Sarah Robbins, Mike Seidle, Sheryl Brown, Scott Wise, and Carmon Wenger.

Erik would also like to thank Kyle for asking him to help with his first writing project, which led to this one, and has led to a years-long friendship.

Erik would like to give a special thanks to his wife Toni and his three children, Maddie, Emma, and Ben, for giving him the support and love to write this book. Hopefully those 3:00 a.m. bedtimes will pay off. Also, thanks to his dad for teaching him to read. Kyle would like to especially thank his wife Rachel and son Caden for being okay with the late nights and working weekends.

We Want to Hear from You!

As the reader of this book, *you* are our most important critic and commentator. We value your opinion and want to know what we're doing right, what we could do better, what areas you'd like to see us publish in, and any other words of wisdom you're willing to pass our way.

You can email or write directly to let us know what you did or didn't like about this book—as well as what we can do to make our books stronger.

Please note that we cannot help you with technical problems related to the topic of this book and that due to the high volume of mail we receive, we might not be able to reply to every message.

When you write, please be sure to include this book's title and author, as well as your name and phone or email address.

Email: feedback@quepublishing.com

Mail: Que Publishing
ATTN: Reader Feedback
800 East 96th Street
Indianapolis, IN 46240 USA

Reader Services

Register your copy of *Branding Yourself* at www.informit.com for convenient access to updates and corrections as they become available. To start the registration process, go to **www.informit.com/register** and log in or create an account*. Enter the product ISBN 9780789759016 and click Submit. When the process is complete, you will find any available bonus content under Registered Products.

*Be sure to check the box that you would like to hear from us to receive exclusive discounts on future editions of this product.

Why Should I Care About Self-Promotion?

1 Welcome to the Party 3

2 How Do You Fit in the Mix? 21

Welcome to the Party

A story.

When Erik Deckers moved to Indianapolis in 2006, he knew one person. When an expected job didn't work out, he searched for another, relying on job boards. He finally found a job at the Indiana State Department of Health.

Erik worked there for nearly 16 months and got to know a number of people in the agency and a few others in different agencies. Rarely, however, did he have the opportunity to work with people on the outside. Consorting with the private sector was essentially frowned upon and attending business-related events during work hours was not allowed. Needless to say, Erik's professional circle was limited to his coworkers and a few journalists around the state.

When Erik left for a private-sector job in 2007, selling direct mail services (interestingly, a job he got through the one guy he knew when he moved to Indianapolis), he realized his former colleagues weren't going to help him in his new efforts, at least not right away.

So, rather than spending every day on the phone, Erik started attending Rainmakers meetings (a local networking organization), a business book club, and local Chambers of Commerce get-togethers. He attended at least two to three events a week, at 7:30 in the morning or 5:00 in the afternoon. By meeting other people in the business world, he hoped to learn about new opportunities, meet possible new clients, and find new partners who could act as evangelists to their clients on Erik's behalf.

Around the same time, he attended a half-day seminar on social media and blogging. Erik had been blogging infrequently up until that point, but he began to take it seriously in 2007. He studied blogging by reading other blogs and books about blogging, then experimenting with some of the new techniques he was learning.

As part of his networking, Erik had coffee or lunch with people he met. He learned as much as he could about them and asked if they could refer him to anyone else who would be interested in learning about his direct mail services. They often asked also about blogging and social media, so he would teach them as much as he could. He spent a lot of time online, blogging, promoting his blog, and communicating on Facebook, LinkedIn, and Smaller Indiana, a now-defunct local social network.

Those connections have led to many opportunities—sales, speaking gigs, blogging opportunities, a job, and even this book—that never would have happened if Erik had limited his job search to just the job boards, and especially if he hadn't drunk enough coffee to float a battleship.

In 2010 when we were first discussing how to write this book, Kyle said, "We need to write it for the you from 2007. We need to create a game plan for that guy on how to brand himself and promote himself online."

When we started discussing this latest edition, we realized the principles were still sound, only some of the tools had changed. In that time, our own circumstances have changed as well. Erik has moved to Florida, while Kyle moved to Massachusetts and then back to Indiana. In both cases, we found we had to re-grow our networks, meet new people, and build new relationships. We basically followed our own advice and built up new circles of friends, fans, and trusted mentors.

And we learned a lot of new lessons about personal branding and networking. This edition reflects what we've learned.

What Is Self-Promotion?

Self-promotion is just what it sounds like: promoting yourself, your events, your accomplishments, your victories, and even your defeats, problems, and hard-won lessons. You do it so you can increase your visibility, traffic to your website, and sales, as well as to get more speaking opportunities, exhibitions, and gigs—more of whatever it is you're looking for.

You promote yourself so you can get even more opportunities, which you can then tell people about.

Self-promotion is also called "branding yourself," because that's actually what it has become. (That, and it's what we wanted to call the book.) Think of it as personal branding because you need to think of yourself as a brand, just like Coca-Cola, McDonald's, Google, or Facebook.

Why Is Self-Promotion Important?

You can't count on people calling you out of the blue to hire you, buy your service, or book you for an event if they don't know about you. The only way to get people to know who you are and what you do is to tell them. And you want to tell as many people as you can who are actually interested.

Self-promotion can help you make those important connections that will further your career and improve your professional standing. It can be as simple as introducing yourself to the organizer of a conference and telling her you are interested in speaking at her next conference, or it can be as involved as writing a book or two and then spending a day emailing every conference organizer you can to get as many speaking deals as you can.

@kyleplacy: Is that a shot at me?

@edeckers: No, not at all, Mr. I-Don't-Have-Time-for-Lunch-Today.

What Self-Promotion Is Not

Self-promotion is not bragging or boasting. It's not acting bigger than you are. It's just letting people know who you are and what you do.

It's perfectly acceptable to promote yourself without looking like an arrogant jerk. People are going to be out promoting themselves and their personal endeavors and small businesses. If you're not, you're missing good opportunities, and others are going to beat you in the competition. They're going to sell their art, get their speaking gigs, get more web traffic, or whatever they're competing with you for.

What Can Self-Promotion Do for You and Your Career?

Without question, self-promotion can make you successful. And if you're already successful, it can make your personal brand huge. You don't become a success without knowing a lot of people and having a lot of people know you. If you want to be stuck in a little gray cubicle for your entire career, never rising above lower middle management, keep your head down and don't attract attention. Actually, put this book down. Stop reading!

But if you want to make a name for yourself, establish a good reputation, finally get that corner office, or even own your own thriving business, you need to promote yourself.

To do that, you need to be passionate about two things: the work you do and yourself. If you're not passionate about what you do, find the thing you're passionate about. If you're not passionate about yourself, seek professional help. The person you should love the most, admire the most, and treasure the most is you. And when you share that confidence in yourself, others feel it, too.

So maybe it's time to change up your life. You want to get out of your cubicle, get off the road, get out of the factory, put down the hammer, or change careers completely. Or maybe you're about to start looking for your first job after college. Figure out what you want to do, make it happen, and then start telling people about it. Let them know that you are good at what you do. Let them come to you for answers and information.

Personal Branding

If you ask 100 people what personal branding is, you'll get 100 different answers. But our answer is this: it's an emotional response to the image or name of a particular company, product, or person.

Think of some corporate brands you have positive or negative feelings toward: McDonald's, Starbucks, Coca-Cola, Walmart, Indianapolis Colts, Chicago Cubs. These brands are popular because they have created a lot of positive feelings in their fans, even if they also engender negative feelings in their detractors. Even companies that people hate are still considered brands, because they're still creating emotional responses.

Similarly, people have emotional responses when they see you or meet you for the first time. These responses can be feelings of joy, pleasure, love, dread, fear, or anger. When they hear your name again, they will either have new experiences and emotions, or they will relive the old ones. The kinds of emotional responses they have depend on you.

✉ *Note*

A brand is an emotional response to the image or name of a particular company, product, or person.

What Is Personal Branding?

Branding yourself means that you create the right kind of emotional response when someone hears your name, sees you online, or meets you in real life.

The "right" kind doesn't mean being someone you're not. It's your personality, your voice, your interests, your habits—everything about you that you want people to know. The information you show to other people, the things you say, and the photos you post should all fit within the theme of your personal brand.

If you're a stand-up comic, the theme of your brand is "funny." You want people to see that you actually are funny, which means posting some of your jokes and posting links to videos of your routine to your blog.

If you're a freelance graphic designer, your brand's theme is "creative." You want people to know you have artistic skills, so you'll show samples of your work through an online portfolio, possibly a blog.

If you're a cost reduction analyst, your brand's theme is "saving companies money." You can demonstrate your knowledge by answering questions on LinkedIn, writing useful articles on your blog, and giving talks to Chambers of Commerce meetings. (We'll talk about your blog in Chapter 3, "Blogging: Telling Your Story.")

Go Brand Yourself

Ask yourself: "What do I want to be known for? What qualities do I want people to associate with me? What is the first thing I want to have pop in their heads when they hear my name?"

Next, create a list of those qualities. Write down everything you can think of in five minutes, even if you think you're repeating yourself. Don't edit yourself and don't leave anything off. This is not a time to be humble or to think, "No one will see me that way." Come up with every adjective and noun you can think of, no matter how outlandish or weird. It may just spur another idea that actually does fit.

Let's say your list looks like this:

Creative	Funny	Interested in people
Musical	Well-read	Detail-oriented
Networker	Outgoing	Singer
Knowledgeable	Songwriter	Teacher
Intelligent	Dedicated	Organized

From here, you need to start grouping things that are similar. In one group, you have musical, songwriter, singer, and creative. In another, you have knowledgeable, intelligent, well-read, and teacher. In a third, you have networker, outgoing, and interested in people. You may have a few items left over, but the important thing is that you start looking for trends and groups.

You can call these groups anything you want, but let's stick with Musical, Knowledgeable, and Networker. These groups are the start of branding yourself. They're the areas you should concentrate on being known for—the areas that can define you for other people. They may know you for more—being a good cook, a budding actor, someone who's fun to hang out with at parties—but those are reserved for your friends, not something you want to focus on professionally. These latter attributes can be an additional side to your brand once in a while, but they shouldn't be the main focus of your personal brand.

How to Build Your Brand

The remaining 14 chapters of this book focus on how to build your brand. You're going to learn what you need to do to promote your personal brand with each of the social media tools and real-world events discussed, whether it's writing a blog post, posting messages on Twitter, or giving a speech.

Before you start, however, you need to understand the foundation of personal branding.

PERSONAL BRANDING CASE STUDY: MIGNON FOGARTY, GRAMMAR GIRL

Mignon Fogarty is the creator of the Grammar Girl podcast and website and the founder of the Quick and Dirty Tips podcast network. Grammar Girl podcast listeners range from CEOs and writers to prisoners continuing their education to ESL students in China. The show has won multiple Best Education Podcast awards and the site has been named multiple times to Writer's Digest's list of the 101 Best Websites for Writers. (Full disclosure: Erik has written a couple language-related essays for her podcast. Despite that, she was still able to manage all this success.)

She is also the author of the New York Times best-seller *Grammar Girl's Quick and Dirty Tips for Better Writing* and has published six other books on writing. She is an inductee in the Podcasting Hall of Fame, and she is often quoted in the media about language issues.

She has also appeared as a guest on the Oprah Winfrey Show and the TODAY show, and has been featured in the New York Times, BusinessWeek, the

Washington Post, USA Today, CNN.com, and more. Mignon has a B.A. in English from the University of Washington in Seattle and an M.S. in biology from Stanford University.

She hates the phrase "grammar nazi" and loves the word "kerfuffle."

How did you decide to go out on your own? When did you find your entrepreneurial calling?

I had my first taste of entrepreneurship in college running a small hair accessory business in my room with my roommate (who later went on to become a venture capitalist). It was quite a thrill to see girls around campus wearing our products. We invested our earnings in capital equipment (a sewing machine), but got crushed when we spent heavily to get a booth at a trade show to sell to retail outlets and couldn't compete with cheaper imported products.

Later, I worked at a series of Internet startups as a very early employee in the late 1990s. I helped build a lot of cool websites, but eventually all the companies died in the dotcom bust, so I worked as an independent science and technology writer/editor. I really love technology and wanted to try podcasting, so I started a science podcast with a friend from one of my previous companies. We did that for about eight months before I branched out on my own by starting the Grammar Girl podcast.

How did social media play a role in your personal brand? What was the very first tool you started using?

Before social media, I was active on a forum where podcasters hung out called the Podcast Pickle. To this day, I am grateful to the people there. They helped me when I had questions about the technical side of podcasting and were a very supportive group. Eventually, most of them moved to Twitter, and I went with them.

The first few years of Grammar Girl, I probably spent about 20 hours per week on social media because it was an easy place to interact with listeners and I enjoyed it. And by being so active, I also attracted people who weren't podcast listeners but were just interested in language. That played a part in developing the brand.

Did any other social tool have as much of an impact?

Twitter was the biggest in the beginning, and was the biggest for years, but ultimately, I think Facebook played a bigger role in growing the brand just because more people use Facebook. I've been on Twitter longer and I'm still much more active on Twitter, but I have about 280,000 followers on Twitter and about 650,000 on Facebook. People seem to spend more time and are more engaged on Facebook.

Has blogging been part of the strategy, or was that just a way to have a written transcript of episodes?

The website has contributed enormously to the growth of the brand. When I meet fans, they almost always say "Your site comes up all the time when I'm searching for help." From my days at Internet startups, I knew about basic search engine optimization, so although the web pages are essentially just transcripts of the podcast, in the beginning I knew enough to format them so they would do well in search. Since then, my partner, Macmillan, has taken over management of the site and has done a bang-up job with more professional SEO. It's getting harder, especially since Google gives answers as web snippets, but it's still incredibly important.

How did you learn to use the different tools?

Mostly, I just jumped in, did a lot of Google searching, and asked questions in forums if I had a problem. These days, I'll also look for a YouTube video if I'm trying to learn about a new tool.

What about your non-online publishing and public speaking? Did those happen as a result of your online work, or did you pursue them separately?

After the Wall Street Journal featured Grammar Girl as its web pick of the day, I was approached by publishers who wanted me to write books and I did a 3-book deal with Macmillan, which was the thing that let me quit my day job freelancing and completely focus on Grammar Girl and Quick and Dirty Tips. I only do public speaking and media appearances when I'm approached—it's not something I've ever put time into building. That's the most amazing thing about having such a strong brand: opportunities just come to me.

I know you like Instagram too. How can a language podcast use Instagram?

I struggled with that question myself for a long time because I'm not a visual person, and I don't have a visually interesting life. I mostly just sit in front of my computer and type! People do seem to want behind-the-scenes glimpses into the lives of people whose work they enjoy, like podcasters and authors, so I try to keep an eye out for things I can post about, big or small.

For example, I always eat an apple before I record my podcast to keep my mouth from sounding dry. One day I took a picture of my apple and described that little behind-the-scenes tidbit. And I was excited when I finished proofreading pages for my tip-a-day calendar, so I posted about that. I go through phases when I post something about the show topic every week, but when I get busy, it's the first thing to go because I'm not sure it makes a difference. I don't feel like I have a good handle on Instagram yet. I'm still experimenting.

What's a big mistake you made or something you wish you hadn't spent a lot of time on?

I wanted to make a grammar game for phones and tablets, and all the bids we got were too expensive, so I learned to code and took most of a year making the game myself with an artist from Macmillan doing the art. The game is called Grammar Pop, and I'm happy with how it turned out—and I loved making it—but it was a terrible, terrible use of my time.

If you had one piece of advice for someone building their personal brand, what would it be?

Be consistent. The power of a brand is that people know what they are going to get.

The Five Universal Objectives of Personal Branding

Whoever you are, whatever techniques you use, whomever you want to reach, five basic ideas, five *universal* objectives, are the same for everyone who wants to grow their personal brand.

1. Discover Your Passion

Passion is fundamental to achieving your goals.

What do you love to do? What gets you out of bed in the morning, fires your imagination, and revs you up? What do you think about when you're daydreaming? How do you spend all of your free time?

Some people are passionate about their work. They love what they do, and that's where they focus their time and energy. These people—usually entrepreneurs—have found a niche that makes them happy, and they want to find a way to make money from it. They wake up early, stay up late, and spend every waking minute thinking about, talking about, and actually doing the work.

In his book *Crush It!*, entrepreneur and social media celebrity Gary Vaynerchuk talks about how he spends hours and hours leaving comments on other people's blogs about wine. It's not because he enjoys leaving comments or because he wants to boost his web traffic. It's because he loves wine. He loves selling it, talking about it, and writing about it. His passion for wine has turned him into a celebrity and helped him sell plenty of wine for his family's liquor store.

Others are passionate about their hobbies. Whether it's painting, playing in a band, fixing up classic cars, analyzing baseball statistics, or collecting vinyl records, some people love their hobbies and pursue them with an obsessive fervor. They view their day job as a means to an end, which lets them fulfill their passion.

And still others haven't found their passion. Or they have no passion at all. They go to work, they come home, they eat dinner, they watch TV, they go to bed. And then they do it all again the next day. The idea of enjoying life has been drummed out of them.

These people are dead inside, whether they know it or not. The only thing that gets them out of bed in the morning is the alarm clock and the fear that they'll lose their jobs if they don't. They eat for fuel, not pleasure. They have friends out of habit, not because they love being around people. They watch TV not because there's anything good on, but because they're afraid of what they'll learn if they're left alone for too long with their own thoughts: Nothing in their lives is truly exciting or enjoyable.

You need to have at least one passion in your life. It can be something you are known for, something you build your personal brand on. Or it can even be something you never tell anyone about, preferring to do in private. But the great thing about sharing your passion is that you get to know people who share your interest and create some beneficial relationships.

All this is our way of saying you need to find your passion if you want to achieve your professional goals. More important, your goals need to tie into your passion because that's how you will achieve them.

If you want to be fulfilled and enjoy earning a living, make sure your goals are achievable through your passions. For example, if your long-term goal is to own a million dollar home and drive an expensive car, you probably won't get there providing knitting lessons to at-risk teenagers.

We won't tell you to change your passions. Don't give them up! If you love giving knitting lessons to at-risk teenagers, by all means pursue it. Just understand that there's not much money to be made giving knitting lessons, so getting an expensive car this way is probably not feasible. If that's what you love to do, make sure your goals align with your passion.

However, if your passion is to create a new social networking tool, and you devote every waking hour to programming and promoting it, you have a better chance of getting the mansion in Silicon Valley and Tesla Model X.

It's a matter of making sure your passions and your goals are in alignment and that you can achieve the one through the other.

We hope you have already found your passion because this book is based on you being passionate about at least two things: (1) yourself and (2) something else.

2. Be Bold

It's okay to talk about yourself.

Despite what your parents and teachers told you, you *can* tell people about your accomplishments. Actually, we want you to do that.

We understand that it's hard to do. You've been taught that talking about yourself is bragging. You're supposed to be humble and quiet about your accomplishments and let your actions speak louder than words.

Think about the past several times you saw somebody boasting about his success, his money, his love life (at networking events, parties, nightclubs, and high school reunions). We can imagine some of the words you used in reference to that person, none of which were flattering, and none of which our editors will let us publish here.

In the movies—like *Mallrats*, *Karate Kid*, *Gladiator*, and *The Princess Bride*—the braggart always gets his comeuppance at the end, receiving some cosmic justice. "See?" you tell yourself. "This will happen if *I* brag about what I do."

The problem is that we associate self-promotion with bragging. We believe telling others about our accomplishments is the moral equivalent of bragging about how much money we make. We associate letting people know we published an article or are giving a talk as the equivalent of showing up at our high school reunion in a $200,000 red Italian sports car.

Nothing could be further from the truth.

Self-promotion seems to be especially hard for people from the Midwest, where we live. We're your typical Midwesterners, only we got over it. We realized we had to be bold without being arrogant. We knew if we wanted to make a name for ourselves, and earn reputations to attract bigger clients and bigger opportunities, we had to overcome this Midwest shyness and be willing to talk about ourselves—a lot.

Self-promotion is just letting people know what's going on in your lives, keeping people apprised of your special events, occasions, and accomplishments.

Table 1.1 shows a few key differences between bragging and self-promotion:

Table 1.1 The Difference Between Self-Promotion and Bragging

Self-Promotion	Bragging
A Twitter message that says, "I just published my book."	A vanity license plate that says, "Gr8 Writer."
Announcing the birth of your child.	Announcing the birth of your eight children at a national press conference.
Telling your friends you're engaged.	Telling people how much he spent on the ring.
Telling your colleagues about your promotion.	Demanding undying fealty from your underlings.

The biggest difference between self-promotion and bragging is the motivation behind why you're telling people. If it's something you're proud of, something you're excited about because you just gotta tell someone, that's self-promotion. If it's something you want people to do, see, visit, or even buy, that's self-promotion.

If you announce something so other people will be envious or think you're cool, that's bragging, and people won't like you.

Creating your online personal brand means showing the best parts of your personality so people do like you. What makes you unique and interesting? Why should they want to spend time with you? Why should they care what you have to say? If you're a fun person, show it. If you're interested in a lot of different things, share them. If you like to create new relationships, seek out other interesting people.

The important thing is to realize that (a) people are interested in what you have to say and (b) it's perfectly all right to say it. Just don't brag about it.

3. Tell Your Story

Your story is what makes you special.

This is the tricky part. We just told you it's okay to talk about yourself, but now you have to do it without talking about yourself.

@kyleplacy: Huh?

@edeckers: Be patient.

Effective personal branding isn't about talking about yourself all the time. As much as everyone would like to think that friends and family are eagerly waiting by their computers hoping to hear some news, any news, about what you're doing, they're not. Actually, they're hoping you're sitting by your computer, waiting for news about them.

Believe it or not, the best way to build your personal brand is to talk more about other people, events, and ideas than you talk about yourself. That's because if you talk about other people and promote their victories and their ideas, you become an influencer. You are seen as someone who is not only helpful, but is also a valuable resource. That helps your brand more than if you just talk about yourself over and over—that gets boring.

But there are other ways you can tell your story, without saying a word. You don't tell people what you believe; you show it by living it.

The next chance you get, watch people. Study what they wear, what they eat, what they drive. Act like Sherlock Holmes to make simple deductions based on what you observe. You can get a clue to their personalities by noticing simple things like clothing and cars.

That woman over there wearing the New York Knicks T-shirt is probably a basketball fan. The skinny guy wearing the running shoes is a runner. The guy wearing a Green Lantern T-shirt likes comic books. And the woman who drove by in the

Toyota Prius with the "Love Your Mother (Earth)" bumper sticker wants to help the environment.

You learned a small part of their personal stories, but they didn't say a word. The symbols people wear and brands they support tell a story. They let other people know, "This is something I believe in, and I want you to know about it."

It's the same for telling your own story. Rather than wearing a sign that says "I love comic books" or sending daily emails to your friends about your obsession with comics, you could write a blog about the comics industry and your favorite titles and characters, or you could publish your own web comic. You could produce a weekly podcast about comic publishing news, cover the news from local and national comic conventions, and even interview other comic artists and publishers. By blogging or podcasting about your passion, you tell the world your story—"I love comic books"—without actually saying it over and over or being a pest about it.

Besides, the sign starts to chafe after a while.

4. Create Relationships

Relationships lead to opportunities.

What's marvelous about social networking and real-world networking is that you never know what kind of opportunities are going to come your way. Without sounding too mystical or cosmic, you must leave yourself open to the opportunities that may arise because of your efforts.

Erik jokes that this is "faith-based networking": You will meet the right person at the right time for the right opportunity. As long as you continue to put yourself in the situations where those possibilities can arise, sooner or later, they will come.

The creation of this book is a prime example of the right people meeting in the right place at the right time. We both belonged to a social network called Smaller Indiana, having joined within the first couple weeks of its creation. We met at the first event that the founder, Pat Coyle, organized on Martin Luther King Day 2008.

During our initial meeting, which was already filled with friendly teasing and Kyle accusing Erik of carrying a "man bag" (something Erik flatly denies even now)—

```
@edeckers: It was a leather messenger bag, I swear!
@kyleplacy: Okay, whatever.
```

—we arranged to get coffee together the next week. In the following months, we continued to bump into each other, get coffee, get lunch, attend the same networking meetings, collaborate on projects, and refer speaking and work gigs to each other. Eighteen months later, Kyle asked Erik to help with another book he was working on, and that led to this one. But it all started with being at the same place at the same time in January 2008.

Whether you're online or out in the real world, treat every person you meet as a possible future resource. You never know if the person you met at the last Chamber of Commerce meeting will become your next employer. The person you have coffee with one day (or even the one who serves your coffee) could become your business partner. And the person who connects with you on Twitter could end up hiring you to speak at an event two months later. (Just remember to be genuine, and do this without being creepy or seeming predatory.)

You need to treat each of these new relationships with care. Nurture them, help them grow, and tell people your story.

"But how will we have time to grow those relationships?" people usually ask. "We have work to do."

That's the beauty of social media. It lets you stay in touch with people in between the times you meet face-to-face. It lets you share your story without doing a big information dump in the first 30 minutes of a one-hour appointment. It lets you find out about a lot of other people all at once, without buying lunch every day. It lets you learn about the details of your lives so that when you do get together, you get to spend more time talking about deeper issues and bigger ideas. And *that* is where those opportunities are going to come from.

5. Take Action

Even a small step is a step forward.

There's an old saying that if you hit a rock with a hammer 1,000 times, it wasn't the 1,000th blow that broke the rock; it was the 999 that came before it.

All the plans in the world don't amount to much if you don't actually put them into action. If you want to be someone notable or be considered an authority in your field, you have to start somewhere.

Although you're not going to become famous with a single blog post or YouTube video, you can't start without your first one. It's a matter of writing post after post, creating video after video. It's publishing those 999 posts or videos that makes the 1,000th effective.

Ask how other people became successful. All of them will tell you that they worked hard—harder than anyone else. They got up earlier, stayed up later, and worked longer in between.

Earlier, we mentioned "faith-based networking" and the idea that you will meet the right person with the right opportunity at the right moment. Whether that meeting was divinely inspired, you also met the right person because you've been to hundreds of meetings talking to thousands of people and communicating the same thing: the kind of opportunities you're looking for.

Just like the rock that took 1,000 blows to break it, you had to meet 999 people before you finally met that one person who changed your life.

We wish we could tell you the secret phrase or handshake that would let you meet that 1,000th person in the first 24 hours of your new personal branding adventure. Unfortunately, we can't. There isn't one. But if you follow even half the steps outlined in this book, you'll eventually get there, and you'll have fun doing it.

Who Needs Self-Promotion?

Everyone needs self-promotion and personal branding. It's how you're going to grow your business, advance your career, and expand your personal network. Few people don't need self-promotion of some kind. (Actually, all we could come up with were spies and hermits.) Even if you work for a large government agency in some half-forgotten division, sequestered away in the basement, working on some underfunded project (*especially* if this is the case; see Chapter 15, "Personal Branding: Using What You've Learned to Land Your Dream Job"), you need to brand yourself.

Self-promotion is for everyone, not just business people trying to get a job or earn a promotion. Even those outside the corporate world can benefit from promoting themselves.

- **Book authors**: Although your publisher—your kind-hearted, giving, generous-to-a-fault publisher—

  @edeckers: Forget it; they said we already blew the promotions budget on the launch party.

  @kyleplacy: Seriously? I knew we should've skipped the lobster.

  —will be doing everything she can to promote your book, it's also up to the authors to make sure they're promoting their book with websites, blogs, Twitter and Facebook accounts, YouTube videos, and several other social media tools and real-world networking opportunities.

- **Musicians**: Musicians are at a personal branding advantage because they're already promoting themselves as a brand. Think of your favorite band and everything you like about them: their music, t-shirts, interviews, website, fan pages, and anything else you can find.

All these things go toward maintaining their public image and persona. As a musician, you'll want to explore every free social media tool where your fans are gathered. It could be Facebook and YouTube, posting videos of your last show, or even a social network devoted strictly to bands in your city or state.

- **Public speakers**: All public speakers, except for the big-name celebrities who belong to speakers' bureaus, must promote themselves to conference organizers, meeting organizers, trade associations, and anyone else who hires speakers.

  You need to provide evidence of your speaking abilities, but thanks to social media, gone are the days of sending out video tapes or DVDs of your talks. Instead, you can refer people to your website where they can watch videos of your talks, download your *one sheet* (a single sheet about your qualifications as a speaker), and even read some of the articles that you discuss in your talks.

- **Entrepreneurs**: This will end up being one of the best marketing campaigns you could run. By equating you with your company, you both become a synonymous brand. When people hear your name, they think of your company, and vice versa. By offering yourself as an expert in your field on a blog and Twitter, people will come to see you as a resource and someone they need to hire for a project or even a long-term contract.

- **Salespeople**: We're seeing a major change in the way sales are done around the world. A lot of sales coaches and experts are telling salespeople to put down the phone and quit making cold calls. They're inefficient, ineffective, and just plain boring (cold calling, not the coaches). Nowadays, salespeople are building relationships rather than databases, providing information and knowledge, and networking with as many people as they can.

  We understand that many salespeople still have to slog out their time on the phones, but by keeping track of your sales funnel (see Chapter 11, "Measuring Success: You Like Me, You Really Like Me!") and finding where your best customers are coming from, you may learn that networking and branding yourself are much more effective than cold-calling some name from a list.

- **Job seekers**: These are people who need personal branding the most. Every element of a job search is focused on what people think of when they hear your name. You email a PDF or word processing document with your skills and experience on it. You have three or more conversations with several people about how your skills and experience can help their company. And nowadays, you're searched online by people who make a hiring decision based on what they find. By carefully planning and creating your personal brand and then living up to it, you can greatly improve your chances to find a new job, compared to those people who still think FaceSpace is just for teenagers and perverts.

Meet Our Heroes

We talk to a lot of people about social media, especially in the small business world. And we have met people who are or were in the same boat as Erik, trying to redefine, or even define, themselves—to launch a new phase of their career, make a name for themselves, or just reach people they've never reached before. These four fictional people are amalgamations of actual people we've worked with, although you can find their "archetype" in most situations. We created them to help illustrate the different lessons in each chapter: the Influencer is well-regarded in their industry, and influences others; the Climber is working their way up the career ladder; the Neophyte is new to an industry or field, even if they've been working for several years; and the Free Agent is the person who bounces around from job to job, less concerned with moving up in rank than they are in finding new challenges and higher salaries. You can see how each of them can apply what we discuss in their own lives.

- **Allen (influencer)** was an account manager for a marketing and advertising agency for 14 years but was laid off six months ago after his agency lost its biggest client. He has many contacts in the agency world and is a member of a professional marketing association.

  Allen is an influencer because he may switch jobs, but he stays within the same industry. Influencers are usually hired because of their network and industry knowledge. A lot of salespeople tend to be influencers, hopping from company to company, but staying within their industry and not actually moving up the career ladder.

- **Beth (climber)** is a marketing manager for a large insurance company. She has been with this company for 10 years, but this is her second insurance company. She has moved up the ranks in this company, as well as with her last employer.

  Beth is a climber because she changes jobs to climb her career ladder, but she will stay within the same industry and even the same company to do it. Her ultimate goal is to become the chief marketing officer of an insurance company, preferably this one.

- **Carla (neophyte)** is a former pharmaceutical sales rep who was laid off after eight years with her company. She is interested in working for a nonprofit, either as a program director or a fund-raising specialist.

  Carla is a neophyte because she is not only changing jobs, but changing industries. This means she is starting over in terms of knowledge, influence, contacts, and even possibly her skill set. A new college graduate would also be a neophyte.

- **Darrin (free agent)** is an IT professional who leaves his job every two or three years in pursuit of more money. He is a free agent because he'll stay at roughly the same level of job, regardless of where he goes, but he can make more money because bigger companies require his expertise. Darrin is not considered an influencer because he jumps industries every time he jumps companies, which means it's harder for him to make a name for himself in any given field.

2

How Do You Fit in the Mix?

Can you remember at least one piece of information from Erik's story from Chapter 1, "Welcome to the Party?" This is what Chris Brogan, one of the top branding and social media experts on the Internet (www.chrisbrogan.com), calls "the storyteller's promise." The storyteller's promise is an agreement that the reader and storyteller/author make at the onset of a story.

What does a storyteller's promise state? According to Brogan, it says, "I'm here as a consumer of your content (or your personal brand). You will give me what I've come to see/read/experience. You won't try to trick me, unless that's part of what I've signed up to see."[1]

In this case, Erik's storyteller's promise is that he will tell you how to build your network through social networking, not about the time he took his dog for a walk and how shenanigans ensued. Erik is going to give you what you expected to see when you bought this book and read the first chapter. You believe we are not trying to trick you by filling the pages with dog stories and shenanigans.

---

1. www.chrisbrogan.com/presentation-and-storytellers-promises/

It would be safe to say that you remembered at least one portion of Erik's story about networking and personal branding. When presenting your personal brand, you're entering into an agreement with the individual experiencing your brand. You're making the storyteller's promise.

When storytellers tell a story, people listen. It's extremely important that your story is not terrible. You don't want to tell a story that people will hate or never remember. Stories are what drive memories. They are intricate to the development of a person, and they're extremely important in the world of personal branding.

There is a story in each of us—our stories are what make each of us different. For example, Erik may have had an encounter with a wild animal at a local restaurant. The wild animal (let's say it was a bear) stole all his food and proceeded to drink his beer.

This is a story, albeit untrue, but it's still a story. The story is unique to Erik, and Kyle could never claim to have experienced the wild animal at the same restaurant under the same circumstances.

@kyleplacy: I did have a talking bear in a green tie steal my picnic basket one time, though.

@edeckers: I think you're thinking of a Yogi Bear cartoon.

The stories that surround you are the first ingredient in building a strong personal identity that enhances your overall brand, whether you're an influencer, a climber, a neophyte, or a free agent.

This chapter can help you define and build your personal story. You don't need to write a book, maybe a few pages. It's a guide to help you discover your personal brand story.

How do you start? Where do you begin this journey to further refine your personal brand story to help you fit in the mix? How do you define your identity? Read on.

The Basics of Building Your Personal Brand Story

The important part of building a personal brand is telling your story. That's a phrase you'll hear a lot from personal branding speakers: "telling your story." (That's because it sounds so much cooler than "narrating your personal history" or "relating your background.")

It has also become an important component of content marketing, which is the art and science of persuading people through education. Good content marketers can tell stories about their products without boring you with a lot of data and features.

Telling your story is what sets you apart and helps you succeed in your marketplace and your career. Your life story, your professional story, or whatever story is most relevant to establishing your personal brand can help you stand out from those who never figure this out.

Writing Your Personal Brand Story

All autobiographies start with a single story. Norman Rockwell has a story, and Bill Clinton has a story. Both wrote their autobiographies, which helped guide their personal brands in the public's eyes, and they're filled with anecdote after anecdote.

Have you tried to write your own autobiography? You don't need to write a book—just a simple bio. You might not even have enough content to write a book, but how about a paragraph?

Your personal brand story is your personal sales pitch. There are three different types: short, medium, and long—a 1-sentence pitch, a 100-word pitch, and a 250-word biography. Each is important because it helps you prioritize and figure out what is most important about *you*. What are you best at? What's your passion? What skills help you in your career? What makes you *you*? The personal brand story is also used in your elevator pitch, which we discuss later in this chapter.

Prioritize Accomplishments

The hardest part about writing a personal brand story is nailing down the right accomplishments. Don't fret. Most people don't know where to start, either because they're modest (don't be; you can't afford to downplay your accomplishments) or lack of direction. Write for the audience you want to reach.

We'll give you some examples to work from. You don't have to do this alone, and certainly not from scratch. Let's look at Kyle's bio and try to break down what is the best and worst in his personal brand biography.

@edeckers: Wait, why are we doing your bio?

@kyleplacy: Because we opened the whole damn book with yours!

@edeckers: Oh yeah. That was awesome.

"Author of three acclaimed books, *Twitter Marketing For Dummies*, *Branding Yourself*, and *Social CRM for Dummies*, Kyle Lacy is the VP of Marketing for Lessonly, a team learning software company in Indianapolis. He leads the company's overall brand strategy, content marketing, product marketing, and thought leadership.

He has an in-depth understanding of the application of social and interactive media for both small and large businesses and regularly speaks on topics ranging from social media adoption to marketing trends across all digital channels. Kyle has been recognized as one of Indiana's 40-under-40 by the Indianapolis Business Journal, Anderson University's Young Alumni of the Year, and TechPoint's Young Professional of the Year. He's also a husband and father of one."

Let's break this down. The bio starts by announcing that Kyle has written three books and spends his time working in marketing at Lessonly. This immediately tells you exactly what Kyle does on a daily basis and gives you a sense of his skills and knowledge.

Next, it establishes his expertise: He wrote three books, regularly speaks at conferences, and has received several awards. His bio covers everything he thinks a potential customer or event organizer would need to know to engage with him in some way.

This all puts the ball in the reader's court and asks that person to make a decision. It could be something small like deciding to follow Kyle on Twitter or connect with him on LinkedIn or hire him to give a talk. A good bio should answer any question someone may have, even if that answer is "no."

Writing Your Personal Brand Biography

Each bio you write, whether short, medium, or long, has its place. You may be at a networking event, for instance, and have only five seconds to give your pitch—so use the short bio. The medium and short types of personal brand biography also have their places in the world of building your personal brand.

We're really tired of elevator pitches, even though they're all the rage with the networking gurus and sales coaches we talk to. Elevator pitches are 30-second speeches you're supposed to give to explain who you are or what product you sell.

The problem is they're about 25 seconds too long. If it takes you 30 seconds to explain yourself to someone, you're probably not going to notice his or her eyes glazing over after the first 15 seconds.

Instead, you should look for a hook. Something interesting about you that you can state in a sentence or two. We've known several friends who have developed their interesting hook that makes everyone want to hear more—the embroiderer who could embroider toilet paper; the real estate agent who used to be a Hollywood sitcom writer; the PR person who helped Hollywood legend Carl Reiner self-publish and promote his book.

Imagine meeting someone whose initial introduction made you say "Oh, wow. What's that like?" Imagine *being* that person. The introduction doesn't even have to be terribly dramatic or exciting. Just something to pique another person's interest. One thing Erik likes to say is that he knows a real rhyme for the word "purple."

@kyleplacy: What is it?

@edeckers: I'm not telling. People have to tweet me to find out.

Think of the coolest thing you've ever done, then build your brand story on that idea. Write your short, medium, and long story, and then practice it several times. Let's say you're a former newspaper reporter who is looking to break into the PR field. Here's how your bio would look:

- **Short:** I'm a former newspaper reporter who covered Hurricane Katrina on the ground, and now I'm trying to get into public relations.

- **Medium:** I'm a former newspaper reporter trying to work as a public relations professional. I worked for the *New Orleans Times-Picayune* as a news reporter for four years, as a sports reporter for another three, and then covered the business beat for six. I've been spending a lot of time volunteering as the PR director for our local Oyster Shuckers Rehab Center, and I wrote a book about Thomas Gardiner Corcoran, one of President Franklin Roosevelt's advisors.

- **Long:** I'm a former newspaper reporter trying to get into public relations. I worked for the *New Orleans Times-Picayune* as a news reporter for four years, as a sports reporter for another three, and then covered the business beat for six. I also served as president of the Louisiana Journalists Association and spoke at our annual conference about the growth of small-town media. In addition, I'm a part-time professional historian, and I wrote a book about Thomas Gardiner Corcoran, one of President Franklin Roosevelt's advisors and part of his brain trust. Because it was a self-published book, I had to do all my own PR work. I scheduled a series of radio and TV interviews, and the book reached Amazon.com's Top 1,000 for 16 weeks in a row, bumping some Twitter marketing book out of the ranking. Finally, I've been serving as the volunteer PR director for our local Oyster Shuckers Rehab Center, garnering about $100,000 in earned media.

The following guidelines should give you a good idea of what we're talking about. And you'll notice that the longer ones seem more suited for a written bio, rather than a verbal introduction. When you introduce yourself, you don't need to recite your written bio word for word. Just make sure you hit the high points.

So what should you do and what should you say during your introduction? Here are a few points you need to remember:

- **Introduce your professional self:** What would you say to a stranger who asked who you were? Kyle would say, "I'm the VP of Marketing for a learning software company." This helps in the development of your one-sentence biography.

- **What do you do?:** Of course, you have to tell people what you do, or they'll have no idea how to use you in their current role. People need to know what you do before you discuss your accomplishments to further solidify your personal brand: "I am a writer and speaker who's been covering digital marketing communication for 10 years." You now have your one-sentence elevator pitch (more about that in Chapter 9, "How to Network: Hello, My Name Is…").

- **What have you accomplished?:** What is the most important thing you have accomplished? For Kyle, it is writing three books and being listed as one of the top business professionals under 40 years old in Indianapolis. Don't list all of your accomplishments. Just pick your top three and let them tell the story of your brand.

- **Write in the third person, talk in the first:** Your bio is used by other people. Your bio is for other people to tell your story. Be sure you write it in third person and make it sound like someone else is describing you. Just, please, don't do this when you're actually speaking to someone. It sounds pretentious.

- **Ask a friend for advice:** Don't believe that you have written a perfect biography. We have each asked other people for their opinions of our personal brand biographies. Have someone else read yours. Ask them to tell you what's missing and what should be taken out. Having another set of eyes to help with the process is going to be the difference between a good and a great bio.

- **Don't forget it:** You cannot rest on your biography any more than you can use the same résumé that you left college with. You're constantly changing and growing, and so is your story. Every project you work on and every client you work with will change your story. You'll have changes in experience, skills, and opinions on your industry. Your top three accomplishments will change as you add new successes. And your career path will change. Your bio needs to change as well, both in the written and verbal form.

You need to use specific language and ideas when you're discussing your bio. Please, oh please, don't buy into that "use memorable, creative terms" or "use an opening statement that will make people ask questions" advice that some networking consultants give.

Many times they'll tell you to use an elevator pitch like "We make your company more memorable." The problem is, everyone does that. It could be a marketing or advertising agency. It could be someone who sells custom logo apparel. It could be the company that does full-color car wraps. It could be the guy who dances outside a store waving a giant sign telling people where to sell their junk gold.

The problem is, all these people will help a company stand out from the competition, which is why you need a hook and not some vague, generic mumblings that applies to nearly everyone in the business world.

How Do Our Heroes Use the Personal Brand Biography?

Let's apply some of the storytelling principles to our heroes from Chapter 1. They're all transitioning from their current roles to new ones and must state their desires and experience in their brand story. If you ran into them at a networking event, what would be their one-sentence pitches? Would you remember them?

- **Allen (influencer)** was an account manager for a marketing and advertising agency for 14 years but was laid off after his agency lost its biggest client. The layoff wasn't his fault, but he was a casualty of the loss. What should his one-sentence biography say?

"I'm a creative director who used to work for one of the largest ad agencies in the state, where I created those Robin-Hood-sells-insurance commercials everyone quotes."

What's positive about this? Allen is creative and professional, has an established marketing and advertising career, and worked for a top agency. You would come away with the idea that Allen is good at what he does.

What's missing? You could argue that Allen could have included something about the kind of job he's looking for, but that could come in a follow-up sentence.

"And I'm looking for a job in another ad agency as a creative director."

- **Beth (climber)** is a marketing manager for a large insurance company. She has been with them for 10 years, but this is her second insurance company. Remember, Beth wants to move up the ranks within the company and eventually become CMO. What would be a good one-sentence biography for Beth?

I'm a marketing manager for Inverness Insurance and have been ranked as one of the top marketing professionals in my industry for the past three years by *Insurance Marketing* magazine.

> What's important about mentioning that she is one of the top marketing managers in her firm? Is it true? We assume it is for one reason: She verified her experience by adding the recognition from a media source.

> If you worked outside the insurance industry, you would have no idea whether Beth was lying, but you would trust the media placement. This doesn't mean you should make up traditional media names to verify your existence. A liar is a liar, plain and simple. Don't lie on your one-sentence personal brand story—or ever.

> What is the difference between Beth's written and a spoken one-sentence biography? For one thing, we hope Beth wouldn't drop the whole "ranked as one of the top marketing professionals" phrase in the middle of a conversation. That sounds a little arrogant. However, it's perfectly acceptable to say this in written form.

- **Carla (neophyte)** is a former pharmaceutical sales rep who was laid off after eight years with her company. She is interested in working for a nonprofit, either as a program director or a fund-raising specialist.

We're actually torn here, because she could use two different stories.

I'm a sales professional who creates relationships between customers and organizations; in fact, I've got more than 200 doctors in my contact list.

and

I'm a former pharmaceutical salesperson making the leap to the nonprofit world.

> The second bio is more of a conversational introduction, something to use when meeting someone in person. The first one is better suited to the written form, especially on a résumé or on LinkedIn (see Chapter 4, "LinkedIn: Networking on Steroids").

> By highlighting that she is a sales pro who specializes in creating relationships between customers and organizations, she's not discounting her last job, but she's not overtly saying she was in pharmaceuticals. She's pointing out the similarities between what she used to do and what she wants to do. The most important part is that she is a relationship builder—organizations want relationship builders.

What's missing? The second bio doesn't say as much about what Carla wants to do. She can easily add "as a fundraiser or program director," and that will fix it. But this is generally short enough to get started.

- **Darrin (free agent)** is an IT professional who leaves his job every two or three years in pursuit of more money. He is a free agent because he'll stay at roughly the same level of job, but he can make more money if he moves to bigger companies.

  Darrin is going to create his one-sentence story with as much validation as possible to win him the largest projects. He needs to talk extensively about his accomplishments while touching lightly on his profession.

I'm an IT professional who has worked for six of the top corporations in the city.

Darrin's biography is less about his profession than it is about his accomplishments.

It is also key to think of the word "trust" when selling yourself as a professional. When people trust your opinion, you are bordering on the ability to become a thought leader to the person who is reading (or hearing) your bio.

What's missing? Darrin needs to be prepared to talk about what he's looking for and what kind of IT work he has done. Darrin also needs a verbal bio, and "I'm in IT" is not going to cut it. That's fine when he's meeting his wife's friends at a party who will end up asking for help with their email, but it doesn't tell a potential employer a single thing. Something more specific, like, "I'm a network security specialist" is more appropriate to tell someone who's in his same field.

PERSONAL BRANDING CASE STUDY: PARK HOWELL

Park Howell is a professional storyteller. He's not one of those guys with the big bushy beard who goes to all the storytelling festivals. Rather, he's the founder of the Business of Story, a marketing agency that helps business leaders and communicators "define their personal brand story to grow their influence, and/or clarify their professional brand narrative to grow their organization and their people.[2]"

Basically, he does everything we discussed in this chapter for a full-time day job. Park has been in advertising for 30 years, has run his own agency for 20, and has been in story marketing for 10.

Park also runs the "Business of Story" podcast, which features authors, screenwriters, makers, content marketers and brand raconteurs (another word for "storytellers") who share their storytelling tips and techniques. Erik was on an episode of "Business of Story" in 2016.

Park has been in business of one type or another since he was 12. When he was in college, he ran a concert-promoting enterprise and then started his own ad agency in 1995. Park has rarely worked for others and has almost always been an entrepreneur.

Of course, Park has a head start on most of us when it comes to defining his personal brand story. As a 30-year professional, Park said, "I have always been fascinated about how to clarify and sculpt the ideal brand story that differentiates an offering and connects with audiences."

He has a 10-step Story Cycle system that he uses on himself, the same process he uses for all his clients. The goal for the process, for himself and anyone else, is to "find your authentic story, focus it, and own it." Park said that owning his own "Brand Story Strategist" market position has helped differentiate himself from all the other executive consultants, coaches, and marketers.

He's also grown his personal brand the same way everyone else in the industry did: through blogging and social media promotion. Park started blogging back in 2007, and he promoted those posts through Twitter, Facebook, and LinkedIn. Now he's publishing on Medium and said he's been having fun with posting images on Instagram, as well as videos on YouTube.

But his most successful social media channel has been his weekly "Business of Story" podcast. Park said it's probably his most successful social channel because it's the kind of content he best likes to produce. (Did we mention Erik was a guest on the podcast in 2016?)

When it comes to writing your own brand story, Park said job seekers suffer from two maladies:

1. Selfie-itis: Most people place themselves at the center of their story when they should make their prospective employer the hero. The job seeker actually plays a more important role as their future employer's mentor or guide (an important role in "The Hero's Journey," a regular storytelling structure. Think Obi-Wan Kenobi from Star Wars). In this role, the job seeker can demonstrate how he will help grow the organization and support his colleagues through his unique knowledge, talent, and passion.

2. Commodity-it is: We're all commodities. It's important that we differentiate ourselves by owning our story. Job seekers don't typically take the time to define their personal brand story before an interview, so they come off as just another number. To stand out, they must articulate through their mentor/ guide role what makes them the most timely, relevant and urgent resource. Focus on what the employer needs first, and then demonstrate through your storytelling how you are the unique answer they're looking for.

As far as the one crucial piece of advice Park wants to share with you goes? "Clarify your brand story and then have the courage to truly own it. After all, the most powerful story you will ever tell is the story you tell yourself. So make it a good one."

Telling Your Complete Brand Story

Your personal brand story will give you your start in formulating your personal brand story. This is the storyteller's promise to the reader, where you give the reader what "they were" expecting. You have to flesh out the story, but in other locations. All of your content—your blog posts, status updates, photos, and videos should build your story like a puzzle.

The following points are more than just a checklist. Your content should fall within one of these groups—these "chapters" or "buckets"—as you live out your personal brand. By putting the right content into the right chapters, you'll tell your story to your readers. And as you put more and more content into each chapter, as you fill the buckets, even latecomers can follow along.

Use the following points as the chapters to help you write your personal brand story. Do this not only as a brand-building exercise, but as a way to create your ongoing story over the months and years.

- **The beginning:** This is where you define yourself. Where did you come from? How did you get here? Where are you going? Write out the answers to each of these questions concisely in a couple of sentences. This is just the definition of who you are and who you want to be as a brand. People want to know your story; you just have to write it. You should end up with two sentences for each question.

- **How did I help?** What situation did you help with? This could be a serious situation that you fixed or any problem you solve on a daily basis. It's up to you to define the problem. Basically, people want to read a story with a problem that needs to be solved. Novelists, playwrights, and screenwriters write about conflict and plot—this is it. Solve the problem by the end of your biography, and you have a real story.

- **Your emotional context:** Engage with people on an emotional level and tell stories that tap into their emotions, rather than relying on statistics and facts. This will help people connect with you. For instance, what significant event took place to make you choose your career path? Use this to let people see you as unique and real. It's not about how 20 percent of people do the thing that results in some other thing; it's about how your high school English teacher said you had real skill as a writer, so you should think about pursuing it.

- **Be consistent:** Build your story by being consistent in the types of stories you tell and the theme around them. All good stories have a rising theme or a story arc. Define your niche (your theme), and build around it. Don't jump all over the place in what you do or talk about; if you're living and writing about your dream of running your first marathon, don't switch gears by writing about your dream of becoming a performance artist. When you're consistent, your story will stick, and your message will reach your intended audience.

- **Remember you:** Don't get too caught up in the words and lose sight of why you're doing this to begin with. Remember those moments in your life that shaped the person you've become. Tell people those moments and get them fired up about your brand. It'll motivate you and make others understand why you're so great.

- **Keep the steam going by firing up others:** You've gotten people interested...or at least gotten their attention. Don't lose steam. Build your story by building up others. The same people who are fired up about you should be the ones you brag about. Shout out to them on Twitter, engage them in conversations, and boast about their accomplishments louder than they do. You want your audience to be loyal, so be good to them first.

- **Connect on their level:** Make your story relatable. Remember, you're not writing science fiction. You're dealing with real life and real situations. Put yourself in others' shoes, and cater to your audience. You defined your audience and know what they want. Give it to them.

- **Keep them interested:** At this point, people know who you are, what you're about, and what you do. Now is the time to make sure they know you're good at it. Share your success stories to reinforce your abilities, and continually invest time in finding new stories. You're only as good as others say you are. Invest in them so that in turn they invest in you. Build your story around an audience that needs you.

- **Edit your work:** Where are you confused? Where are you confusing others? You can define and redefine your brand if it makes sense. Look back through your story to fix any holes you may have.

After you finish writing a couple of sentences for each point, you will have a basic understanding of what you want to accomplish and how you are defined as a person. You will end up with a short bio to help describe, define, and relate to individuals in the professional world.

The Law of Anecdotal Value

Peter Sagal, the host of "Wait, Wait, Don't Tell Me," a comedy quiz show on public radio, once said that he was told by a professor to "Choose the experiences in life that offer the most anecdotal value—that is, look for the opportunities that have the most likelihood of producing a cool story." He said he has tried to live by this directive, which he calls "The Law of Anecdotal Value."

As the hosts of the Moth storytelling podcast say, "live a story-worthy life."

This is an important piece of advice, and one we thought worth offering here because it encourages us to actually do stuff that's interesting and worth repeating to others.

Remember, the whole basis for your personal brand is to build an interesting personal story, to actually do things worth telling other people about. It means getting out of the office and doing things. It means going out for drinks, coffee, or dinner once in a while, instead of going straight home. It means going to festivals or taking mini vacations with friends. It means going to conferences and spending time meeting new people. It even means reading books. And best of all, it means not watching television every night.

We have yet to hear an interesting story that starts with, "One night, while I was watching TV…"

We want to encourage you to do things that add value to your own life. Throughout the rest of this book, we're going to tell you to share interesting things that are of value to the people in your network. But we don't want you to spend all your time amassing other people's interesting information. We want you to be a source of interesting information and stories yourself.

Living an anecdotal life—a "story-worthy" life—usually means being passionate about things you enjoy doing, or want to achieve, and then working and thinking about how to get it done. We talked about passion in Chapter 1, but it's worth mentioning again: You will not be following the Law of Anecdotal Value if you just sit around and watch TV night after night or sit in your cubicle day after day without dreaming of, and working toward, your next big thing.

Plenty of people live their lives without passion and without doing anything. They don't have anything to inspire them, and they don't try anything new. Some people eat the same food, go to the same restaurants, and drive the same route to the same job they've had for 20 years because it's easier to do that than to work a little harder to accomplish something a little better.

These people don't want More. They are happy with Good Enough. Good Enough is easy because it doesn't require any work. But the problem with Good Enough is that it sucks the life and motivation right out of you. Once you have achieved it, there's never a reason to reach for More.

If you want to follow the Law of Anecdotal Value, it means you won't accept the status quo and do only what you need to do to earn the next paycheck. It means you'll actually do something that takes some time and effort. This book is filled with case studies and testimonials from people who have worked to do more in life, and as a result, have dozens of stories to tell; we've chosen a few of our favorite social media professionals and asked them to share their stories with us.

Surround Yourself with Passionate People

If you want to lead that story-worthy life and have interesting stories to share, surround yourself with people who have a passion for something in their lives. It doesn't have to be the same passion as yours. You want to surround yourself with people who love what they do as much as you love what you do, if not more.

Whether it's someone who loves her work or loves her hobby, find a way to spend time with that person—she'll sweep you up in her energy, and you'll add her fuel to your own fire. Her energy will be contagious—as yours will be to her—and you can feed off each other's ideas and passions.

As you spend more time with these people, and learn from them, you'll learn new stories to tell, discover new ways to tell them, and best of all, you'll create your own stories. Next, you have to share them with other people to get them to stick.

Sharing Memories and Stories

You can tell your story by using a lot of different tools and technologies. We'll cover them in Chapters 3 ("Blogging: Telling Your Story") and 7 ("Say Cheese: Sharing Photos and Videos"), but first we want tell you why it's important.

Think about your family's best stories. What are the stories that get told and retold during family gatherings? What are those stories that are passed down from generation to generation, father to son, mother to daughter? These are the stories that family legends are made of.

There is no reason you can't have stories like that or that they need to stay only with you. One of the cool things social media lets us do is to share those stories with each other.

Both of us have heard stories from friends and colleagues like Jason Falls, a notable social media practitioner and Erik's co-author on another book (you can read his case study in Chapter 15, "Personal Branding: Using What You've Learned to Land Your Dream Job.") that we repeat to our own audiences. These stories have become memorable, and occasionally legendary, in their retelling because they're interesting things that actually happened to these people.

But here's the important thing: You have to tell these stories. You have to be willing to share those stories with people—whether it's writing it up as a blog post, posting it on Facebook, or letting your videos and pictures tell the story for you and putting them online for others to see and share. Stories help people understand and connect with you better; certainly better than lists of data points and proclamations.

If you're not comfortable sharing parts of your life, don't share them. No one said you had to tell everything you were doing, show photos of every aspect of your life, or reveal every personal detail you'd rather keep private.

"There are just some things I don't want people to know about," we often hear from social media resisters.

Fine, don't share those things. If you don't want people to know where you live, don't put your house on Swarm. If you don't want people to know you're on vacation, don't post photos to Facebook while you're out. (In fact, that's a very important safety tip! Never tell people you're on vacation. Only post photos and updates when you get back.)

Share the parts of your life that you feel comfortable sharing and keep the rest of the stuff private. Rather than relying on the ever-changing, always-complex Facebook privacy settings to keep your stuff hidden, just don't put it up in the first place. If you live in a small town or a suburb, don't put that on Twitter. Instead, put the nearest big city in your Twitter bio.

Just remember that to build relationships with people and get them to know and like you, you need to reveal some parts of yourself to make yourself seem more human. That's how sharing memories, knowledge, and visual content through social media will help you build your personal brand.

Ten Do's and Don'ts of Telling Your Story

Everyone should follow certain rules when embarking on their personal brand journey. Read, reread, and read again the points made in this section of the chapter. They will help guide you through the situations you will face while building your personal brand.

1. Don't Post Pictures that Would Shock Your Mother

Every social networking site lets you post pictures. Whether you're on Facebook, Twitter, or LinkedIn, you can post pictures of yourself to help tell your story. Don't be stupid when it comes to your picture posting and professional storytelling.

It's safe to say that an employer doesn't want to see you doing a keg stand or flashing the band at a concert (especially a symphony orchestra). Post pictures that strengthen your story and completely avoid pictures that you would be ashamed to show your mom. The general rule of thumb is to imagine your mom, your boss, and your biggest client are in a car together, driving by a billboard with your photo. If you would be embarrassed for them to see it, don't post it.

2. Don't View Your Personal Brand Story as a Sales Pitch

Plenty of people dislike getting sales calls during dinner. Or ever. The same is true of your personal brand. Don't create your story as a sales pitch. If you treat your personal brand as a conversation rather than a sales pitch, your readers will trust you. If the whole point of your brand is just to sell, sell, sell, you're a breathing advertisement. And we all know how people feel about advertisements.

3. Don't Post Something You'll Regret

Imagine a situation in which an employee posts something extremely negative about a client, a business partner, or even a whole city she's visiting, and it's seen and shared by hundreds of people online.

We know people who have posted a nasty or negative comment at a time when, frankly, they should not have been posting anything after having spent months trying to cultivate an image of being a respected professional.

The people used Twitter or Facebook to share their comments and meant them as a joke. They then realized the error of their ways and deleted the offending posts. However, it was too late because people had taken screen shots or even retweeted and shared them with hundreds and thousands of other people. The fallout in those cases has been staggering.

For example, in May 2017, Denver Post sports writer Terry Frei tweeted that he "was very uncomfortable that a Japanese driver—" Takuma Sato"—(won) the Indianapolis 500 over Memorial Day weekend."

The backlash was immediate and enormous. Frei apologized a few hours later, giving his reasons why he made the statement, but he was released by the Denver Post the following day.[3]

---

3. http://www.complex.com/sports/2017/05/sportswriter-fired-racially-insensitive-tweet-takuma-sato-indy-500-win

What would you do if an employee embarrassed you and your company with a misguided tweet? What if it was a potential customer or vendor? Or even a job candidate? Would you fire the person? Probably. Would you do business with them? Doubt it. Would you ever hire them? Absolutely not.

The old World War II phrase "Loose lips sink ships" fits here. Everything on the Internet is saved, whether it's Google's cached pages or by Archive.org (a site that saves web pages as they're created; Erik has found stuff he wrote back in 1996). Remember that everything is being read, and everyone is listening to what is being posted. You're not invisible.

4. Don't Ask for Things First; Ask for Things Second

Your role in building your personal brand is twofold. To help other people, and then to help yourself. When we help others, we all succeed, not the other way around. When Erik offers to help Kyle with a project, Kyle is more likely to help Erik when he needs it. But if Erik asks for help first, Kyle may be busy at the time and can't help out. And later, if Kyle needs help, Erik will remember that, and he'll be "busy" as well.

@kyleplacy: Is that why you couldn't help me set up that blog site last week? You're so selfish.

@edeckers: How hard is it to help people move? I spent 12 hours loading and unloading that damn truck.

@kyleplacy: I was at my sister's wedding!

@edeckers: My back still hurts!

The important lesson is to give before you ask. By doing so, you'll build up goodwill, and people will be more willing to help you. (We'll talk more about this idea in Chapter 9.)

5. Don't Get Distracted

It's easy to get distracted when you work on your personal branding. There is so much to do, so much to say, and so much to accomplish that it can be hard sometimes to focus on a specific task. It's easy to get distracted by all the things you "ought" to be doing and tools you "ought" to try. But being active does not mean being effective.

Remember that focus is key when it comes to telling your story. If you lose focus and slip, brush yourself off, drop the thing that distracted you, and refocus your efforts. By refocusing your efforts, you can more easily meet your goal.

@edeckers: Squirrel!

@kyleplacy: RT @edeckers: Squirrel!

6. Don't Underestimate the Power of Your Network

Your current network should mean everything to you. These are people who know about opportunities, deals, and projects that you may never hear about otherwise. They are the people who can connect you with individuals who could change your career, your company, and your life.

Rather than trying to figure things out on your own, ask your network for help. If you want to be connected, you have to let your network do its thing. However, remember to not badger your network into helping you all the time. Ask for help when it is needed, and then be sure to be effusive and public with your thanks.

7. Do Invest in Yourself

Invest in yourself by always staying informed about what's going on in your industry. Read blogs from your industry and allied industries, attend seminars, read books, and listen to podcasts.

You want to be ahead of the game compared to your peers. Read and talk to people to improve your knowledge. Investing in yourself is one of the most important aspects of your personal development and growth.

8. Do Invest in Other People

When you invest in other people, they invest in you. This could be as simple as sending an email or Twitter message for someone. When you give, you will receive. When you help others grow and find new opportunities, they'll return the favor. If you ignore them, they'll ignore you when you need their help. (We'll discuss this extensively in Chapter 9.)

9. Do Be Visible and Active

It's just as important to stay visible in the world of social media as it is to invest in yourself. In fact, staying visible and involved is a form of self-investment.

You can be visible by sharing information on a daily basis and staying in front of the influencers, clients, and network connections that matter. By being visible, you maintain awareness of your personal brand.

10. Do Take Some Time for Yourself

Read this last one carefully: You will most certainly be overwhelmed with the amount of information you receive, content being processed, content being shared, and stories being developed. You need to take some time for yourself. This means turning off everything you're doing and spending time with family or friends. If you don't, you'll get caught in the never-ending process of personal branding and be completely void of your own winning personality after a couple of years of grinding yourself into the dust. And we like you just the way you are.

II

Your Network Is Your Castle—Build It

3 Blogging: Telling Your Story 43

4 LinkedIn: Networking on Steroids 75

5 Twitter: Sharing in the Conversation 95

6 Facebook: Developing a Community of Friends 119

7 Say Cheese: Sharing Photos and Videos 141

8 Other Social Networking Tools 169

9 Googling Yourself: Finding Yourself on
Search Engines 183

10 Bringing It All Together: Launching
Your Brand 205

11 Measuring Success: You Like Me,
You Really Like Me! 225

3

Blogging: Telling Your Story

Blogging is an easy way to publish your thoughts, ideas, and insights, and it can be done without any web coding. You can showcase your best work and invite others to comment on what you've done.

And a blog is easy to start: You sign up for a free blogging platform, pick a theme to make it look nice, buy a domain name that's easy to remember, write some blog posts, and promote it to your friends and family.

Blogging should be at the center of your social media campaign, because it's the anchor for all your efforts. Your blog is the place where you send everyone. It's the collection of all your knowledge, the hub of your personal branding wheel, the virtual spot where you plant your personal branding seed and say, "This is where I will grow." And despite the know-it-all wags who have claimed "blogging is dead" for the last ten years, a blog is still the most important piece of online real estate. (It's also the centerpiece for most corporate content marketing, too.)

If you're an artist, you'll upload photos of your work to your blog. If you're a consultant, you'll share your thoughts about your industry. If you're looking for a job, you'll write about industry issues to demonstrate that you understand what your potential employer is dealing with. And if you're a nonprofit, what better way to keep donors up to date with different research, political developments, and current events than by blogging?

It's not impossible to have a personal branding campaign without a blog, but it's difficult. You need a central place to showcase your thoughts, ideas, and work.

Remember, two of the personal branding universal objectives (see Chapter 1, "Welcome to the Party") are to tell your story and to be bold. You need to tell people about yourself, and a blog is the best way to do it. You can keep a record of what you've done, where you've done it, and what you were thinking when you did it. It's a journal of your professional accomplishments that show your value to an employer, a client, or your industry in general.

What Is Blogging?

To begin, you need to register on a blogging platform, like Blogspot or WordPress. Today's blogging platforms make it easy for anyone, even non-programmers, to share photographs and videos online and to post articles for the world to read.

Before these different blogging platforms, any web updates had to be done via HTML coding. If you wanted to post a new article, you had to place your new article above the old one, format it via HTML, and upload it via File Transfer Protocol (FTP). If you were really good, you could add a new pre-written article in about 1520 minutes. Now, it's just a matter of entering text in a window that looks like an email window, formatting it, and clicking the "publish" button.

Take a look at Figures 3.1–3.3 for examples of what an email window, a Blogger window, and a WordPress window look like.

Most blogging platforms are just as easy to use as your email. Your subject line is your headline, and you type the content in the body. You format the text with the formatting buttons, which look an awful lot like the ones at the top of any word processing program. In an email, you click "send," and the other person receives your email in seconds. In blogging, you click "publish," and your post is published in seconds.

✉ *Note*

In the second edition of this book, we said there were more than 40 different blogging platforms. Now, in 2017, it's closer to 100, including emerging new sites like Medium and Ghost, as well as LinkedIn and

Facebook, that provide publishing space. Still, we're going to stick with the most popular ones: WordPress, Blogger, Tumblr, and (now) Medium. We'll mention others at times, but when we discuss blogging, we're primarily thinking of these four, and especially WordPress because it's what we use for our clients.

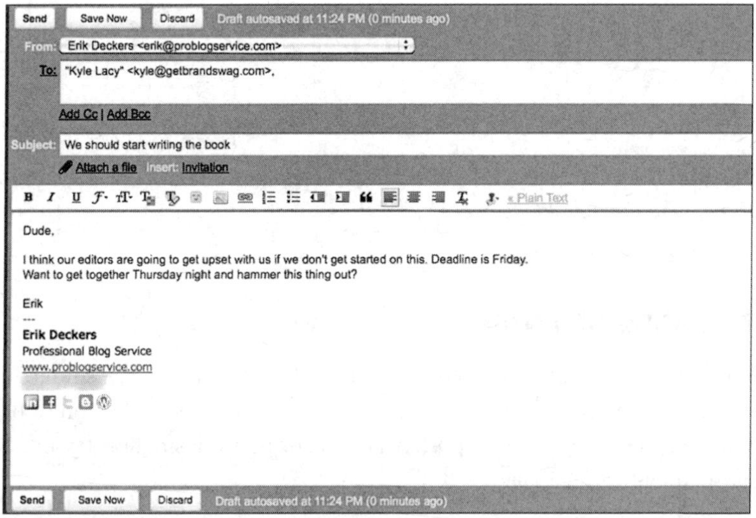

Figure 3.1 *A Gmail window.*

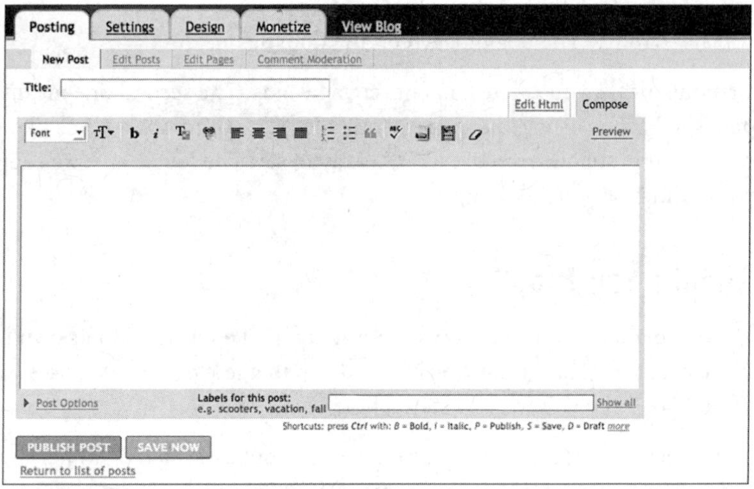

Figure 3.2 *A Blogger.com window. Google owns Blogger and Gmail, which may explain why these two look similar.*

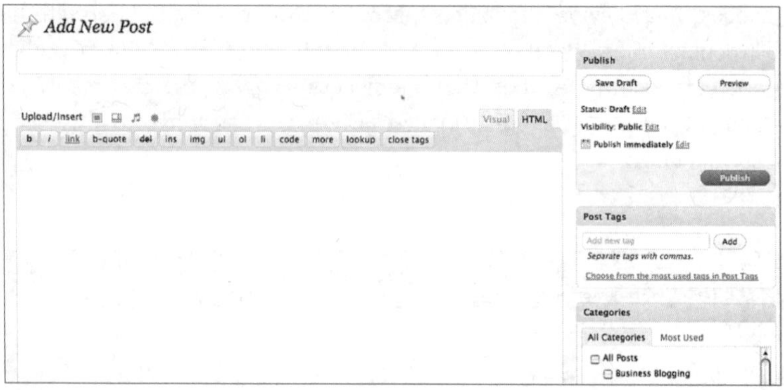

Figure 3.3 *A WordPress window. Whether you use WordPress.com or self-hosted WordPress. The window looks like this.*

A Clarification of Terms

There is a difference between a blog and a post. People use the terms interchangeably, but there are actually two strict definitions. A *blog* is the collection of blog posts. It is *not* a single article or post. An *article* or *post* is a single entry in a blog, similar to an entry in a diary.

- Wrong: "I wrote a new blog today."

- Right: "I wrote a new post today."

- Also right: "I blogged today."

- Really wrong: "The dog blogged on the floor again."

The first one means you created an entirely new blog. The second one means you just published a new article on your existing blog. The third one sounds like you picked up a virus somewhere, but it's still okay to say. The fourth one we slipped in when the editors weren't looking.

Why Should You Blog?

There are as many reasons to blog as there are blogs. People have their own reasons to start one, but they can usually be boiled down to a few major categories. See if one of these fits why you want to start a blog.

- **You want to establish your expertise:** You could start a blog to help your chances in a job search, to launch a public speaking career, or to show all those jerks from high school that your knowledge of mollusk mating habits was not useless.

This is also a good way to improve your own knowledge in your field: You need to keep up with your industry in order to tell your readers about it. So, if nothing else, blogging forces you to stay current on your knowledge, and establishes you as an industry expert.

- **You want to market or sell something:** Businesses use their blogs to engage directly with their customers and help them make buying decisions about their products or services. This is called content marketing, and it's all the rage in marketing circles.

  You may not sell anything on your blog, but you can sell things because of it. You can showcase your products and drive people to your website to increase sales. Many businesses have embraced blogging for marketing, which is why we know it isn't going away any time soon. When the business world picks something up, it'll be around forever. (It's 2017, and plenty of businesses still have fax numbers.)

- **You have something to say:** Whether it's personal observations about life, political beliefs, or knowledge you want to impart, you want a place to publish your thoughts. Even if you write your blog for just three people, it's important to have a platform to stand on. We know bloggers who started out writing for only a few friends and now measure their readers by the tens of thousands each month.

  It's worth noting that sharing personal beliefs on a blog for professional branding can backfire. Potential employers may read your blog, and getting too personal or too controversial can keep you from getting the job. So if you want to use your personal blog as your platform to talk about the current political climate, just be aware that your employer may think differently than you.

- **You want to share your passion:** Many blogs are about someone's passion or hobby. Photographers, collectors, and writers have all showcased their talents or acquisitions through blogging. Whether it's the photographer who uploads her best wedding photos or the antique tractor collector who's showing off his latest steering wheel, bloggers have shared their passions with other people like them.

- **You want to be a part of a community:** The great thing about sharing your passion is that people who share that passion will soon find you. If you write about marble collecting, other marble collectors will find you on the search engines and any networks where marble collectors hang out. You can share information via your blogs, talk about upcoming events, and eventually meet face to face at the Marble Collecting Convention. (Yes, there actually is one. Erik gave a TEDx talk about it once.)

- **You want to make money:** You can make money from blogging, but it can be difficult. There are three basic ways: ad sales, freelance blogging, or affiliate blogging. Our good friend, Douglas Karr (MarketingTech-Blog.com), is one of the most widely read bloggers in Indiana, and his blog has been one of Ad Age's Top 150 blogs. But he makes just a small amount of money from ad sales each year.

  Freelance blogging or **ghost blogging**, is writing blog posts for other companies, and they pay you for it. Erik's company is a ghost blogging company.

  Affiliate blogging is selling things for other companies through your own website or blog. For example, you set up a system in which you are an affiliate of Amazon.com. You create a page that has a link to this book in Amazon's system. If a visitor to your page buys our book, you make a small commission.

  Some people, like Heather Sokol, have built small businesses that do nothing but affiliate sales (see Figure 3.4). They create several blogs, write posts about different products for them, and then promote them via search engines and social media so people will buy their affiliate products or services.

Figure 3.4 *Heather Sokol runs Inexpensively.com as part of her affiliate blogging network. This is one possible way to make money from blogging.*

PERSONAL BRANDING CASE STUDY:
JONATHAN THOMAS, ANGLOTOPIA.COM

Jonathan Thomas loves England, even though he lives in Indiana. He's dreamed of living in Britain for most of his life, so he and his wife started the website and print magazine *Anglotopia* for Anglophiles, people who love the United Kingdom, its history, and its culture.

Jonathan started the website in 2007 and had actually just celebrated its 10th anniversary when we asked him to participate in this case study.

"I started *Anglotopia* because I couldn't find a website that ticked all my Anglophile boxes," said Jonathan. "I needed extra money, so I thought I could make money at this newfangled blogging thing."

Jonathan started *Anglotopia* with two goals in mind: to make extra money and to return to England somehow. It's worked out—he and his wife have since made ten trips to England, some paid for by others, most paid for by them. And now running *Anglotopia* is his full-time job.

Although he hesitates to use the word "blog"—he thinks of each installation as a publication—he has two, uhh, online publications: *Anglotopia*, which focuses on British travel, culture, and history, and *Londontopia*, a site dedicated solely to London.

Erik first got to know Jonathan back when they were both travel writers for the state of Indiana, and Erik, a mild Anglophile, has been a fan of *Anglotopia* ever since. Meanwhile, Jonathan took what he learned as a Hoosier travel writer and started using it in *Anglotopia*.

"*Visit Indiana* was my first real experience as a blogging superstar, as local tourist authorities were happy to host me and I got paid to do the blogging," said Jonathan. "I got to see some really cool parts of Indiana."

Anglotopia has opened up a few travel doors for the Thomases too. Jonathan said he's taken some trips with support from someone else. Most recently, a major airline arranged for him and his wife to fly free in business class on a research trip. They were also given a tour of the airline's heritage museum that's normally closed to the public.

"We were treated like VIPs, and it's a great feeling to be taken seriously. Even after ten years, it still feels good to be taken seriously," Jonathan said.

The site once even led to a job offer and a chance to move to England permanently. The fact that he had built the blog from scratch and did all the marketing himself was a big boost. He had just started following the CEO of a London startup on Twitter, and the CEO tweeted about a digital marketing job at his company. Jonathan asked if they would be willing to sponsor a visa. The CEO said they would and encouraged him to apply.

He and his wife flew over (another airline flew them for free in exchange for writing about the trip—a common travel writing exchange), Jonathan worked in the office for a week while he did a series of formal interviews, and at the end of the trip, he was offered the job. Sadly, he turned it down when he and his wife discovered she was pregnant, and they wanted to have the baby in the U.S.

A few years later, Jonathan was laid off, so he made *Anglotopia* his full time job (he was already making more money at it than he was at his actual job), and he hasn't looked back. He's been working on it full-time since 2011, and he has no desire to work for anyone else. Social media marketing has always been important to *Anglotopia's* success, but Facebook has been the biggest help.

"A few years ago we exploded from a few thousand fans to over 100,000. Now we're at 225,000 fans," Jonathan said.

One important lesson Jonathan has learned is that advertising to high web traffic is no longer the way to make money. It used to be that Google would pay a lot of money for clicks, but Facebook changed its algorithms as a way to force businesses to pay to promote their posts, which slowed their Facebook traffic (and thus, their Google payments) to a trickle.

So *Anglotopia's* biggest product now is its audience. Jonathan sells access to a very specific niche that is valuable to advertisers. As one of the leading Anglophile websites, Jonathan is reaching an audience of devoted fans, and advertisers are willing to pay for that access. He markets their products across all of *Anglotopia's* social media channels and in an email newsletter.

Through it all, and by focusing solely on his blog, Jonathan has created some great opportunities for him and his family.

"There's the big advertising/marketing deal with a huge international company. There's getting offered your dream job because someone can clearly see what you've done on the Internet," said Jonathan. "There's being flown for free to Britain or getting comped free hotel rooms or discounts on car rentals. All because you run a publication."

He sometimes wonders whether a real job would be less stressful, but he wouldn't want to give up what he's doing.

He said, "This is so much more rewarding."

Choose Your Blogging Platforms

All of the platforms we discuss in this chapter are completely free to use, including WordPress.com and Tumblr. Some of them have additional upgrades you can buy, but they're optional, and you can run your blog without them.

If you're not technically savvy or don't know anyone who is, we recommend that you start your new blog on Blogspot, WordPress.com, or Tumblr. You can set one up in less than 30 minutes, and the hardest part will be choosing which theme you want to use (graphic design elements, such as background, colors, and photos). But after you're up and running, it's a breeze to add new content.

Blogspot.com/Blogger.com

Blogspot was called Blogger before Google purchased it in 2003. Now, typing in either URL will get you to the same place. It's one of the most widely used blog platforms around the world. It's easy to use, and it integrates seamlessly into other Google properties like Picasa (photo sharing), YouTube, and Google Analytics (web analytics software).If you've signed up for a free Google account of any sort, whether it's Gmail, Google Analytics, Google Drive, or even YouTube, you have a Blogspot account.

Blogspot is also a hosted blog site, which means your blog lives on Google's servers. You don't have to mess with server storage or updating and maintaining software, and it doesn't cost anything.

Although many advanced bloggers look down their e-noses at Blogspot, it's one of the most widely used of all the blogging platforms because it's easy. However that also means it's limited in what it can do. It doesn't have the add-ons and plug-ins that WordPress does, although it does allow users to create separate pages.

Note

Let's define a few terms:

Add-ons and plug-ins are features you can add on or plug in to a blog to increase its functionality. Pages are extra pages you can add to a blog, which are accessible from the front page. This lets it work more like a website than a traditional blog. This is a fairly new development in the blogging world, so it is not available on every platform.

The URL for your blog will look like "http://bobscrumrunner.blogspot.com" (or whatever name you choose; this is one we created for the book. You can actually visit it.), but Blogspot has a feature that lets you cloak your blog behind your purchased domain. (See the later section "Purchasing and Hosting a Domain Name" for more information.) The upside of cloaking is that your domain, BobScrumrunner.com, is always visible. The downside is that there are no specific URLs, like "http://bobscrumrunner.blogspot.com/2009/12/18/my-trip-to-the-twine-museum.html." The original domain is the only one to show up in the address bar. This means you can't copy the longer URL that sends someone to a specific post.

Erik runs his humor blog, ErikDeckers.com, on Blogspot.

WordPress.com and WordPress.org

WordPress is a more advanced, powerful, and sophisticated platform than Blogspot. WordPress is open source software, which means a community of users and developers are freely working to improve it and add new features. You can choose from two versions of WordPress, depending on how much effort you want to put into it: WordPress.com and self-hosted WordPress (also known as WordPress.org).

- **WordPress.com** is a hosted blog site, like Blogspot. You don't worry about server space, paying for usage, or maintaining a server. WordPress.com is a little more basic than WordPress.org, which means it's suitable for the beginning blogger who is happy with using templates and having limited functionality. WordPress.org is a better fit for more technically inclined bloggers who want to learn new software.

  A WordPress.com URL looks like: "http://bobscrumrunner.wordpress .com," but WordPress.com will also, for a fee, let you choose your domain name (but won't cloak the longer URLs, which is good), buy extra storage, post videos with a WordPress player, and eliminate ads. But other than those options, it's free. (If you have a WordPress.com blog already, go to the dashboard and click the Upgrades button for pricing. There are currently three options, Personal, Premium, and Business, which let you add more features, customization, and even storage space.)

- **Self-hosted WordPress/WordPress.org,** on the other hand, is software that you download and install onto your server—it's self-hosted. This takes some technical know-how. If you're technically savvy, have the patience and willingness to learn, or can bribe a geeky friend with a nice lunch, you can tackle this version. If you plan to become a blogger of some note, or plan to have a lot of features, you need a self-hosted WordPress blog (you can download the software at WordPress.org and install it on your own server, or use a web host like GoDaddy which has "one-click installation." You don't have to start here, but you'll want to get here sooner rather than later.

WordPress.com and self-hosted WordPress both let you create pages. Rather than writing code to create different pages, you can click buttons to create a new page for any topic or subject, like speaking videos, photos of your art, or any products you sell. Creating a new page is as easy as creating a new blog post.

✉ *Note*

Posts are regular blog posts listed in reverse chronological order on the home or blog page. Pages are static and not listed by date. An About page is a good example of a static page.

A self-hosted WordPress post will have its own URL—such as "http://www.bobscr-umrunner.com/blog/2010/04/12/I-met-Elvis-at-conference"—and the long URLs won't be cloaked. This is crucial to help your blog posts be found more easily on search engines.

The great thing about self-hosted WordPress is that it's fully customizable and has literally thousands of plug-ins and add-ons for your blog. With these plug-ins, you can do all this and more:

- Block spam comments.
- Ask readers to take a survey.
- Optimize your blog to be found more quickly by search engines.
- Integrate your Picasa or Flickr account.
- Create an e-commerce site.
- Create your own shortened URL based on your domain name.
- Show visitor locations and stats.
- Post your workout results.
- Post the Turkish lira exchange rates in your sidebar.

Basically, we could write an entire book with nothing but WordPress plug-ins, and it would be out of date the second we sent it to the publisher. That's because new plug-ins are constantly developed and released, and old ones are dropped by their developers all the time.

Both of us use self-hosted WordPress. for client blogs. We also have our work blogs on our own servers using the self-hosted WordPress software; Kyle's is at KyleLacy.com; Erik's is at ProBlogService.com.

Other Blogging Platforms

At least 100 other blogging platforms are available. All of them are free, although some of them offer premium upgrades as WordPress.com does. Several are increasing in popularity.

Tumblr

Tumblr (no "e") lets you post text, photos, and videos just by uploading or emailing them to your blog. Unlike the other platforms, however, users can follow each other and see their posts aggregated on their own dashboard.

Basically, if Kyle follows Erik's blog, both blogs appear on Kyle's dashboard. If he follows a third blog, his dashboard includes that one as well, but Erik's does not. You just need to click the "Follow" button in the upper-right corner (see Figure 3.5) to follow someone's blog.

Figure 3.5 *A Tumblr blog. Note the "Follow" button at the top right of the window. That's how you follow a Tumblr blog.*

Tumblr has been embraced by younger users as an acceptable substitute for WordPress—it's great for anyone who wants to have a blog presence but doesn't want to bother with a self-hosted WordPress site.

Tumblr lends itself to the rapid response, on-the-go blogging that a lot of mobile phone users want without all the hassle of messing around with something bigger and more complicated like a WordPress blog. If you snap a photo on your mobile phone or have a random thought or even write a short article (100–200 words), it's great for Tumblr. There's even a dedicated mobile app, and you can email any text, audio, video, and photos from any mobile phone.

Another reason Tumblr has been embraced by a lot of younger users and social media pros is that it's a community. Like we mentioned, it's easy to follow each other's blogs (just like Twitter), which lets you connect with other users, building your own community of favorite Tumblrs. And as you follow other Tumblrs, you can see their own blogs in your feed. However, there's no way to divide Tumblr feeds into separate groups like Twitter (see "Chapter 5, Twitter: Sharing in the Conversation"), so if you follow a lot of people, you'll be overwhelmed by the resulting feed.

You can also integrate your Tumblr blog into your Google Analytics app, auto-promote new posts on Twitter and Facebook, and fully optimize it for search engines.

On the downside, Tumblr is not a great fit for long-form writing, and it doesn't have any plug-ins. It's intended to be a simple micro-blogging service, rather than a full-blown blog or extensive communication tool.

If you want something for short, pithy comments and lots of photos and videos, Tumblr is a great tool for the beginning blogger. But if you want to write longer blog posts, it can't handle the posts very easily. And if you decide to export your blog to another blogging platform, such as WordPress, it can be rather convoluted.

Actors Wil Wheaton, Mark Ruffalo, and Felicia Day are famous Tumblr users, as is David J. Peterson, the guy who created the Dothraki and Valerian languages for *Game Of Thrones*.

Medium

Medium has just sort of burst on the scene over the last few years, becoming a major publisher of notable writers, artists, and thinkers. Large publications began shifting their written content over to Medium and sharing their work there rather than on their own websites. Even President Obama pre-released his 2015 State of the Union Address on Medium.[1]

Medium is different primarily because it does something no other blog platform does: It emphasizes the quality of writing over the most popular (that is, most read) articles, to ensure the site's readers only get the good stuff. The editors will often pick their favorite articles, called—what else?—Editors Picks. These are often based on Total Time Read, reviews, and total engagements.[2]

If you write an outstanding article, but someone else writes a schlocky article and gets 5,000 friends to read it, your article can still be placed higher because it's better. So Medium forces you to really polish up your writing skills and bring your A-game.

Medium has an enormous audience with millions of visitors each month. Think about what that can mean for your brand if you got only a tenth of a percent of that.

Those millions of visitors can also lead to better search rankings for your Medium articles than your own blog. (But if you publish on Medium, be sure to publish on your own blog a few days earlier, and then post a link back to the original article. That's so your blog will be recognized by Google as the "canonical" or original source of the article.)

Medium also has a strong community of fellow writers. Not only can you find potential collaboration partners, but you can link back to each other's articles, which will also contribute to your overall traffic.

---

1. https://medium.com/@ObamaWhiteHouse/president-obamas-state-of-the-union-address-remarks-as-prepared-for-delivery-55f9825449b2

2. https://medium.com/@yourfriends/how-we-curate-guidelines-and-principles-fdcf43e049c5

Bottom line, we don't recommend Medium as your primary publication. It's a great publishing platform because it's widely read, but as the old saying goes, "don't build on rented land." What will you do with all your original content if Medium ever goes out of business? More importantly, why would you put more effort into getting traffic to someone else's blog over your own?

Remember, you want traffic to *your* blog. That's *your* reputation, *your* readership, *your* thought leadership, and that's all that counts if you ever want to review products, get sponsors, or attract a conference organizer's or editor's attention. So publish to your blog first, and then republish to Medium.

Which Platform Is Right for You?

So which platform is best? We're going to give you one of those maddening answers that people give when they don't want to make a choice.

It depends.

It depends on what your level of commitment will be, what your level of technological expertise is, and how much time and money you want to spend on your blog. Table 3.1 shows a few questions to ask yourself before you choose your blogging platform.

Table 3.1   Choosing Your Blogging Platform

Issue	Platform
Money is a concern. You want free.	Blogger, WordPress.com*
You want stability and ease of use.	Blogger, Medium, WordPress.com
You need convenience and speed.	Tumblr
You want to customize.	Self-hosted WordPress
You want to use your blog as an e-commerce site.	Self-hosted WordPress
You need multiple pages, like a website.	Blogger, WordPress

*Self-hosted WordPress is free as well, but it's your server hosting that actually costs money.

Setting Up a Blog

Setting up a blog can be quite easy. Blogging platform companies want to get as many people to sign up as they can, so they make it as easy as possible to use their services. Basically, if you have ever set up another social network profile, even Twitter or Facebook, you can set up a blog. Like we said earlier, the hardest part of the process is choosing a theme to use.

Just go to one of the blog platforms we listed, or any of the others we didn't, and follow the step-by-step instructions. No programming, no coding, no dealing with technical issues (unless you choose the self-hosted WordPress option). Just fill in the blanks, and you're done. But we can give you a few hints to make your blog more successful.

- **Choose an easy-to-say URL:** When you tell people where your blog is, you want something you can actually pronounce without difficulty. No special characters, weird spellings, or special abbreviations. When Erik set up his Blogspot account, he made the mistake of getting a URL with a dash: http://laughing-stalk.blogspot.com. After a few years, he got so tired of telling people "laughing dash stalk dot blogspot dot com" that he had to purchase his name as his domain name—ErikDeckers.com— and forward it to the website. Of course, now he has to make sure people spell his first name correctly, but it's a lot easier than explaining that stupid dash.

- **Choose a professional-looking theme:** If you keep the default theme that comes with your new blog, you'll be branded as an amateur or a poseur until you change it. Pick something you like but is easy to modify. Depending on which theme you choose, this can actually be one of the hardest parts about blogging. Not because you need any technological know-how to make it happen, but because there are dozens, hundreds, or even thousands of choices, depending on which platform you pick. (Self-hosted WordPress has the most.) Find one you like, and stick with it. If you're going for a serious, professional image, be willing to spend a little money on a theme. They're professional looking, well-designed, and optimized for search engines, making them well worth the cost.

- **Set up an RSS feed:** Regardless of which blog platform you choose, we recommend FeedBurner.com as a way to measure your RSS feed. (RSS stands for Really Simple Syndication, and it's the way you get your new blog posts to your readers, who can see them on an RSS reader, like My Yahoo! or Flipboard.)

Tip

All WordPress blogs come installed with an anti-spam plug-in called Akismet. Follow the directions on your blog dashboard for installation. Even if you have a self-hosted WordPress blog, you still need a WordPress.com account to activate Akismet.

Purchasing and Hosting a Domain Name

Your domain name is crucial when setting up your blog and your personal brand in general. This is the first thing search engines key in on when they index a website or blog. If your domain explains what it is you do, who you are, what you sell, and so on, you get a lot more search engine juice. (That's one of those technical terms we use to sound cool.)

You don't need to purchase a domain name when setting up your blog. But you may find that as you get further into this and become more proficient, you want to have a special domain name. You can purchase this before or after you set up your blog.

For example, if you sell abstract French art, you should get a domain that has some variation of those words in it, like "LesliesFrenchArt." That will tell the different search engines what your site is all about, and they'll know how to index the site. They'll know what keywords and hyperlinks to look for, and they'll make sure the "best" hyperlinks to your site have something to do with either art or France.

✉ *Note*

Generally, it's a good idea to purchase your name as a domain name. That makes it easier for people to remember, helps you when you try to show-case yourself to hiring managers, and even helps you be found more easily on search engines. If you share a name with someone famous, add your middle name or initial to your domain name to set yourself apart.

We strongly recommend that you use a domain registrar like GoDaddy (GoDaddy.com), Network Solutions (NetSol.com), or other independent registrars, as opposed to purchasing a domain through a blog hosting provider. You could run into a couple of dangers with the latter:

- They charge more than your typical registrar for a domain. (You can get them for $9.95 or less from GoDaddy.)

- They may try to keep your domain if you ever try to switch to a different provider.

If you work with a reputable domain registrar, you can avoid those problems.

Getting Inspired

First, if you've never considered yourself a writer, now is the time to start thinking of yourself as one. You're writing blog posts, therefore, you're a writer. And writers have processes. They have procedures. They have their favorite places to think, their favorite ways to find ideas, and their favorite ways to get inspired.

Pay attention to where you get your ideas, and start writing them down. Maybe you like to come up with ideas sitting in a coffee shop with a Moleskine notebook in front of you; so get a latte and buy yourself a notebook. Maybe your ideas come in the middle of the night; keep an index card and pen on your nightstand, and write down ideas when you wake up. (Do not try to remember them the next day. That never works.) Maybe you get inspired in the shower, so get a low-flow shower head and take longer showers. Or maybe a meeting with a colleague triggers an idea, so send yourself an email, or write in your notebook, as soon as the meeting ends.

Whether it's music, exercising, or meditation, you need to find the things that inspire you to write, and then you need to start doing them. Combine those with your preferred sources for material, and you can start creating more blog posts than you'll know what to do with.

What Should You Write About?

You've got your blog set up. You've followed most of the advice we've laid out so far, and you're ready to start writing. Maybe you even wrote the obligatory "This is my first blog post" post. (Go back and delete that. That's amateur hour. Also, we both did that on our blogs.)

Hopefully you've figured out what to write about before you set up your blog. If you didn't, and you've waited this long to figure it out, we'd like to commend you on following our advice so closely.

We'd also like to ask you to buy five more copies of this book.

Figuring out what to write about can be what makes or breaks your blog. Although your subject matter is up to you, we can tell you that having a focused, specific topic is going to make your life much easier than if you have a broad, general topic. That seems rather counterintuitive, but it's true. You will have much more to write about if you narrow your focus to something small than if you write about something huge.

Say you want to blog about marketing. What's there to write about? Well, for starters, there's advertising, direct mail, marketing campaigns, marketing strategy, billboards, and Internet marketing. Most general bloggers we know can generate 10–20 posts about marketing, and then they're tapped out. The topics are too broad to cover without either going overboard and writing 50,000-word textbooks or getting stuck after writing their "this is my first marketing blog post" entry.

But if you make your blog about marketing strategy, you're getting somewhere. Your blog can be about creating strategies, critiquing other strategies, and even doing case studies about a company's strategy. Drill down a little more. How about "social media marketing strategy for nonprofits?" Even better. Now you can focus strictly on that one small niche about how nonprofits can improve their marketing efforts and raise more money. And because you're so tightly focused, you'll have an endless supply of topics to discuss.

By focusing on this niche, you're also more likely to catch the attention of nonprofits who want to improve their fund-raising and marketing. And—get this—they will want to hire the person who told them how to do it: you.

That's right. You've been giving a certain nonprofit all this free advice, and the management figures there must be a whole lot more rattling around in your head. That's why they'll pay you a lot of money to show what that "more" is and to help it get better at what it does.

ρ Tip

Check out the book *Free: The Future of a Radical Price* by Chris Anderson for an explanation of why giving stuff away for free will end up making you more money than if you charged for that same information in the first place. Believe it or not, if you blog about social media marketing strategy long enough, you'll be asked to give talks at conferences, get hired to consult at $100 per hour, and be asked to write a book, where you package your blog posts and your conference talks into easy-to-carry book form and sell it for $29.95...uhh, we've said too much.

Heather Mansfield writes the *Nonprofit Tech For Good* blog (NPTechForGood.com; see Figure 3.6), in which she tells non-profits how to use technology to reach members and donors. She writes about several different topics, all centered around non-profits and non-governmental organizations (NGOs) and how they can use social media technology to increase their reach. She also holds webinars, offers training, and travels around the world teaching her nonprofit and NGO clients how to use the plethora of technology out there.

Figure 3.6 *Heather Mansfield writes the* Nonprofit Tech For Good *blog as a way to promote her personal brand as a social media trainer, author, and speaker.*

Heather owns a company that specializes in training and consulting, so by writing constantly about topics in this area, she also establishes her own expertise, which makes her an attractive option to nonprofits that need her help using social technology.

By focusing on this very specific niche, Heather can plumb the depths of the topics that matter most to her audience: nonprofits that need help raising money from donors and volunteers.

Table 3.2 General to Narrow to Niche—Finding Your Specialty

General	Narrow	Niche
Cooking	Italian cooking	Gluten-free Italian cooking
History	American history	Civil War history
Business	Sales	Selling to large corporations
Marketing	Internet marketing	Email marketing
Finance	Personal finance	Personal finance for Millennials
Writing	Journalism	Running a weekly newspaper

Use these examples in Table 3.2, which compare a general topic to a narrow topic to a tightly focused niche, to help you figure out how to find your own niche.

If you're not sure how to focus your niche, ask your social networks what areas they think you should focus on. This is especially helpful if you're following a lot of people in your chosen industry.

Finding Subject Matter

One of the best places to find subject matter and writing topics for your blog is other blogs. This is especially true as you try to establish your place in your field. You want to be noticed by other bloggers (so they'll write about you and introduce you to their audiences), and the best way to do this is to write about them.

If you want to establish yourself as an expert in your field, writing about the latest developments in your chosen niche will show you're keeping up with the advancements in thinking and technology. You can become a resource to your readers by being the first to tell them about all the great stuff you've been reading. Not only should you share those articles via Twitter, but you should blog about them. This lets you add your own thoughts to their ideas and helps you set yourself apart from the Me Too crowd who only repeat what they've heard.

Here are some other places to find blogging ideas:

- Newspapers

- Trade journals

- Questions from customers

- Comments on previous posts

- Something you heard on the radio or saw on TV

How to Write a Blog Post

When you find your niche, figuring out your subject matter is very easy. But your blog is more than just an opinion column. Use different formats that can drive your topics and determine what you write about:

- **Personal versus professional topics:** Many bloggers who try to create a professional image worry about whether to write personal posts. They don't want to put too much information about themselves in public or confuse their personal life with their professional life. We don't think that's an issue. Social media has blurred the line between our personal and professional lives anyway, so there's nothing wrong with letting some of your "public personal" life bleed over into your professional life.

  As dreadful as some people may think personal blogging is, it's going to make you more accessible and likable. People will get to know you and feel a closer connection to you by reading what you think about personal topics like your favorite TV show or your adventures in find- ing a babysitter to watch the kids on a Friday night. Although this may not seem as important—because it frankly doesn't do squat for your credibility and expertise—it lets people get to know you. When they get to know you, they'll trust you. And when they trust you, they'll want to be a part of what you're doing.

  Remember, as part of your personal branding objectives (see Chapter 1), you're creating relationships. To create relationships, you need to be personable in order to build trust, which leads to the opportunities you're trying to create.

- **List posts:** This is a big favorite with readers, and it seems to generate more blog traffic than any other type of post. "Five Secrets to Successful Blog Writing" always gets more attention than "How to be a Successful Blog Writer." People are attracted to these because they're finite, they hold the promise of being short, and they're an easy read.[3] You can

---

3. http://www.newyorker.com/tech/elements/a-list-of-reasons-why-our-brains-love-lists

spend a little time on several topics and explore a few ideas at once. Later, if you're ever stuck for another article idea, you can come back to your list, pick an item from the list, and expand on it.

However, the list is starting to fall out of favor with some people, especially thanks to sites like BuzzFeed and Upworthy with their "27 Secrets About Your Favorite Movie. #18 Will Amaze You!" posts. So, if you're going to use a list post, do so sparingly, keep it brief, and avoid trying to amaze us.

- **Authority posts:** These establish your authority on a particular topic as your "messages from on high." Here, you can pontificate, philosophize, and predict. Talk about industry trends. Predict what issues your industry will face in the coming year. Review new books or technology, and give an opinion about whether you think they're great or they suck.

- **How-to posts:** These are more specific and factual than authority posts; they're for teaching processes, while authority posts are about expounding on viewpoints. For ideas, check out message boards for questions in your field or industry. Answer customer emails, especially ones you have to answer over and over. (In the future, you can just send customers a link to that post.) Write out step-by-step instructions whenever you can and include diagrams or photos, if possible.

- **News article and blog responses:** Find a post by someone in your field that you can respond to. State whether and why you agree or disagree (be polite), and present your own thoughts. Don't just say, "Here are five reasons why entrepreneurs should outsource your bookkeeping" and then repeat the five reasons. List a couple of reasons, but then add a couple of your own. Now you've contributed to the original author's conversation and maybe given him something to think about. You've also added to the body of knowledge about entrepreneurship.

  As an added benefit, if you link back to the original post, the author will see the link, which can increase the chances of him linking back to you and participating in your conversation as well. And that can introduce your blog to his readers.

- **Product reviews:** Review new products, services, restaurants, companies, software, tools, whatever you happen to be involved in. Because you're the expert, you're going to teach people about what's out there. Introduce people to the new offerings in your industry, and give an unbiased opinion about them. If you're a restaurant reviewer or travel wrier, review different restaurants and travel destinations. If you're a woodworker, talk about the new tools on the market.

Writing for Readers vs. Writing for Search Engines

A few years ago, there was a big debate in the industry about whether the quantity of posts was more important to search engine rankings than the quality of the writing.

Generally, people who write a lot of posts are concerned with winning search engine rankings—how high they rank in Google or Bing—because higher rankings mean more visitors. People who try to write better posts are more concerned with winning additional readers.

That argument was put to rest in 2011. Google wants quality writing over quantity. If you have to sacrifice quality to produce a lot of mediocre, poorly written content, save your time. Focus on producing the best writing you can and forget trying to produce as much content as you possibly can. The Google staff have said over and over again in the last six years that they want high-quality content and do not want anyone resorting to search engine optimization (SEO) trickery anymore. They've begun ignoring a lot of the old tricks—keyword stuffing, anchor text, putting the keywords in the headline, and so forth—and look at things like how long people spend reading your posts, whether people link back to your site, and even whether it's mobile-friendly and loads quickly. They're no longer concerned with the things that worked even two and three years ago, and some of those tricks can even get you penalized.

It's About the Quality of the Writing

You can tweak your blog's SEO to win search all day long, but if people don't like what you have to say or you say it poorly, they won't stick around, let alone come back. Just because they showed up once doesn't guarantee they'll show up again. That's where quality writing comes in.

It is true that people come to your blog through search engines, where you can hook them with good writing. But there are so many additional ways to bring them around: Twitter, Facebook, speaking opportunities, networking, and so on. Bringing them in via search is great, and it's still the most popular source of website traffic for both of us. But we focus more on writing great articles and sharing great ideas.

Bottom line: This is a fine line to walk. We don't think you should ignore search engines because that traffic will be a big part of your audience. But don't ignore writing well for the sake of tricking search engines.

Google Expects You to Write Good Stuff

In early 2011, Google updated its search engine algorithms with a new version called Panda, and with it, it started paying closer attention to a website's quality. They wanted to make sure that people were writing good copy and designing attractive sites. Plenty of search engine spammers—also called

"Black Hat SEO"—were trying to trick the search engine into ranking their sites first, and one of the telltale signs was poorly written or very short copy—100 words or so, also called "thin" content. To combat it, they began blacklisting all sites that used these black hat techniques, and began rewarding high-quality content instead.

They have released several updates since then named Penguin, Pigeon, Pirate, and Possum. They've even released several updated versions of Penguin since then.

In short, Google is always changing and updating its search algorithms to punish cheaters and ne'er-do-wells and to boost people who create high-quality content. If you want to keep up with the changes, pay attention to sites like SearchEngineLand. com and Moz.com. Those are SEO professionals who understand the minutiae of Google's changes. But unless you want to become an SEO pro, just focus on the things you absolutely can control, like the quality of your work.

But how do they measure quality? While Google can't tell if your writing is any good or not, their algorithms have a few factors they look at, and those are things you can control.

There are more than 200 signals Google checks, but just three make a big difference (and they're things you can control), according to most SEO experts. They are: time spent on a site, bounce rate, and click-through rates.

- If people spend only a few seconds on a site, Google assumes they didn't like what they read. So Google assumes the content is poorly written and lowers the page's search rank. It counts when people click a link to visit a site and then hit the "Back" button to return to the search results. They conclude the shorter the time, the worse the site must be.

- If people bounce on a site (visit one page and then leave again; visiting a second page means they did not bounce), Google assumes the site wasn't easy to navigate or wasn't good enough. Again, they measure whether a user hits the "Back" button. (However, don't fret if you have a high bounce rate on your blog posts. That's normal.)

- If people don't click a site when it's near the top of the search engine rankings, the Google bots assume the description wasn't even interesting enough to get people to visit the site. (It's like having a store that wasn't interesting enough for people to walk into.) Because Google can measure whether people click a result, they can also tell when people don't click a result.

So, if you want your site to do well on Google's search engine, make sure you write great content. Make sure it's beautiful and easy to navigate. Include photos, videos, and other content to get people to linger on your site. Include "Previous Post/Next Post" links to help people get around as well as "Related Posts" links. (There are WordPress plug-ins to help you do this; there aren't for most of the other blog platforms we discussed.)

In short, be a good blogger, and you'll be doing good SEO. You don't even have to be awesome at it. Considering most people do not do a great job of blogging, you can do a passable job and surpass most bloggers out there.

How Often Should You Post?

Basically, we recommend posting new content once a week for most blogs, and as much as two or three times a week. Anything less and you look like you can't commit to a simple blogging schedule, you don't have good follow-through, or you've just abandoned the blog completely. And because you're trying to create a positive personal brand, this is something to avoid.

Regular posting makes it easier to be found in the search engines for your particular search terms because search engines want fresh, new content on a regular basis. The more you post, the more they visit your blog. The more they visit your blog, the higher your possible ranking.

More important, you need to post consistently. If you post once a week, publish on the same day. If you post daily, post it at the same time. That way your readers will know when and how to find you, and your readership will build more quickly and reliably than if you were to post every 715 days, without rhyme or reason.

But don't feel like you have to publish something when you don't have anything to say. We both tried that, publishing every single day, and while it did have a positive effect on our traffic, the quality of our work suffered. We both fell into the trap of writing about anything just so we could keep up that crazy publishing schedule.

Plenty of people publish every single day, and we can tell you that the quality of their content suffers greatly. Not only are they scrambling around for ideas, but they'll give the bare minimum of time to their work.

We even know a few bloggers who boast that they write all five days' worth of content in a couple hours on a Sunday afternoon. And it shows. It shows that they spent roughly 20 minutes on a single blog post, with another 10 minutes the following morning for a quick edit. As a result, their work has deteriorated, and their readers take them less seriously because they're not coming up with anything new or they're singing the same songs over and over.

How Long Should Your Posts Be?

A few years ago, we would have told you a decent blog post should be in the 350–450 word range.

"350 words?!" new bloggers would exclaim. "I can knock that out in a quick email."

Except this has changed. Now, while 300 words is still an acceptable amount, we're writing blog posts that are 500–700 words; Erik frequently writes in the 1,000–1,200 word range, and he still has plenty of readers.

When you consider that the average newspaper column runs about 550 words, you can see why blogging has become so popular among readers: your average blog reader is like your average newspaper reader. They have the reading level and attention span of a sixth grader.

This isn't true of everyone, and we're not suggesting you dumb your work down. We're also not suggesting that readers are dumb. (Not all of them anyway.) Rather, people have grown to expect most text to be written at this level.

Think of it this way: When you're jogging or riding your bike, you can probably run or ride one or two miles per hour faster than your usual pace, but you don't because it doesn't feel comfortable. You want to stick with a rate that feels good so you can keep doing it.

Our brains work the same way. Yes, we can read at a higher level. We all learned to read, and most of us graduated from high school at least. But that doesn't mean we want to read at a high school reading level all the time. Thanks to years of journalists and marketers writing at the sixth grade level, we expect it. The reading is easier and requires less mental bandwidth; we're more likely to stick with something at our accustomed reading level.

So if you want to make your posts readable, write them like a newspaper article. Not only are they at a sixth grade reading level, they're written for someone who gets impatient and abandons an article halfway through it.

Newspapers are also readable because of the tone and voice the writers use. Many newspaper columnists have regular readers because of their particular writing style. Adopt your own style, but make sure you're friendly, conversational, and factual. Your style can be anything from your frequent choice of certain words, to the length of your sentences, to the complexity of your words. It can be the tone you take when discussing certain issues or even ending every question with "huh," because your "?" key is broken. Find a style that suits you, stick with it, and hone it until it's something you and your readers enjoy.

Newspapers figured out a long time ago that people abandon articles around the halfway point, so they started putting the most important information first, second-most important information next, and so on. Most newspaper articles get boring about halfway through because they're giving nothing but background information, so you can skip that part. Likewise, when you're blogging, just stop writing when you get to the less important information and you'll be around 500–700 words.

Be sure to answer the "who, what, where, when, why, and how" of each article, which is standard on all news articles. (Read several news stories in your local newspaper. Nearly all the news stories will answer the "5 W's and 1 H" in the first couple sentences.

Now, there's no magic number of what a blog post should be. We recommend 500–700 words because that's what people will typically read these days, especially if they're reading your blog on a mobile phone.[4] But even then, there are plenty of people who want 300-word posts, and plenty who want 2,000-word articles. Just pay attention to your analytics and see what's performing the best on your site.

But My Posts Are Too Long!

This is another frequent problem we see: What do I do if my blog posts are too long? In some cases, bloggers want to cram as much information into a single post as possible, as if they're trying to make up for lost time. They try to make several points and cover several ideas at once.

Don't worry about lost time. You'll have plenty of opportunity to get your information out to people. But if you want to write longer posts, go ahead. Like we said, there's no hard and fast rule about how long a post should be. You just need to make sure your writing style and your subject matter are compelling enough to keep people engaged to the end.

Still, if your posts are too long, the problem may not be too many words; it may be too many ideas in one post.

In our blogging talks, we recommend that people follow the mantra "one idea, one post, one day." Talk about one idea, not two or three, put it in one post, and publish once per day. If you try to double up on any of those areas, you're going to have problems keeping readers interested because your posts will become cumbersome and complex.

As you're writing, see if there is a natural "crease" in your writing. Is there a place where it would be easy to break the post into two places? Maybe you're talking about the importance of getting durable, hard-wearing luggage for business travel, and you start talking about choosing the right kind of luggage for vacation. If you look closely, you could probably split the post into two different ones: one for business luggage and one for vacation luggage. There's no need to combine the two, so just split them into two separate posts, which takes care of two days of writing.

---

4. https://www.orbitmedia.com/blog/blogger-trends/

SEO Through Blogging

SEO is the art of making your blog appear at the top of the search engines. By focusing on a few keywords and optimizing your posts for them, you can improve your chances for appearing at the top of Google and Bing.

We may have come down a little hard against SEO earlier, but we still think it's important. You don't want to ignore SEO completely, but you also don't want to focus so much on it that your writing sucks.

These factors have largely fallen out of favor with Google, although they still give some weight to them. If nothing else, these help Google understand what your articles are about.

- **Keywords:** Everything is based on keywords, or the words or phrases that each post is about. That's the thing the search engine zeros in on. Choose your keywords carefully, but don't go for the big, generic keywords, like "history" or "marketing." You'll never win that search. Instead, go for long-tail keywords, like "19th century Midwest agricultural history" or "email marketing best practices."

  However, Google is more concerned about topics than specific keywords these days. Their bots understand language better, and they understand synonyms.

  Seven years ago, if you wanted to write about your cheeseburger restaurant, you might write a post about "Minneapolis cheeseburgers," "cheeseburgers in Minneapolis," and even the "best Minneapolis cheeseburgers." Then you'd have to do it all over again for "hamburgers." Now Google understands that "cheeseburger" and "hamburger" mean the same thing and that putting them in an article about Minneapolis means it's about that topic.

✉ *Note*

The term "long-tail" is from Chris Anderson's book, *The Long Tail* (Long-Tail.com). It's the 20 percent in the 80/20 rule. Or as Anderson says, the two percent in the 98/2 rule.

Think of it as a special sales niche: 98 percent of people want to buy a big generic product, and every store is fighting to be #1 in that market. But by appealing to the two percent who don't want the generic product, you can expend less energy and comfortably sell to them. So, this means that if you can win enough long-tail searches, you'll do as well or better than the one person who tries to win a single search for the 98 percent.

- **Headlines:** This is the first place to put your keyword. If you're writing about direct mail response rates, your headline should be something like "5 Tips for Improving Direct Mail Response Rates." (Notice we used the 5 tips list post idea.) This tells the search engine what you're writing about and tells the spider what it should be looking for when it crawls your site.

- **Anchor text:** Search engines also pay attention to whether you put your keywords inside your hyperlinks. **Warning:** If you do this too often, or if you're too on the nose, Google will penalize you. When we published the second edition of this book in 2012, this was an important tactic; now, it can cause you a lot of trouble. Instead, they want you to use "editorial text" inside your links. That means they'd rather you link a sentence like "A recent state of the email marketing industry report from Emma," rather than linking "email marketing best practices" every chance you get.

- **Body copy:** The actual text of the blog post needs your keywords. If you're writing for SEO, you want to shoot for about a one percent keyword density. That is, out of every 100 words, you should use your keyword one time. But don't stuff in the keywords, and don't make it obvious that you're trying to cram it all in.

- **Backlinks:** This one is important for SEO. The more links that point back to your blog, the more important Google thinks your site is. However, these have to be high-quality backlinks. One of the things that prompted all the Google changes in 2009–2011 with Panda, Penguin, and Hummingbird were people creating link farms, single pages with thousands of backlinks on them. Now, they want high-quality links on pages and websites that are related to your own site, such as a link from a bed-and-breakfast site to your travel blog. But links from restaurant supply stores? That can cause you some problems.

How Does This Apply to Our Four Heroes?

We've been saying blogging is important, and that it's for anyone who wants to build their personal brand. So let's see how our four heroes would use blogging to find a job or further their career:

- **Allen (influencer)** spent 14 years as an account manager in a marketing agency, so he has a lot of expertise in account management, marketing campaigns, and ad creation. He's also looking for a job. Blogging is going to be a great benefit to him for two important reasons. First, hiring managers use search engines to research candidates. Allen wants to make sure that hiring managers find him instead of finding absolutely nothing. Second, Allen wants to show that he knows a lot about account management and agency life. We would also suggest that he interview different professionals about agency life and issues in the industry. People like to talk about themselves, so this strategy will put him in touch with people who might otherwise ignore him if they think he's only calling them about a job.

- **Beth (climber)** wants to be the CMO in the insurance industry, possibly at her current company, but not necessarily so. Insurance marketing is a specialized niche, which makes it ideal for blogging. Beth can't write about insurance specifically, which violates all kinds of industry rules and laws. But she can write a variety of posts about things that insurance touches, like safe driving tips for teenage drivers, ways to reduce the risk of a home fire, and how to protect your family while traveling.

- **Carla (neophyte)** has left a career in pharmaceutical sales and wants to become a program director or development director at a nonprofit. Although the for-profit and non-profit worlds are quite different, some of the ideas are the same, like getting people to give you money in exchange for something. Carla can use her blog to explore the connections between sales and fundraising, which will be of interest to other fundraising professionals. And because there are so many openings in fundraising, Carla can use this blog as an introduction to potential bosses, as well as a selling point when she's asked an interview question like, "So how can selling techniques help you with fundraising?"

- **Darrin (free agent)** is an IT professional who spends his days troubleshooting computers, and he moves from employer to employer every two or three years. He's almost a commodity in the IT field, so he needs to distinguish himself from every other IT professional. A blog is the best way to do it. Darrin can write about things like balancing the need for network security and the growing use of social media in the corporate setting or providing basic computer security information for non-IT personnel. By adopting a style that's friendly and easy to follow, Darrin can become the computer troubleshooting expert, which makes him more attractive to larger corporations with IT professionals who do nothing but fix computers.

The Do's and Don'ts of Blogging

We asked our Twitter friends to give us some do's and don'ts about blogging for newbies. (See, this is the kind of thing you get if you follow us on Twitter: We ask you to help write our book, and you might be put in it!) Our friends came through for us. They gave us a lot of great advice, which we include here.

What's not so surprising is that we got more do's than we did don'ts. More people have good advice for things to do rather than things to avoid. Either that, or we just know some really optimistic people.

Do's

- Resist the urge to talk about the blogging itself. "Well, it's been a while since I last posted." Just get to the point.—@JuneCasagrande

- It's a long-term play. Stay committed. Integrate it into your day-to-day schedule and routine.—@RosserJobs

- Have the same attitude as a shooting guard in basketball: When you're on shoot it. When you're off, shoot until you're on again.—@thechuck-chapman Write from the heart.—@dave_kellogg

- Write about something you have passion for!—@mandyboyle

- Blog often. Don't worry about perfection. Just get your words out there!—@robbyslaughter

- Invite guest bloggers and submit guest blogs to others.—@edeckers

- Always check a twitter handle or blog URL before mentioning; it might not be the right business or person. (Learned myself the hard way.)—@kellyjknutson

- Maintain a consistent posting schedule. Readers and search engines both love fresh, interesting content.—@mandyboyle

- Blogging is about community. Don't expect people to read your blog if you aren't reading and commenting on theirs.—@JustHeather

- You will not be making any money blogging nowadays. Advertising is a shell game. Running a blog is now about the opportunities it creates.—@jonathanwthomas

- Re-read each post before you click "Publish." It will save you some embarrassment.—@4ndyman

- I try to sit on a new piece for 24 hours then re-read, but I still post mistakes.—@randyclarktko (response to @4ndyman. Conversation abounds!)

- Unless you are a copy editor, use and trust one.—@randyclarktko

- Use alt text with images. Most people forget to. It can boost SEO and help when browsers don't display images.—@mandyboyle

🔍 *Tip*

"Alt text," or "alternative text," was originally created so people who used screen-reading software (software that lets people who are blind use a computer) could tell what was in a photograph. If you post a photo of your daughter riding her bicycle, you would write an alt tag that says "My daughter riding her bicycle." That way, the screen reader users would know what this photo is about.

However, search engines also use alt text, so you can give yourself an SEO boost by including alt text inside your photo descriptions. However, don't go nuts and try to cram keywords and search terms into each photo.

Putting "Kyle Lacy talks about social media, social networks, social marketing, blogging, Twitter, and Facebook marketing at his KyleLacy.com blog" into every alt text of each photo may trigger alarms on the search engine, and you'll be penalized for keyword stuffing. Also, your blind readers will hate you.

Don'ts

- Don't assume people are as informed as you are. Spell terms and ideas out once in awhile.—@sunnysocial

- Don't think of topics all by yourself. Find help from Google Reader, StumbleUpon, guest posts to share the load/inspire.—@DanOnBranding

- Don't leave spam or half-hearted comments.—@edeckers

- Don't make your blog one big commercial.—@edeckers

- Don't neglect grammar and spelling.—@dave_kellogg

🔍 *Tip*

One problem that Microsoft Word users have is that copying a post from Word and then pasting it into a blog window adds a lot of extra HTML characters that are viewable when published. One way to eliminate this is to copy the Word version, open Notepad (the free word processor on Windows), paste the text into Notepad, and then copy it again. This strips out all the extra HTML, and you can then paste it into the blog window.

Our favorite tip came from our friend and fellow blogger, Meghan Barich, who summarized this entire chapter in one tweet.

- Do be social. Do ask questions. Do have a sense of humor. Don't be boring. Don't blog at people. Do blog to engage.—@meghanbarich

A Final Note on the Rules of Blogging

When we were first writing this book in 2010, Erik met with Jason Falls, a noted social media consultant and writer (and Erik's eventual co-author on *No Bullshit Social Media*), on the day he was writing this chapter. Erik asked Jason, "What's some advice for blogging newbies?" Jason is a seasoned blogging expert, so we'll just let him speak for himself:

> Take all of the "rules" with a grain of salt. I've seen not only with my own blog, but with some of the most notable blogs in the world, that sometimes the rules don't apply. Until recently, I've never tried to win search terms, so there's never been a concentrated effort to optimize my blog at all. I win a lot of important search terms, but I've never focused on that. I focus on providing great content and let everything else take care of itself.

In other words, as Jason said, you can ignore everything we've advised in this chapter. As long as you're writing with passion and providing well-written content, people will come to you. Even seven years later, this is still great advice.

Or as our friend and popular Hoosier aficionado Tony Troxell (@IndianaGeeking) put it, "If I had listened to the tips, I would have given up back in '04."

4

LinkedIn: Networking on Steroids

Imagine this.

You walk into a networking event. You are pleasantly surprised to see your closest business contact and friend standing at the front of the room talking to one of your clients. You are also surprised to see the majority of the people being close connections of yours.

At first, you think this is a surprise party and you're about to look for your mother, but then you notice another group farther away (who are also smiling at you). You recognize some of the faces but can't place their names. Looking closer, you become aware of multiple groups of people spread wide throughout the building who you've never seen before.

Just then, your friend walks up and asks if you'd like to be introduced. Absolutely. After all, you're there to network.

So you're introduced to each new person. The group grows larger, and more people enter the room. One by one, you're introduced to every one of them, and your network keeps growing.

Finally, money starts falling from the ceiling, and you smile because, hey, free money.

No, this isn't some creepy dream. (Although the money thing would be pretty cool.) It sounds funny but this is how LinkedIn builds your personal brand.

LinkedIn is an in-person network that uses the power of computer algorithms and data analytics to connect you with people you know and suggest people to meet who share your interests and career. Erik calls it "Facebook for Grown-Ups," and Kyle calls it the "White-Collar Connection Point."

It's like playing Six Degrees of Kevin Bacon, but without the bacon.

@edeckers: Mmmm, bacon...
@kyleplacy: Not that kind of bacon.

LinkedIn gives you the opportunity to connect with people who can push your personal brand to new heights. It's a social networking site much like Facebook, but with 630 million fewer people and higher incomes.

LinkedIn boasts a membership of approximately 500 million users,[1] and 75 percent of them earn $50,000 per year or more in salary.[2] Talk about a professional networking site.

What makes this site valuable? LinkedIn is exactly what it sounds like: A networking site that helps you "link" to other professionals and build a web of ultimate personal branding domination through new connections. LinkedIn gives you the opportunity to connect with people who can connect you with other people who can connect you with other people, and so on, such as a connection to a former co-worker, which leads to them connecting you to a potential employer.

To start in the world of LinkedIn, you need to understand some of the basics.

The Basics of LinkedIn

Your LinkedIn profile is the window into your professional soul. You can technically view the profile as your online résumé, but it is so much more than that. Résumés can be extremely boring, but a LinkedIn profile allows you to shine.

It's a way to promote the professional side of your personal brand. It's the link to your best skill sets, the recommendations of your peers, your professional personality, and a place to share your knowledge. It's the ideal place to demonstrate every aspect of what makes you valuable to an employer or a client. We have talked extensively about how your personal brand builds trust and tells a credible story. Your LinkedIn profile is another chapter of that story.

---

1. https://blog.linkedin.com/2017/april/24/the-power-of-linkedins-500-million-community

2. http://www.pewinternet.org/2015/01/09/demographics-of-key-social-networking-platforms-2/

What Are Degrees of Connectedness?

We'll discuss this later, but just understand that LinkedIn—all of networking, in fact—is based on knowing someone who knows someone. Those are the degrees of connectedness.

Let's say Kyle and Erik are connected on LinkedIn. That makes us **1st degree** connections. And Sarah is connected to Erik, but not to Kyle. That makes Kyle and Sarah **2nd degree** connections—there are two degrees of separation between Kyle and Sarah. Then, Ernesto is connected to Sarah, but not to Kyle, which makes Kyle and Ernesto **3rd degree** connections.

Or, to put it another way, Kyle and Erik are friends. Sarah is the "friend of a friend," and Ernesto is the "friend of a friend of a friend."

One of LinkedIn's strengths is that Kyle and Sarah can connect through Erik, and then Kyle and Ernesto can connect through Sarah. (We'll talk more about the real-life application of this in "Chapter 12: How to Network: Hello, My Name Is…" We mention it now because everything you'll do on LinkedIn is built on making these connections to build your network.)

What's in a LinkedIn Profile?

The first step to establishing your presence on LinkedIn is creating a profile. After that, you can start connecting to people you know who are also on LinkedIn.

The Employment Section

The profile usually focuses on employment and education history (see Figure 4.1), not a list of your hobbies or your favorite movie. We're going to leave that to Facebook. Remember, this is for your professional brand.

To fill out your profile page, begin by filling in information for your current and former jobs. The entries will include job title, employer, industry, dates, and a short description of what you accomplished at the job.

But don't simply list your job responsibilities; that's not very interesting, and it doesn't set you apart from everyone else. List your accomplishments instead. (And if you can assign a number or dollar value, that's even better.) For example, write "Grew sales by 23 percent in two years"; "managed $2 million accounting software system overhaul"; or "led marketing campaign that increased web traffic by 200 percent."

Set aside at least 60 minutes to fill out your LinkedIn profile, and then tweak and adjust it for a few days afterward. It's easy to fill out, but it needs to be completed fully to do its best work for you.

Figure 4.1 *This is an example of a completed LinkedIn profile with all the information associated with your personal brand.*

LinkedIn also looks up your employer to see if they're in the LinkedIn database. That can help you find people who used to, or still, work at the company. This way, you connect with people you already know and start building your network.

After you have filled out your professional information, upload a professional picture, and then fill out your educational experience.

Your Photo/Avatar

We can't stress enough how important your photo (also called an avatar) is to your social media profile, not just LinkedIn. And it's important to use the same picture on every social network site on the Internet—it's part of your personal brand.

If you don't want to use a photo, at least use something that absolutely looks like you. Not your company logo, not a group photo, and not you standing on the beach with the sun behind you. Not your dog, not your kid, not you as a kid.

If you're meeting someone for coffee or at a networking event for the first time, they need to be able to know how to find you. What's the point of having a bad picture on a professional networking site? It's like going to a networking event with a mask on.

You can decide to take a professional head shot yourself or hire a photographer to take it for you. We recommend the latter. We also assume you understand your photo should not involve a swimsuit or a keg stand.

Education

After you figure out your picture situation, you need to fill in your educational experience. List the different schools and institutions you attended after high school, including their names, degrees earned, years attended, awards won, additional activities, and any awesome accolades you're able to add.

`@kyleplacy:` Knock it off with the alliteration.
`@edeckers:` Awww...

Remember, the more information you list, the better. You never know when you'll have something in common with a potential employer.

 Note

LinkedIn uses all this employment and education history later to help you search former and current colleagues and classmates.

The employment and education information make up the basics of your LinkedIn professional profile, but you also have the chance to fill out a short summary to help people understand exactly what you do and why you do it.

The Summary

This is basically a short description of your professional experience and skills. Remember your personal brand story discussed and built in Chapter 2, "How Do You Fit in the Mix?" This is a great place to use your medium or long story. It's the traditional career objective you would put on a résumé, but you get to add a little more and make it more thorough than you have room for on a paper résumé.

(Also, don't put a career objective on your résumé. It's always some variation of "I want a job using my skills." Of course you want a job! Save the space for something else. Depending on how much information you have on your résumé, you'll need every inch you can get.)

LinkedIn uses keywords to track and categorize profiles for use in searching. An employer may use LinkedIn to search for job prospects, or a fellow networker may be searching for you. Be sure to use keywords you want to be known for or found under. And don't overload the career summary section by using the same keywords over and over. Instead, use words that describe your position, your field, and any useful skills:

"Creative and hardworking young professional focused on corporate public relations. Led two 80+ student organizations while also studying as a full-time student. Worked at two different internships with a PR firm in Washington, DC. Strong written and oral communication skills with a passion for public speaking."

What makes this an effective summary? It describes what makes the individual special and unique, "who they are, and what they like to do." They used keywords like public relations, PR, communication, and public speaking.

Your Websites

There's also a section to list any websites that you're associated with: personal and professional, your blog, your RSS feed, and your creative portfolio (see Figure 4.2). There's also a place for you to list interests, affiliated groups, and honors. This lets people find out more about you beyond your LinkedIn profile.

Tip

When you list your websites and blogs, you can select "My Website," "My Company," "My Blog," "My RSS Feed," "My Portfolio," and "Other." If you select one of the first five options, they show up as that name on your profile. But if you select "Other" (see Figure 4.3), you can spell out what that other site is. Type in the name of your blog, your website, whatever. Then, when people see your profile, they see the name of your company, the name of your blog, and so on. That link is more informative and interesting than the other options.

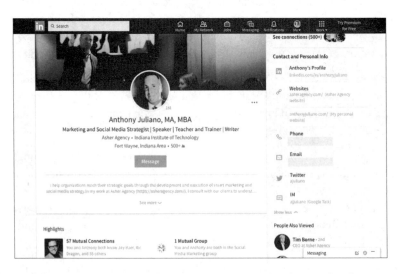

Figure 4.2 *This is an example of what someone sees when he searches for your profile. You want him to connect with you outside of LinkedIn using your website or a blog.*

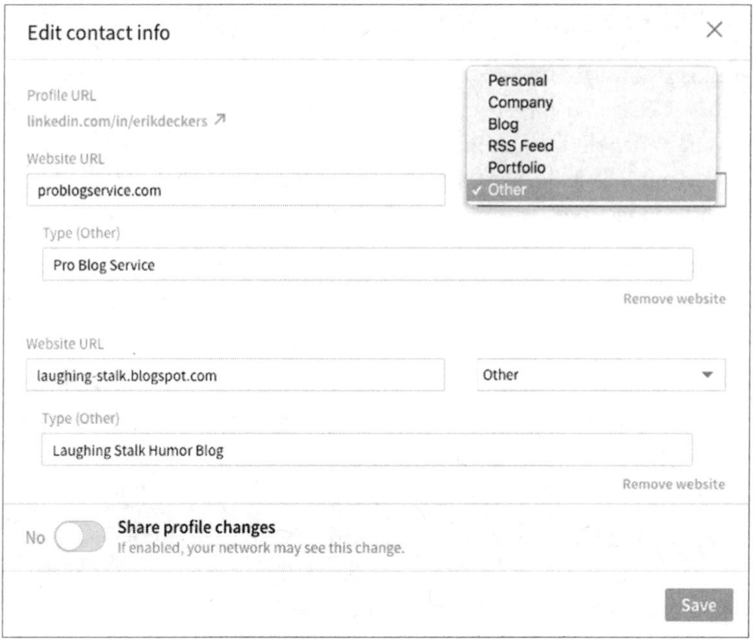

Edit contact info   ✕

Profile URL   Personal
linkedin.com/in/erikdeckers ↗   Company
                                               Blog
Website URL   RSS Feed
                                               Portfolio
problogservice.com   ✓ Other

Type (Other)

Pro Blog Service

                                                         Remove website

Website URL

laughing-stalk.blogspot.com   Other   ▾

Type (Other)

Laughing Stalk Humor Blog

                                                         Remove website

No ⚪ **Share profile changes**
      If enabled, your network may see this change.

                                                              Save

Figure 4.3 *Don't just select "Company" or "Blog" on your profile. Select "Other," then specify what that other thing is. Customizing the name of that particular site is so much more interesting than just plain old "Blog." Blurg.*

🔍 *Tip*

Don't link to your Facebook profile in your website section. Try to create a boundary between your personal and professional life. Although truly industrious hiring managers may search for you on Facebook, there's no need to make it easier for them. (At the same time, don't post anything on Facebook that could harm your professional reputation. Even restricting your Facebook profile to "Friends Only" isn't sufficient.)

After you fill out your profile, check whether it's 100 percent complete. LinkedIn shows your status for completion, and it's not difficult to hit 100 percent. Just follow their suggestions, and you'll complete it before you know it. If only life were this easy!

If you haven't hit it yet, you need to figure out what needs to be done to reach that mark. A complete profile shows that you mean business, and that helps with LinkedIn searches. It shows potential connections that you're using LinkedIn properly, and it isn't just some half-finished, rarely visited network to you.

Cool LinkedIn Features for Personal Branding

LinkedIn is a powerful tool. It's more than just a résumé or network-building site. It isn't just a set-it-and-forget-it social network. You actually need to use LinkedIn if you want to benefit from it. Just like every other social network, you get out of it what you put into it. So, use the full range of features to make the best of your efforts and connections.

LinkedIn offers some cool features to help you build your personal brand. The company was bought by Microsoft in 2016, and it has undergone several dramatic changes since then. Focus on these features as you first get started.

- **Personal URL**—You can personalize your LinkedIn URL. So rather than having a long URL filled with all kinds of letters and numbers, you can have one with your name in it, like "www.linkedin.com/in/WinstonChurchill" (assuming your name really is Winston Churchill).

- **Groups and Subgroups:** Look under the "Work" tab at the far right of your screen. Join a few groups to build deeper relationships and gain new connections. You can find groups for your community, your industry, or even your job function. You can find some of the best discussions and most influential contacts within your groups. They're great resources for announcements, sharing upcoming events, starting discussions, and finding valuable information. But only join groups and subgroups because you have a genuine interest in what the group is about; it's easy to get overwhelmed by them.

- **Jobs:** We really like the "Jobs" function on LinkedIn, because you have a better shot of networking your way into a job. LinkedIn will show you how many first and second degree contacts as well as fellow school alums work at any given company. If you know one of those people, they might be able to refer you to the right person. Or at the very least tell you if it's a company worth applying to. Also, you can customize your job searches for certain cities and industries, and you can even save those searches as email alerts.

- **Articles:** If you've read Chapter 3 on blogging, then you understand the importance of publishing your work online. We highly recommend you publish on LinkedIn, too. However, we recommend you publish on your blog first, wait a few days, and then republish the same content on your LinkedIn profile. This way, your blog content is canonical, or recognized as the original source material. The same is true with the blogging platform, Medium.

Making Contacts on LinkedIn

Of course, a networking tool is not much good without a network. And although you can search for people on LinkedIn, there's an easier way to make connections.

We all have personal contacts who can expand our LinkedIn network, so it's time to build that database and connect with them. There are a couple of ways you can build your list, and it starts with your email contacts list. You can also find contacts by searching for names, companies, schools, and cities. Finally, LinkedIn has advanced search functionality to reach people you don't know directly.

After you find your people, invite them to connect. Afterward, check out the people they know and connect with them. Just ask your newly minted connection for an introduction, or peruse their list, click on someone's profile, and hit the "Connect" button.

Tip

Please, please, *PLEASE* rewrite the introduction message—"I'd like to add you to my professional network on LinkedIn"—before you connect with someone. At the very least, it tells the other person how you know them, especially if they don't recognize your name off the bat. At best, it shows that you actually want to connect with that person, and aren't just too lazy to make an effort to tap out a few sentences of introduction. We know people who delete connection requests if the requester couldn't be bothered to rewrite that introduction message.

Using Your Email List

Of all the tools you have at your disposal, your personal email list is the most important one you have. It's your initial contact list, filled with people you have already communicated with. They're the people who already know why you want to connect with them.

The easiest way to start is to download your email database from your email client (like Outlook or Apple Mail) or use your Gmail or Yahoo! email. LinkedIn can connect automatically, or you can upload your list yourself. LinkedIn will then find every address connected to a LinkedIn account. The only thing you have to do is connect. It's that easy.

Tip

We recommend that you get a Gmail account and synchronize it with your work email. You never know when you're, um, not going to have ready access to your work email address any more. Then keep it up to date and clean. Also make this your primary personal address, instead of an email from your cable company, phone company, or work. If you change jobs or move away, your email address becomes obsolete. Finally, every social network we have seen lets you add contacts through your Gmail account.

Just connect your email account, and LinkedIn pulls in your contacts and shows those who have already joined (see Figure 4.4). This allows you to connect with friends, colleagues, co-workers, vendors, and so on. The same process happens when you upload your email list.

However, you have a chance to confirm any connections before they're automatically made. That allows you to avoid connecting with someone you'd rather keep at arm's length.

After you connect to someone, remember to take a quick look at their connections. These are people you may not know but they could be valuable to your network. Remember, your connections can be your best marketers. They're the ones who spread your message and brand faster than anyone.

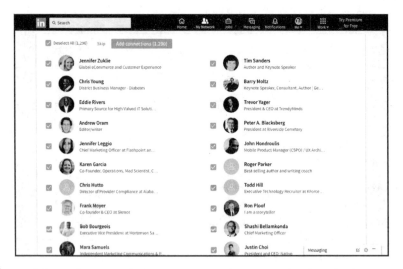

Figure 4.4 *By allowing LinkedIn to connect with your email address book, you can build your network with personal connections.*

Other Ways to Connect: Colleagues and Classmates

After you fill in all your education and work history, LinkedIn can find other people who shared these experiences with you. Whether it's the woman who worked in the cube next to you, the guy who sat behind you in Psych 100, or even someone you never met from your graduating class, LinkedIn gives you the tools to easily connect with all of them.

When you upload the address book or database to LinkedIn, you can check or uncheck the names of people you'd like to connect with. You can bulk connect with every person in your database automatically, or pick and choose.

You're also asked to invite nonmembers to the site by email, although we don't recommend it. The only time you should invite nonmembers is when you're sure they will appreciate the invite. If they're the type of people who might freak out that you "sent another email," it's probably best to keep from sending that or any other message. And keep in mind that they may be on there under other email addresses. Do a quick search before you invite them via the email addresses you have.

You're making some great progress. You've created a profile and connected your email list. The next step is growing your network into something that can help your overall brand. You can ask your LinkedIn network for introductions to people you do not already know. Remember the second- and third-degree section from the party at the beginning of the chapter? Let's get this party started.

Building Off Your Second- and Third-Degree Network

Building your network on LinkedIn does not stop at your first-degree connections. The power of LinkedIn lies in connecting with people outside of your immediate connections. It would defeat the purpose if you attended a networking event and chatted only with people you already knew. By connecting with people you know, you can build a platform to reach their connections. This is where the second- and third-degree connections come into play.

- **Second-Degree Contact:** This is the more important connection. Being connected to a person by second degree means there is only one person between you and the other individual. LinkedIn allows for second-degree connections to contact each other.

- **Third-Degree Contact**—A third-degree contact is a harder shell to crack because you're not directly connected to that person through one other contact—two people are between you and that contact, and you can be third-degree connected to literally tens of thousands of people. "Oh what a tangled web we weave, when first we practice to achieve."[3]

---

3. Take *THAT*, Walter Scott!

The second-degree contacts on LinkedIn are the more important connections to you in this web of networking. LinkedIn puts the degree of connectedness—first, second, third—next to a person's name when you're looking at his profile or at a connections contact list.

By connecting to second-degree contacts, you can build your network past your initial contact list to people who could be extremely helpful to you. You can build an army of people who could become powerful evangelists for your personal brand.

Transforming Your Contacts into Connections

So, why should you turn your contacts into connections? What does that even mean? What is the difference between a contact and a connection? And can we squeeze one more question into this paragraph?

A contact may be less important than an actual connection, because it tells you how closely you have connected.

- **Contact:** A contact is someone you have met (online or offline) at least once, so they know your name and occupation. They may appreciate the initial connection on LinkedIn, but would hesitate to share their entire client list with you. Remember, the entire point of LinkedIn is to build your network to get introductions to individuals who are second and third degrees from you. To do that, you need to get each of your contacts to become a…

- **Connection:** A connection is a cheerleader. Not the pom-pom kind, but the rabid fan kind. There's a level of trust and a relationship there, something you don't get if you're a LION (LinkedIn Online Networkers; see the "Do's and Don'ts about LinkedIn" below). A connection is someone who will share your message whenever asked and will connect you with the necessary people to make your goals a reality. You want to try to turn every contact into a connection. It may not happen, but that doesn't mean you shouldn't try.

So, clearly, the important question is how do you turn contacts into connections? Here's how.

1. Build Trust

LinkedIn was built to create connections between trusted contacts. So how do you do that? Offer them information they think is valuable. Share content through your status updates that helps them. Rather than trying to connect with anyone and everyone—that's what LIONs do—you should build a smaller, more valuable network by connecting with people who will actually benefit from your content.

2. Recommend Your Friends

You must give to receive. Write recommendations, and you will receive them in return. By recommending people you have worked with, your relationships with your contacts will grow deeper. People put greater stock in recommendations because they're sincere.

3. Get Involved in Your Contacts' Groups

Get involved with groups that share your common interests. This introduces you to more possible contacts, and you can identify your relationship with people as part of a shared group. The more groups you join, the more opportunity there is for you to make contacts. But don't just join to join; be selective. Participating in a group builds the deeper connection points that can strengthen your relationships.

4. Stay in Touch

LinkedIn offers the opportunity to connect with people who may not use sites like Twitter and Facebook. Remember, LinkedIn is made up of professionals who (usually) use it to connect only with other professionals in their industry. LinkedIn is great for staying in touch.

The Importance of Recommendations

Out of all the features LinkedIn offers, recommendations are one of the most important. Recommendations give you additional credibility with people—they're open letters of reference. And the best way to dominate with your personal brand is to get qualified and stellar recommendations.

If you've had a good business relationship with another LinkedIn member, ask them for a recommendation. Don't ask just to rack up a bunch of recommendations, though. This isn't a contest. You want people who know you and can honestly write a good one. (We have both been asked for recommendations by people we didn't even know. We very politely declined.) Then return the favor; writing recommendations also helps complete your LinkedIn profile.

Look for ways to give and receive the appropriate recommendations that can help further your personal brand. Do you want to be known as a good speaker? Ask for recommendations from people who have seen you speak. Do you want to be known as a strategist? Ask clients who have been successful because of the strategy you created. And remember, you must give before you receive. Give recommendations to the people who have helped you over the years, and they more than likely will return the favor.

So what makes a good recommendation? Remember our friends from Chapter 1, "Welcome to the Party"? Our four heroes are devoted LinkedIn users, and they each have gathered recommendations that are useful for their personal branding objectives.

- **Allen (influencer)** is looking for a new job after working at the same ad agency for 14 years. Allen should ask his supervisor, a co-worker, and a client he worked with for recommendations. Here is an example of a recommendation for Allen from one of his clients:

"Allen has been nothing short of extraordinary at managing our projects with our company. They were continually delivered on time, on target, and on budget, with every detail covered. Thanks, Allen, for being such an asset to our company!"

   Notice that the recommendation feeds into Allen's strengths as an account manager and strengthens his commitment to managing customer accounts the right and successful way.

- **Beth (climber)** wants to move up the ranks within her company to become CMO. How should Beth use recommendations? She needs recommendations from her superiors and co-workers to show upper management that she is fulfilling her company goals.

   Recommendations can help her get past the manager who may not share positive information with the higher-ups of a company. Here is an example of a positive recommendation for Beth:

"Beth has been extremely effective at building marketing platforms that help our team at Company X. She is a go-getter and has consecutively hit her goals and helped our team meet its expectations."

   Beth has a recommendation that feeds into her ability to meet her goals, which is extremely important when climbing the ranks of any company. Remember to include information that can help in your internal promotion meetings. Also, do not hesitate to ask for recommendations from individuals of different departments within the same company. They could end up being extremely powerful for your personal brand development.

- **Carla (neophyte)** is a former pharmaceutical sales rep who left after eight years with her company. She is interested in working for a nonprofit, either as a program director or a fund-raising specialist.

   Carla has an interesting problem because her previous job was as a pharmaceutical sales rep, which has nothing to do with being a program director. There are two things Carla could do. She could ask her sales manager at the pharmaceutical company to give a recommendation based on her ability to create relationships with doctors and other medical professionals, which could help her get a position as a fund-raising specialist. Or she could ask him to talk about her ability to manage several different clients and projects, which could speak to a program director position. Here's an example of the former:

"Carla was extremely effective in creating strategic relationships with doctors at private practices and helped in securing those relationships over an extended period of time. The relationships she handled have resulted to an increase in sales at our company!"

- **Darrin (free agent)** is an IT professional who leaves his job every two or three years in pursuit of more money. He's a free agent because he'll stay at roughly the same level of job, regardless of where he goes, but he can make more money because there are bigger companies requiring his expertise.

  Darrin should follow the same path as Allen when asking for recommendations. He should ask a client or co-worker to discuss his ability to deliver for high-level clients. It is important that he get recommendations from bigger companies because they are his target market; smaller companies will probably not help him in his personal branding endeavors. Here is a good example:

"Darrin is a skilled IT professional who provided me with quality service when I knew very little about the field or my software. He was patient and knowledgeable and communicated well in explaining to me what his plans were in designing my software and internal communication solution. He listened well and provided choices for me based on the type of systems I was going for at the time."

You may feel overwhelmed because there are so many useful tools to use for LinkedIn and personal branding. But if you want to choose one of the top features to further your personal brand, it's Recommendations. You are giving people the opportunity to tell their story of interacting with you as an individual and how you helped them. Now that's powerful!

PERSONAL BRANDING CASE STUDY: ANTHONY JULIANO

Anthony Juliano is an exemplary relationship builder, not only in his adopted hometown of Fort Wayne, but in the state of Indiana (he's originally from the Boston area). He's the vice president and general manager of the Asher Agency, a marketing agency headquartered in Fort Wayne, where he's spent the last 13 years.

But more people know him because of his work based on LinkedIn. He's taught college classes on it. He's spoken about it at national and international conferences. He's trained a wide variety of businesses on how to use it. And he's written a social media column for a regional business journal, as well as other publications and blogs, that explain it.

Anthony isn't a LION, though—a LinkedIn Online Networker who tries to amass as many contacts as possible. Instead, he focuses on the quality of the connections.

He said "There are a lot of people who are probably more naturally talented and smarter than I am, but clients choose me because they trust me. It's what I've built my whole career on, and trust will continue to be the primary element that determines my success."

That's what puts him top-of-mind for many people: He earns their trust and they remember him for it. Anthony said people he hasn't talked to in months or years will remember him and ask for help. He said this happens nearly every week, and it's what gets him most excited about his work.

He prefers LinkedIn over other networks because it's focused entirely on our professional lives.

"It helps us stay in touch without the labor intensity that often comes with staying in touch. It fills in the gaps between real-world conversations. It's absolutely critical to helping me stay top-of-mind with my connections and helping them stay top-of-mind with me," he said.

It's that "top-of-mindedness" that gives Anthony "dozens of success stories." He's gotten speaking gigs, new clients, and even new co-workers through the platform. He's also used it to solve his own problems. He was recently looking to refinance his home and did a quick search on LinkedIn to find someone in the mortgage business. He only had one connection who met the search criteria, and that person ended up getting the work.

Anthony tells his students and clients that to be a LinkedIn power user means they should post status updates regularly, at least once a day. The biggest mistake he sees is that a lot of users only rely on their profile to tell their story.

"That's the starting line, not the finish line," said Anthony.

"If you only use the profile, your connections have to think of you out of thin air, seek you out, and digest everything on your profile. Status updates eliminate those issues by putting you in the newsfeed conspicuously, meaning you don't have to be thought of randomly or sought out."

To be honest, that's sort of how we landed on Anthony for this case study.

"It's interesting to note that a LinkedIn update is what generated this conversation with you. If I hadn't posted an update about my LinkedIn class, you may not have remembered me as someone who spent a lot of time with LinkedIn," he said.

(In our defense, we were already thinking about Anthony, but his posting about the class reminded us to ask him at that moment.)

His big tip for LinkedIn users building their personal brand? Know exactly what problem you solve in the world and for whom.

"Most people haven't articulated their value, and they try to reach everyone with their story," Anthony said. "In today's environment, if you try to be all things to all people, you'll end up being not much to anyone."

Ten Do's and Don'ts of LinkedIn

Don't you love the do's and don'ts section of books? We do.

```
@kyleplacy: This is the only part of the book I'm actually going
           to read.
@edeckers:  But isn't this your chapter to write?
@kyleplacy: Yeah, so?
```

There are plenty of rules to apply when building your personal brand with LinkedIn. These are the top 10 we share with our audiences. They are the ones you should take extremely seriously if you want your personal branding campaign to be a success.

1. Do Upload a Professional Picture

This should be self-explanatory, but it's surprising how many starfish, cars, sunflowers, people standing on the beach at sunset, and dogs we see on LinkedIn profiles. Honestly, who puts a picture of their dog on a professional networking platform?

It's bad enough when people do it on Facebook and Twitter, but this is a professional network.

The point of LinkedIn is to further your networking ability online as well as offline. You want people to recognize you when you walk into a networking event. And that doesn't happen with a picture of your dog, you in a group, a picture of your kid, a picture of you as a kid, or you at the beach.

```
@edeckers:   Ooh, I hate the "standing on the beach" photos.
             They're too small and they're backlit so I can't see
             who they are.
@kyleplacy:  What about the photo of people standing in the
             mountains?
@edeckers:   Those too. They try to show the entire mountainscape,
             but the person is the size of a gnat in the photo.
```

Upload a professional picture to all the platforms you join. We know you'll want to be fun and creative on those other sites, but don't do it if you're trying to create a professional image. (That means no selfies either.)

2. Do Connect to Your Real Friends and Contacts

Just like we tell children not to talk to strangers, the same applies to your LinkedIn profile. It's crazy to see how many people connect with strangers all over the world because they want to build up their network.

Connecting to hundreds of strangers will not help your network in LinkedIn. They don't care about you! They will not help build your brand. Why would you build a network of people you don't know and will never know? Remember, you want to create connections (deep relationships), not contacts (someone whose email you just happened to get).

The value of your network comes from the quality of your relationships, not the quantity. Although LIONs abound on LinkedIn, they don't actually add value to their network. They just have a lot of people they're connected to.

As a test, Erik has asked LIONs for referrals to one of their connections, only to be told, "Oh, I don't actually know them; they're just in my network." LIONs don't actually provide any real value to the people they connect with, so don't become one!

3. Do Keep Your Profile Current

Here's a hypothetical. Erik is hanging out with Kyle, and there is a funky smell coming from somewhere. Kyle asks Erik where that smell is coming from, and Erik nonchalantly says he hasn't changed clothes in three days. Does that change the way Kyle interacts with Erik? Of course!

```
@edeckers:   What the hell? Why did you pick that example?
@kyleplacy:  See what happens when you leave me alone with the
             manuscript?
```

Just like Erik neglected his appearance (hypothetically, dammit!—Erik), the same idea applies to your LinkedIn profile. If you neglect your profile, people will tend to forget and avoid you. Neglecting your profile doesn't help you in the least, and at worst, it shows you're lazy.

4. Do Delete People Who Spam You

In life and in LinkedIn, there are bad apples. Sometimes contacts or connections abuse the system and spam your Inbox with some new multilevel marketing scheme or a new product or service they're selling. It's polite to ask them to stop and rethink their strategy. They could be new to this, and maybe they made a mistake. But if they continue to abuse your connection, delete them. They're wasting your valuable time by making you wade through their mess. Get rid of them.

The latest trend has been for salespeople from web development firms to connect with dozens, if not hundreds of people, who immediately pitch their web company (with nearly identical emails). Erik disconnects with those people when it happens and often reports them as spammers. If only a few people do that, LinkedIn may suspend their account.

5. Do Make Your Summary Look Its Best

Do you ever read an email, newspaper, or blog post with a terrible headline? Of course not. Your summary has the same effect on your LinkedIn profile. Be extremely concise and specific when writing your summary. Get people excited about reading your profile and connecting with you. Express what you are passionate about. It may even be helpful to have a co-worker or close connection review your summary.

6. Don't Use LinkedIn Like Facebook and Twitter

There's a time and place for professional and personal content when building your brand. LinkedIn is a professional network, and although it's important to share some personal content, don't use LinkedIn as a personal network. And certainly no cat videos or animated gifs. That's what Facebook is for.

7. Don't Sync LinkedIn with Twitter

Similarly, don't automatically blend LinkedIn with Twitter. There are tools that will automatically repost your Twitter messages to LinkedIn.

Don't do this ever. If you're using Twitter correctly, you're communicating with people, asking and answering questions, giving shout-outs to people across the country, and even making plans for lunch. People on LinkedIn don't want their feeds filled with your constant tweets.

The same is true of Facebook: Don't push your Twitter feed into your Facebook account.

8. Don't Decline Invitations—Archive Them

When a stranger asks you for a connection on LinkedIn, archive the invitation instead of deleting it. There could be a time when you meet this person, and you can refer to the previous invitation to connect with them. When a connection is archived, it's easier to keep track of.

9. Don't Ask Everyone for Recommendations

There's no hard and fast rule about the number of recommendations you should have. There's no minimum, and some people think there's no maximum. Just remember that not every recommendation is important.

You do need to have at least two recommendations to reach 100 percent completion of your profile, but they need to be valuable recommendations. Here are a couple tips to follow:

- **Make sure you know the person:** This seems obvious, but unfortunately it's not. If you don't know the person who's asking for a recommendation, send a nice note that says, "I'm sorry, I don't know you well enough to do it justice." You don't need to give a recommendation to someone you don't know; similarly, you don't need to accept one either.

- **Ask your best clients:** Happy clients are the best referral and recommendation sources for you. Make a list of 10 people to ask for a recommendation. You don't need 20 or 30, because 10 people talking about you is more than enough to strengthen your personal brand.

10. Don't Forget to Use Spelling and Grammar Check

Do you check the spelling and grammar on your résumé? Your profile is technically a résumé, and we've all been taught that our résumés have to be laser-perfect. Spell-check everything! If you lose a job or a position because you misspelled a word, you have to buy five more copies of this book.

@kyleplacy: Ooh, and attend one of our seminars!

@edeckers: Yeah, at full price!

5

Twitter: Sharing in the Conversation

Imagine a social networking site where millions of people connect on a daily basis. You throw yourself into a networking event with millions of people chatting in succinct 35-second conversations. In 140 characters, they update the world on everything from the vital to the mundane, from the inspirational to the just plain silly, from the passions that drive them to what their pet ate for breakfast (which can be extremely entertaining and valuable). We're either talking about a weird Alfred Hitchcock-meets-Adam Sandler movie or Twitter. We know it sounds odd. We know it's hard to understand at first. We know you have no idea where to begin. It's also safe to assume that you've probably disregarded it as yet another site where people share things you don't need or want to know. However, Twitter is actually extremely valuable to your personal brand.

The truth is Twitter has revolutionized the way people communicate daily, and this revolution has spread over every inch of the globe.

Twitter is a platform that enables the instantaneous sharing of your blog or website's content, which means you have the opportunity to publish your opinions and ideas—through "tweets"—to potentially reach millions of new readers, and you can do all this between sips of your latte, beer, or single-origin cold-brew coffee. (Don't get us started.)

Tweets are the brief messages you send out to your followers. They are the lifeblood of the Twitter universe. The 140-character post is the engagement tool that prompts the conversation from other users. You can essentially say whatever you want, link to whatever you want, and show pictures and videos of whatever you want. But keep in mind, as you build your personal brand, that everything you do is a reflection of you.

Remember, it's the content that makes the personal brand, and Twitter is the perfect site for sharing those ideas and passions that make you unique. The quickest, easiest way to share information and content—and thus, create your brand—is Twitter.

The question you need to answer is this: Does this tool really matter to you? In a sea of other social media tools, does this one even make a difference? Can Twitter actually have an impact on personal branding in 140 characters or fewer? (Hint: We wrote a whole chapter on it, so you can guess what the answer is.)

Why Should You Use Twitter?

Do you care about 328 million people paying attention and understanding your message? Okay, you won't get 328 million, but you can get hundreds and even thousands of people interested.

Twitter has been growing exponentially since its creation in 2006 and now boasts upward of 328 million active users around the world (as of the first quarter of 2017)[1].

Now, that's a big number. It's bigger than the entire population of the United States. It's more than 7 percent of the world's population. It's a massive network of people where you can promote yourself. Ridiculous amounts of content are shared on Twitter (upward of 500 million tweets per day[2]) or 6,000 tweets per second. When we wrote the second edition of this book in 2012, that number was only 200 million tweets per day and 2,340 tweets per second.

Admittedly, a few of these are a complete waste of time to most people, but others might appreciate pictures of avocado toast or pets eating dinner.

For example, the marketing director of a pet food supplier would love to know what her customers use on a regular basis. Food journalists might find the latest new

1. https://www.statista.com/statistics/282087/number-of-monthly-active-twitter-users/

2. http://www.internetlivestats.com/twitter-statistics/

food trend on Twitter. And people visiting your hometown may appreciate hearing about your favorite local restaurant. With so many different people on Twitter, 100 percent of your tweets will be relevant to someone, just not everyone.

In other words, tweets are changing the way we communicate to the masses—and they can change the way people perceive your personal brand.

It's just a matter of figuring out which tweets are important to your audience.

What Can Twitter Do for You?

There are many reasons to use Twitter to share your content. For one thing, it's an established tool whose vernacular has entered the everyday language: hashtag, tweet, "find me at kyle p lacy" (@kyleplacy). Everyone uses these terms so much, even most non-Twitter users have a basic understanding of what they mean.

It's also worth repeating: Twitter is one of the premiere platforms to build your personal brand on. Remember when we discussed the goals of building your brand in Chapter 1, "Welcome to the Party," and Chapter 2, "How Do You Fit in the Mix?" This is the place to do both of those things quickly and easily.

Finally, Twitter has a lot to offer you in regards to meeting your personal branding objectives and goals.

- **You can establish your expertise:** We talked about blogging and establishing your expertise in Chapter 3, "Blogging: Telling Your Story." Blogging helps you share your story with anyone who comes to your site. To increase its reach, you need to share that story, and Twitter is the perfect place to do so. Remember your fellow 328 million Twitterers? (Twitterati? Tweeple?) You can share your story with as many of them as you can convince to listen to you.

- **You can market your personal brand:** Twitter lets you share your expertise with people around the world. It's possible to find people who work in your industry (or the industry you'd like to work in), follow them, and even create a list of those people. For example, if you wanted to work in a software startup company in your city, you could create a private list of the startup owners so you can pay attention specifically to what they're saying. Then just respond to the appropriate messages as you find them as a way to get on their radar.

- **You can communicate directly with potential clients and employers:** Essentially, Twitter is a communication medium. People use it to communicate with different people all over the globe. This is not only a medium to simply share content and ideas, but to discuss them as well.

- **You have access to all kinds of research:** You can use Twitter to research blog content or to find marketplace trends. What are your peers writing about? What are they reading? What's trending across the country or around the world? Check it out, and create your own responses. Twitter even has a trends feature that tells you the popular topics of the day. You can also listen to what other people are saying about your product, service, marketplace, or industry. Just set up a column with a particular search term or hashtag, then follow along with all the related tweets that appear in the column.

- **You can share breaking news:** We can't count the number of times we've seen breaking news on Twitter before we saw it on the mainstream news. People share news stories from their corner of the globe, and thanks to the power of retweets and sharing, any story can travel around the world several times in as many minutes. And then you can read the different reactions and analyses (some from professionals, many from enthusiastic amateurs), and find links to stories you might not have otherwise found.

- **You can also track your competitors:** You'll be amazed at how much content your competitors share on Twitter. Because Twitter is so widely used, it's extremely easy to gain valuable content from your competitors, including things like, "Had a great meeting with @ABC_Widgets about possible marketing plan!" Use Twitter to make decisions on how to market yourself to clients just by watching what your competitors are sharing. Set up a private list—make sure it's private, because people are notified when they're added to a public list—and add your various competitors to keep an eye on them.

- **You can find people who share your passions:** Plenty of different personal passions are shared daily on Twitter. Millions of tweets are posted every day just about the things people like doing for fun; your interests are in there too. Just do a search for whatever inspires you and connect with the people talking about it.

You want to connect with passionate people because they share content. It helps when you find individuals who are passionate about the same things. Kyle and Erik share a passion for the city of Indianapolis (and now Erik is learning about Orlando), and they connect with people daily who live in their respective areas.

Erik also connects with other food lovers in his new city to find new restaurants to visit. And Kyle finds new music venues by following local musicians. Our passion for our cities helps us grow our personal brands because of the direct contact we make with other individuals.

PERSONAL BRANDING CASE STUDY:
@HAGGARDHAWKS

Q: So what is Haggard Hawks exactly?

A: Haggard Hawks is primarily a Twitter feed that posts about obscure words, language trivia, and etymology facts (see Figure 5.1)—so-called, I should point out, because the etymology of the word "haggard" lies in the world of falconry.

I'm Paul Anthony Jones, a writer and non-fiction author based in Newcastle in the UK, and I produce all the online material for Haggard Hawks.

Figure 5.1 *@HaggardHawks is a great place to learn about clever words that make you feel smarter for having read them.*

Q: How long have you been doing it?

A: I set up the Haggard Hawks Twitter feed in December 2013 alongside the release of a book I had written about etymological connections, *Haggard Hawks & Paltry Poltroons*. The account has been running ever since.

Q: What got you started on Twitter, and how did that build up your Haggard Hawks brand?

A: After a lot of cajoling from friends who thought I'd enjoy it (they were right!), I set up a personal Twitter account about a year or two before I set up Haggard Hawks. I followed a few fact and trivia accounts myself so I knew that there was certainly an audience there to connect to. I had also briefly experimented with running a Twitter account alongside my first book back in 2012; that account had fared well, but nothing like Haggard Hawks, which seemed to find a niche very quickly.

I think two main things helped build the account in the early days. The first was interacting not only with my followers, but with other accounts providing similar language- or literature-orientated material. Just replying to other tweets and answering and asking questions was enough to make the account more visible and to keep those who were already on board engaged in what I was doing.

Secondly (and in retrospect, this one sounds somewhat daft!), realizing that the account had a potentially global audience through Twitter was key. At the very beginning, I would just post the Haggard Hawks tweets from my phone as and when I remembered—entirely unscheduled and irregular.

I would keep a dozen or so tweets in my drafts and post one while I was waiting for the kettle to boil, standing in a queue, or commuting to work. The problem with that (aside from the obvious) was that there was no point at all in posting something at 8:00–9:00 a.m. UK time, if half my followers were fast asleep in North America. After a bit of research online, I started using Tweetdeck, and then Hootsuite to schedule the tweets in advance so that the account stayed active even when I was not.

The next biggest developments followed from there: Blogging about the account on The Huffington Post was a lovely break, and off the back of that, Haggard Hawks was named by *Mental Floss* magazine as one of the best language accounts to follow in an article back in 2014. Setting up a tie-in blog and publishing online word quizzes and games helped enormously too. I always think providing sharable content and links to content outside of Twitter is just as important as posting material direct to Twitter itself.

Q: What has been one of the coolest things you've managed to do?

A: Live tweeting the 2016 presidential debates was a lot of fun ("An abydocomist is a liar who boasts about their lies" went particularly well), and judging by the feedback it received, it helped make watching them more tolerable!

But speaking personally—and considering I started Haggard Hawks by tweeting random words from my phone—one of the coolest things has been seeing the account grow to the point where it's now attracting some high-profile followers. I can remember a friend of mine asking if I could pick one person in the world to follow the account who would it be. I said J.K. Rowling. Two days later, there she was.

Q: Do you now use Twitter differently than you used to?

A: Although there's a full Haggard Hawks network now—a website and blog, a Facebook page, a YouTube channel, an Instagram account, and an email newsletter—the vast majority of my time is still spent on Twitter. It plays a huge part in Haggard Hawks' identity online, and I imagine it will continue to in the future.

I'm always looking at new ideas and looking for new material to post or blog about, but the core of it all is continuing to post tweets daily and keeping the Twitter account as active as possible.

Q: Do you get more traffic from Twitter or from other channels?

A: Despite all those different channels, I still get most of my traffic via Twitter; and yes, I do feel how I use Twitter has changed—but I feel like it's only recently that I've noticed it!

Because the Haggard Hawks tweets are always scheduled a good few days in advance (and have been for so long now) I feel like I lost sight of the fact that Twitter is a live stream of information. When events happen or major stories break in the news, Twitter is always abuzz with the most up-to-date developments, and it's only in the last year or so that I've started more overtly live tweeting or subtweeting what's in the news.

The scheduled tweets are all still posted throughout the day, of course, but I find myself dropping in on the account more often these days to post more apposite words, and the response to that has by and large been superb.

Although the words that take a swipe at politics or politicians are understandably dividing (I can still remember a tweet calling Haggard Hawks "an ignorant non-voter from the new world order across the pond" when I happened to post a word that wasn't too complimentary about President Trump), it seems most people appreciate having an armory of words to describe what is going on around them. Relevancy is key.

Q: Any interesting language feuds with someone like @OEWordHord, the Old English word of the day Twitter account?

A: One of my favorite good-natured Twitter spats was the ongoing rivalry between the libraries on Orkney and Shetland in the far north of Scotland, and so I would love to say that Haggard Hawks has a nemesis of its own, but, alas, no! Although a friend of mine keeps threatening to start an account called Furious Falcons and tweet entirely made-up words just to wind me up, so watch this space....

Q: Has using Twitter led to interesting opportunities for you personally?

A: Haggard Hawks has definitely opened doors for me as a writer. I've lost track of the number of times I've been approached through Twitter or through the website to write articles, provide quotes or comments, review books, give interviews, or the like. And, again, as a writer, there's not a doubt in my mind that having the account there alongside all of my other work helps make me a more salable prospect in the eyes of publishers.

Q: Are people seeing you as more of a language "expert" just by virtue of tweeting old words?

A: It's curious, because my background is in language—I have a Master's degree in linguistics—but the disciplines I have ended up dealing with through Haggard Hawks are very different than what my academic interests were.

At university, I was involved in a mixture of toponymy (place name origins) and psycholinguistics (how the brain stores and deals with language, and how to fix or rebuild that when things go wrong). Philology, lexicography, grammar, and just generally digging up old words aren't necessarily involved in either of those, and I'm certainly nowhere near as well versed in those subjects as others are who deal with them as their stock-in-trade and always have done.

Nevertheless, I'm often approached to write or comment on them simply because of my involvement with Haggard Hawks, but that can be advantageous: It encourages me to improve that more academic side of what I do online. If I really don't feel confident or experienced enough to do the work required, I will pass the opportunity over to a fellow blogger or Twitterer I'm in touch with who will doubtless do a better job than I could and will benefit from the new contact or the wider exposure.

Q: You're based in the UK, but you have fans from around the world. Are there any surprises or unusual trends?

A: The problem with running HaggardHawks single-handedly is that I have to make judgment calls—often essentially blind!—about how well known or obscure these words are in all the regional varieties and dialects of English of all those who follow the account. I and every other British speaker might think a word odd or obscure, but a Canadian English speaker or a New Zealand English speaker might think very differently.

But then of course there's the problem of slang: I can remember stumbling across the word "diddle" in the Oxford English Dictionary, where it has a variety of lovely meanings like "to walk unsteadily like a child," or "to sing without distinct words"—the kind of thing you do when you're singing along to a song and it reaches a part you don't know the lyrics for. Thinking nothing of it, I posted it to Twitter. Only to find out that in American slang it means "to masturbate." Lesson learned.

Q: Do you know any rhymes for "purple" or "orange?"

Good question! There's an old myth that says "silver," "orange," and "purple" have no rhymes, but unfortunately it's not true. "Silver" rhymes with "chilver," an old dialect word for a ewe lamb, and "purple" rhymes with "hurple," meaning "to draw your arms and legs together" or "to crouch or cower." But nothing—not even lozenge, no matter how many times I'm told it!—rhymes with "orange."

Q: Aha, but "sporange" rhymes with "orange!" It's part of the sporangium, which is the part of the plant that shoots off spores.

A: Ha! You know, I've had the sporange debate before, and we were both sorely disappointed to find out it's pronounced "spuh-RANJ", with stress on the second syllable. The hunt for a rhyme for orange continues!

Q: I just checked. It appears that the British pronunciation is "spuh-RANJ," but Americans pronounce it like it rhymes with orange.

A: Superb. I'd put money on the pronunciation changing just so that we can say it rhymes with orange. But I'll still take it!

Q: What's one tip you would share with new Twitter users?

A: Provide content and keep things relevant. Posting one or two tweets a day and then wondering why you haven't been contacted by absolutely everyone who follows you isn't going to help anyone, nor will ignoring trends and losing sight of the fact that social media is a live, constantly updating stream of information. In my experience, the more content and the more relevant your online material is, the more visible your brand becomes.

How Do You Use Twitter?

Are we past the point of proving that Twitter is a viable platform? If you've read this far, hopefully you're ready to join the twitterati, the millions of people who use Twitter on a daily basis to build their brand. It starts with your profile.

Creating a Twitter Profile

Your Twitter profile is your Twitter home base, much like your website/blog is your home base for your business. It's where you connect with people and follow others to build your personal network. You can customize your settings and background and send or receive direct messages.

When you create your Twitter name, make sure it's easy to remember and has something to do with your real name. If your name is Kyle Lacy and your Twitter handle is @394ldkf, you're not going to be very memorable in the world of Twitter. "394ldkf" just doesn't roll off the tongue.

The best solution is to use your actual name in your Twitter handle. If your name is already taken, try different variations. Kyle used @kyleplacy because @kylelacy was already taken by another Twitter user. It's normally a great idea, until his friends started sending notes and letters to Kyle Placy.

@kyleplacy: Not funny anymore, people. I've heard them all!

@edeckers: How about Ky Leplacy?

@kyleplacy: Shut up.

@edeckers: Or Kyl Eplacy?

@kyleplacy: Or Ed Eckers?

@edeckers: Truce.

After you come up with your Twitter name, upload a nice photo. As a friendly reminder, upload a nice photo of yourself, not your dog or a Mercedes. (We all know it's not your car anyway, so quit trying to fool people.) Remember that people want to get to know you, not your dog. Your picture should be an accurate representation of you.

Finally, fill out your profile information, including your bio. Be sure to fill it with relevant information, and don't cram it full of #hashtags. That's just annoying and looks more than a little desperate. Your bio lets people learn what you're about and who you are. Also, add your blog or website URL and your hometown. (Or, if you're concerned about safety and privacy because you live in a small town, put the name of the nearest big city.) Give people the opportunity to connect with you as many times as possible.

Finding Followers

The next step is getting followers to your Twitter account. Your goal may not be to have hundreds of thousands of followers, but you do need a few friends. Friends (or followers) on Twitter give you the opportunity to share your message with other people.

You can add people as followers to your account in a few ways.

First, introduce yourself by following other people. Make your tweets public/not private so anyone can read them. It's likely that when you follow people, they'll check out your Twitter page, so they should be able to see what you've tweeted about.

Search for people based on keywords. Using Twitter's search function, look for keywords about your industry or hobbies. Follow the people who use them, and see if they'll follow you back. Make sure your bio is written to let those people know why you're following them. If you're a physical therapist, and you want to connect with other physical therapists, make sure your bio says "physical therapist" in it.

Don't follow everyone though. Be selective and find the best possible audience for your work.

✉ *Note*

> "Following" is Twitter jargon for "connecting with." Although it sounds rather stalkerish—"Hey, I'm following you. Are you following me?"—you'll get used to the parlance after a short while. Although it's not the puppy dogs and rainbows of Facebook—"Will you be my friend? She's my friend!"—it's not as creepy as it sounds.

Next, import your email contacts. When you launch your account, Twitter asks if you want to import contacts from email providers like Gmail and Yahoo!. Enter your email information and watch what happens: Twitter pulls all your email contacts and cross-references them with the Twitter database. It tells you which people in your email database use Twitter.

Click a button, and Twitter will follow everyone from your email database. And remember that if you follow all these contacts, they may follow you back. You will get a better response rate from people following you from your email list because they already know your name (or at least they should).

Sending Out Tweets

Let's get to tweeting! This is where the true fun begins in the world of Twitter. "Tweets," "tweeting," and "being tweeted" are less about that little yellow bird from Bugs Bunny cartoons and more about sending messages to other Twitter users.

Remember to start conversations. You can direct tweets to other users by asking questions, sharing news, or just putting up something to see if people will react (see Figure 5.2). By starting conversations, you build relationships with other Twitter users. The point of using Twitter and social networking is to build your brand, and the only way to accomplish this is to share content.

> **Erik Deckers**
> @edeckers
>
> Have to edit 6 pages before I go to bed. So I did what any writer would do. Cleaned an electric fan that has not been cleaned in 10 years.
>
> LIKES
> 12
>
> 12:33 AM - 31 May 2017
>
> 2   13   ♥ 12   ili

Figure 5.2 *This is a tweet Erik (@edeckers) sent out when he should have been working on this book. Part of Erik's brand is "humor writer," and so he sends tweets like this to support that and to see how much of a response he can get.*

 Tip

Content makes the tweet. Remember, the more content-rich your tweets become, the more people will read. This is done by linking your blog, including photos or gifs, and even using popular or commonly-used hashtags, like #GameOfThrones, #MakeAMovieBoring, and #PersonalBranding.

Retweeting Content

"Retweeting" is forwarding a tweet you found particularly interesting, sort of like forwarding an email. Users who like a tweet might retweet it to their followers, which amplifies your reach and can be seen as a compliment. It means that the content was interesting enough to be passed along.

If you want one goal for Twitter, it is the retweet. There is no function more powerful and more apt to spread your message (and personal brand). It is viral and word-of-mouth marketing at its finest. Retweeting is a way to share content without looking like you're copying and pasting.

Just as you would not plagiarize a research document, you wouldn't just copy and paste someone else's tweet. The same repercussions could occur. People don't like it when you steal their tweets, comments, content, or sandwich, and retweeting avoids all this. It says, "this other person wrote this tweet, which I wanted to share with you." You can earn those retweets in a few different ways:

- **Don't talk about yourself too much:** The more interesting your tweets, the more likely they'll be retweeted, especially if you include a link that leads the reader to even more interesting information. Links also give your information more credibility. Most people don't want to hear about what you had for dinner. Instead, tweet about things relevant to your industry, a newsworthy story, or even something humorous or emotion-grabbing

- **Remember who your audience is:** You're not tweeting to 5-year-olds, so your tweets can use grown-up language. When you post content that has substance, people may respond to it and retweet it. Try asking for advice or an opinion about something. Questions that evoke conversation will more likely get retweeted.

- **Tweet about how to do something:** Some people are on Twitter to learn, so provide them with your expertise and know-how.

- **Include photos:** A few years ago, you would have had to leave space to include a URL for any photo you included or even to add a person's name to a retweet. Now you don't have to do either of those things. Twitter has fixed it so photos and retweeted names don't take up any of the 140 character limit.

- **Write a quote:** When responding to a tweet, you can reply or retweet it. If you reply, you answer someone's tweet with your own, and another person can trace back through the chain to see your discussion. A regular retweet is just forwarding a tweet to your network. But quoting a tweet means you write a response above the original tweet, which lets people look at the previous tweet that elicited your response. This is a more effective method of replying, because Twitter does not share your regular replies with your entire network, only the people who follow you and the person you're replying to. At least with quoting a retweet, you increase the reach of your message.

The basics of Twitter are important, but there are also advanced features. Now if only there were a way you could manage the account more effectively to fully grow your brand. Oh, wait—there totally is! There are a few apps that can help you in your Twitter domination.

Applications for Twitter Domination

So far, we've talked about using Twitter as your primary source to share and tweet to your little heart's desire. However, the website can be a little hard to navigate if you start getting ungodly amounts of followers (which you'll get, just because you're awesome). We're talking Lady Gaga famous!

@edeckers: Dude, settle down. We don't want to promise that.

@kyleplacy: What? She's got a few thousand followers. How hard can that be?

@edeckers: No, she's got nearly 67 million followers.

@kyleplacy: Oh. Uh, never mind.

So, how do you navigate Twitter without opening multiple tabs on your browser?

Tip

We recommend using Google's Chrome for your Internet browsing. There are several plug-ins and extensions that can make your personal branding campaign easier and more efficient. Plus, it's more stable and less vulnerable to viruses and phishing attacks.

Twitter is a great tool on its own because you can engage with readers all over the world in just a few minutes a day. But you can get even more out of Twitter with a few different third-party applications designed to make the site even more useful for the professional.

Well, sort of.

When we wrote the second edition of this book, there were several apps for mobile, web, and desktop usage, but many of them have gone away. Now, a few are left that are worth using, but the selection has gotten a lot smaller over the years.

Regardless of when you read this, just do your research into the existing Twitter applications. There should always be a few that make using Twitter easier and more efficient, so even if the three on our list are gone by the time you want to use such an app, you should still be able to understand how to use new tools that replace them.

TweetDeck

This is the application we use the most to manage our multiple Twitter accounts. Sure, you could use the Twitter.com home page , but if you've got more than 100 followers, it's like trying to drink from a fire hose. TweetDeck is ideal for anyone getting started or for those people who have thrown up their hands and shouted, "I just don't get Twitter!"

TweetDeck helps you manage multiple Twitter accounts, schedule tweets, and use different columns for different lists, search terms, and users. You can add several Twitter accounts, which is useful if you need to manage accounts for different clients, or if you want to have two accounts, one for work and one for personal use.

You can set up columns and place followers into it, or set up a search column for certain terms like a #hashtag or "specific phrase" (use quotes so you get exactly that phrase and not just a combination of the words). You can even set up a search column to only show tweets from a specific city.

And because Tweetdeck is owned by Twitter (which is why you can't share to other social networks anymore), you can still use all of Twitter's functionality, like tweet analytics and watching trending terms.

Hootsuite

This is a web-based social media tool used by a lot of social media professionals, because you can plug-in your Twitter, Facebook, LinkedIn, Google+, WordPress, Instagram, and YouTube accounts. It's ideal for social media marketers who have to oversee several different networks but don't want to bounce between them all on their phone or laptop.

Hootsuite is the deluxe version of all Twitter applications. Although TweetDeck can be easier for some to use, Hootsuite gives everything you need to dominate in the personal branding world.

You can do the following with Hootsuite:

- Using its publishing function, you can schedule tweets for pre-posting throughout the day. Hootsuite lets you schedule in 5-minute increments, like at 10:15 a.m and 10:20 a.m. The paid version lets you schedule at odd times, like 10:17 a.m or 10:26 a.m.

- Manage and monitor different Twitter accounts, like a work account and a personal account, or integrate two other social accounts. If you use the free version, you can add three social networks to your profile. But if you use the Professional plan for $19 per month, you can add as many as 10 social networks. (Frankly, you shouldn't need more than five at the most, but they don't have a five-network plan.)

- Create search columns to monitor a keyword, such as the name of your business or your industry. You can have more than one stream/column of a single network on your Hootsuite page, but you can only add up to 10 streams per tab.

- Create multiple tabs for your networks within Hootsuite. This will help you keep an eye on several networks at once.

- Track links and clicks with its ow.ly URL shortener. You can also create basic analytics reports. If you need to analyze more data, you can upgrade to a paid plan.

There are plenty of ways to use Hootsuite in the world of promoting yourself through Twitter. Whether you pre-post tweets to be sent out during the day or track clicks for links you have tweeted, Hootsuite is, in our opinion, the best application to use for total social media management (see Figure 5.3).

Figure 5.3 *The different columns in Hootsuite represent different ways to manage and organize your social networks.*

BufferApp.com

We can't finish the web-based applications section without discussing BufferApp. BufferApp is similar to Hootsuite in that you can schedule your posts to multiple social accounts. You pre-set a posting schedule—say, between 8:00 a.m. and 5:00 p.m. Eastern time—and add several posts to your queue (your "buffer").

Then, Buffer sends out your updates at evenly-spaced intervals. If you post 10 updates in one day, it will send them out roughly once per hour. Post five updates, and they'll go out every two hours.

On the free plan, you're allowed 10 posts per day. On their paid plan, you can post 100 updates per day.

Deciding What's Best

Twitter applications are intended to enhance your Twitter experience. Twitter.com does not offer the functionality that most applications offer, such as watching multiple columns, scheduling tweets, or operating multiple accounts.

So which one should you choose? It depends on whichever one you feel most comfortable with. Test them all before you start using them regularly, and remember that the tools aren't as important as what you do with them. One app cannot help you more than another, any more than one kind of pen can make you a better writer. Get the app you like best, and then get going.

What Should You Tweet (and Not Tweet)?

This is a struggle for a lot of people. They're caught up in trying to figure out what to tweet, how to tweet, and when to tweet—it can be frustrating. They start to question and doubt their efforts so much that they stop tweeting altogether. Or they worry that their content is monotonous and lose sight of why they wanted to tweet in the first place (personal branding).

Ultimately, people lose motivation and slowly begin tweeting in circles, sending empty, meaningless messages. Or they race around, not sure where to start, so they just start throwing up anything and everything they can think of. Avoid the embarrassment of poor tweeting habits with these tips:

- **Tweeting for current topics:** How many journals have you started, only to toss them aside after two weeks of struggling to think of something profound to write about? You're trying to write to future generations for posterity, in the hopes that someone will think you're interesting 50 years from now. Forget that. Just write about stuff happening or you're thinking about right now. Just tweet anything semi-interesting. Then do it again and again. Learn what is important, and make tweeting a habit.

- **Sharing is caring:** This is crucial on Twitter. If you love reading another user's tweets, chances are someone else will, too. People love following new Twitter users who post interesting content, so introduce them to your network. Sharing is more than just retweeting other people's tweets, though. It's about sharing a variety of great content, too—links, questions, pictures, articles, videos, announcements, and so on. Share what you know and who you know. When you've hit a rut, find more to share. There's plenty of information out there worth passing on.

- **Engage and begin a conversation:** Don't have anything to say? Then engage with someone else and begin a conversation. It's amazing how powerful a simple conversation can be if you show someone you're listening! In this weird six-degrees-of-Kevin-Bacon world, one conversation (even on Twitter) can lead to an endless amount of useful resources and information. This is what Twitter is for! And the only way to expand your network is through conversations. No one knows who you are until you've introduced yourself, right? You can't be a wallflower at a party, and you can't be a wallflower on Twitter.

The point here is to share your opinions and ask questions. Use (and grow) your resources and network just by sitting at your computer or using your mobile phone. Ask and answer new questions, and be a point of reference for someone else.

- **Be consistent:** Remember the times when your head is completely empty and words escape you? It happens to everyone. If you lack a topic or questions to ask, you can still tweet. Rework old ideas, revisit old stories, relate funny stories, crack a joke. You can even repeat an old tweet by adding "ICYMI" ("in case you missed it") and pasting in the original content. Your followers are not all paying attention to you at the same time of day, so drop the occasional ICYMI tweet to reach those who truly might have, well, missed it.

- **Be active, not annoying:** You know the little kid who talks constantly? That one kid who chatters, makes a lot of noise, and is a general nuisance? Don't be that kid. The difference between being active and annoying is important. First, you don't need to tweet 100 times a day to be consistent or relevant—tweeting too much can lose followers for you.

  Next, this means don't tweet the same thing over and over. Although we said you can re-send previous tweets, we didn't mean 10 times a day. It also means don't tell us what you had for breakfast every morning or that you're sick, healthy, going to lunch, back from lunch, tired, wide awake, going to work, or heading home. You've created all this chatter, and it doesn't do a thing. Remember to focus on your content, and refer to the five principles we talked about in Chapter 1.

  Your content is what drives your personal brand, and if your content is just endless chatter about your immediate surroundings, that's not as interesting as you might think.

- **Be relevant and surprising:** We don't mean to sound like a "365 Platitudes for a Joy-Filled Life" calendar though.

```
@edeckers:    Is there really such a thing? Do you think we
              could pull that off?

@kyleplacy:   I don't know. Do you think we could get these
              guys to publish it if we wrote it?

@YourDamn     Boys, just focus on this project for now. One
Editor:       thing at a time. Also, no, you can't.
```

So without being all Rebecca of Sunnybrook Farm about this, we think you should post some stuff that will make people happy or interested in you. Share an interesting article you read, a blog post you wrote, a meeting you had with another social media friend, a conference you're attending, a video you uploaded, a video of your latest conference session, or an interesting blog post from your social media friend. You can talk about other things as well, but when you're first starting out, make sure you're making a positive contribution to your content stream.

- **Be goal-oriented:** Do you feel like you're not going anywhere? Now is the time to sit back and revisit your goals. Why did you create your Twitter account? Why are you creating your personal brand in the first place? What are the goals and ideas pushing you to becoming more well known in your field? Remember, your goals should guide the steps you take. If you want to be a stand-up comic, tweets about estate tax reform will not do much for you. Figure out which tweets take you a step toward that goal and which ones take you a step back.

- **Take a break:** When you feel stuck and lose motivation to tweet, don't force it. You're allowed to take a day off. You're allowed to shut down and throw a Frisbee to your dog. You're allowed to have a drink with that special someone. And you're allowed to tweet things that are silly, angry, unusual, or just don't have anything to do with your overall strategy. Whether your goals are big or small, users want to follow someone they can relate to. They want to know you're a human being, not a marketing machine. Social media is not all about constant self-promotion. It's not all about "me, me, me," but neither is it all about "you, you, you." Sometimes it's just about "Here's what I like" or "Here's something that bugs me." Remember, this is your personal brand, and that includes your identity when you're off the clock. So your Twitter messages need to be a mix of building your personal image and brand and helping others build theirs.

PERSONAL BRANDING CASE STUDY: @MUSLIMIQ

Qasim Rashid—@MuslimIQ—is a best-selling and critically acclaimed author of three books on Islam and human rights, including *Talk to Me: Changing the Narrative on Race, Religion, & Education.* He is a practicing attorney, former visiting fellow at Harvard University's Islamic Studies program, and the current national spokesperson for Ahmadiyya Muslim Community USA. Also, he's a vocal supporter and defender of women's rights and the Black Lives Matter movement. So, he has a lot of conversations on social media from people with questions, people who want to argue, and people who just want to be mean.

Qasim has embraced social media as a way to push back against the misinformation about the Muslim faith. He said his priorities are religious freedom, racial justice, gender equality, and also dad jokes. (No, seriously!) He uses social media as a way to focus on these priorities efficiently and effectively. Whether he's speaking for himself or serving as part of the True Islam education campaign (@TrueIslamUSA), Qasim pushes back against the distortion from groups like Daesh and the Taliban.

"I want it to be known by example that a Muslim is one who stands for peace and opposes terrorism in all its forms," said Qasim.

He has especially taken to Twitter as a way to promote dialogue and understanding, and to test ideas, concepts, and strategies to "push back against ignorance and hate."

He said, "If an approach is successful on Twitter, I know that approach to a problem is worth writing about in an op-ed or even a book. And by 'successful,' I mean something that goes viral."

Qasim does a lot of writing. He was inspired by Mirza Ghulam Ahmad, the founder of the Ahmadiyya Muslim Community, who said, "we must wage the true Jihad of the Pen to combat ignorance, fear, hatred, and bigotry with education, love, compassion, and empathy." So Qasim picked up his pen, wrote three books, and continues to write numerous articles and columns every week, as well as a few dozen tweets each day.

All his hard work may be paying off. He said one of the best parts of his day is when someone tells him his commentary made him reconsider his negative views on Islam and Muslims, and advocate for "pluralism and education."

"That bridge building is the key to peace, and that's what the true Jihad of the Pen is all about," he said.

Nevertheless, he still puts up with a lot of nastiness online—and he combats hatred and bigotry with love and compassion. How does he manage to do it day after day? He said, "With class, humor, and by adhering to the Qur'an 25:64, 'When the ignorant address you, say peace and carry on with dignity.'"

Social media has been a bright spot for him, too. Many of Qasim's speaking requests come though social media, and he enjoys that. Plus, he said, "I got to do this interview!" (So we've got that going for us.)

Qasim has five pieces of important advice for people building their personal brands:

"First, know what you believe and why you believe it. Second, stay consistent. Third, be committed to your brand. Don't jump on the viral trend that has nothing to do with your brand. Fourth, maintain expertise in your area of branding. Fifth, be sure to have fun. This is literally your passion, so enjoy it," he said.

The most important thing to learn from Qasim is that you must remain committed to your ideals and be willing to defend them. Qasim does that with grace, dignity, and humor. Especially with his dad jokes. As fellow dads, Erik and Kyle can attest to their brilliance.

Seven Do's and Don'ts While Using Twitter

You can use Twitter to effectively further your personal brand in a lot of fun ways. You'll get even more out of it if you keep in mind these rules governing the world of Twitter:

1. **Do be yourself; don't be a fake:** Personal branding is about being honest and being real. When it comes to sharing content on the Internet, make sure you're telling the truth. And when you're sharing content, make sure you're sharing both professional and personal information. Remember: Your personal identity is what crafts your professional brand.

2. **Do learn the art of following and unfollowing:** When using Twitter, you will have multiple people following your account every day. This is based on the content you share as well as the people who are retweeting and following your account. Don't be afraid to unfollow people if they post too many updates, don't post interesting information or anything of value, are only posting spam, or are mean and abusive.

3. **Don't automatically follow people just because they follow you:** Check out their profile bios and the content they share. Decide if they will be valuable to your efforts (or at least aren't a bunch of filthy spammers).

4. **Do not, Do Not, DO NOT be a yo-yo follower:** These are the people who will follow as many people as they can, wait for follow-backs, and then unfollow them a few days later. They do this so they can repeat the process and cheat the system. You can spot these Twitter cheaters, because they'll have tens of thousands of followers, but will only have a

few hundred tweets. Nobody gets those numbers without being a celebrity. Seriously, do not ever do this. It's just as bad as hiring someone to follow you with thousands and thousands of empty accounts. Their number of followers is high, but nothing good will ever happen. It's like giving a concert to a room full of mannequins. Sure, the room's full, but there's no one to actually hear you. Plus, Twitter can suspend them for cheating. Yo-yo followers are not good people.

5. **Do practice "Giver's Gain":** It means you give without expecting anything in return. For Twitter, you should share other people's content more than your own, often at a 9:1 ratio (tweet about yourself one time out of every ten; the other nine should be about someone else). When you share their content, they're more likely to share yours in return. In the world of personal promotion, you need to have loyal fans who spread your content for you. Remember, content gets other users to notice you. Share others' work, and they'll build your brand for you.

6. **Do tweet your content on a regular basis:** People have different ideas on how often you should tweet. We have heard everything from five to 20 tweets a day. There's no magic number, but we always tell people to share at least three tweets a day. Don't shoot for 20 a day, but if you want to post 10–12, nothing's stopping you.

7. **Don't lose track of time:** We call Twitter "the best, most fun waste of time you could ever have," and we've both spent more time than we should on the tool. Other people panic at the amount of time they think they should spend on it. When you're starting out, focus on 30 minutes a day. At first, that may be the time you spend creating your profile or sending your first few tweets. But as you get better at it, 30 minutes at once is too much, so divide it up into a few blocks of time throughout the day. Eventually you'll be a Twitter master who can get a lot done in half that time. If you need to, use BufferApp or Hootsuite as a way to reduce the time you spend on Twitter or use the timer on your phone and set an alarm.

Twitter Tips in 140 Characters or Less

We asked our Twitter friends to give us some tips on using Twitter for personal branding. And our friends came through for us. They gave us a lot of great advice:

- Be yourself on Twitter. People will either love you or hate you but at least it's you.—@mooshinindy

- Twitter is a conversation. Take some time to listen to what is going on and respond.—@virtualewit

- Twitter is as good as the people you follow.—@lookwebdesign

- Tweet 80% content your readers will find helpful and 20% self-promotion.—@watsonk2

- Find the perfect balance between the quantity of your tweet versus the quality.—@edeckers

- First—get followers. Second—keep followers. Sounds easy right?—@edeckers

- Pay it forward—giving is as good as getting, and social capital is invaluable.—@jennielees

- Identify. Engage. Respond. Repeat.—@chadrichards

- Simply be genuine and share useful information as in time it will come back to you.—@jillharding

- Don't constantly change your avatar as it's one of the main consistencies in your brand.—@bnyquist

- If you murder someone, don't tweet about it. Bad for the brand.—@brianspaeth

- Focus on building conversations, and relationships and the followers will come.—@roundpeg

- Be mindful that your horse precedes your cart. Relationships are key.—@fleurdeleigh

- Employ a content lure strategy. You point users to helpful content in exchange for influence.—@edeckers

How Should Our Four Heroes Use Twitter?

You can use Twitter to further build your personal brand through content sharing and network building. How should our four heroes use it to further their personal brand in their respective industries and networks?

- **Allen (influencer)** is searching for a job in an advertising firm as an account representative. Twitter is extremely important to him because his potential employers use it as a corporate communication platform. Plus, Allen can connect with influencers in the advertising industry or connect with individuals who work at local ad firms where Allen is trying to get a job. Remember, this is all about building a network and relationships, and Twitter is an ideal tool for that.

- **Beth (climber)** wants to be a CMO at an insurance agency. This is where the use of Twitter can become a little dicey. Beth's main problem is the lack of use of Twitter within the insurance world. Her industry is heavily regulated, and corporate attorneys do not look on social networking favorably (it can be done, but attorneys tend to worry that way). However, Beth can use it for personal communication by sharing her expertise on all things marketing and as a way to distribute and share information related to her work.

- **Carla (neophyte)** wants to switch from being a pharmaceutical rep to a nonprofit role. She can use Twitter to start networking within the nonprofit world. Like Allen's advertising prospectives, directors and volunteers use Twitter constantly for news, information, and distribution to help further their messages. Carla should share information on the nonprofit world and retweet individuals who are already involved.

- **Darrin (free agent)** wants jobs at his current level of responsibility, but with more pay, so he's in the same situation as Carla, using Twitter for development, networking, and content sharing. Darrin should also attend networking meetings and connect with people he meets on Twitter to further his conversations and increase the size of his professional network.

6

Facebook: Developing a Community of Friends

Imagine a single lamp lighting a desk deep in the dormitories of Harvard University. A scrawny college student types at a computer, working on a project with his roommates. In 2004, Harvard sophomore Mark Zuckerberg began developing a new kind of website for fellow students to track their social lives. He called it Facebook. And it changed the world.

It quickly caught on among students, and membership was first expanded to include Stanford, Yale, and Columbia universities and then to most universities across the U.S. and Canada. By 2006, anyone in the world could join, and many did.

There are 2 billion monthly active Facebook users as of June 30, 2017[1]—people sharing content and creating relationships. And there are 1.32 billion daily users.

In just 13 years, Mark's student project has become the biggest social network in the world. At 2 billion users, that's bigger than any single country.[2]

1. https://newsroom.fb.com/company-info/

2. https://www.cia.gov/library/publications/the-world-factbook/rankorder/2119rank.html

You're probably already on Facebook, but you may not be getting the most out of it. You could use this incredibly powerful tool for personal branding. The main purpose of using Facebook is to create a community and connect people. Connecting with people and creating community can help fuel the influence behind your brand. Influence creates viral marketing within a community. More on that later.

When it comes to Facebook users, 82 percent of all 18–29-year-olds are on it, but so are 79 percent of 30–49-year-olds (their parents). And 56 percent of people over 65 are on it.[3]

People still assume that only young people are using Facebook, but that bubble got popped years ago. Now nearly everyone is using it, regardless of age. They're sharing content, thoughts, ideas, and opinions. And each one of them builds some type of identity, whether personal or professional, with Facebook.

Why Should You Use Facebook?

Facebook exists to help people connect and stay in touch. Where LinkedIn is an extremely professional site, Facebook is truly the personal tool for your personal brand. Many people use Facebook as a way to share pictures, opinions, and content about their personal lives—cat videos, pictures of their kids, and their thoughts on the 2016 presidential campaign. (If you missed it, count yourself lucky. We both nearly quit Facebook by October 2016.)

Others add a page to their account and a community site around their organization, brand, or personality. Some still use it as a community site to gather different groups of people into an online group or fan page. (More on professional pages later.)

What we have found over the years is that the essence of your personal life has an impact on your professional brand. Plenty of professionals sell their products and services in direct association with their personal lives. What you do, see, and involve yourself in daily relates to your job.

And in a growing freelance and small-business economy, it's not uncommon to be friendly with your clients, blurring the line between personal and professional. That can be good or bad.

An example: An insurance agent creates a Facebook group page for her son's Little League team and uses it to help promote her business. We're not talking about being awkward like, "Your kid might break an arm with that bat! Are you insured?" We're talking about using the team as the middle ground to connect with the other parents.

---

3. http://www.pewinternet.org/2015/01/09/demographics-of-key-social-networking-platforms-2/

When you create a common association with other people, they're more likely to join the group. Eventually you can enter into deeper conversations with other parents because of the relationship built from the team—and let it be known that you're an insurance agent, for example.

However, people who are Facebook friends with their colleagues, clients, and networking groups often forget the #1 rule of personal branding: Don't post anything you wouldn't want your boss, client, and mother to see on a billboard.

Another example: So, a web designer gets into a heated online shouting match with someone from the other side of a political argument, complete with insults. The web designer's client sees it and doesn't actually care about the argument either way. But she's so shocked at her web designer's behavior that she cancels her business relationship with him.

Is that fair? No. Are we saying you should hide who you are on Facebook? Absolutely not. We're just saying don't be mean to people in general. And maybe don't friend your damn clients for just this reason!

Facebook is the website to make that connection happen. Are the parents of the other children on the team prospective clients? Probably. Could the insurance broker create a connection with other parents because of her kid's baseball team? Definitely.

```
@edeckers:   Do you think @YourDamnEditor would let us use
             our kids to market the book?
@kyleplacy:  I don't see why not. We've been acting like children
             the whole time.
@Your
DamnEditor:  Amen!
```

We do not condone the use of your children to sell your products. (Well, maybe a little, if they're adorable.) We do condone finding similar interests and circumstances to create connections with people. And Facebook, if you can balance it properly, will let you create a greater connection between your personal and professional lives. It can strengthen personal relationships in a way that can turn into professional relationships and vice versa.

With nearly two billion people using Facebook, you're more than likely going to know someone on the site already—unless you're a hermit, which raises more questions than we have time for. If you already use Facebook, you're aware of the staggering amount of time most people spend on it every day. If you haven't yet joined, trust us: People really, really like to use Facebook. Consider some of these statistics:

- More than half of all users—1.57 billion—log on to Facebook daily with a mobile device; 1.18 billion are desktop users.

- The average Facebook user has 155 friends.

- On average, more than 300 million photos are uploaded per day.[4] (Half of these are of people's feet at the beach.)

Used correctly, Facebook can be a great tool for building your personal brand. You need to learn how to share information safely and tastefully, and you need to know what the site can do for your personal brand.

What Can Facebook Do for You?

You may be among the millions of people already logging into Facebook every day or every hour, using it to catch up with old friends, reconnect with former classmates, and share your latest baby pictures with your family. Just as you use Facebook as a social support system, you can use it to build professional networks and enhance your personal brand. Facebook has a variety of built-in tools to do all these things.

Reconnect with Old Classmates and Coworkers

It might be hard to imagine reconnecting with your long-lost friends from high school or college, but they could still be great connections 10 or 20 years later.

Facebook lets you reconnect with just about anyone. It's just as important to reconnect with people you've lost touch with—from high school, college, and previous jobs—as it is to expand your network with new people. The more people you connect with, the more opportunity you can have in the future to grow your network and brand.

How can our hero, Allen, use Facebook to reconnect? Allen (influencer) could reconnect with old classmates and past co-workers to build his network in the advertising field. He graduated with a double major in design and marketing. His classmates from college are probably involved in other advertising agencies or ad firms. He can connect, network, and build a relationship to further his search for the job.

Professionally Brand Yourself

There are two types of pages in Facebook: personal and professional. You don't need to use your personal profile for your personal brand strategy, especially if you want

---

4. http://www.facebook.com/press/info.php?statistics

to keep your personal life completely separate from your professional. Instead, use a page for your professional identity and a personal profile for your private life.

How could our hero, Darrin, use this feature? Darrin (free agent) needs to start building a personal brand to build his identity among the IT and corporate professionals in his local area. He must create a page to further his professional brand, gain influence in his industry, and fetch bigger clients.

Be Philanthropic

What could be a better way to build your personal brand than to support a cause? Facebook Causes is an application that makes it easy for you to support different causes and to persuade your friends to give to each cause. Every brand, including the personal ones, should have a philanthropic side to it. When you support different causes, you build your personal brand story.

If you were to ask entrepreneur or business professionals how they became successful, the majority would say "philanthropy." When you give your money and time to an organization, you have the opportunity to network with other individuals associated with the organization.

How might our hero, Beth, use this feature? This is a perfect example of something Beth (our climber) would use to further her network in the corporate ranks at the insurance company. By supporting causes (through Facebook) that the company supports, she can show her commitment to the company and share that commitment with the rest of her Facebook network. In some cases, she may even be asked to join a local board of directors, which will help her meet other influencers in her community.

Find Local Events

Networking is extremely important to building your personal brand (see "Chapter 12, How to Network: Hello, My Name Is...") Facebook Events helps you find events in your area to attend to meet new people. The more people you meet, the more opportunity you have to expand your territory and spread your personal brand story.

How can Carla use this feature? This function is for the networker among the heroes. Carla (neophyte) is completely starting over from being a pharmaceutical rep to looking for a job in the world of nonprofits. She needs to network with people in her new field and attend events to meet those individuals. She can use Facebook to track events, add them to her calendar, and find out who else will be attending each event. (She should also spend a lot of time on the Causes pages.)

There are plenty of ways to use Facebook for personal branding. The first step is to create your own personal profile.

What You Should Know About Facebook

Like all social networking sites, Facebook has different elements and uses specific terms to describe its features and functions: the pages and personal profiles (see Table 6.1). Remember from the Twitter and LinkedIn chapters that when you connect with individuals on the sites, they are described in different terms; a Twitter friend is called a "follower," and a LinkedIn friend is called a "connection."

On Facebook when someone connects with you on your personal profile, he becomes a friend. When an individual connects with you on your page, she becomes a fan. You want friends and fans!

Table 6.1   List of Important Facebook Vocabulary

Personal profile	Your personal page on Facebook
Applications	Fun and interactive elements that can be added to your pages
Discussion board	Area on the page where fans can engage in topic-based dialogue
Wall/News feed	Your personal page that logs all activity on Facebook by your friends and your profile
Poke	An awkward way to say hello
Status update	A way to let your friends in on your activities and feelings
Tag	A way to let your friends know they are in a picture posted to your page
PM/Private Message	A message sent between two friends on Facebook

The professional page is Facebook's way to give businesses Facebook accounts. Facebook calls these professional pages, well, "professional pages," but for clarity, we refer to them only as "pages."

To truly take advantage of Facebook as a personal branding tool, you need to build a personal profile and a page to house, store, and create the communication funnel that can nurture your Facebook network.

Professional Page vs. Personal Profile

There are two types of pages you can create on Facebook: the personal profile and the professional page (see Table 6.2). Facebook personal profiles are meant to represent a single individual and not an overall entity, so personal profiles and professional pages have unique content and offer different Facebook functionality.

What type of page should you create? A Facebook personal profile or a professional page?

To start, just use the personal profile. But as you gain some notoriety as a speaker, writer, business leader, entertainer, actor, musician, or anyone in the public eye, then you'll want a professional page.

All pages must have a personal profile connected to them. Profiles are the keys to every page you develop. You can have multiple pages associated with one personal profile, but you can't have a page without a profile.

You can use your individual profile for business or for your personal life, but it's usually best to keep them separate; after all, you might not want potential clients seeing pictures of you three drinks into your best friend's wedding. We've all been there.

The point is, there is information that you want to share with your family and friends that you don't necessarily want to share with business associates. If you want to keep a Facebook profile completely private, lock it down in the privacy settings and keep it separate from your page.'

Table 6.2   Differences Between Facebook Pages and Personal Profile

	Personal Profile	Page
Who is allowed to use the page?	Individuals.	Businesses and individuals.
Can you invite friends to the page?	You can mass invite people to your personal profile by email.	No. However, you can invite people to join your page from your personal profile page.
Can you update your status?	Yes.	Yes.
Can you mass message your friends?	Yes.	No. You can only send a page update to your supporters.
Are applications allowed?	Yes.	Yes.
Is there a limit to the number of friends you can connect with?	5,000.	No. You can have an unlimited number of fans.
Can you run analytics applications on the page?	No.	Yes. Pages have analytics to measure the effectiveness of your content.

After you set up your personal profile, you can next set up a page to reflect your business (and personal brand). A professional page is particularly useful if you hope to gain thousands of followers because, unlike personal profiles, pages have no caps on the number of friends who can connect to the page.

Kyle experienced Facebook's limit when his personal profile hit the 5,000-friend mark and he wasn't allowed to add more friends. He then created a page to manage the friend overflow from his personal account and turned them into supporters of his professional page.

Needless to say, having to create a page after spending so much time on his personal profile was a pain. If you plan to grow past 5,000 friends, create a page right after creating your personal profile. (Or just don't be so greedy.)

The Basics: Creating a Personal Profile

When you first visit Facebook.com, you're asked to register with the massive Facebook database. The straightforward form asks for your name, birth date, and email address. Next, fill out your personal profile by uploading a picture of yourself; share personal information, including where you've worked and gone to school; and search for people you know in the database (see Figure 6.1).

Like Twitter and LinkedIn, Facebook makes it easy to find your friends in the database. If you use a public email program, such as Google Mail or Yahoo! Mail, to register your Facebook account, Facebook searches for your contacts in your contact list. When you find people you know, send them an invitation to become a Facebook friend and link their profile to yours.

Facebook also asks for current and former employers, bio, hometown, likes, and interests. The likes and interests portion of your profile is a great opportunity to build your personal brand. It's up to you to decide how much information you want to share on Facebook, but this will help you connect with new people. (Later, we'll talk about security and different profile filters you can create to block people from receiving certain pieces of data.) We recommend filling out the information you are comfortable sharing.

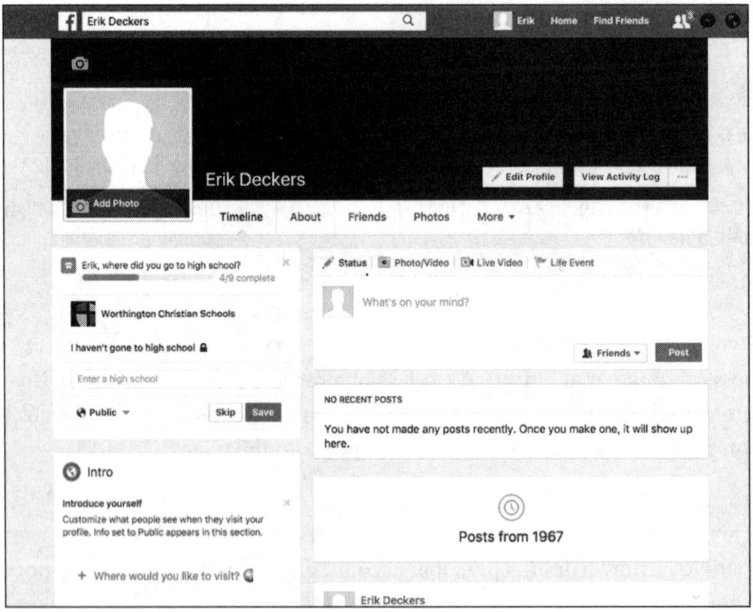

Figure 6.1 *After you create your account, you are asked to enter additional information into your personal profile.*

One of the most important part of this process is choosing your profile picture. We have talked about this at length in other chapters, but we'll look at it again. Keep your professional persona throughout every social network. Your picture should be current and focus only on you. To upload a great Facebook profile picture, follow these tips:

- Use quality profile pictures for all networks. This is extremely important for your personal brand and your Facebook profile (or professional page). What is a quality photo? It's a picture of your wonderful face. It should also be professional and fit your personality.

- A picture from spring break is probably not your best portrayal, and a group photo of you and your friends is not helpful. Use the same professional, high-quality photo on each of your social network sites, from LinkedIn to Twitter to Facebook. If you would like to show a more personal side to your profile, use different photos for your personal and professional pages.

- Make sure your photo was taken with a decent camera, and crop it in tightly so your face is nicely framed.

- Be approachable. You don't have to smile, but don't look sad and downcast either. We're drawn to happy-looking professional people.

Finally, some people change their profile picture every few months, while other people (Erik) will keep theirs for a few years. Regardless of what you do, people must be able to recognize you from your profile picture.

Stay in Control of Your Profile

After you set up your personal profile, you have to decide who can access your profile as well as how it appears to the public. Facebook provides tools that give you specific control. The first issue is the privacy settings and controls of your Facebook profile, and the second issue is your customized URL. You can use both tools to your advantage.

Your Personal Page Privacy Settings

Let's be honest: Facebook is not completely private. You can keep your friends and family from reading your content, but Facebook still has access to everything you post on their network[5], including your private messages[6] to other people.

---

5. https://www.facebook.com/privacy/explanation

6. https://qz.com/940488/youre-about-to-help-facebook-understand-how-your-private-messages-make-you-feel/

This is not meant to scare you away from using Facebook. We only want to make you aware of why you should use the privacy settings.

You may be thinking, "I'm a brand, so I'm not concerned about my personal privacy. I want to show my brand to all who will look, listen, and be enraptured by my personal branding prowess."

Are you done now? Keep in mind, you're not invincible. You need to understand the potential security problems you could face.

It's hard for Facebook to keep up-to-date with all the hacking and scams happening inside the network. Hackers phish for your information so they can break into your account and steal your information to sell to others.

"Phishing for information" means exactly what it sounds like. Hackers create a code that pulls information from a large number of people. This could include family member names, home addresses, phone numbers, email addresses, and other pertinent information. Everything can be public if you're not careful.

You can prevent hackers from getting your data. The first way is self-explanatory: Do not share information you would prefer others not have. Second, use Facebook's privacy settings to block your information from the bad guys as well as people you didn't like in high school, and keep your personal information as secret as possible.

Setting Up Your Privacy Settings for Your Personal Account

Phishing scams and hackers aren't the only security threats users face on Facebook. You need to keep your personal brand safe, and that starts with determining how you'll set up the privacy settings for your profile. Remember, all content in your profile is public and open to the Internet community until you lock it down.

When you log in to Facebook, your main screen shows your stream and other tools to interact with the world of Facebook (refer to Table 6.1). Before you begin exploring, you need to secure your account to your comfort. Go to the far top right of the window and click the little arrow. When the drop-down menu appears, select the "Settings" button. Next, click "Privacy Settings" on the left side of the window. Check out Figure 6.2 for a screen shot of the options.

On the Privacy Settings page, you have several options for choosing who can see your content and what they can see. Below that are "Timelines" and "Tagging Settings" (where you manage whether you can be tagged in other people's photos), and the "Blocking Setting" (where you block stalkers and rude people).

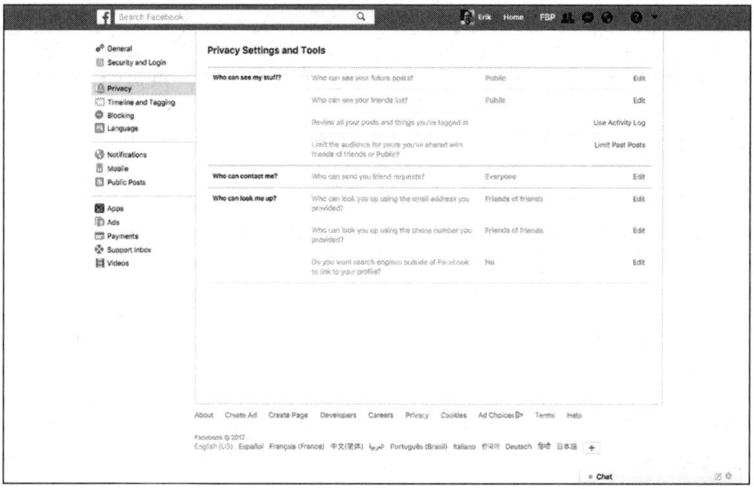

Figure 6.2 *The privacy settings box gives you additional options for personal profile security.*

You have three basic settings to choose from: "Everyone," which makes your profile completely public; "Friends of Friends", which requires placing a certain amount of trust in the people your friends know; and "Friends Only," which means that only your Facebook friends can see your content. You can further customize your settings for who can see future and past posts, and your friends list. Click the "Edit Settings" button next to each to set your privacy.

Tip

Your privacy options are your personal preference. There is no absolute rule for the use of Facebook. But think long and hard about what you would like to share and what you would rather not share with just anyone.

Part of security is also protecting your name. When you create a website, choose a URL that exemplifies your brand. When you get an email address, use your name, or a variation of it.

The same applies to Facebook URLs and usernames. So, don't pick a name like HotDudez89 as your Facebook name, because that will also be your Facebook URL. (Similarly, don't pick that for your email name, because that's what you'll be using when you communicate with potential employers.)

Working with Your Customized URL

When you join Facebook and create your personal profile, you are given an automated URL, such as "http://www.facebook.com/id=20392023/". This ID is your "name" on Facebook.

Needless to say, this URL is overly long and hard to remember. Your personal name is extremely important to your personal brand. Facebook lets you change that username into a customized URL; you can use your name in your link instead of an ID number. Kyle's company has a Facebook URL that's similar to the company's website: "https://www.facebook.com/lessonlyapp," instead of something long and complicated.

To set up your Facebook customized URL, go to the General section of your settings. Check out Figure 6.3. The General button is on the top of the left sidebar.

You'll see a place for you to set your customized URL for your personal profile. You need to set your name so another user cannot steal it.

Your new customized URL is the personal destination to your brand. Users can enter your Facebook username as a search term on Facebook, which makes it much easier for people to find and connect with you.

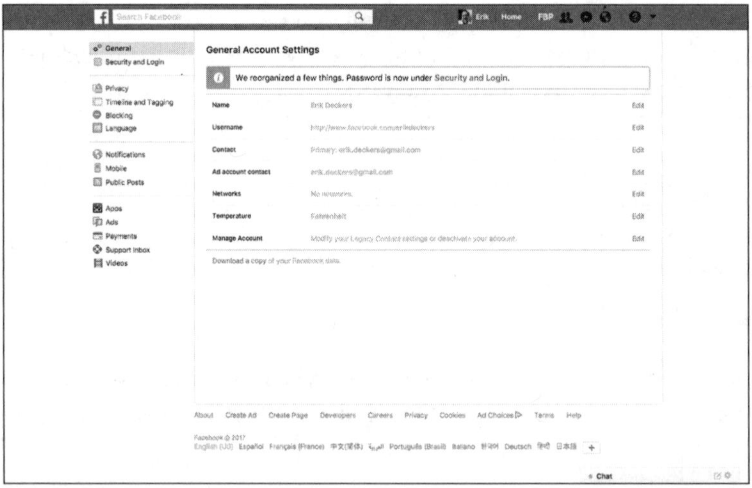

Figure 6.3 *You can customize your Facebook URL. We strongly recommend you use your own name, or some variation of it.*

Now that your personal profile is set, you can build a Facebook page that allows you to share your content with your network of friends. You can build relationships, find places to visit, causes to support, and events to attend.

Using a Professional Page for Personal Branding

Facebook pages are extremely important when creating your personal brand and telling your story. Why? They can reach millions of people in the blink of an eye! The main purpose for using Facebook is to create a community element around your brand. When you have a community, you can experience the beauty of viral communication. Use a page to promote your personal brand for these four great reasons:

- **Facebook reaches billions of people:** With nearly 2 billion users, some of them are bound to like your brand, and a professional page makes your brand accessible to them. Unlike your personal profile, your professional page has no limits to the number of Facebook supporters that can like it.

- **Facebook pages allow for community-based relationships to develop:** Having your brand on a page is an outlet to post all things about you, but not all things deeply personal to you. A page separates the personal from the professional. It allows you to maintain your professional presence on Facebook.

- **You can share business updates and post videos and pictures** for the people who joined your page and want to know the latest news. A page allows professional relationships to develop because people are on the page for professional purposes. A page also lets you grow your professional community in step with your personal community. It gives your audience an outlet to reach you without cluttering up your Inbox.

- **Advertise through Facebook ads:** A professional page gives you plenty of opportunities for paid advertising, whether you just want to promote your brand or sell something. You can create ads that appear on Facebook sidebars. You are in complete control of who you want your audience to be. Target your desired product/service demographic, and verify results with your analytics.

When you set your desired demographics, Facebook tells you how many potential users are available to click your ad. Say you want to run an ad for the Humane Society and reach single females between the ages of 40–55 who live within a 10-mile radius of your zip code. Facebook can tell you that 5,403 women meet the criteria and use Facebook. You can test ads you create to see what works best. The ads can promote your page or your website. By using the "Like" button, you can see how influential your ad is to the Facebook demographic.

Facebook ads (see Figure 6.4) are based on a pay-per-click (PPC) and pay-per-impression (also called CPM, which means "cost per thousand impressions." M is the Roman numeral for 1,000) model of payment. PPC is when a user clicks on your ad, and you pay a price you previously set. CPM happens every time your ad is shown, whether it's clicked or not. Once you reach a set budget amount, your ad stops showing for the day.

The price for PPC varies so much. Facebook fluctuates their best cost based on the amount of use in a given 12-hour period. To stay relevant, look at the amount Facebook asks you to spend. You set the budget and can change it at any time.

Organic content (status updates) usually get a better click-through rate than paid ads. Although Facebook ads are amazing for driving users to your pages, don't lose sight of organic (unpaid) content. You need to measure the influence of both types.

- **Facebook analytics provide insight:** Only a professional page lets you use Facebook Insights, an analytics package, equivalent to Google Analytics (see Figure 6.5, which is not our data). With Insights, you can gather data about your readers, including which posts get the most reactions, when users visit your page most often, and the demographics of your page's fans. This helps you understand and expand your base. Without this, you would have to do extensive research to find the same information.

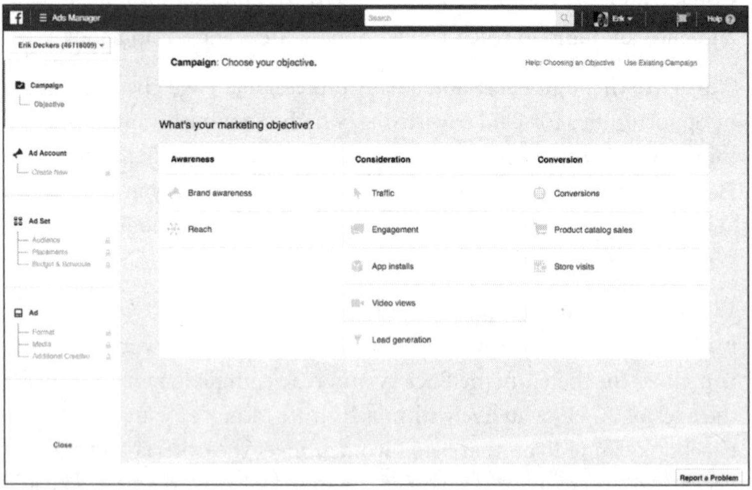

Figure 6.4 *Target your message to your company's key demographic to make your Facebook ad campaign successful.*

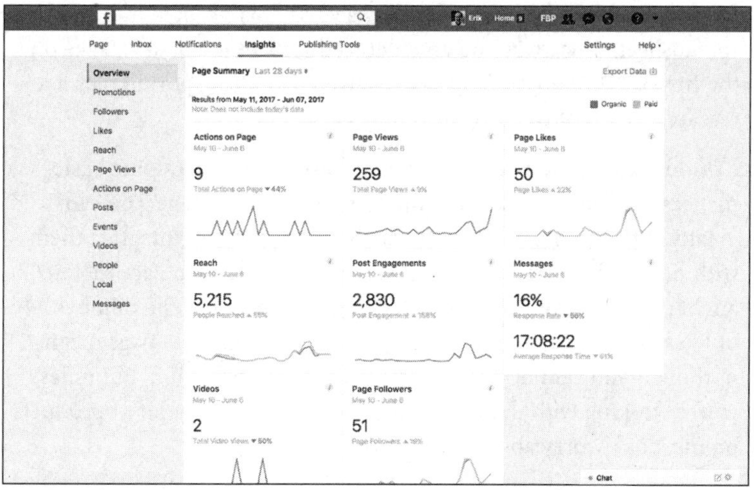

Figure 6.5 *Facebook Insights provides you with qualified information that helps you make content and fan growth decisions.*

Using Insights to Track Your Content Growth

Facebook Insights allow you to gauge who your connections are in terms of gender, age, location, and language. Instead of wasting time on extensive research, these charts show who and where your target audience is. The system is extremely valuable for anyone using professional pages to build a company brand on Facebook.

The Insights data is easy to understand and use to see the growth of your page and demographic information. Play around with the data a little bit to understand the different aspects of the tool. The Insights application gives you four extremely valuable tools for building your personal brand on Facebook:

- **Measure interactions and engagement:** Insights allows you to measure how your fans interacted with the content you shared on the page. When you post a story to your wall and a fan likes and comments on it, that's an interaction. The more interaction your content gets, the more likely your fans will come back for more.

- **Capitalize on content:** Use the interactions numbers to determine what content users find most interesting. Give your audience what they want. When you see increased interactions, it means your content has been watched and read by your fans. You need to share more of that type of content. You also can now see analytics for referral traffic and stream stories in the dashboard to get an idea of what people are sharing and not sharing.

- **Save and export data:** Insights allows you to export data into a spreadsheet. This gives you an enhanced view of the data you see on the Insights dashboard. This also lets you save the exported files and research different trends over months at a time.

- **Conduct advanced research:** Insights also lets you see some basic metrics relative to the activity on your professional page. You can greatly expand on the analytics capabilities when you integrate them with more robust tracking systems that link directly to Facebook to answer some of your more direct business questions. The number of likes and the gender of those who visit your business page mean nothing if you cannot do anything with that information. But unless you're working with thousands of visitors and selling a lot of products online, don't worry about this just yet.

Setting Up Your Professional Page

When you're ready to set up your professional page, you'll find that it's not much more difficult than setting up your personal profile. The important thing is to visualize how you want to portray your professional persona, and then build your page with that vision in mind.

First, select "Create Page" in the far right menu at the top of the blue Facebook bar where you can start the process. Once you start, you'll be shown a list of options: "Local Business;" "Company or Institution;" "Brand or Product;" "Artist, Band, or Public Figure;" "Entertainment;" and "Cause or Community." Choose an option, then add some content.

The Facebook page (as shown in Figure 6.6) is already constructed, and you can see the places to upload your photo (or logo), your cover photo, and other important pieces of information and content. The page has much of the same content as a personal profile except it caters to the public-facing aspect of your personal brand.

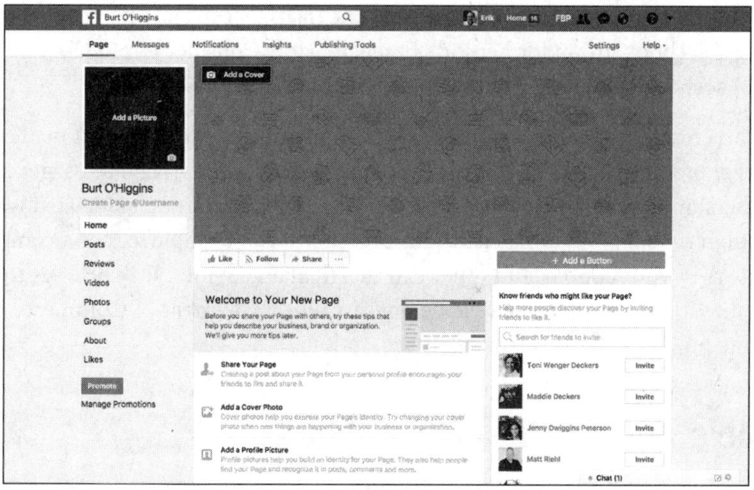

Figure 6.6 *Just like the personal profile, a page gives you additional fields to fill in pertinent information for your business or brand.*

Top Four Tips for Using Facebook

Keep these tips in mind every time you log on to your Facebook account:

1. **Realize your brand is public on Facebook:** If you're not using the security settings discussed earlier in this chapter, your profile page is completely public. More than likely, a Google search of your name can even bring up your Facebook profile. Is your mom looking at your profile? How about your boss or ex-spouse? Remember, share content that is reasonable and won't cause you trouble.

2. **Write on your friends' walls:** Remember the wall from Table 6.1? The Facebook wall is a personal feed that records everything your friends do on Facebook. Writing on your friend's Facebook profile wall is a great way to build relationships. Don't just post messages on your wall—go to theirs and send them a special note, like a birthday wish or a congratulations for a special accomplishment.

3. **Create events on Facebook and invite your friends:** Facebook lets you invite your friends to the events that you host or are just attending. This can help you get more people to your events.

   Just don't invite all your out-of-town friends, because they won't be able to attend anyway. It can be rather spammy if you invite all of your friends to an event, so limit the invitations to people who live less than an hour away.

4. **Join a Facebook group:** Remember the insurance agent who created a Facebook group for her kid's baseball team? Consider joining a Facebook group or two to help promote your personal brand.

You can create or join groups on Facebook depending on your subject matter or personal brand story. After you join a group, you can send private messages to other members or comment on their profiles. You could start a group associated with your high school graduating class, fans of a sports team, employees of a company, members of your church, and other extracurricular activities. Erik belongs to several writing groups, while Kyle belongs to a local Chamber of Commerce group and one on the future of space travel.

Ten Do's and Don'ts of Facebook

First things first. Tear out this portion of the book and post it above your computer or on your mobile device.

@edeckers: Don't have them tear out pages from the book! That's destroying books. That's just wrong.

@kyleplacy: But then they have to buy more books.

@edeckers: Tear, readers! Tear like the wind!

@kyleplacy: Or I suppose they could photocopy them.

1. **Do upload a real picture:** Upload a picture that is real and has some type of substance to it (that is, not a photo of you as a baby, your baby, your dog, or a photo with you and friends). Both your personal and professional pages should have the same photo for consistency's sake.

   After you have established your personal brand and accomplished some goals, you can switch pictures on your personal and professional pages, but for now, stick with your head shot.

   See Figure 6.7 for an example of Kyle's personal page and Figure 6.8 for his professional page photo.

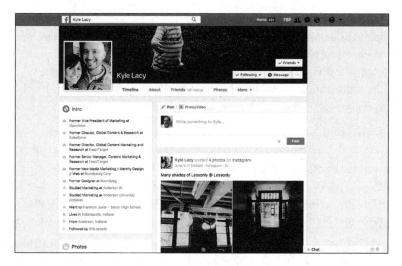

Figure 6.7 *This is Kyle's professional page and professional photo he uses to develop his professional and personal brand.*

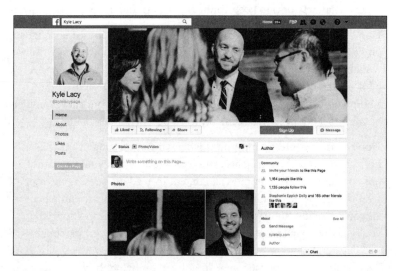

Figure 6.8 *Kyle shows the more laid-back and human side to his brand on his personal page.*

2. **Do share industry-specific content:** Post content that highlights your personal interests and your professional areas of expertise on your personal and professional pages (not your personal profile). If you're interested in marketing, you might post a link to an interesting article.

3. **Do use your email to find friends:** Earlier, we talked about importing your email contact list to find friends on Facebook. If you have not already completed this step, we want you to put down this book and complete it now. Seriously, do it. Importing your contact list is one of the more important things you can do on your personal profile. It helps you connect with users that you already know in the real world.

4. **Don't "Build on Rented Land":** Several years ago, businesses put hundreds and thousands of dollars into Facebook Markup Language (FBML) pages, only to have Facebook drop FBML and introduce frames. Later, after they had persuaded businesses to put a lot of effort and energy into new business pages, they throttled their reach to only one percent of their total followers, unless they paid a promotional cost.

   The lesson? Never put your best work or all your content onto something that you don't own. This is why we told you to set up your own blog and website in Chapter 3. You control the content, you control the reach, and you're in charge of it all. You don't want to build the home of your dreams on someone else's property, so don't rely on Facebook (or any other social network) to keep your content safe and in your total control.

5. **Don't use inappropriate language:** "Duh, I would never use bad language on Facebook. That stuff is permanent." Some people do. (We know *you* wouldn't. We were talking to your friend who's thumbing through this book.) Keep things clean, and keep the content great. Don't drop the f-bomb on your Facebook wall because you're mad at your cable company or got into a political disagreement. You'll be a better person for it.

6. **Don't spam people:** Spamming is when you share content that has nothing to do with your goals or objectives. It's when you constantly post promotional or commercial content instead of focusing on your relationships. Why would anyone want to become your friend when all you do is post about the stuff you sell? People want to know what you're trying to accomplish in the world. If we go to your personal profile and all you have is content and no interaction, you're more than likely spamming your followers, or at least annoying them.

   This also applies to game invites. If you invite someone to a game and they don't join, don't ask them again. No means no. (Also, if people keep doing it to you, you can block all invites from that particular company.)

7. **Don't tag everyone in a picture:** Don't tag anyone in a picture that they're not in. And be aware, some people don't like to be tagged at all. They should lock all that down in their security settings, but don't take it personally if they demand to be untagged. They're thinking about their own safety and security, so respect that.

8. **Don't sync your Twitter profile with your Facebook page:** Facebook updates are completely different from Twitter updates. Twitter users can read hundreds of different updates, and write a few dozen, in one sitting. You don't want to flood a user's timeline with your Twitter chatter. If anyone ever suggests this, just ignore them and re-examine your entire relationship with them.

9. **Don't invite people to your professional page over and over:** After you set up your professional page on Facebook, you will be asked to invite friends to "like" your page. Some will accept, and some will do nothing. Don't take it personally. It's okay to invite users a couple of times in case they accidentally missed it, but don't request the same friends over and over again. No means no. People get annoyed when they're asked to do something repeatedly. Request more than three times, and you become an awkward stalker. And no one likes a stalker.

Facebook Tips in 140 Characters or Less

We asked our Twitter friends to give us some tips on how to use Facebook for personal branding, marketing, and self-promotion. As always, our friends came through for us. They gave us a ton of excellent advice!

- Always make sure your profile pic is of you. —@talk2RyanMitch

- Funny, sports, and food mixed in make you human. Don't be a robot! —@mbj

- Converse. Create and convert. Converse with people. Create content and then convert people to fans. —@MrDrewLarison

- Share timely information in your market. —@tojosan

- Take a look at the "People You May Know." You may find connections you haven't thought of. —@TimChaize

- Remember to look at your Insights in order to track progress of content. —@aims999

- Read the Facebook TOS [terms of service]. It will benefit you in the long run. —@MrsRachelLacy

- Be sure your profile pic is clear and well-lit. —@fleurdeleigh

- List interests that best differentiate you, but don't overdo it. —@edeckers

- Don't underestimate the importance of your "Favorite Music" section. —@kyleplacy

- Pay attention to the lists on Facebook. Sort your friends, colleagues, and family. —@igc

7

Say Cheese: Sharing Photos and Videos

There's an adage among social media marketers: "Photos perform better than plain; videos perform better than photos."

It's also easily provable. Bloggers the world over can tell you that any post where they have a photo has a higher read rate than a post without it. When Erik was a travel writer at the Indiana Office of Tourism Development, they found that posts with photos got 25 percent more traffic than text-only posts, and posts with video got 15 percent more traffic than posts with photos. These trends still hold true in 2017.[1] Why? Because we're a visually-oriented society. We grow up watching television and seeing photos. Because Google has been pushing us toward both video and mobile phone usage and combining the two, it makes sense that more than half of all video content is watched on mobile phones.[2] The short of it is, you need to embrace these technologies for your personal branding and use photos and videos whenever you can.

1. https://blog.hubspot.com/marketing/visual-content-marketing-strategy

2. http://go.ooyala.com/rs/447-EQK-225/images/Ooyala-Global-Video-Index-Q2-2016.pdf

This doesn't mean placing photos of you on every blog post, or that you should create a series of video blog posts. (Although you can if you want; it wouldn't hurt anything.) Rather, it means you should strategically use photo- and video-sharing sites and consider them part of your personal branding arsenal.

Why Video

Google declared 2010 to be the year of video and they've been promoting and growing their video efforts ever since. And because they already owned YouTube, they did everything they could to make videos easy to watch and share. They added YouTube videos to Google search results, so you could watch any videos on your search subject. Even now, video is expected to be 74 percent of all Internet traffic.[3]

In addition, in 2015, the Pew Research Center has found that 72 percent of American adults watch videos on video-sharing sites.[4] Split among age groups, 82 percent of 18–29-year-olds watch videos. Perhaps surprisingly, our parents and grandparents do, too: 34 percent of people 65 and older watch videos online.

This means that because video is so widely accepted, it's a great tool for building your brand. Your colleagues watch it, hiring managers watch it, and decision makers watch it. Video has become so important, for a number of different reasons, that it's hard to ignore, especially if you want to succeed. That's not to say you'll fail without it, but it will certainly make your branding journey easier. Take note:

- **YouTube is the #2 search engine in the world**[5]: And Google is #1. Think about the ramifications of that. Not only does YouTube demand more market share than Yahoo! and Bing, it means Google owns first and second place in the search engine market. It also means that if you optimize your videos well, you can easily start showing up in top search results for that video topic.

- **YouTube is also the #2 social network in the world:** Behind Facebook. A 2014 Pew Research study found that 77 percent of Internet users were on Facebook and 63 percent use YouTube.[6]

3. http://www.kpcb.com/internet-trends

4. http://www.pewresearch.org/fact-tank/2015/02/12/5-facts-about-online-video-for-youtubes-10th-birthday/

5. http://cohlab.com/blog/youtube-the-second-largest-search-engine.html

6. http://www.pewresearch.org/fact-tank/2015/02/12/5-facts-about-online-video-for-youtubes-10th-birthday/

- **Google declared 2011 to be the year of mobile:** Google made sure that the videos that they promoted so heavily in 2010 were easily viewed and shared on mobile phones in 2011, and we're still reaping the benefits in 2017 and beyond. The long and short of it is this: If you produce an awesome video, you're likely to get some significant views from people on mobile phones. Figure 7.1 shows the popularity of mobile viewing on Erik's YouTube channel.

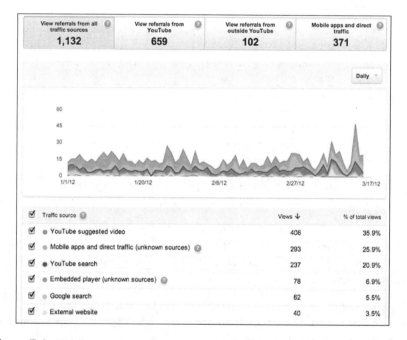

Figure 7.1 *Mobile views on Erik's YouTube channel is nearly 24% of the total views. This can be much higher for other video producers.*

- **Videos are easily and quickly viewed:** With mobile phones, you can watch a quick video embedded in a blog post or on a website and move on, so short videos are especially interesting to people. The average view time of a video is around 4 minutes and 30 seconds, although that time may be longer if your video is longer and good.

- **Videos have a positive effect on search engine optimization (SEO):** If you use videos on your blog or website, it helps your site to be found more easily on the search engines. "Chapter 9, Finding Yourself on Search Engines," discusses this more, but for now you should consider using videos whenever possible.

Where to Put Your Videos

Where you host your video is up to you. Only a handful of video sharing sites are left (there were 80 when we published the second edition of this book). Some are general video-sharing sites like YouTube and Daily Motion. Others are specific to a certain type of video, like FunnyOrDie.com for comedy and humorous videos, while still others are more specialized, like Vimeo, for people who are passionate about creating top-notch videos.

@edeckers: Have you checked out FunnyOrDie? They've got some awesome videos up there.

@kyleplacy: Is that why you were late getting your part of this chapter in?

@edeckers: I was researching! I had to make sure they had comedy videos on there.

@kyleplacy: But 8 days late?!

@edeckers: I had to be really sure.

Also, many of the common photo sharing sites now support video, like Snapchat, Instagram, and Facebook Live. We'll discuss those later.

You only need to focus on the one or two sites that you prefer. Some people think you should upload your best videos to more than one site, especially those that people visit and browse over, just like any other massive content site, like online news or StumbleUpon.

People browse these video sites to see what they can find, so you can either be a big fish in a small pond, or a small fish in one of the most popular ponds in the world. There are benefits to either approach.

YouTube

Believe it or not, YouTube was originally envisioned as a video-dating site, but when it went online in 2005, users uploaded every kind of video so they could share them on MySpace. Since then, it has become the number one video-sharing site in the world, with more than 300 hours of video uploaded to YouTube every hour[7] (compare that to 60 hours every hour in 2012), and more than 4.95 billion videos viewed per day.

That should tell you a few things:

- It's easy to shoot a video. All you need is a smartphone, a cell phone with video capabilities, a digital video camera, a digital camera with video capabilities, or a laptop with a built-in video camera.

---

7. http://www.statisticbrain.com/youtube-statistics

- It's even easier to upload a video. YouTube wouldn't have so many thousands of videos uploaded if it weren't easy.

- YouTube is everywhere. Basically, if you have a Google account of some sort—Gmail or Google Drive—you have a YouTube account. Just sign in with your Gmail account, and click the "Upload" link in the upper-right corner.

Figure 7.2 shows you the YouTube upload window, and the different upload options, including a drag-and-drop feature. Just drag a video from your computer desktop or another folder to your YouTube window, and it handles the rest.

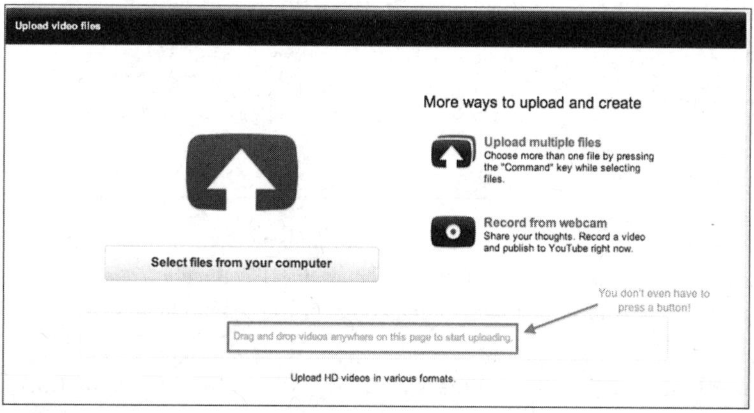

Figure 7.2 *Uploading videos to YouTube is one of the easiest things you can do on the Internet. It has several different options to choose from to fit whatever technology you use.*

After you upload a video or two, you can start sharing them on your various social networks. You can even set YouTube to automatically notify Twitter when you upload a new video. Go to the "Settings" tab in your account, and then choose the types of notifications you want to share. Figure 7.3 shows the "Sharing Settings" screen.

Vimeo

Vimeo is a video-sharing site for people who are serious about their videos. According to the website, Vimeo is "a respectful community of creative people who are passionate about sharing the videos they make."

These aren't just people shooting videos with a cell phone camera of a guy getting hit in the groin with a football. These are professional and enthusiastic amateur videographers who have great gear, excellent editing skills, and interesting subjects. Vimeo has channels for people interested in the arts, nonprofits, comedy, nature, and sports.

For instance, Rand Fishkin of SEOMoz uploads videos of his talks and his Whiteboard Fridays. The rock band Modest Mouse has released several videos here; indie movie producers and documentary filmmakers post their movies; and even the White House kept an official video channel on Vimeo during President Obama's tenure.[8]

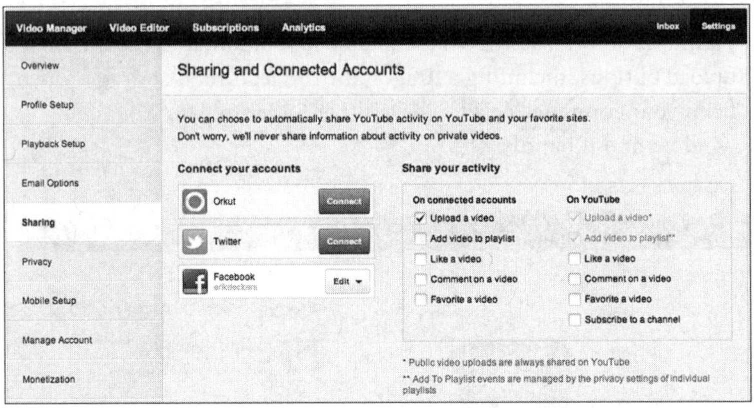

Figure 7.3 *On YouTube, you can share videos, favorite them, add them to a playlist, and even edit them online. You can subscribe to others' channels, leave comments on their videos, and embed their videos, and yours, in your own blog posts or website.*

If you can shoot and edit some great video, you will be in some august company among Vimeo's videographers.

Periscope

Periscope is a video app that lets you stream live video to be shared by other people with the Periscope app. It was bought by Twitter before it launched in 2015, and immediately became a big hit.

As you stream the video, people can tap a little heart at the bottom of the screen to show you how much they like what you're doing.

Erik's friend, Dewey McGeogh (pronounced Magoo), became something of a Periscope celebrity by creating an almost-daily show where he would just share random thoughts and stories that happened throughout the day. Other times, he would perform under his drag character, Lady Winifred, and perform a sort of tiny talk show.

---

8. https://vimeo.com/obamawhitehouse

Dewey and Lady Winifred would often get several hundred viewers each broadcast, with a few hundred regulars. It got to the point where Dewey was on almost every night, unburdening himself, or Lady Winifred would regale her listeners with her stories and jokes.

Periscope also has a map function that lets you explore videos broadcast from different parts of the world. Want to practice your German or French? Check out some of the broadcasts from Berlin and Burgundy. Want to see what's happening in Melbourne or Johannesburg? You can use the map to zoom in on the videos in those locations and just listen in.

The nice part about Periscope (which some people may also think is a downside) is that only the broadcaster can be seen, not the viewers. So you can be strictly anonymous while you watch, but everyone will know who you are while you're broadcasting.

Unfortunately, trolls often target individuals on Periscope, leaving harassing and disgusting comments. It's possible to eliminate a lot of this by only allowing comments from people you follow first. You can also block people from viewing your videos if you're harassed during an actual stream. (Dewey used to do this live, making jokes about the troll, much like a comedian calling out a heckler.) This isn't much different from YouTube or other publicly accessible sites and comment functions, but it can be a bit distracting when you're trying to record a live video and someone makes a nasty comment. Dewey used to call his trolls out live and then make a point of visibly blocking them.

Finally, while Periscope's videos can only be played for 24 hours after the initial broadcast, it is possible to save them—to your mobile phone's photo storage, for example—to be shared and shown later on Facebook and Twitter. With a little work, you can even save someone else's video as well.[9]

Facebook Live

After seeing the success of Periscope, Facebook decided they wanted to get into the live video-streaming business (which severely cut into YouTube and Periscope's popularity.[10])

You can stream live videos via Facebook Live, which your Facebook friends can all watch from within Facebook. The announcement about your video appears right inside your Facebook stream, and it will also appear in other people's news feeds based on your relationships with them and how often you interact at other times.

---

9. https://blog.iqtecture.com/2017/04/22/how-to-save-periscope-videos/

10. http://www.adweek.com/digital/youtube-beefing-its-live-video-game-compete-facebook-and-periscope-172246/

(So if you want to build up a big audience for your Facebook Live videos, be sure to build up solid relationships with a lot of people during your downtime.)

People can also watch the video later, as long as it's still showing up in their Facebook feed. And unlike Periscope, Facebook Live videos are automatically saved forever.

Erik's wife Toni is a jazz singer, and she has streamed some of her performances on Facebook Live, as well as singing the national anthem at a couple local minor league baseball games, allowing friends and family from all over the world to watch. She'll sometimes get a couple hundred views for each show, including post-performance viewings. While that's not enough to build a career on, it is a way to reach new people, as her friends share the videos on their Facebook streams, where their friends could also watch it.

Facebook Live is also a great way to show what's happening around you, whether you're out with friends, at a theme park, at a bar or restaurant, or just sitting at home sharing some random thoughts. On the social justice side, there have been people who stream their participation in protests, and even routine traffic stops and police shootings are regularly streamed for the whole world to see.

Whatever you share, just make sure you're doing the things that support your professional brand. We're not saying you can't have fun or participate in social causes you think are important. But make sure you're not going to harm your brand that you've worked so hard to create.

Shooting Video With Regular Digital Cameras

You can shoot videos with just about any type of camera, whether it's your smart phone or video-enabled cell phone. It can be a $150 digital video camera you plug in to your computer, a $3,000 professional digital camera, or the little camera that is build into your laptop. You can even record what's happening on your computer monitor with screen recording software.

There are too many different camera options to go into them all here. But there are a few things you'll want to look for if you decide to get your own camera to shoot video without your phone:

- **High-definition capability:** The current maximum resolution of a typical laptop or computer monitor is 1080p (pixels), although they're getting better all the time. Make sure your camera is at least 720p and can shoot 30 and 60 fps (frames per second). Some phones, like the iPhone 7, can record at 1080p and even 4K at 30 frames per second. Translation: Videos look great on high-definition TVs and monitors.

- **Read the customer reviews:** While we were researching this chapter, we found a lot of inexpensive cameras online. You can get an HD (high-definition) video camera for as little as $90, and the quality is pretty good. Any less than that, and you're going to have problems. As you research a camera, visit different sites that sell that camera and read the reviews. They'll tell you more than any marketing brochure ever will.

- **Look for built-in lighting:** This isn't a deal breaker, but if you can find a camera with a built-in light, or even a slot to add your own, that's always going to be a better option than a camera that doesn't have a flash. It adds some cost to the camera, but it's worth it.

- **Get a microphone jack:** Again, this isn't a deal breaker, but if you get a camera with a mic jack, you can plug a cheap microphone into it for better sound than the built-in microphone provides. Because the audio is nearly as important as the video, make sure the camera at least has a decent built-in mic. Read the customer reviews for this information, too.

Recording Screen Capture Videos

You can also use tools like Camtasia, OBS Studio, or Flashback Express to record screen captures—record the things you're doing on your computer screen so that you can show people later how it looks, and you talk through what you're doing. (Use a decent microphone for better sound quality, too.) This is great for sharing presentations and giving demonstrations.

If you need a free screen capture program, OBS Studio and Flashback Express are available for both Windows and Mac computers, and won't put ugly watermarks on your videos or limit their length. But if you want a professional package, consider Camtasia, which costs $199. Other free and shareware video recorders are out there, too.

PERSONAL BRANDING CASE STUDY: LYNN FERGUSON & MARK TWEDDLE

Lynn Ferguson is an award-winning writer-performer and highly acclaimed comedian. She has appeared in numerous Edinburgh Fringe Festivals, worked as a staff writer for the *Late Late Show,* and was a script consultant for the Pixar movie *Brave.* She was also the voice of the hard-to-understand Scottish chicken from the movie *Chicken Run.*

Lynn is now a regular storyteller and host for The Moth Story Slam and can often be heard on their weekly show broadcast and podcast. She and her husband Mark Tweddle also created the YouTube video series "ThisDayTo-day," a comedic look at different days in history, like the day Anne Boleyn was arrested and imprisoned by her husband, Henry VIII (May 2, 1536) or Canada Day (July 1, 1867). She and Mark write and perform short humorous lectures, or enlist some actor friends to do it, like Alfred Molina, Kurtwood Smith, and Gina Yashere, so far creating 482 episodes.

Mark has worked in a number of different business areas, including manufacturing, travel, IT support, and even the defense branch of the UK government. Surprisingly, despite being married to a professional performer, Mark struggled with public speaking for years, until he worked on a story with Lynn.

Because YouTube is not only social media, but also a search engine and a video distribution network, Lynn and Mark were able to get their content out and get feedback and make direct connections with people.

"ThisDayToday was our big experiment," said Lynn. "We didn't overthink it. We just got started based on a conversation that writing agents wanted a half-hour sitcom written as an example piece of work for me. So we decided that if I was going to have to write something, why not actually make it... and why not give it to them in 30 individual minutes?"

The thing Lynn and Mark especially like about their videos is that they're a permanent record of how fast the couple can work, how decisive they can be, how well they work together, and how they constantly improve their work.

"Our YouTube videos steadily got longer, and we also started writing to the voice of the actors we used, like Alfred Molina's Valentine's Day video,"[11] said Lynn. (It's gloriously filthy. Trust us.)

Notice that Lynn and Mark worked on improving their work as they went on. They didn't seek to reach a certain level of perfection before they launched. They launched and improved.

"Like most projects, the enemy of progress is perfection," said Mark. "Just get started and keep improving; don't wait until you have a perfect personal branding strategy and copy."

These days, Lynn and Mark own YouTellYours, a storytelling school and coaching practice that teaches people how to tell stories, whether for public performance, to improve their public speaking, or even develop their own personal brands. They also offer private coaching for people performing in plays, giving TED talks, and testifying as trial witnesses. Lynn is the Chief Story Wrangler and teaches all the classes, while Mark is the Chief Operations Officer, making sure the business runs efficiently.

Of course, social media hasn't been the panacea for them that many social media gurus want you to believe. That's because many businesses only use

---

11. https://youtu.be/aGQ9Wop2xxc

it to promote, promote, promote their work; but all we users really want is to talk to someone—not to be shouted at.

"Often, I think it serves more as a comfort for new clients who've just found or met us that we are real and the business is working," said Mark. "We experimented a little with Facebook ads for specific events, but they've not been overly successful. I think social media is at its best when it's conversational."

Having said that, Lynn and Mark admit that social media has helped them leverage the local success of their classes and coaching internationally.

"The photos of events, videos of storytellers, and so on all help give social proof to potential clients throughout the world, which we then steer to our online classes," said Mark.

The whole process, from Lynn's early days as a standup comic to working on award-winning shows and movies and to Mark's realization that he actually enjoyed (or at least wouldn't die from) public speaking, has been a process of self-discovery and growth, especially around developing their personal brand.

"The coolest part of this journey is that by trying to describe your personal branding, you are also discovering more about yourself," they say, in near-perfect unison. "The more you understand yourself, the better you get at making decisions. particularly with regard to the projects that you undertake."

What Should I Make Videos Of?

The great thing about personal branding and videos is that you can make videos of anything you want. Rand Fishkin, founder of search engine optimization tools company Moz.org, makes Whiteboard Friday videos, where he shares the latest SEO research his organization has done. Years ago, entrepreneur and Internet personality Gary Vaynerchuk built his personal brand by making wine-tasting videos, and he's still constantly producing social media marketing videos today. And Lynn Ferguson created ThisDayToday to feature her talents on YouTube.

You can record videos of book reviews for your industry. Have a friend shoot a video of you giving a talk at a conference. Give a three-minute presentation on a piece of information. Turn one of your blog posts into a video presentation.

Whatever you choose, a video can be one of the most powerful ways to grow your personal brand. It lets people see and hear you; it can help you get speaking engagements; it can put you in touch with new people who have never met you; and in some cases, it can even help you find a job, or build a personal empire centered around one thing that you love to do.

The best way to figure out what to make a video of is to go back and reread "Chapter 3, Blogging: Telling Your Story" about finding your niche. Whatever you write about on your blog should also be the subject of your videos. This way, you can share some of your ideas in an entirely different format, which could even lead you to a whole new audience.

Why Post Photos?

Photos are one of the first things that come to mind when people think about sharing. And it's so easy to do now, even with the most rudimentary flip phones— they're still out there, trust us. Erik has a friend who carries one, which can take pictures, and then he texts them to his Twitter account.

Photos are proof that you've done something interesting or seen something cool. It's a way to share remarkable stuff with friends, or show yourself in action teaching a seminar, performing on stage, or even giving a demonstration . You can provide a visual element to anything you're working on, like a blog post, website, or even a single tweet.

Thanks to sites like Facebook, Instagram, and Snapchat, people are sharing millions of photos every day with their friends, family, and even complete strangers. It's the ultimate in sharing and community building.

Again, just remember to post photos that are appropriate to your brand, and make sure you understand your audience.

Where to Post Your Photos

The places where you post your photos dictate who's allowed to see them and who you want to see them. Using public photo-sharing sites like Photobucket, Pixabay, and Google Photos are great for a general catch-all place to put your photos, especially if you want to let other people use them. They're ideal for storage and sharing, as well as finding photos you can use in your own content, like embedding a photo in a blog post. (Just read the section on Copyright below first.)

Instagram and Snapchat are communities of sharing, as is Facebook. These sites are also for sharing, but they're used more for community building, storytelling, and showing friends what you're doing at that moment.

When we last wrote this chapter, we were recommending Google Picasa, Flickr (owned by Yahoo), and Photobucket. Instagram was barely a blip on anyone's radar, and it was used more for creating "artistic" photos with filters.

But now, Picasa has been replaced by Google Photos, Flickr is on its way out, especially after Yahoo was sold, and Instagram, which was acquired by Facebook, is now the premier photo and short video sharing app. Photobucket is still going strong, growing from 9.6 billion photos to 15 billion in five years,[12] but recently implemented a controversial pricing plan that upset many of its users.[13]

Regardless of which photo sharing apps are around when you read this chapter, some of the principles will be the same: People love seeing photos, so use them often; there will always be a major photo-sharing site available; and never, ever depend on a photo-sharing site as your only backup for your photos. Make sure you have an external hard drive for them, too.

Google Photos

Google Photos (or just Photos for short) is Google's photo-sharing and storage site, which replaced their Picasa photo brand. It's tied in to every other Google property, too—Blogger, Gmail, Google Drive, and YouTube. Post a photo to your Blogger blog, and it's uploaded to Photos. Upload photos to Photos, and you can store them on your Google Drive.

Photos gives users 15 GB of storage, which can take a while to fill up if you don't take extremely large photos. It has unlimited photo storage if you let Photos reduce the size of your uploads. You can also increase your storage size to 100 GB for $1.99 per month or 1 TB for $9.99 per month (at the time of this writing).

A desktop uploader called Google Photos Backup makes it easy to upload photos to your Photos account. You can make them public, share them only with people who have the URL, or keep them completely private. (Google stopped supporting Picasa, which was a much better organizer and uploader, but you can still find ways to download it if you hunt around online.)

Other cool Photos features include embedding photos in your blog posts; creating online albums and collections; a few basic photo-editing functions like Instagram-style filters and cropping; and even facial recognition.

Photobucket

Photobucket, which has more than 15 billion photos on it, works just like the other two sites, with sharing, editing, and storage capabilities, as well as letting you print some of your favorites. You can upload photos and videos, then share them to Twitter and Facebook as well as Pinterest and Tumblr.

---

12. http://blog.photobucket.com/about/

13. http://www.zdnet.com/article/photobucket-endures-user-backlash-after-breaking-images-with-ran-som-demand/

A mobile app will let you share photos and upload them to your Photobucket account, and a mobile editor will let you add frames, stickers, and special effects (you may want to avoid the stickers and special effects if they clash with your professional image). Oh, and if you actually want to improve the photo, you can crop, rotate, and change brightness as needed.

While we were working on this edition, Photobucket implemented a new pricing structure that angered many of its users, breaking 3rd-party hosting links (that is, embedding a Photobucket user's photo on your blog post). The plan that allows 3rd-party hosting costs $399 per year (as of this writing), and many users have threatened to leave the site.[14]

Instagram

Instagram is a photo tool that applies special filters (at this time, it has 16 different filters) to the photos you take on your mobile phone to give them an interesting, professional, sometimes retro look. You can then share them through your Instagram account as well as Facebook, Twitter, and Tumblr. (You can also use a tool like IFTTT.com to create an automated process that will post your photos elsewhere. IFTTT and Zapier are tools that let you create automated processes like reposting photos or sending you text alerts when severe weather is in your area.)

Instagram, despite what *some* curmudgeons might say, is more than just a series of filters to make photos look old. It's a sharing community where people get to share their experiences and likes and dislikes. People use it to raise awareness of public issues, share things that are important, and celebrate special events.

Certain companies have embraced it, and some people have even become famous by using it. There have been several independent designers and people marketing it to teenagers and Generation Y (ages 18–28, as of this writing). And plenty of people are using Instagram to become famous, especially fitness instructors, comedians, and makeup artists.

You can use #hashtags for any number of causes, topics, and events, as well as create daily stories about the things you're seeing in your life. Whether it's a stream of photos or videos, you can even annotate your content for some added information or humor.

One word of caution. Don't use more than 3–5 hashtags for a single photo. We've seen people drop in 12–15 hashtags on a single photo, and it not only looks like the person is desperate and trying too hard, but it's boring to read when it appears on someone's Twitter feed or Facebook stream.

---

14. http://www.zdnet.com/article/photobucket-endures-user-backlash-after-breaking-images-with-ransom-demand/

Snapchat

Started in September 2011, Snapchat was barely a blip on our radar in 2012 when we published the last edition of this book. It was something the kids were doing—they took goofy photos, shared them with their friends, and the photos were automatically deleted within 24 hours. It was a great way for kids to share photos with their friends, without worrying about them being found 10 years later when they're looking for a job.

Now, Snapchat has become a major tool for marketing and personal branding people alike. In fact, if anything, teenagers are getting worried because, like every other social network they join, their parents joined and immediately made it not cool anymore.[15]

@edeckers: MWAHAHAHAHA!

@kyleplacy: MWAHAHAHAHA! (Man, being a dad is fun!)

You can still take photos and short videos, share them with people in your network (we recommend being a little choosy), and use them to tell your Daily Story. (Imagine taking a series of photos throughout the day to show what you're doing and where you've been. That's your Daily Story.) While most people use them just to show what they're doing throughout the day, they're especially useful for events, conferences, or even weddings.

You can also add fun filters and lens effects to your photos, including animal ears and whiskers, funny hats, the local weather and time, face distorting filters, and anything else that might make your photo stand out and look funny, or weird. (Not that we're judging or anything. We are, but we're not going to say it out loud.)

There's also a "Discover" feature that lets you watch Snaps and daily stories from a number of major publishers like ESPN, BuzzFeed, CNN, Mashable, and People. Their social media folks are always taking pictures and connecting them to different news stories and features. And Snapchat also has a video communication function that works a lot like a regular video chat except that the chat is deleted when you're finished. It also has a direct chat feature called, well, Chat.

To be honest, neither of us are big users (or fans) of Snapchat. For one thing, we like the permanence of other tools like Instagram. We also like the possibility of connecting to new people, like you can with Instagram and Twitter; Snapchat requires you to be friends with people to view their content, although you can grow

---

15. https://www.forbes.com/sites/curtissilver/2016/07/05/snapchat-use-rises-among-adults-to-the-chagrin-of-teens

your network to include strangers. Don't get us wrong—it's a great tool because it allows millions of people to do fun things with their photos. But for serious personal branding, where we're trying to get speaking gigs and jobs, Snapchat is low on our list of priorities.

Facebook

Facebook is the ultimate photo-sharing site because it's all about being social and sharing memories and good times with your friends. That, and it has more than 250 billion photos on it, and more than 300 million new ones are uploaded every day. This is the place to post your fun photos of you and your colleagues, you and your friends, or just things you find interesting. While Photobucket and Google Photos are devoted to photo sharing, Facebook is more about the social aspect of photos (similar to Instagram and Snapchat).

Just remember that you're playing on Facebook's playground. If they, or you, ever decide to delete your account, those photos are gone forever. And because Facebook is well known for changing the way they do things, this is more likely than you might think.

Copyright: Understanding Creative Commons

So we've talked about sharing photos with people, which implies that people are willing to share photos with you. They are. They want you to see them, admire them, and comment on them. But can you borrow them and use them in your own blog posts and presentations? That's a whole different thing.

The short answer is "no."

Basically, copyright means this: If you created it, you own it. If you own it, you get to say what other people do with it. The "default setting" for copyrighted material is that you can't use it without express written permission. That means that unless someone sends you an email or letter that says, "Sure, you can use my photo/video/audio file/written text!" you can't use it. Ever. Not ever.

Even if the photo was taken by a friend of yours. Even if you're giving him "exposure." Even if you're really famous. Even if you think someone else's photo/video/audio file/written text is wonderful, and it gives you a warm feeling all over, and you want to share it with the world—not even then can you use it.

However, in some instances you can use someone's content without their express written permission. You don't even have to ask because they gave it to you in advance. This is called Creative Commons.

Creative Commons

Creative Commons basically says that some rights are reserved, but not all. If you see "all rights reserved" on an image or story, that means that every right you can think of is reserved by the content owner to do with it what they will. But "some rights reserved" means that the owner is letting you, the user, use it in certain instances. Maybe it's to share with people, maybe it's to remix and add your own flair, or maybe it's to build upon and combine with something else, like reading all your slam poetry over someone else's great music tracks.

Regardless of what it is, Creative Commons gives you, the creative individual, a chance to share your content with people and a chance to use other people's content legally and with their blessing.

Table 7.1 shows some of the different licenses available from CreativeCommons. org. If you create and upload a work to a CC-compliant site, like Photobucket or Pixabay, you can choose which license you want to grant.

If you use someone else's work, you need to make sure you abide by its creators' licenses, represented by buttons including "Attribution," "NonCommercial," "ShareA-like," and "NoDerivatives." Creative Commons buttons and images are used in strict compliance with its licensing policies, which you can find at CreativeCommons.org.

Table 7.1 A few Creative Commons license buttons that you can find at CreativeCommons.org

Symbol	License
(cc)	**Creative Commons:** This is the CC logo. If you see it, you may use the content you find. If you don't, assume you can't.
(i)	**Attribution:** Give credit to the creators, including their website.
(NC)	**NonCommercial:** You can use the creator's content in any manner except a commercial manner (that is, you can't make money from it).
(SA)	**ShareAlike:** You can use the creator's content in any manner, but you have to grant the same rights to anyone else with your new creation.
(=)	**NoDerivatives:** You can copy, perform, or exhibit only original copies of the work. No modifications or editing.
(cc)(i)(NC)(SA) BY NC SA	A sample of a Creative Commons button you might see on a website. This one gives Attribution, NonCommercial, and ShareA-like permissions.

We had to ask permission from the Creative Commons people to use this. Ironic, no?

Creative Commons was created as a way to help copyright law keep up with the rapid growth of the Internet. Let's face it; copyright laws are often outdated and may be modified by people who still have a tough time understanding the nuances of the fax machine. There's no way they can keep up with the rapid changes apps like Instagram, YouTube, Vimeo, and Pinterest are throwing at us. Creative Commons enables people to use online content with permission, and without fear of getting into legal trouble.

So unless you have the creators' written permission, or are complying with their Creative Commons wishes, don't use their content at all. Ever.

When you do use someone else's Creative Commons content, be sure to give credit. Either include their name in the caption, or put something at the bottom of the page or post. For example, post "Photo credit: Kyle Lacy (Wikimedia Commons, Creative Commons 2.0)," then link to the person's page where you snagged the content.

Embedding Videos and Photos in Your Blog

Embedding videos and photos is easy. The only platform that makes it difficult is WordPress.com, unless you pay the annual fee. (Believe us, we've tried. There's no way to trick the system, even if you add streaming windows instead of actually embedding the video.) Still, it can be much cheaper than paying for server space for a self-hosted WordPress blog, which does let you embed videos and photos. So, decide who you want to pay for a blog (if anyone).

We'll show you a couple of different options for adding photos to WordPress and Blogger. If you can figure either of these out, you can figure out how to add photos to any other blog platform as well. We'll also show you the only way you need to know to add YouTube and other videos to your blog platforms.

Adding Photos

The technique is nearly always the same from platform to platform. Every blogging platform has an "Add Image" or "Add Media" button on the main formatting bar. Figures 7.4 and 7.5 show the WordPress and Blogger buttons for adding videos and photos to your blog.

Click the appropriate button and follow the instructions. You either need a photo saved to your computer—WordPress lets you even drag and drop the photo to your browser window—or have the URL of a photo on another website.

Figure 7.4 *The WordPress "Add Media" button is just a single button, unlike on other blogging platforms, which have both "Add Photo" and "Add Video" buttons.*

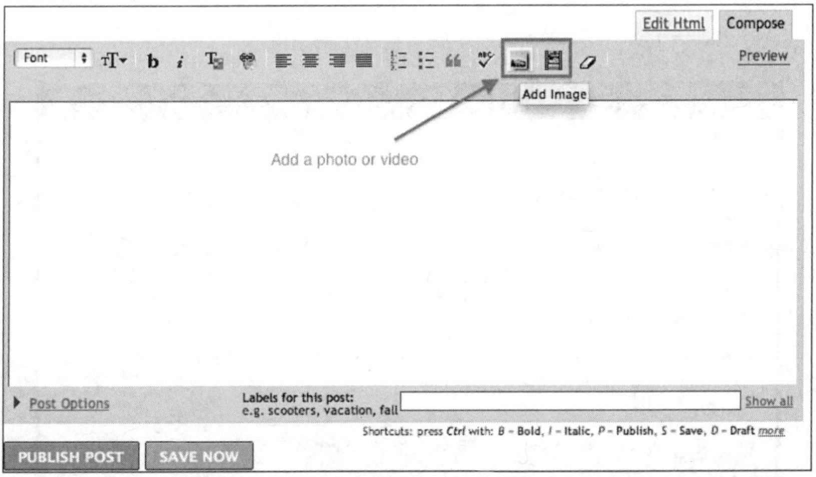

Figure 7.5 *The Blogger "Add Photo/Add Video" buttons require you to choose between file formats. That's easy.*

After you open the "Add Media" dialog window, you see several fields of information to fill in. Figures 7.6 and 7.7 show the WordPress "Add Media" window. To add a photo from another site, you just have to right-click the photo, copy the link, and then paste it into the URL box in the appropriate place.

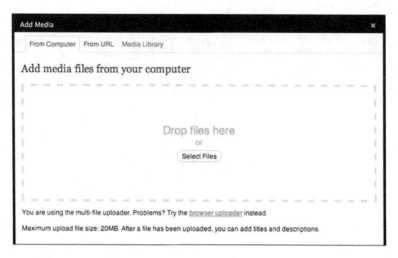

Figure 7.6 *To add a photo or video to WordPress, you can just drag and drop from your computer desktop to this window in your web browser. WordPress takes care of the rest.*

Figure 7.7 *If you would rather keep the photo or video in its original site, just get the URL (right-click, and then select "Copy Link"), and paste it into the URL field.*

- **You must fill in the URL and title box**—That tells the blog and the search engines what the photo is called, which is especially useful for SEO.

- **Be sure to use ALT text**—We discuss that further in the section on SEO, but that's something that people who are blind use to understand what an image is. The more descriptive it is, the better they can "see" it with their screen reader.

- **Write a caption**—Sometimes a caption is useful to explain why the photo is relevant. Remember to include a credit to the photographer.

- **Set the alignment of the photo**—Erik always likes using align-right for the first photo in a blog post and align-left for the second photo. If you don't set the alignment here, it can screw up the body of the text and make it look terrible.

Adding Videos

Adding videos from YouTube and other video-sharing sites is also easy. The platforms usually provide the code from their sites and let you copy and paste it to wherever you want.

Figure 7.8 shows the YouTube embed code box. You get to it by clicking the "Share" button underneath the video, and then clicking the "Embed" button. Select the size of video you want, then copy the code, and paste it into your blog window. (Make sure you use the HTML interface, not the Visual interface, when you paste it. Otherwise, your post will just show a string of code.)

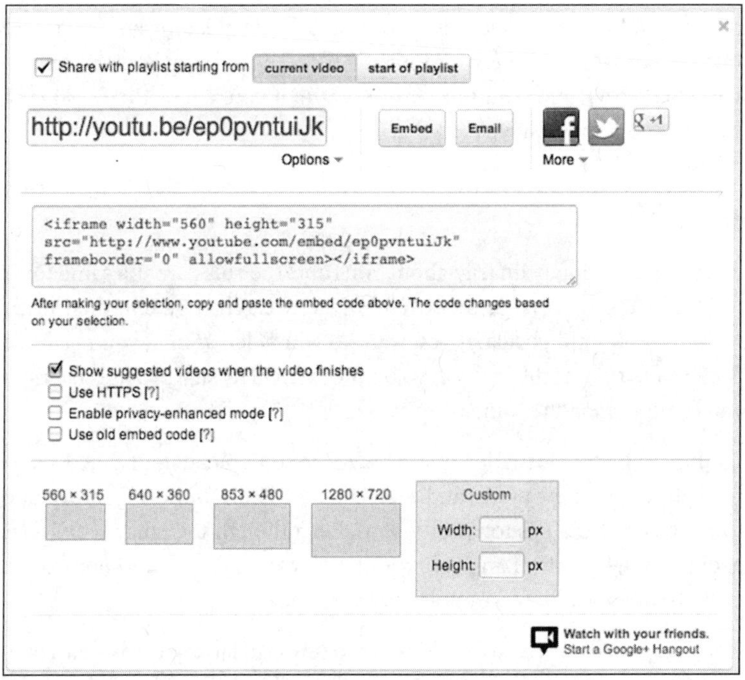

Figure 7.8 *Adding videos to your blog posts is easy. Just grab this code and paste it into the post.*

One exception is a self-hosted WordPress page, which lets you paste in the URL of a video you want to use and give it a title. Click the "Insert Into Post" button, and you're done. You can see how simple it is in Figure 7.9. This method lets you save space on your own server, although it can be risky if your video is ever taken down by the original creator. Then you're left with nothing but a big empty box where something cool used to be.

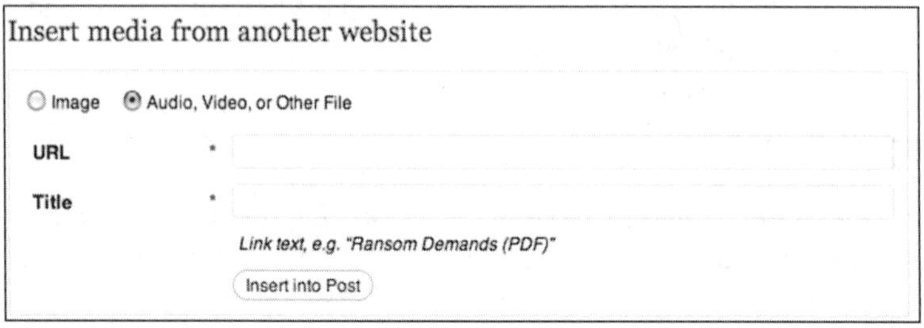

Figure 7.9 *Or if you don't want to host videos on your blog, you can link to them while they're hosted elsewhere, like YouTube or Vimeo.*

SEO for Videos and Photos

Your photos and videos—especially your videos—are great for boosting the SEO for your blog or website. After you finish "Chapter 9, Finding Yourself on Search Engines," come back and read this section again; if you're new to SEO, this will make more sense after you've read that.

YouTube SEO

Although we're talking primarily about YouTube, the rules are the same for Vimeo. Keep in mind, though, that as the second biggest search engine in the world, YouTube is the 800-pound gorilla. If you want to win video search, you need to do what YouTube wants first, and then worry about other video-sharing sites later. But the rules are pretty much the same throughout.

Doing SEO on a YouTube video is simple. After you upload your video, go to "Video Manager," find your new video, and then click the "Edit" button. There, you can take some basic SEO steps for your videos. Even though they may seem obvious, few people do it; by optimizing your video, you can make it stand out from the rest Figure 7.10 shows different examples of how to use these tips.

- **Use keywords in the title**—Pick just a few crucial keywords that you want your video to be known for. In this video, Erik picked "Alex Rossi," "press conference," and "Indianapolis 500."

- **Use keywords in the description**—Make sure to write a 1–3 sentence description that uses a few of the keywords from the title.

- **Keywords are tags**—You should actually start in the "Tag" field to start figuring out your keywords. What do you want your video to be associated with? Pick 2–5 keywords, and then use the most important ones in your title and description. Leave the ones you didn't use in the tag field. Don't try to force them into the description or title.

- **Specify the date**—Make sure you fill out the date the video was taken, not the date you upload it.

- **Specify the location**— Google's search results are locally focused (see "Chapter 9, Googling Yourself: Finding Yourself on Search Engines"), so this can help your video show up in someone's localized search results.

- **Choose the best video thumbnail**—It doesn't have much to do with SEO, but it does affect the click rates on the video. Pick a thumbnail that represents the entire video, rather than just the first frame of the video. Otherwise, it could end up being the opening credits or a blank screen, which doesn't look interesting enough to watch.

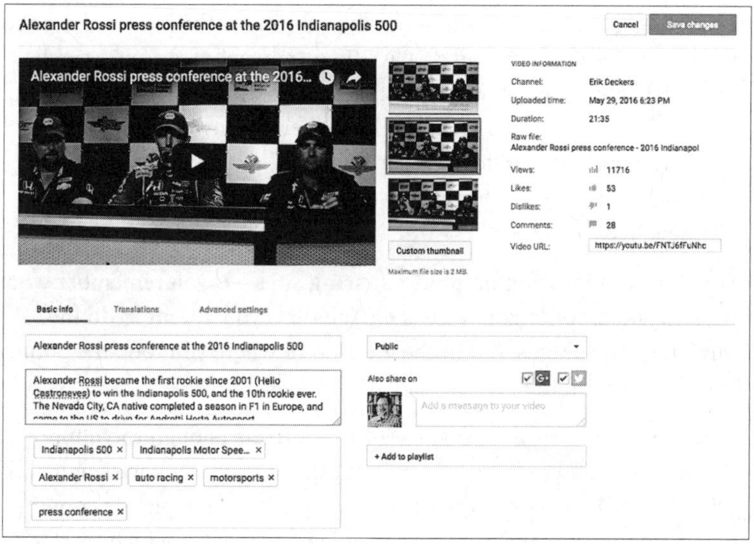

Figure 7.10 *Video SEO can help a video be more easily found on YouTube or Google.*

Photo SEO

SEO for photos is just as important as it is for videos. For one thing, Google occasionally drops images into their search results. For another, photo-sharing sites are also search engines. People use them to look for interesting photos and to find photos they can use in their blog posts and presentations.

SEO is important if you want your photos to be found and used by other people. While it may not help your SEO directly, it can boost your personal brand. You don't know when one of your photos will be seen by someone else who wants to learn more about you.

- **Use keywords in the title**—Don't keep the original filename from your camera, like "IMG_0017.jpg." That tells the searcher nothing about what the image is, and so it will absolutely never be found.

- **Use a keyword-rich ALT text**—If you embed photos in your blog posts, you can use ALT text to describe the photo, but be clear about what the photo is. The primary use for ALT text is to let people who are blind use screen readers to access your content. The ALT text describes the image so that they know what it is, so if you're cramming it full of keywords, you're not being a good SEO practitioner or a good host to your visitors.

- **Use keywords as tags**—When you upload your photos to Instagram and Google Photos, add tags about the subjects of the photos. These are important because if you don't have them, your photos aren't searchable. Maybe you renamed the photo, but if you used only one keyword, no one can find it based on any of the others. Many photo and video sites use comma-separated keywords, instead of space-separated keywords. That means that every comma you put between a word or phrase makes it its own keyword.

- **Use date and location on photo-sharing sites**—If you remember what we said about optimizing videos on YouTube, you'll want to do the same for your photos. Put in the location of where you took the photo and the date you took it.

  However—and this is crucial—we cannot stress enough the importance of personal safety and security, especially if you have small children, or you're worried about your own safety. Many photos contain data about where they were taken (called EXIF data), which means someone with the right software can find the place where the photo was taken. You can turn off the EXIF data in the settings section on your mobile phone. There is also software that will strip out EXIF data from your photos. Use that before you ever post your photos online.

- **Remember not to stuff keywords**—We've talked a lot about keywords in this section, but it's important that you don't stuff your keywords. Calling a photo "Orange on an orange tree in an orange grove in Florida" or writing "here is a photo of an orange that I took while we were at an orange grove in Florida" could mean that Google thinks you're spamming them, and they will act accordingly, either dropping your site's rank, or even dropping the site completely from the index.

- **Make sure your images are small**—Well, smallish. We're not saying they should be a half-inch in size, but make sure you edit the photos so that they're a reasonable file size.

When most people take a photo, they have the resolution on the highest possible setting. The end result is sometimes photos that are 44 inches wide and 300-dots-per-inch resolution (which is laser printer quality). A photo like that could be 100 MB in size easily. But if you put that on your blog, it will take several seconds or even a minute to load.

Google has said it measures how quickly a website loads and takes that into ranking consideration. A huge picture takes longer and lowers your rankings. So use a photo editor—such as Preview for Mac or Photo Viewer for Windows—and reduce the size of the photo to no more than 1,000 pixels wide and the resolution to no more than 100 dpi (the size and resolution of most laptop monitors). When you embed the photo, set the width of the photo between 300 and 600 pixels.

The Video Résumé

Video résumés are becoming more popular, especially among 20-somethings in creative roles, because it gives them a chance to stand out from everyone else they may be competing against. Impress the hiring manager with your video résumé, and you may get invited in for a real interview. Just remember though, your video résumé is like a real résumé. It's not supposed to get you the job; it gets you the interview. The interview gets you the job.

@edeckers:	Slipping them 50 bucks doesn't hurt either.
@kyleplacy:	$50? Are you serious? I had to give my intern director $100 before she'd hire me!
@YourDamnEditor:	Guys, we are NOT advocating that people bribe their potential employers in ANY way. Got it?!
@edeckers:	Yes, ma'am.
@kyleplacy:	RT @edeckers: Yes, ma'am.

- **Look like a professional**—Your video résumé needs to look as professional as you would if you were going in for a real interview. Put on a suit or work-appropriate attire and have a simple, clean background for the shoot—not in your kitchen, not in your bedroom with dim lighting. Make it look great. If you need to go to a friend's place or borrow an office, do it. Don't do what one candidate did and use a flowered bed sheet for a backdrop.

- **Use good equipment**—Use a mobile phone that's not more than two years old or get a decent digital camera that can shoot in high definition. Use a tripod or set the camera on a stable surface. Don't record this with your laptop camera; the quality is there, but the angle is usually such that viewers will either be looking up your nose, or you'll look at your image on the screen, which will look like you're looking down at your keyboard.

- **Sound is important**—This is essential. The sound must be clean and clear, so it sounds appealing. Although the video quality is important, you can't use your laptop camera, so don't use your laptop microphone either. Get a mic with a decent sound quality. Even a $10 microphone from an electronics store can do the trick.

- **Lighting is also important**—Make sure you're well lit. It's best if you can shoot this during the day when you have great ambient light. If not, use some desk lamps as spotlights. Be sure to check and adjust your settings as you need to. You don't want to be in the dark or so brightly lit that you appear washed out.

- **Speak clearly**—Speak slowly and enunciate, in a conversational tone, like you would on the phone. Don't mumble; don't speak too quickly; don't shout. Also, speak conversationally, rather than reading from a script. Practice several times so you can get it just right.

- **Use the right format**—You can upload videos to YouTube in most formats, but mp4 works the best. It works on YouTube directly and on smartphones, and it can be downloaded and opened with a regular video browser.

- **Answer anticipated questions**—Rather than run through a laundry list of your accomplishments and experiences—that's what your paper résumé is for—use the video résumé to answer any questions you're likely to be asked: Why do you want to work here? What's the biggest challenge you've ever faced? What's a success you've had? And if there's time, list one or two major accomplishments.

- **Keep it short**—Keep your video to two to three minutes long. The closer to two minutes, the better. If you have so much stuff that you're going over three minutes, you have too much information. Remember, the purpose of the video résumé is the same as the paper résumé: to get you an interview. So focus on that step, not landing the job.

You can host your video résumé on YouTube, then embed it in your blog's "About Me" page or host it on a video résumé site, and point potential hiring managers to it.

Many hiring managers express a positive interest in video résumés and like to see them. If you're in the right kind of industry or applying to a more forward-thinking company, by all means, give a video résumé a try. Just know that some companies aren't as progressive as others and may be a little wary of video résumés.

A Cautionary Note About Video Résumés

Although we like the creativity and boldness of video résumés—correctly created, they can show passion, energy, and vibrancy—and we think they can be used to great effect, we also want to urge extreme caution about using them. Here are a couple of reasons:

- Mind the U.S. EEOC (Equal Employment Opportunity Commission) laws and rules. It is against the law to not hire someone based on "race, color, religion, sex (including gender identity, sexual orientation, and pregnancy), national origin, age (40 or older), disability or genetic information."[16] Companies can be sued if a candidate thinks they weren't hired for any of those reasons. But unless an employer writes a letter that says, "don't hire this person because they are _____," you'll have a hard time proving you were discriminated against.

- But EEOC laws don't stop non-hired candidates from trying. To prevent that, many companies and government agencies will not look at personally identifying information on your résumé.

  In fact, some administrative assistants have been instructed to mark out any information, such as group memberships, that can identify a candidate's race, religion, national origin, and age. If your résumé is laden with that information, it can be tossed. For that reason alone, we're a bit iffy on video résumés, especially aimed at larger companies.

@kyleplacy: Can I be not hired for being too attractive?

@edeckers: Uhh....

@kyleplacy: What? Why aren't you saying anything?

@edeckers: I don't know what to say without hurting your feelings.

---

16. https://www.eeoc.gov/laws/practices/

- Video résumés are still not widely accepted as a practice. If you're in a creative industry where people expect and condone this kind of behavior, you'll have some luck. But if you want to work in a traditional industry, don't send one.

Even though the business we're in—technology, startups, and entre-preneurial ventures—loves the wild creativity and daring of a video résumé, we don't know a lot of bankers, government managers, or insurance executives who love wild and daring anything, let alone when it comes packaged as a potential lawsuit waiting to happen. If you're applying for a job in a traditionally buttoned-down market, you may want to hold off on the video résumé.

Photos and Video Tips in 140 Characters

- Lesson #1: Learn about framing your subject. —@mmercenary

- A blank wall does not make a good background for your video. Pick something with visual interest. —@RockyWalls

- If you're using your smartphone for videos and photos, use an app like Instagram that will automatically share them with your favorite social sites. —@edeckers

- Say your name and give a URL in your video for when it gets separated from your description when shared. —@SteveGarfield

- You are producing a web video to convince your audience to convert on your call to action, not to win an Oscar. —@RockyWalls

- For video.... If your subject doesn't move, don't make it move. —@DaddysInCharge

- It's okay to break some of the rules you learned in journalism school. —@LeilanMcNally

- When interviewing w/a handheld camera or smart phone, the closer your subject, the better the audio. —@RockyWalls

- Learn the camera by shooting with the manual at hand. "Why is this shot so dark?"...look it up, experiment w/settings. —@mmercenary

- Learn the rules of design (composition, etc.) so you know when & how to break them, because you will break them, and it will be good. —@dezrad

8

Other Social Networking Tools

According to Wikipedia, there are more than 200 notable social networks in the world. And when they say "notable," they mean it. A notable social network has more than one million users, and it can cover any topic, from vampires to knitting enthusiasts to book lovers. For authors in the technology world (like us), it is an absolute pain to keep up with all the changes in technology from social networking to mobile phones. We can only imagine what it is like for the normal (non-nerd) person to keep up to date.

When we first wrote this book in 2010, we wanted to give you a brief overview of the main social networks of the time like LinkedIn, Facebook, and Twitter. They are still extremely important; however, we have witnessed an uptick in smaller sites that you could effectively also use to build your personal brand. It seems like a new social networking site explodes onto the scene every day. And many of them tend to promise untold amounts of fortune pertaining to content and personal branding development. Some sites that are valuable, but many, many others you should ignore.

After reading this far in the book, we hope that you fully understand the value of top sites like Twitter and Facebook. But how do you sort through the rest of the story? How do you figure out which of the new sites are best for your personal branding quest?

Fear not! We are here to lead you through the new social networking mire as new networking tools pop up on a regular basis. This chapter defines the top five social networking sites that may be new to you but are building the social networking and personal branding scene by the minute.

Google+

When we wrote about this in 2012, Google was calling their Google+ network a Facebook rival, and we even said, "it might actually succeed."

It didn't.

A few features and social products make this social network unique and some are similar to that of Facebook or Twitter. Although Google+ may look like it's dying to the outside world, there are actually plenty of enthusiastic Google+ users.

The great thing about Google+ is that it's a small community of rabid fans, people who truly love the network and have created or found a small group of people who also love what they love. Google+ will never replace Facebook, but it sure does attract people who love a wide variety of topics. These features are among its users' favorites:

- **Stream:** This is what you see first when using Google+. It's the area of your page that shows what your friends have posted since your last visit. It's like your Facebook feed, but more, well, Google-y.

  Want to know how to update your Google+ status? Look at the top of the stream in Figure 8.1. Erik's stream starts there. If Erik wants to share something new with his network, he types into the box that says, "What's new with you?" Type your content into the share box, and include any links or photos you want to add. You can share text, photos, videos, and links—all the juicy content you want to produce to build your personal brand story.

- **Collections:** This is sort of like your blog home in the Google+ world. There are collections on just about any topic, from productivity to underwater photography to history's greatest last stands. You follow a collection just like you would follow a Twitter account, and you'll receive notifications whenever a new post is added to it.

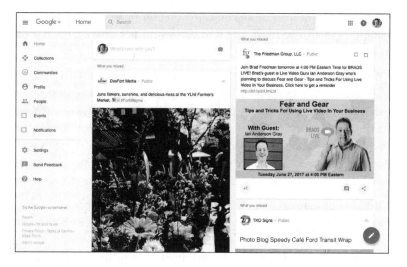

Figure 8.1 *Type in your updates just like you would in Facebook, LinkedIn, or even Twitter.*

- **Communities:** This is the group or forum function of Google+, similar to LinkedIn's. And just like Collections, there are Communities for
  just about every topic you can think of. When we were working on
  this edition, we found Communities for travel photography (531,000
  members), Marvel fans (630,525 members), and radio control airplanes
  (95,514 members).

If you want to find a place where you could develop your expertise in a subject,
Google+ may be a nice place to start. You can find a small group of experts to learn
from, and you can jump in and join the discussion right away. As you write new
articles or read other articles and blog posts, you can share all of that in a Google+
community, which can also help boost your personal SEO efforts.

Quora

We talk a lot about using social networks to display your expertise and tell your
story. There is no better site on the net to display your intellect than Quora, a social
forum that enables users to ask and answer questions on varying topics that relate
to their professional or personal lives. It is truly a knowledge engine. Frankly, it's
one of the easier places to write new content and share it with others.

You have three ways to join Quora: through Facebook or Google or by email.
Fill out your profile, add some credentials like education and experience, upload
a good photo of yourself, and select a few topics you know a lot about. Then,

choose some areas of interest and start looking for questions to answer, or just ask a question or two yourself. Use it to build your personal brand in a variety of ways:

- **Build thought leadership:** Any question-and-answer site (like LinkedIn) lets you ask insightful questions that pertain to industry trends or new topics entering your network. When you ask or answer a thoughtful question, you show that you are building your knowledge and staying on top of industry trends. You can also share your answers on Facebook and Twitter, or you can copy the URL of your answer and add it to a LinkedIn status update.

- **Build your network's knowledge:** By answering others' questions, you are adding to the knowledge of your personal network, which creates a foundation of trust. When you answer questions thoroughly, you can become the go-to person for that industry, which increases your visibility and presence in the market.

- **Stay in touch:** Quora enables you to follow certain individuals and topics related to your industry and your passions. By keeping in touch with people in your network, you may be the first to hear and respond to trends relating to your industry.

- **Link everything:** Like many social networking sites, Quora lets you link to your blog, other social networks, and your company website. Share your knowledge with those networks, but don't overshare your thoughts.

- **Vote up often:** The site also lets you vote on answers and questions relating to your niche. If you agree with someone's answer to a question, you can vote it up so that it appears higher on the list of answers. This will increase your visibility as well as that of the person you voted up; your name appears next to the "Vote Up" button, and his name appears higher in the list of answers. This builds your credibility with key players in the Quora world.

Quora has settled into a nice groove as a question-and-answer social network. And that's all you can do with it—people ask intelligent questions and give intelligent answers. There's no sharing of cat videos or annoying gifs. It's a place to learn and teach. Quora is the best place to gain credibility and focus within a given trend or industry.

Meetup.com

While Meetup.com doesn't fall within the strictest definition of a social network, it does something other social networks don't: encourage people to step away from their computers and meet each other in person, focusing on their shared passions for computer coding, filmmaking, business networking, creative writing, speaking conversational French, LGBTQ issues, dragon boating, kite flying, tiny houses, or beekeeping. Figure 8.2 is the opening screen of the Meetup website, where you can explore different groups in your area to find the ones that interest you.

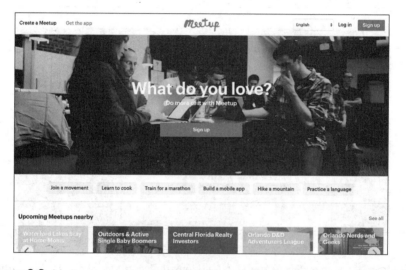

Figure 8.2 *Meetup.com is a great place to find people who share your passions and interests and meet them in the safety of a public place.*

Because we're big fans of real-world networking and meeting people face-to-face, you know we're big fans of Meetup.com.

When Erik moved to Orlando, he immediately started looking for different writing groups, social media groups, and business networking groups in the community. He used different keywords like "writing," "creative writing," "social media," and so on.

He tried out several different ones, stayed with the ones he really liked, and now has one group he regularly attends, the Writers of Central Florida or Thereabouts. He even became the emcee of a humor-based open mic night. Figure 8.3 is the home screen for his writers group.

To get started on Meetup, create an account, and then fill out your profile. Select as many personal interests as you can to find the groups that might appeal to you. It's better to start off with too many and pare it down, because you're more likely to find the groups that appeal to you this way. Many of the groups use several similar tags—writing, creative writing, short stories, aspiring authors, fiction writers, and so on—but you'll start to notice patterns and find more popular tags , while weeding out the low-value tags that might not yield very many interested (or interesting) people.

After you find your groups, visit their Meetup pages. Look for groups that meet regularly, have met recently, and have another meeting coming up soon. If you find a group that hasn't met in a couple years, drop it because there's a good chance they won't be meeting again any time soon.

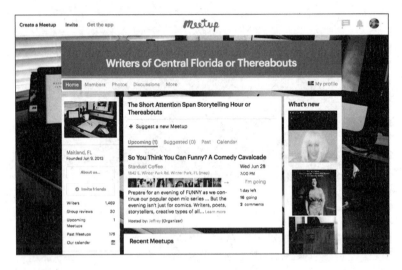

Figure 8.3 *Erik was able to find a writers group that suited his particular needs: the chance to stand up in front of a lot of people and be the center of attention.*

Keep an eye out for the number of members too; that's a good indication of a group's health. A group with only 20 members doesn't have a good chance of surviving very long, but a group with a few hundred members will, even if 95 percent of them don't attend the meeting. (Of course, if you start a group, you'll pull your hair out trying to figure out why 95 percent of the people who joined never show up anymore.)

Don't forget to connect your Facebook profile to your Meetup page, because it's a great way to see which of your Facebook friends are also using the network. You can see which groups they've joined and which ones they spend a lot of time visiting. They can even give you some recommendations about which groups to join or avoid, and when you attend your first meeting, you'll already know someone, which can make taking that intimidating first step a little easier.

Email Newsletters

We're a little torn on the use of an email newsletter for a personal brand. It's a great idea for companies to use. The marketing team can reach customers, potential customers, and even partners and vendors.

But it may seem a little odd and puffed up to have your own personal newsletter. We understand the feelings—we're both from the Midwest, and so something like having your very own newsletter seems a little like bragging. However, this is not so much about "look at all the cool stuff I'm doing" as it is "look at all the important industry knowledge I want to share with you." Still, we can see why having an email just about Kyle Lacy or Erik Deckers would be more than a bit arrogant.

Instead, your newsletter should be on some aspect of your personal brand—the skill you want to be known for, the industry you're trying to break into, or even one of your personal ventures, like your professional speaking career or consulting. We know several solo musicians who have their own email newsletter, as do several speakers, actors, and even writers. Erik has had an email newsletter through Yahoo Groups since July 2001 where he shares his weekly newspaper humor column, while Kyle has a newsletter associated with his website, KyleLacy.com.

@kyleplacy: Yeah, and I noticed you just signed up for it last night!

@edeckers: I didn't know you still had it. I thought I signed up for it years ago, and I figured you weren't publishing it anymore.

@kyleplacy: Do you even read my blog?!

Of the few dozen email providers out there, we specifically like MailChimp because it has a free option for small subscriptions (as many as 2,000 subscribers and 12,000 emails per month). Otherwise, just Google "free email newsletter" or "free email newsletter services" to find several different options.

The best way to start your newsletter is to sign up for the service, put the subscription box on your website, and then publish an issue once a month or even once a quarter.

But be careful that your subscription popup box doesn't get too obnoxious on the mobile version of your website. Google will penalize your site, mobile, and desktop, if your interstitials—email popup boxes—cover more than 25 percent of the mobile screen.

You can always write new articles to share with people, but a great source of newsletter content can be your regular blog. Paste 100-word snippets of the month's best posts into your newsletter template, with a "Read More" link, so people can click it to read the rest of the article. Not only does this boost your blog traffic, but you can measure those clicks inside your newsletter provider's site to see which kinds of articles generate the most interest among your readers.

Podcasts

Podcasts are the radio shows of the 21st century. Although podcasting's roots go way back to the 1980s, it really started to catch hold in 2004. Back then, you could produce these little radio shows and share them online for other people to download and listen to on their own time.

While the concept hasn't changed much—they're still pre-recorded shows that you can listen to at your own convenience—podcasting has matured and grown as an industry. Now, 112 million Americans have listened to a podcast at least once and 67 million listen to them monthly.[1] (No one seems to track the global listening numbers.)

Podcasting as a form of personal branding is taking hold as more people are finding their passion, and then taking to the online airwaves to talk to people about the thing they love or want to be known for professionally.

Listen to Podcasts

Before we discuss whether you should podcast, and lose the interest of those of you who don't want to, we want to make a strong push for you to listen to podcasts on a regular basis.

You can find podcasts on nearly every subject, especially ones related to the thing you want to promote as part of your personal brand. If you're an accountant, there are accounting podcasts (probably). If you're in marketing, there are plenty of marketing podcasts. There are writing podcasts for writers, book review podcasts for book lovers, beer podcasts for home brewers, cooking podcasts for home chefs, and parenting podcasts for parents. (Dave Delaney in Chapter 12, "How to Network: Hello, My Name Is. . ." had a parenting podcast with his wife Heather for several years. Or check out *One Bad Mother* or *Mom and Dad Are Fighting*, from two editors of Slate magazine.)

Why Podcast?

Park Howell, the personal branding storyteller we mentioned in Chapter 2, has his own podcast, "The Business of Story" (BusinessOfStory.com), in which he talks about the importance of storytelling to film makers, TV writers, actors, and even marketers. He does it to support his own work as a professional business storyteller.

---

1. http://www.convinceandconvert.com/podcast-research/the-11-critical-podcast-statistics-of-2017/

Mignon Fogarty from Chapter 1 started the "Grammar Girl" podcast to tell people how to use grammar and punctuation, then turned it into a small empire of advice-based podcasts at QuickAndDirtyTips.com. She's managed to also turn that into a series of New York Times-bestselling books. Australians Kate Toon and Belinda Weaver run "The Hot Copy Podcast" (HotCopyPodcast.com), which is for and about copywriters and their craft. They don't talk about creative writing, long-form journalism, or even any type of nonfiction. They only talk about copywriting, because it is a great way to promote their own copywriting webinars and learning materials.

Not that financial gain is the only reason to have a podcast, but it certainly helps. If nothing else, some podcasters make only enough money to cover their hosting costs, while others make a decent living as a result of their podcast—landing new clients and paid speaking gigs—but not as a professional podcaster.

What Do You Need?

One of the benefits of podcasting is that the barrier to entry is fairly low: All you need is a microphone and some audio editing software, like Garage Band for Mac or Audacity for Mac or Windows. It doesn't have to be complicated—you just want to be able to take out any flubs, mistakes, and long pauses.

You can also drop in some theme music. Search for "Creative Commons music" and check out sites like CreativeCommons.org or FreeMusicArchive.org for a good opening theme. Don't just pick your favorite song off the radio, because it's protected by copyright laws and you'll have a team of lawyers who want to have a quick and expensive word with you.

Of course, there's a higher bar of success. You don't want just any old microphone; you should invest in a high-quality one, like a Blue Yeti or Audio-Technica ATR2500-USB Cardioid Condenser. A quick bit of research will show you any number of choices, many of them $150 to $200.

You also want to find studio space where you can soundproof, or at least sound deaden, the room so you can get that full studio effect without any ambient noise spoiling your recordings.

What Should Your Podcast be About?

As far as your subject matter goes, go back and reread the section in Chapter 3 on finding your niche. Everything we said there will be true for your podcasting niche as well. You want to find the area you want to be known for. But be careful you don't pick a well-populated niche, like business or marketing.

There are already hundreds and hundreds of podcasts in those two fields, and although it won't take a lot of effort to get good at podcasting, you'll find you spend much more time promoting your podcast to get people to listen to it than you spend producing it.

So focus on a particular niche within marketing—brand storytelling, copywriting, cable TV advertising, the history of print advertising, and so on—and spend your time doing that. You may not get as large an audience as you had hoped, but you'll have a group of devoted fans.

If you can't find a topic that works for your business interests, but you still want to produce a podcast, then start one about your favorite hobby. If nothing else, this introduces you to a whole new audience of people who might never know you otherwise.

For example, Scott Monty (former social media director at Ford) and Burt Wolder (professional copywriter) have hosted the "I Hear Of Sherlock Everywhere" podcast (IHearOfSherlock.com), and they now host the much shorter "Trifles" podcast, which focuses on details in the 60 original Sherlock Holmes stories.

Producing the Podcast

Try working with a co-host, or at least do a regular interview show. People often get bored hearing the same voice over and over for several minutes without a break and tend to tune out. But having a couple of voices can help hold a listener's interest.

Marty Wilholt and Larry Niece produce "The Eephus Podcast" about weird happenings and unusual events in professional baseball. The two work from a pre-written story, but intersperse each episode with off-the-cuff comments and jokes, which makes it much more enjoyable to listen to than a single reader droning on and on without a break.

Additionally, commit to a schedule of podcasting. Produce a few episodes in advance—called "having a few in the can." Try to have a month's worth of podcasts waiting for upload. This way, you always have a built-in buffer in case something goes wrong for a week.

Once you get into the rhythm and flow of things and know you'll never pre-empt your podcast production schedule, then you might be able to flirt with disaster and produce your latest episode the week it airs. Otherwise, be diligent and work ahead.

You'll also need to decide whether you want a video or audio-only podcast. Generally, we recommend audio podcasts (despite telling you in the last chapter that video is ideal content). If your video podcast is just you and a co-host sitting and talking on camera, that's not as interesting as you might think.

Sure, you and your co-host are both good-looking, but viewers can only look at attractive people for so long before they get bored. Besides, producing video can be more difficult and time consuming, plus it uses up more high-speed bandwidth. If you've got the capabilities for high production values and can do things like split-screens and switching camera angles, like on an interview television show, then use video. Otherwise, stick with audio only.

PERSONAL BRANDING CASE STUDY: JOHN J. WALL, MARKETING OVER COFFEE PODCAST

John J. Wall has been a regular podcaster since 2005 when he started a short podcast called "The M Show." Two years later, he started producing the "Marketing Over Coffee" podcast with co-host Christopher S. Penn. It's a high-level marketing podcast geared toward professional digital marketers, and Erik has even been an interview guest. (He's hoping this case study will snag him another invite. . . .) John is also the VP of Marketing at EventHero, a trade show and event management registration tracking system.

"Marketing Over Coffee" is a once-a-week show that explores the latest developments in marketing technology, especially web analytics, digital marketing trends, and, lately, artificial intelligence, and machine learning. They even have sponsors who support the show, which is a goal many podcasters have but not many realize. Still, that's no surprise: the show is downloaded more than 10,000 times every week, which is more reach than the average speaking tour.

John enjoys doing the show because it has allowed him to connect with people all over the world.

"If you had told me 10 years ago that I'd be able to talk with people like Seth Godin, Simon Sinek, and David Meerman Scott [leaders in the social media and marketing worlds—Erik & Kyle] on a regular basis I would not have believed you," said John.

Both John and Chris have been able to meet their favorite authors, talk to people from all over the world, report live from Dreamforce (Salesforce's major annual event), and even get recognized for their work by *Inc.* and *Forbes* magazines.

But best is knowing that he's not only built up a reputation for himself thanks to the podcast, they've also been able to help other people do their jobs better.

"When people look to you for tips, tricks, and insight to help them be better at their job, they consider you a friend," said John. "I always love how when

I meet a listener, they tell me great stories. They know that we already have a lot in common and I'm going to understand what they do for a living. Every marketer has great stories and jokes that nobody around their family dinner table understands."

(It's true. When someone laughs at "yo mama is so mean she's got no standard deviation," you know you've found a fellow marketing analytics junkie.)

Of course, like true statistics, podcasting does have its ups and downs. John says one of the things he likes least about podcasting is something he says he stole from Seth Godin: "Knowing that half the shows will be below average."

John says that sometimes producing an episode is like capturing lightning in a bottle, and other times, he and Chris are fighting the episode every step of the way. But as long as listeners find something useful, or are at least entertained, he's pleased with his work.

If you decide you want to get into podcasting, John suggests getting three essential things: a subscription to Zencastr, a cloud-based podcast recording service; a set of professional headphones (John actually makes his own brand that he modifies for podcasting and sells online); and, an audio editing program that also offers a corresponding Udemy online learning course (like Audacity, Blender, or Handbrake).

In the end, John is so invested in podcasting, even his personal branding advice is influenced by it: "Be able to introduce yourself (and your brand) clearly and concisely."

We couldn't say it much clearer ourselves. (Or is that "much more clearly?" Well, we messed that one up!)

How Does This Apply to Our Four Heroes?

Now that we've given you a few new tools to use, let's look at how our four heroes would use this new information:

- **Allen (influencer)** spent 14 years as an account manager in a marketing agency, so he has a lot of expertise in account management, marketing campaigns, and ad creation. He's also looking for a job. Allen needs to do some additional networking at his regular American Marketing Association meetings—he can look on Meetup.com for any local meetings of marketing professionals, creative types, or even just straightforward business networking groups. He can also use Quora to help answer questions for other marketers, which will boost his credibility for potential networking targets. Finally, podcasting might be a good outlet for him to share advanced marketing ideas, which he can then share with potential clients and employers. He could even consider interviewing those same people as a way to introduce himself to them.

- **Beth (climber)** wants to become the chief marketing officer at her current employer. Insurance marketing is a specialized niche, which makes Quora an ideal tool. She can answer questions and build her reputation with fellow professionals, which can give her more opportunity to showcase her knowledge. She can also use an email newsletter for other insurance marketing professionals, if she wants a way to specifically reach people in that field. This can help her become a thought leader to the entire industry, not just her company.

- **Carla (neophyte)** has left a career in pharmaceutical sales and wants to become a program director or development director at a nonprofit. Although the for-profit and nonprofit worlds are different, some of the ideas are the same, like getting people to give you money in exchange for something.

- **Darrin (free agent)** is an IT professional who spends his days troubleshooting computers, and he moves from employer to employer every two or three years. He's almost a commodity in the IT field, so he needs to distinguish himself from every other IT professional. Google+ is currently used more by the technical elite, making it the perfect site for Darrin to start networking with individuals within his space and sharing cutting-edge information. Quora is another good choice because he can share knowledge with people with questions he can answer.

9

Googling Yourself: Finding Yourself on Search Engines

Some people call it ego surfing, others call it reputation management. Whatever you call it, and no matter how egotistical you think it sounds, you need to search for yourself on search engines.

Why?

Because your potential employers, clients, and even former classmates are searching for you. People who are deciding whether to hire you (or to reconnect after "that awkward way we left things back in high school") are going to search for your name to see what they can find out about you.

Do you know what they'll find? Are you sure that they won't find anything that makes you look bad?

More important, are you confident that they'll find things that make you look good?

In 2017, Forbes reported that 75 percent of HR professionals are required to research a candidate online before making a hiring decision. Meanwhile, 60 percent of employers screen candidates via social media. They've rejected candidates because they were turned off by provocative photos and videos: evidence of drinking and drug use, bad-mouthing previous colleagues and employers, and poor communication skills.[1]

Silly Facebook pictures, an offensive tweet, and even a rarely seen blog post in which you used some colorful language—any of these can get you rejected quickly, and you'd never know why.

Similarly, well-written blog posts, interesting videos, and a clean online footprint can move you through the hiring or sales process.

But if nobody can find anything—if you haven't done anything to catch Google's attention—then you'll go unnoticed, un-contacted, un-hired.

The only thing worse than being found on Google for something bad is not being found on Google at all.

Have You Ever Googled Yourself?

Take a few minutes. Google yourself—see what you can find.

@kyleplacy: Heh. Google yourself.

@edeckers: Man, grow up. That's just—oh, I get it! Ha! Good one!

@kyleplacy: Why would you tell people to do that?

@edeckers: That's how I do it.

@kyleplacy: So people have to change their search engine habits to suit you?

@edeckers: I don't see a problem with that.

What did you find? Did you find the websites and profiles you hoped to find? Or did you find some embarrassing information? Or did you find someone else with the same name and no mention of you at all?

How deeply did you dig? Even though the average Google user typically only looks at the first results page, you need to click the "Next" link and look at more results. Better yet, go into your Google settings and set the number of results on one page to 100. This will save you a lot of clicking.

---

1. https://www.forbes.com/sites/johnhall/2017/03/12/the-case-for-online-reputation-management-by-the-numbers/#ab795a63f6f6

Keep digging until you've seen at least 100 results and make sure nothing bad has been said about or by you. If there has been, don't worry. We'll discuss how to fix that shortly.

Next, set your browser to "Private Browser" (Firefox) or "Incognito Browsing" (Chrome), which makes your browser and Google think you have signed out, and are an unregistered anonymous user.

✉ *Note*

> If you have any kind of Google account—Google Drive, Gmail, YouTube, and so on—you have a Google identity, and if you're logged in to any of them, Google knows who you are. Google tries to deliver search results that it thinks you want to see. These are not the same results as everyone else gets, especially if they're not connected to you in any way whatsoever (more on that later). If you want to see what everyone else sees, sign out of Google or do an incognito search, so Google can't tell who you are.

Did you get different results? Did you appear more or less prominently on the pages? The results you see when you're anonymous are closer to what strangers see, like hiring managers at other companies, conference organizers who want to invite you to speak, and potential clients who check to see if you're worth calling. Because they have never met you and aren't connected to you online, these objective results are the ones strangers are likely to see.

This distinction is important because we don't want you to do a basic search and think everything is just fine. It's what other people see that you need to be most concerned about.

What Do You Want Others to Find?

For now, we're going to approach this as a job candidate. Whether you're looking for a job, trying to book a speaking engagement, get hired as a consultant, or just to show up an old high school friend, we want you to put yourself in the shoes of someone who is trying to get hired for a new job. In some ways, every situation is a job search of sorts. Your job is to speak at a conference or work for a new client. And rubbing your high school friend's nose in it? Just a bonus.

`@kyleplacy:` Do you have issues about your high school days?
`@edeckers:` "Most likely to live at home" my ass! I'll show them!

The whole point of your résumé, and your countless phone and in-person interviews, is to demonstrate how qualified you are for the position. You want to demonstrate that you know your stuff—you're up on the important topics, worked on those issues, and have brilliant ideas for dealing with them.

In this way, your social media footprint is an extension of your résumé and a glimpse of how much you know about the issues, what your personality is like, and how well you'll fit within the organization. Think about what your different social networks say about you:

- **Blogging:** Your deepest, biggest, most profound thoughts on the areas that affect your industry.

- **Twitter:** Your sense of humor, your willingness to share information, and a look at what you think is important and valuable.

- **Facebook:** What you like and don't like, support, and even your decision-making abilities. (Did you post a photo of you drinking heavily? Could demonstrate poor decision-making.)

- **LinkedIn:** A bigger, more robust version of your résumé, as well as your networking connectivity.

- **YouTube:** Your ability to speak in public or at least communicate with others.

Why do we talk about these tools in the chapter on search engines? Because that's where people will find your content. If someone—say, a potential book editor—searches for your name, these results can show up, whether it's the good stuff you want them to find or the bad stuff you hope no one ever sees.

@kyleplacy:	I think she was impressed by my LinkedIn profile.
@edeckers:	I'll bet it was my humor blog that sold her.
@YourDamn Editor:	Boys, don't flatter yourselves. I just needed to make sure you weren't felons.
@kyleplacy:	Uh, yeah, not felons.
@edeckers:	Yes, not felons at all. Especially not felons. In Texas. I mean, not in Texas. We're not wanted for a felony in Texas.

Basically, you want people to find the good stuff. You want them to discover your brilliant thoughts on a particular topic, appreciate that you're witty, and see that you can get along with others. The reason we've been talking about all these networks is the whole reason for this chapter: being found on the search engines. Because if people can find you, it makes your job search (Chapter 15, "Personal Branding: Using What You've Learned to Land Your Dream Job") or getting speaking engagements (Chapter 13, "Public Speaking: We Promise You Won't Die") so much easier. Our editor even checked us out online before she signed us up to write this book.

(Don't worry; we talk about reputation management and hiding negative information in "The Value of Reputation Management" later in this chapter.)

Search Engine Optimization

Search engine optimization, or SEO, is the art and science of getting your website or blog ranked at the top of the search engines' results. It uses a variety of techniques drawn from a variety of sources, and opinions vary about what works, what doesn't, how much of something works or doesn't, and so on.

 Note

(We focus on Google in this chapter primarily because they control nearly 80 percent of the desktop search engine market and 94.5 percent of the mobile search market.[2] So while there are other search engines out there, we're going to focus on the search engine that 8 out of 10 people use.

No one knows for sure because Google won't tell. SEO professionals have ways of doing their testing, and they're pretty sure they know what's happening. But Google won't confirm it.

Google is not only withholding this information from the end users, they don't even tell themselves. According to industry legend, Google employees who work on its algorithms are not allowed to share what they're working on, for fear that someone has too big of the Google piece. (It reminded us of the Monty Python "Funniest Joke in the World" sketch. You can see it at http://bit.ly/MPFJITW.)

So people—SEO professionals, mainly—try various things on different websites. They try certain techniques and test the results, make a few tweaks here and there, and measure what happens. Once they do something that improves their search results, they publish their efforts on their company blogs as a way to demonstrate their knowledge and win new clients.

With enough people doing this and sharing what they find, people have put together what works and what doesn't on the search giant. If you would like to learn more, check out SearchEngineLand.com and Moz.com.

What SEO Used To Be

To explain SEO, let's go back to March 2011, when it seemed like every SEO professional had everything figured out. They read all the right blogs, knew all the right

---

2. https://www.searchenginejournal.com/august-2016-search-market-share/172078/

moves, and used all the right techniques. Some of them—the ones whose names were never mentioned in polite society or who were spoken about in hushed tones—had even developed techniques that, if they were ever confirmed or proven, would bring a screaming mob of Google employees to their doors with torches and pitchforks.

@kyleplacy: Chill out. It's search engine optimization, not freaking Frankenstein.

@edeckers: That's the last time I read Mary Shelley before a writing session.

But SEO had some basic rules that most people knew about. It wasn't cheating; it was the way Google had asked people to create and lay out their pages, so that Google's bots and spiders could properly index a page and know exactly what it was about.

Except the cheaters went and ruined it for everyone. People were publishing single web pages with thousands of backlinks on them, articles that had been poorly written just so they could stuff them with keywords, and other tricks to cheat the system.

So Google did away with it all, and said they wanted to focus on other areas: original, well-written long-form copy; easily-navigable websites; backlinks from authoritative websites; and mobile-friendly blogs and websites.[3]

The techniques that were crucial to successful SEO in 2011 don't work as well today. Nevertheless, these website components must still be included in every page:

- **Keywords:** These are the topic or subject of a single article or even an entire blog. The keyword or key phrase for this book is "personal branding." But, unlike what did before 2011, we don't have to use the phrase "personal branding" over and over in every article we create. For one thing, Google abhors keyword stuffing, and they'll penalize websites that engage in it.

- **Titles:** The title of a blog post should have the keyword in it, but only so the search engines know what the page is about. You might call a single blog post "5 Personal Branding Secrets You Can Use Right Now," but we could just as easily call it "5 Secrets to Develop Your Personal Brand," and Google would still understand the topic.

- **Body copy:** The ideal keywords-to-copy ratio used to be two percent. That is, you needed to use your keyword or key phrase twice for every 100 words. That no longer applies, although you should use your keywords a few times in your various articles. But don't obsess about it, and

---

3. https://www.searchenginejournal.com/4-important-ranking-factors-according-seo-industry-studies/184619/

don't ever try to cram in the keyword as many times as you can. That will certainly get you penalized.

- **Anchor text:** Back in the day, it was always a great idea to use your exact keywords inside a hyperlink, like this: "Click here for more **personal branding** secrets." That's an exact keyword match, and it's a dead giveaway that we're trying to cheat. So, now, instead we say "**Click here** for more personal branding secrets."

- **Backlinks:** Backlinks are links on other websites that link back to your sites. These are still important, but only if they come from authoritative websites created by companies and people who have proved themselves to not be filthy, rotten cheaters. The best way to earn a proper backlink is to write a guest post for a friend's or colleague's blog and link back to your own. Doing this will also improve your reach and audience, which can only help your branding efforts.

What SEO Looks Like Now

We mentioned it earlier, but it's worth stressing again: Google only wants to see high-quality content that people find interesting, well-written, and original. They don't want repeats and "me too" articles about "the five secrets of personal branding" or "what the new Wonder Woman movie can teach us about personal branding."

Instead, focus your efforts on creating content with the modern techniques Google now expects in all sites:

- **Quality content:** Now, rather than focusing on keywords, Google would rather see fully-developed content that thoroughly explores the depths of a particular topic. It's not uncommon to see blog articles more than 1,000 words long, rather than the 300- to 500-word articles everyone was writing just five years ago.[4] It's also important to explore new ideas and topics. Seriously, if we see "Five Content Marketing Secrets" with "Write good content" as the primary secret, we're going to scream. It's been said hundreds of times, so people are unlikely to read it.

- **Mobile-first usability:** Because so many people are using mobile phones for their searches, Google is giving preference to mobile-friendly websites or blogs, even if the searcher is using a laptop. That means a mobile-friendly site will rank higher than a non-friendly one. If you're using Blogger.com, WordPress.com, or even a Tumblr blog,

---

4. https://www.coredna.com/blogs/long-form-content

you're already covered; those are automatically mobile-friendly. But if you have an older website or a self-hosted WordPress site that doesn't use a mobile plugin (like WPtouch, Touchy, or Superfly), your site won't be mobile-friendly.

- **Encryption:** This makes your website an "https" site and not an "http" site. Encryption is available on the free blogging platforms—Blogger, Tumblr, WordPress.com—but you have to get it for a self-hosted WordPress site. Talk to your web host about getting an SSL Certificate (that stands for Secure Sockets Layer) for your site.

- **<h1> and <h2> tags:** These tags are how the subheads at the start of a section of a single page or article are inserted into the page. The headline to this section, "What SEO Looks Like Now" would be marked up with an <h2> tag to make it stand out. It's okay to slip a keyword into an <h1> or <h2> tag, but don't try to get one into every <h> tag you use.

- **Time on site:** Google assumes that the more time a person spends on your site, the more interesting it must be. If visitors stick around for a few seconds and then leave, the site must be poorly designed or poorly written. If they stay for a while, then the page must be well done. (Or your visitor passed out before he could leave.) You can see your time-on-site stats on your Google Analytics page (see "Chapter 11, Measuring Success: You Like Me, You Really Like Me").

- **Bounce rate:** You have a "bounce" on your site if people come to a single page and then leave. Basically, they hit it once and are gone, just like bouncing a ball. But if people visit a second page on your site, there's no bounce. (The bounce rate on your analytics measures the people who came and left without visiting a second page.)

- **Click-through rate:** What happens when a particular page appears near the top of a search page and no one clicks it? Google assumes that the site is so awful or unrelated to the search—usually because of the description—that no one even wanted to go there. This is the equivalent of having a store in the mall that no one visits because they don't like what they can see from the outside.

- **Page load speed:** Does your page load quickly, or does it take a lo-o-o-o-ong time to load, causing your readers to die of sheer boredom as 37 pictures of your cat load in your latest blog post? Nothing is more frustrating than waiting for a page to load, and people will hit the Back button rather than wait for 10 seconds for a page to appear.

These are not 100-percent absolute factors—remember, no one knows for sure, and Google's not telling—but based on the research of several SEO professionals, including our favorite, Rand Fishkin of Moz.org, Google seems to care most about these factors. At least 200 factors go into calculating a website's search ranking. These are just a few, but they're the easiest ones to control on your own.

How Can You Influence These Factors?

When Google released its Panda algorithm update, it chilled the hearts of SEO professionals—especially the black-hat ones—who had perfected their link-building software system to give them thousands of links with the click of a mouse. Although that didn't make them go away, it certainly reduced their effectiveness.

Instead, it put the focus on the quality of the blog and website, whether people would actually want to read and explore it. It began to look at how good a website was, rather than how popular it was.

So, if you want a high-ranking blog, you need to focus on the quality of what's on there and whether people want to read or watch it. Get them to stick around, and your site can outrank the blogs and websites of people who put little to no effort in keeping theirs up to date. Focus on these four areas to help improve your search engine rankings:

Quality of Content

Basically, this means you have to write well. Or at least not poorly.

@kyleplacy: Didn't we just complain about this kind of "secret?"
@edeckers: Yes, but we're the ones saying it, so it's okay. Besides, we probably said it first.

Years ago, many black hat SEOs were using article spinners to take a piece of content—in our industry, we call everything "content," rather than "written text," "videos," or "photos" (it usually means written text, but we're never satisfied with calling things by what they really are)—and run it through a piece of software called an article spinner.

The spinner would then rewrite the text so it was different enough from the original text that Google wouldn't think it was the same thing. Then you'd get something like this:

The rotator would then recast the words, so it was unusual from the primary words that Google wouldn't deduce they were the identical objects. Later you'd receive an item such as this.

It's just awful. Not only is it unreadable, it's annoying to anyone who stumbles across one of these. You'd think it was written by someone who translated it from English to French to Mandarin to Pig Latin and back to English.

So Google decided to penalize sites like this. One way they can tell how bad things are is to look at the time on site stats. Because no one bothers to read bad writing, if enough people come to this page and leave quickly, Google knows the site stinks.

But this also means that if you write well—if you focus on the quality of your writing, avoid misspellings, and actually string some coherent thoughts together without rambling— people will stick around longer.

This also means that the length of a single piece of content is important. A 100-word blog post is probably not going to win a lot of searches, but visitors might read a 1,000-word article, especially if it's well written. You can also make it easier to read by breaking sections up with <h2> subheads, and using short words, short sentences, and short paragraphs. If people see a lot of white space between short paragraphs, they're more likely to read more.

Quality of Design

You need an attractive website, but don't spend thousands, or even hundreds, of dollars to make it look cool. Good design doesn't bring people in, but bad design makes people leave. If they come to your site and see that it looks awful, they'll leave again a few seconds later, affecting your time on site and bounce rates.

Using some of the blogging tools we described, you can create an appealing website for a few dollars or even free. The point is, you don't want to have a site that looks like it was built in 2010. Set up a blog, get a good-looking theme, and you're all set.

You can either pay for a professionally-designed theme or find a gorgeous free theme for just about any blog platform you choose. WordPress.com, Blogger.com, and other hosted blog platforms have themes already available when you first create your blog. In most cases, they have been fully tested and optimized to work with the platform. Some of them cost money, but most are free. You can usually swap out a theme for another easily, but you may need to ask a techie friend for some help for some of the minor details.

Ease of Navigation

How easy is it to get around your site? You don't want to make it difficult for people to get around, and you certainly don't want them to follow a series of links down a rabbit hole only to have to hit the "Back" button several times to get to where they were going. Make the navigation easy to use, not only so they can find their way around, but also so they're encouraged to stay longer.

If you want to reduce bounce rate, make it easy for someone to find another piece of content on your site that they would like to read. Include a "Related Articles You Might Like" link at the bottom of every post or "Newer Posts" and "Older Posts" links. These can help get people to click to a second page on your site, thus lowering your bounce rate. Depending on your blog platform, you can get plug-ins to put these kinds of links at the bottom of each blog post. Otherwise, you have to hand-code it.

While we're on the subject of navigation, consider page load speed again. You want to be sure to do a few things that affect your speed:

- **Use low-resolution photos:** When people take photos, they often have their cameras set for high resolution and large sizes. You could basically print a poster with some of the sizes people upload for pictures. We've seen photos that are 22 inches across and 300 dpi (dots per inch) resolution. And people unknowingly load these giant images onto their blog. A photo this size can take several seconds, if not minutes, to load. To avoid this problem, open an image with your computer's photo viewer and re-size the image to no more than 900 pixels wide and 150 dpi resolution.

- **Host your videos elsewhere:** Don't upload videos to your blog or website; instead, host them on a video-sharing site like YouTube and embed them in your blog. That saves all the load time of the video and puts the bulk of the work elsewhere, plus you don't pay for video storage on your server. (Chapter 7, "Say Cheese: Sharing Photos and Videos" explains embedding videos.)

- **Avoid overloading on Javascript:** You may find interesting scripts to add to your blog, but many of them use Javascript to run. These take time to load, plus they chew up a user's processing speed. If you can, avoid them completely.

  If you can't, find a non-Javascript alternative or see if you can place the scripts into an external file, not within your regular HTML code. (If you don't know what this means, ask a knowledgeable friend to help you out; if your site is big enough, consider hiring someone to help with this. It could be worth the effort and expense.)

- **Eliminate unnecessary plug-ins:** If you use self-hosted WordPress and you've experimented with several plug-ins, be sure to delete the inactive ones. You can't just deactivate them and leave them in place. WordPress checks every plug-in to see if it's running, including the deactivated ones, which slows the page speed.

- **Avoid Flash:** Flash is not a good user experience for many reasons. It takes up a lot of computer resources to run; it's unreadable by search engines (which means they have no idea what's in it); and it takes quite a while to load, which hurts your page load speed.

Add Video

Video may be one of the most important SEO tools you can use. Entire books have been written about videos, video SEO, and video marketing. Companies specialize just in making Internet videos. And these videos have a huge impact on SEO.

That's because Google declared 2010 to be the year of video. They put a lot of attention and energy into getting people to use and promote videos on YouTube, their video-sharing site. (It's no coincidence that they called 2011 the year of mobile and made the whole Internet experience—including videos—something worth doing on mobile phones.)

To help drive this change, Google included videos in their search results. So, when you search for certain topics, you see YouTube videos in the results. Search for something like "lawn mower repair," and videos show up in the results in addition to the "how to" and "where to" pages.

And, as we mentioned in Chapter 7, YouTube is the #2 search engine in the world, right behind the #1 search engine in the world—you guessed it—Google. That means that if people want to learn how to do something, like clean a computer keyboard or replace a carburetor, they'll go to YouTube to see a video on how it's done. (While we were writing this edition, Erik searched on YouTube to learn how to replace the air conditioning filter in his car, and managed to do it without blowing anything up.)

So, what does all this mean for your personal brand? Major implications for your SEO efforts:

- **You need to make videos:** Videos are more important than ever, period. And people will view them. Create videos of yourself doing whatever it is you're passionate about, whether it's about repairing a lawn mower, reviewing a new compute product review, or riding the latest theme park ride.

- **You need to optimize your videos:** Be sure to use keywords in the title and description of your video. Also include links to your blog or website, especially if it's embedded in your site. If nothing else, this tells people how to find you.

- **Don't try to win search on Google; win it on YouTube:** Only a few videos on YouTube are properly optimized, usually by video professionals and SEO geeks. If you optimize your videos, you can more easily win a YouTube search. Because Google pulls search results from YouTube, your top videos are more likely to rank well in Google.

Reverse Search Engine Optimization

Reverse SEO is regular SEO but with a different intention. With regular SEO, you want to push your page to the top of Google's search rankings, like a blog or LinkedIn profile. But with reverse SEO, you want to push a result out of the top rankings—usually a negative post, whether as a result of your own doing or someone else's. You can do this by ranking other content higher than the negative content.

Say a highly-ranking online newspaper article mentions you for something you don't want to be known for.

```
@kyleplacy: Oh, wait! Is this that time that you—
@edeckers:  No.
@kyleplacy: Or was it that time that you forgot to—
@edeckers:  No!
@kyleplacy: I know! I know! It was that time when you crashed
            your—
@edeckers:  No!
@kyleplacy: You're no fun.
```

For whatever reason, you can't have the article removed from the original site, and it keeps showing up whenever anyone searches for your name. You need to replace it by getting as much other, better content online as much as possible.

By doing reverse SEO, you can push that negative piece out of the results. Try a few of these tactics to use reverse SEO to protect your reputation:

- **Start a blog:** If you completely ignored the advice in Chapter 3, now is the time to start a blog. Go back and reread the chapter, and don't continue until you start one. No, seriously! Do it now! We'll wait for you.

- **Focus on more than one property:** If you focus all of your energy on one property, like your blog, you may get that to the top of the search results, but the offending content will still be second.

- **Use videos:** We already talked about the power of YouTube. Be sure to create a few videos and upload those. Embed a few on your blog to see if you can get other bloggers to pick them up as well.

- **Write guest posts:** Write guest blog posts for other people. Aim for high-traffic blogs with writers who will promote your work.

- **Purchase your name as a domain name:** Pick your favorite domain registrar, like GoDaddy or Network Solutions, and purchase your own name. Forward it to your blog or at least set up a free website with Google, and point the domain there. Point your other social networks there, too.

- **Optimize your LinkedIn profile:** LinkedIn shows up high on Google results. See Chapter 4, "LinkedIn: Networking on Steroids," for more information on how to optimize your profile.

What if You Share a Common Name?

Erik considers himself lucky. He's the only one with his name in the entire country. There are three or four other Erik Deckers in Belgium, but as he says, "I totally own those guys on Google." Kyle's rather fortunate, too. There are only a handful of Kyle Lacys in the United States and certainly only one Kyle P. Lacy, which is why @kyleplacy is a good Twitter handle.

Most of the people we know have a somewhat uncommon name. But what do you do if you have a fairly common name, share your name with a celebrity or athlete (our friend Douglas Karr shares a name with a movie director named Doug Karr, and Erik has a near-match with Eric Decker, wide receiver for the Tennessee Titans)?

@edeckers: I had that guy on my fantasy football team.

@kyleplacy: How'd he do for you?

@edeckers: I don't know. I was losing so badly, I quit paying attention by week 7.

Worse, if you're already known for something you'd rather not be, then you have a problem.

When someone searches for your name—say "Doug Karr," hoping to find the owner of the Marketing Tech blog—what they'll see instead is a results page filled with movies the other Doug Karr has made, but nothing about our friend. It can get confusing, especially when you want people to know who you actually are.

Erik once pitched a campaign to a possible client who had a rather uncommon name; still, he had a couple of name twins. One guy, who lived in the same state as the client, was convicted of real estate fraud, which is a felony. The felon and Erik's client, a respected former sports reporter, shared the same name, but had a different middle initial. The client decided to not worry about it, since he realized most people wouldn't actually confuse him with a convicted felon. However, he started publishing more work with his middle initial a little more often.

This is when you need to consider renaming yourself, at least professionally.

We're not talking about changing your name like Chad Ochocinco did (the former Cincinnati Bengals wide receiver who legally changed his name from Chad Johnson to match his jersey number, #85). Rather, we're talking about how you use your name.

For example, even though our Doug—Douglas Karr—is known as "Doug" to friends, he needs to use "Douglas" online so people don't confuse him with the other guy. Similarly, Christopher S. Penn of the "Marketing Over Coffee" podcast goes by "Christopher S." so he's not confused with the actor Chris Penn or the NFL player of the same name.

Consider one of several re-naming options:

- **Use your middle initial:** It worked for Christopher S. Penn.

- **Use your middle name:** The odds of someone having the same first, middle, and last name as you are remote.

- **Use your full name:** Both Douglas Karr and Christopher Penn use their full first name, even though they go by their nicknames when they're around friends.

- **Do the first initial, middle name thing:** A lot of lawyers do this. Actually, this is one of the only professions where you tend to see it. Of course, it's a little confusing because you never know whether to use that first initial when addressing the person.

- **Change your name:** This is a huge pain, and something we don't recommend lightly. But noted blogger and consultant (and fellow Pearson author) Penelope Trunk changed her name several years ago to escape some past personal issues, and it seemed to work out for her.

Of course, once you re-name yourself, you need to make this change as public and permanent as you can. It means changing the name on all your different social networks or even starting new ones.

For example, Douglas Karr uses "@douglaskarr" as his Twitter handle. He's "Douglas Karr" on LinkedIn and Facebook. He even uses it for his domain name, "douglaskarr.com." Rather than fighting a constant battle with the movie direc-tor, our Doug is taking the path of least resistance and changing what people call him. After they meet him, they can call him whatever they want. But when it comes to online usage, he can be found only by the name that best serves his purposes.

This tactic can also work well for reverse SEO. You can reverse SEO your old name down the search engine rankings by creating a variation of your name and using that everywhere you can—new Twitter handle, new Facebook and LinkedIn names, and even new blog site and domain name. Eventually, your old name will be pushed down the search engines as it's replaced by newer, better content associated with your new name.

Search Engine Tools

We've used "Google" and "search engines" almost interchangeably in this chapter. Although that's not to downplay other search engines, we mentioned earlier that Google has nearly 80 percent of the desktop search engine market and 94.5 percent of the mobile search market. So, most people who search for you will use Google. You can optimize for Bing and Yahoo too, but don't spend a lot of time there. Be sure to check your Google Analytics to see which search engines are bringing the most traffic, and focus on them.

Use these Google tools to find your name on the search giant:

Google Alerts

One of the greatest discoveries we ever made was learning that you can save Google searches and have the results emailed regularly. Rather than visiting Google day after day and running the same searches, you can save your search and have it emailed to you once a day, once a week, once a month, or as new results are found.

Because you're monitoring your own name, which is the most important facet of your brand, select the "Every Day" option. While you're at it, you should also create Google Alerts for your company, key names, and phrases from your industry. If you're looking for a new job, create alerts also for the names of people and companies you might want to work for.

Visit www.google.com/alerts and set up your alerts. We recommend you have the service return "All Results" rather than "Best Results" when you start. Then, when you start getting too many results to track, switch back to "Best Results."

TalkWalker.com

Back in 2013, a spate of articles and posts wondered whether Google Alerts was dying, so people started scrambling around for an alternative.

That's when Talkwalker.com emerged as the best alternative and a way to keep your regular search alerts coming in. Just like Google Alerts, you can ask TalkWalker to look at websites, news articles, and blog posts and report its discoveries once a month, week, day, or as new results are found.

It may even be a good idea to set up searches on both tools, because they don't always report the same results.[5]

Google Image Search

You can search Google Images at images.google.com to see what pictures are out there with your name attached to it. Occasionally you get results that have a photo on a page that has your name on it, but it's not of you. Sometimes it's a photo you took and is on your blog or website; sometimes it's a photo of you that someone else took; and occasionally it's a photo that's not you and it's not on your website. We're not entirely sure why this happens because the photo hasn't been tagged with your name, you're not in the alt text, and there is nothing to make anyone think the photo is of you. But there it is.

So, you need to check your Google Image Search once in a while to make sure you approve of any photos online with your name on them.

Conduct this search with the Safe Search turned off. Not because we want you to see dirty pictures, but because if there are pictures associated with your name on R-Rated and X-Rated websites, you need to know it. Warning: This may be a problem, especially at the office, so you may want to do this search at home.

Bing

Microsoft's search engine once held a strong partnership with Facebook, showing you what your Facebook friends had shared in your Bing search results. For example, if you searched for Japanese woodworking videos, and your friends had shared some, those would show up in your results.

Facebook also used to provide search engine results from Bing, which made it one of the top search engines in its own right. However, since partnership ended a few years ago, the main thing Bing has going for it now is that it does deeper data mining than Google. And since Microsoft bought LinkedIn, you can get more professional data from a Bing search—yet one more reason you should boost your LinkedIn profile. Figure 9.1 shows what a Bing search turns up for Erik's professional presence.

---

5. http://www.matthewwoodward.co.uk/experiments/which-is-the-best-web-monitoring-tool-talkwalker-vs-google-alerts/

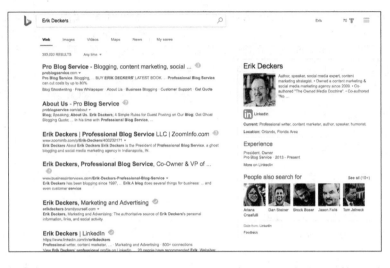

Figure 9.1 *A Bing search for a person is likely to show his LinkedIn profile on the right side of the results page because Microsoft bought LinkedIn in 2016.*

Yahoo!

Yahoo! was once the premier search directory on the planet. It was one of the first, and it eventually turned into an entire portal, offering all kinds of news, content, and other services. Although it was originally known only for search, that quickly became one of the smallest services it offered. They currently get about 300 million searches per month, compared to Bing's 400 million and Google's 1.6 billion.[6]

Yahoo! was recently purchased by Verizon, which plans to merge it with AOL, their other recent purchase. No one is sure what will happen to the search pioneer after that, so if you can use it by the time you read this, be sure to search for your name on the engine to see what other Yahoo! users might find.

The Value of Reputation Management

Reputation management is basically just making sure your online brand—your reputation—is positive and that people see you in the best possible light, which is the whole point of this entire book. But it's important to discuss reputation management as an area of practice because you may need it one of these days.

---

6. https://searchenginewatch.com/2016/08/08/what-are-the-top-10-most-popular-search-engines/

Reputation Management Tools

Online tools let you do everything we've talked about up to this point. A couple of them are free, or have freemium models (free + premium = freemium). Others let you try out their system for a short time, usually 30 days, before they start charging you. If you have a particularly sticky situation or a spotted reputation, you may want to consider trying one of these tools.

> ✉ *Note*
>
> A freemium service means that there is a free component and a premium component. You can use the network for free, but you can't take advantage of all of its features. Some sites have a limited free trial—it can only import three links, or monitor three accounts—while others have robust free offerings, but charge for elite usage—being able to view everyone outside your network and having unlimited messages.

BrandYourself.com

BrandYourself is a reverse SEO and reputation management tool that looks at your name's Google ranking and shows you where and how to add positive content, which will bury unwanted results.

You are assigned a grade, A through F, for your search results; a percentage score based on how much you have boosted your best links; and a progress line to show you how well you're moving up the search rankings. Figure 9.2 shows the BrandYourself score screen.

Google Dashboard

Google knows a lot about you. And if you use any Google properties, or have in the past, you may want to know what they track and to see how much they know. Log into Google Dashboard with your Google credentials (Gmail, YouTube, Blogger, or whatever you use to access any Google properties).

Google Dashboard knows your websites, your analytics profile, your Gmail contacts, and any Google properties that you've claimed, like Blogger and YouTube. You can access your saved Google Alerts, see your Android phone information (if you use an Android phone), and even check out your Google Voice number.

```
@edeckers:  Everything! They know EVERYTHING, Kyle! MWAHAHAHA!
@kyleplacy: Knock it off!
```

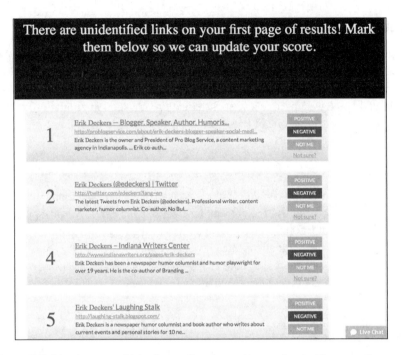

Figure 9.2 *You can see which of your Google results may be positive, negative, or not related to you. This helps boost your online reputation.*

Unlike BrandYourself, this tool does not give you a score based on your visibility or sentiment. You can get a basic idea of your visibility if you use Google Analytics, but no percentage scores, grades, or badges, or anything cool like that. But if you're a regular Google product user, it's interesting to see how tied in you are to all their search products.

Google's Dashboard can tell you when your personal data is released on the web, like your phone number or email address. It's more of a review of what you're doing on Google, but we've both used it a few times and found some old setting or other still connected to our Google account.

How Do Our Heroes Use SEO?

All four of our heroes monitor and manage their online reputations in the same way, keeping their profiles clean, monitoring what can be found and what has been said about them through Google Alerts, and making sure they put out good content to help them be found on Google, Bing, and Yahoo!. They also participate thoroughly on Google+, including adding people from their professional networks to boost their search engine rankings. Of course, they want to make sure they put out the stuff that's related to their next job or industry, as well as sharing that kind of information on Google+, Twitter, and LinkedIn.

If they happen to have made make a mistake in their past, and there's something they wish weren't online, they can use Reputation.com or BrandYourself.com, as well as practice some solid reverse SEO, to remove the negative information from the front pages of the search results.

Reputation Management Tips in 140 Characters

We asked some of our Twitter friends for reputation management tips, and here's what they shared.

- Use the same photos w/filename across social accounts. —@BTutterow

- Just live right, and then it is easy to be authentic and the reputation follows. —@TahiraCreates

- Establish, curate, and promote profiles, i.e., @résumévu and others to help establish a presence and story. —@Mah1

- For businesses, have policy for responding in place; set up industry alerts because your biz is affected by industry news. —@CharleneBurke

10

Bringing It All Together: Launching Your Brand

Some people have called it the campaign of the century. Others have called it the best campaign ever run in the political arena. Still others proclaimed that the use of the Internet was absolutely genius and won the presidency. In 2008, then-candidate Barack Obama and his team created and launched a personal brand that redefined the idea of a political campaign. They planned and developed a story, and then they built that story into a campaign centered on change.

The campaign redefined the idea of using traditional and grassroots promotions. The Internet, blogging, Facebook, and the creation of content were used to win the hearts and minds of the American public. Obama's people accomplished this by planning and launching the best personal brand campaign on the face of the planet. And they used the tools and strategies talked about in this book! Whether you're running for President of the United States or you just want to get a new job, the same strategies and principles apply. Social media isn't just a matter of politics. It's strategy, planning, measurement, and implementation.

This book is about planning to launch your personal brand into the market and make the most out of your skills and attributes. President Obama's first presidential campaign is the most famous case study of how to plan and launch a personal brand, and many other business people, artists, musicians, and the like, have followed his lead. Ever since we published the first edition of this book in 2010, countless people have used it to launch their own personal brands, ultimately landing new jobs, getting new speaking engagements, gaining more readers, finding more customers, selling more products, and even signing publishing deals.

Everything launched into the world, whether a product or business, has one common characteristic: The creator has a plan, and with the plan comes a campaign. President Obama certainly did not launch his bid for presidency (his personal branding campaign, if you will) without a plan.

It's not a good idea to launch anything new without a plan—"If you fail to plan, you plan to fail," goes the old saying. To successfully launch your personal brand, you must build a campaign.

So far, we have given you the ideas and tools to create, test, and promote your personal brand. In this chapter, we'll give you a roadmap for introducing your personal brand to the market.

Launching a successful personal brand requires more than creating online profiles, posting regular updates to your blog, and keeping track of your site's analytics. You also need a solid campaign to launch your personal brand.

What Is a Personal Brand Campaign?

What does it mean to create a personal brand campaign? Now you know how to define your brand story, and you understand you need to have some sort of campaign to launch that brand. That's essentially what President Obama did, right? To fully build your campaign, you should understand what it means.

A personal branding campaign builds your network, including the customers, readers, organizers, and hiring managers who're aware of your personal brand. You've gained their trust enough to interact with you through your positive message (your story).

Your personal brand campaign is the succinct planning and implementation of your promotional vehicle that leads to awareness. In this way, your personal brand is positioned for the right transaction. Because your network trusts you, they come to you when they're ready to make a transaction.

What do we mean by "positioning" and "transaction?"

Positioning is where you fit in your overall marketplace, depending on what you sell. It's determined by what you offer to the people interacting with you.

(See Chapter 2, "How Do You Fit in the Mix?") You're also positioning yourself against the competition. How are you different? How are you similar? What can you do better than anyone else?

A transaction is the acceptance of your personal brand by other people, which can lead to any number of things depending on your story. You sell your product. You are hired. You get booked to speak. You land the publishing deal. People click the link to read your blog.

The final outcome of defining your position and transaction is what we call "the positioning and transaction statement." It's basically your tagline. Remember the short personal biography you wrote in Chapter 2?
You can use that as your positioning and transaction (P&T) statement. It's a catchy, memorable phrase or sentence that expands on the uniqueness of your personal brand.

We want you to get a piece of paper and outline the following questions. Yes, right now. Write down Table 10.1.

@edeckers: Wait, write down "Table 10.1" or the stuff actually inside Table 10.1?

@kyleplacy: What? Just write. . . You know what? I can't even with you right now.

@edeckers: BOOM! #DADJOKE! NO ONE IS SAFE!

Table 10.1   Setting Up Your Positioning and Transaction Statements

Positioning
Who is your competition? List three individuals or companies.
How are you different from your competition? List three differentiators for each competitor.
How are you similar to your competition? List three parallels for each competitor.
Transaction
What does your transaction look like? How do people "buy" from you?
What is your end goal?
Positioning and Transaction Statement
Write down one sentence about what makes you different from everyone else that supports your end goal.

It is important to fill out this information to get a better idea of how to launch your campaign to make the greatest impact. How do you apply these ideas to it?

Kyle uses his positioning and transaction statement as a way to keep focused while building his brand.

In answering the positioning question, Kyle listed other social media writers, speakers, and thought leaders. After researching the competition, he understood what makes him similar and different. He described how his location and experience, being a published author, and working for a company like Lessonly set him apart.

Keep in mind, though, that the things that make you different from one group could also make you similar—and appealing—to another group. In answering the transaction question, Kyle defined his goals, focusing on how to meet his personal goals as well as those of his employer. The transaction is the fulfilling of the goals.

After much hard work, sweat, and tears (Kidding. Sort of. Kyle's a bit of a crier—

@kyleplacy: C'mon man! It was dusty.

@edeckers: Curious how it's always dusty when ESPN's 30 for 30 stories are on.

—Kyle's positioning and transaction statement is this:

I'm a mid-level digital marketer positioning my personal and company brand as the premiere thought leader in online training and learning software.

@edeckers: Who cries at the drop of a hat.

@kyleplacy: Knock it off!

It covers his aspirations to write, teach, and consult on ideas that change business, especially social media and technology. His main differentiation is being an experienced and successful author in the digital space.

How Do Our Heroes Build Their P&T Statements?

- **Allen (influencer)** was an account manager for a marketing and advertising agency for 14 years but is looking for a new job. Remember Allen's short brand bio? He wrote, "I'm a creative professional in high-level marketing and advertising, and I used to work for one of the top agencies in the country."

  Allen will position himself as a creative, high-level account manager with plenty of work experience, which he wants to show off. He wants also to exude the creative passion that makes advertising firms great.

  Allen must write a positioning statement that demonstrates how he is different from his competitors. A transaction in Allen's world would be a new job. He should build his personal brand story to get in front of hiring managers—usually the principals—at advertising firms. His skills in networking and spreading his message will be fundamental to landing a job in the near future.

Unfortunately, Allen's personal brand bio does not fully represent a P&T statement. Allen needs to do the research on his competition and then define himself differently. By filling out the information from Table 10.1, Allen can further solidify what makes him stand out from the competition.

He can use that information to build a P&T statement: "I'm a creative marketing professional who has built several successful national advertising campaigns for Fortune 500 clients."

How did Allen change his personal brand bio? He showed a success statement. What makes Allen different from his competition is the level and size of clients he has successfully helped.

- **Beth (climber)** is a marketing manager for a large insurance company and wants to move up the ladder in the firm. Beth's transaction is going to be meeting new people, networking, and advancing in her company.

What was Beth's short personal brand bio? "I am a marketing manager for Inverness Insurance and have been ranked as one of the top marketing professionals in my industry for the past three years by *Insurance Marketing Magazine*."

From a positioning standpoint, Beth does a good job of explaining why she is qualified for the position. But navigating the politics of the corporate world is difficult. Still, she can define how she is different from other candidates.

The majority of Beth's competitors are insurance marketing managers, including her co-workers, so it's important to find areas of distinction. Her transaction is aimed at getting promoted in her company. With that in mind, she can pinpoint the information she needs to build her positioning and transaction statement and eventually her brand launch campaign.

Beth's personal brand bio fits quite well with her P&T statement. However, she needs to tighten the statement to make more impact. "I am ranked one of the top insurance marketing professionals by *Insurance Marketing Magazine*."

This is a simple and succinct statement. What makes Beth different from her peers? She is ranked one of the top in her industry by an objective third party.

- **Carla (neophyte)** is a former pharmaceutical sales rep who was laid off after eight years with her company and is interested in working for a nonprofit. Remember Carla's personal brand bio: "I'm a former pharmaceutical salesperson trying to make the leap to the nonprofit world."

Carla is similar to Allen, except she has to completely reinvent herself. It is going to be harder for her to define her competitors because the world of nonprofits is completely new to her. She has to do some major research to define her competition.

Her transaction is twofold: She wants to get a job, but she also wants to completely change her brand story. Carla's P&T statement should be designed around how to evolve to become competitive in a new environment.

Carla's is going to be the more extreme change between her brand bio and P&T statement. It is going to take creative thinking to define what makes her stand out from the competition: "I'm a former business professional who wants to make a difference in the nonprofit world by using the sales and networking skills learned in the corporate world."

How did Carla change her statement? She defined what makes her different from other nonprofit professionals. She worked in the corporate sales environment and understands how to build and sell a successful product. Notice that she also dropped "former pharmaceutical salesperson," because she found that the term "salesperson" could have a negative effect when pitching herself to an organization. She also appealed to the emotional side of the reader by saying she "wants to make a difference," which makes her P&T statement even more powerful.

- **Darrin (free agent)** is an IT professional who leaves his job every two or three years in pursuit of more money. Darrin's short personal brand bio was great for his P&T statement: "I'm an IT professional who is trusted by 10 of the top corporations in the city."

  Darrin's transaction is getting a better-paying job over the course of his campaign. What does he have to do to build out his ability to sell? He has to define his P&T to fully understand how to launch his brand story.

  Darrin's competitors are extremely active in the space because of the fast-changing world of technology. He must be extremely comprehensive in defining what makes him different from his competitors. His personal brand bio actually works quite well for his P&T statement, but he needs to add one thing to the mix: "I'm an IT professional who implements technology solutions that drive success for the top 10 corporations in the city."

  What did Darrin do differently? He added why the top 10 corporations in the city trust him. When you create something that makes another individual (or organization) successful, it needs to be built into your P&T statement.

You now have a better idea of how to build the beginning of your campaign by writing your P&T statement. Remember, you can use your brand bio as a positioning and transaction statement, but fill out the information in Table 10.1 to fully understand what makes you different. You can't launch your personal brand campaign if you don't know how you're unique.

Why Is a Personal Brand Campaign Important?

Did you read the first part of this chapter and nod in agreement? (Or at least want to?) It's easy to understand that you have to plan to be successful. You've heard it from every success guru on the planet. However, there's more to planning than just building a system. It's about designing a system to launch your story—the key word being "launch."

The significance of launching your personal brand story into the world should not be taken for granted. You don't want to simply create another promotional campaign that oozes into existence. You want to build something that will spring into the world and create change. The term "launch" is significant in itself. Let's look at the definition:

> To send forth, catapult, or release, as a self-propelled vehicle or weapon: Rockets were launched midway in the battle. The submarine launched its torpedoes and dived rapidly.

You are the submarine. Chills, we know.

```
@edeckers:  I am the walrus, goo goo g'joob.
@kyleplacy: What the hell are you talking about?
@edeckers:  It's a Beatles song.
@kyleplacy: Oh yeah, my dad listened to them.
@edeckers:  Shut up.
```

The concept of launching something into the world is a powerful proposition, especially for your personal brand. The launching of you is more significant than the launching of any Snuggie or Reverse Flush Toilet campaign could ever be. This is the personal brand story that will build your life from here on out. It's the line you've drawn in the sand.

Before you get into the planning details, understand a few issues that should guide your branding campaign:

- **You want to be compelling:** People are overloaded. You know exactly what we're talking about. People are constantly bombarded with an onslaught of branding messages. Make sure yours is new, personal, and compelling, or your story won't get much attention. Your P&T statement help define what will make your campaign compelling.

- **You want to be different:** Developing your personal brand story helps you understand exactly what makes you different in the marketplace. Your campaign should share this with the world creatively and interestingly.

- **You want to create a professional demeanor:** When you create a plan to deliver your personal brand story, you set yourself up for not only sounding and looking professional but also being professional. When you plan for something, you are becoming the professional you need to be to achieve your goals in life.

- **You want to be constant and consistent:** You can't just launch once and wait for something to happen. People are busy, so they're not going to see your messages the first time. You need to publish your message regularly. (This is where luck comes in.) You also don't want to be a pest, so professionalism is important. Don't send the same messages over and over every 10 minutes.

We know you've invested a ton of time already in developing your personal brand and learning about the tools to share your brand story. We want to further solidify your desire to champion your personal brand by creating the launch campaign, so spend some time developing a plan to help you completely understand your personal brand story. When you build a campaign to champion the work you've completed, you create more meaning in your work than ever before.

PERSONAL BRANDING CASE STUDY: SHERYL BROWN

Sheryl Brown was a huge fan of the Bionic Woman Jaime Sommers growing up. She even had her own motivational quote: "Be bigger, better, and more bionic today!" So when it came time to create her social media persona as an adult, she picked "@BionicSocialite" as her Twitter handle. It's the running theme behind every other network that followed.

Sheryl has spent several years working for a financial services brokerage as their lead digital marketer, showing brokers and agents how to use social media to promote their own personal brands while remaining compliant with the various laws and regulations governing financial communication. She opened her own digital marketing agency, BIONICSocial, where she continued serving the financial services industry, providing guidance and education about online marketing. Then, a week after we wrote this case study, she landed a new job at another financial services brokerage.

She became a renowned digital thought leader several years ago when she spoke at the LIMRA financial services conference, where she met Gary Vaynerchuk, one of the giants of social media marketing. They talked for a while that morning.

"He told me I had hustle and good energy," said Sheryl. "Then he got on stage and told everyone they should follow what I'm doing. Oh boy! It was busy from that point forward."

Sheryl's bionic persona became her recognized brand when she was asked to write for several publications, which put her name, face, and knowledge in front of thousands of people. It took a while for that brand to catch on at work, but that changed when her CEO saw her in action.

"When I came to Ash Brokerage, I wasn't doing social media for business. I was using social media more for networking personally," said Sheryl. "Then one day, our CEO noticed I knew 'everybody.' He said I needed to work on their social media presence. Ash Brokerage is the largest insurance broker-age office in the United States, so I knew that was going to be a big job."

She tackled their internal social media and created a roadmap for her col-leagues to use social media properly, developing what the brand would look like coming from each of her colleagues. This movement then piqued the interest of their carriers and vendor partners, which led to interest from financial service professionals around the country. Soon, Sheryl became a regular speaker and trainer for brokerages and agencies around the country.

Of course, the various rules and regulations were a veritable minefield. These regulations remain a problem because there are no official social media rules in financial services. So, Sheryl and her brokers created a few ground rules, like never disparaging a person, place, or thing, and they would never talk about products or quote premiums online.

(Erik helped the CEO of American Family Insurance, Jack Salzwedel, write a book in 2013. At that time, Jack explained that American Family had the same online philosophy of never talking about products online. It has kept them out of trouble and with a strong online presence for years.)

Sheryl told all 400 employees to use their best judgment, and they were given social media access at once. They've never had one issue in the last six years.

Sheryl said her favorite thing about social networking is being able to reach out to someone who would have never known her. Erik and Sheryl met at a marketing conference in Boston in 2013, even though they lived two hours from each other in Indiana at the time, and they have stayed in touch via social media ever since.

"You can leverage data, understand someone's humor (or lack thereof), learn about their family, and see what they're eating for dinner all due to social networking. It's sheer brilliance —those not leveraging this are missing out." said Sheryl.

Some of the coolest things Sheryl has gotten to do because of social media include meeting Gary Vaynerchuk and Seth Godin, having friendships with Ann Handley (Chief Content Officer of MarketingProfs) and Gini Dietrich (CEO of Arment Dietrich). She's also gotten a "hey" from 90s rapper and dancer MC Hammer, which is pretty awesome.

"I can't imagine my life without social media," said Sheryl.

Nevertheless, she still believes in the power of snail mail for connecting with people. She sends out cards and hand-written letters to friends, because she loves the experience of pulling a letter or card out of the mail herself.

When it comes to one piece of advice Sheryl has for you, Dear Reader, she said:

"Follow people you admire and emulate some of what they are doing. Don't copy everything, but jump and build your parachute on the way down. You are going to have failures, like I did and still do now and again. Also, be open to learning because it all changes every single day. Regardless of titles like "guru," "ninja," and "experts," we are all just users of a product trying to keep up."

Building Your Personal Brand Campaign

Now that you understand the why of a personal branding campaign, it is time for the implementation. You can launch a campaign in hundreds of different ways, but they all have three phases: developing, implementing, and automating.

Developing Your Personal Brand Campaign

Your personal brand campaign is based on how you use the tools we've described. You've set up your different social networks. You've differentiated yourself (P&T statement and personal brand bio) and started using tools to promote yourself. Now is the time to show the world what you've built! We're going to start with your calendar as the center of your campaign.

Let's assume you use some type of calendar. Whether it's Google Calendar, Microsoft Outlook, or a paper day planner, you need to have one. (We like Google Calendar because we're both Gmail users, but any calendar will do.) It's going to be extremely important to managing your campaign.

An important area of campaign management is blocking out certain parts of every day to accomplish tasks associated with your campaign. You can apply the following time blocks to any area of your business or personal life, and they'll help you manage your time effectively. The most important thing to remember is to stick to what you planned.

Think of your typical work day. What's going on throughout the day? You have a presentation to write, meetings to attend, phone calls to return, and your boss is still waiting on that TPS report. Or maybe you have a business to run, which means a lot of sales calls and meeting with clients. After work, you need to go grocery shopping and run a few errands.

It's important to block out time in your day to spend time on your campaign. You've already spent so much time building and tweaking the system you might as well stick to it, right? Set aside 30 to 60 minutes every day to use the social networking tools of your choice.

Tip

Block out at least 30 minutes, but not more than 60 minutes, at once. You want to develop a habit, not overwhelm yourself with things to do.

The whole point of the calendar is to keep you productive so you can accomplish your goals. How does that look?

- **Set your time:** Find two 15- to 30-minute time blocks. You can place the blocks at the beginning and end of your day or during lunch, whatever is convenient for you.

- **Respect your time:** Would you call a prospective client to reschedule a meeting because you needed to run to the store or pick up office supplies? No. The same rule applies for your time block. Do not schedule other things during your personal branding promotion time.

- **Adjust your time:** If certain times of the day don't feel productive enough, move the time block. Adjust and change it depending on how and when you do your best work.

So, what do you actually put in the time block? We're glad you asked!

Implementing Your Personal Brand Campaign

In short, you're going to use different components of what we've already discussed—blogging, Twitter, LinkedIn, Facebook, photo sharing sites, video sharing sites, and so on.

Build a daily task sheet (or use a to-do app like Todoist or Wunderlist to assign your daily tasks) to fully understand what you need to accomplish during your time blocks. Table 10.2 gives you an example of a campaign launch task sheet. Finish this task sheet every day, and you'll be well on your way to success.

Table 10.2   A Campaign Launch Task Sheets

Daily Activity Sheet

The following activities will be completed on a daily basis:

Facebook

- Post one status update.
- Answer messages and postings on your wall.
- Friend at least five people from your local area.
- Send one message to a friend with personal content.

Twitter

- Follow 10 people.
- Pre-post five tweets using Hootsuite or Tweetdeck.
- Respond to @ replies with conversational content.
- Respond to direct messages.
- Send one tweet telling your followers to follow a friend.

LinkedIn

- Connect with two people or ask for a connection.
- Answer one question posted to a LinkedIn group.

Blogging

- Comment on two blogs.
- Work on your weekly blog post.

Weekly Activity Sheet

The following activities will be completed on a weekly basis:

Facebook

- Tell a success story.
- Share a funny story.
- Announce good news—tell about awards your company has won, welcome a new client, share presentations, or post on a blog.

Weekly Activity Sheet

- Upload a picture.
- Run a promotion campaign.

LinkedIn

- Post one question to a LinkedIn group.
- Connect with one person for a face-to-face networking meeting.

Weekly Twitter

Send out three #followfriday tweets.

Aim to complete these tasks daily and weekly, and your social media use will become a habit. We're online promoting our personal brands at least an hour every day—a few minutes here and there, of course—because we know how effective it can be in promoting our work. If you've heard of us before you read this book, it already worked!

Automating Your Personal Brand Campaign

As you built your campaign launch task sheet, you may have realized it's easy to automate some of the tasks in the list. Good for you! That's going to save you a lot of time.

Tools like HootSuite that will let you preschedule content on a number of different networks. It can also help you share content from your blog and others. This is how you automate part of your workload.

You want to automate the posting of some of your content so you can focus fully on measuring and tweaking your efforts. Also, creating high-quality content is key to the distribution of your campaign, so you want time to do that. Plus it lets you either cut back on the actual minutes you spend, or it gives you more time to continue to develop your campaign.

Understand, too, what can be automated and what can't or shouldn't be. For example, you can automate the posting of blogs and other articles, and you should schedule your blog posts to publish at a specific time of the day.

When Erik schedules a blog post, it's either for 8:00 a.m. or 1:00 p.m. on a weekday. That gives him a deadline to push for, and if he misses it, he needs to try again for the next day. He can queue up the blog post a few days or hours in advance, so he doesn't always have to be in front of his computer at that time.

But when Kyle schedules a tweet, he can use a random time—say, 8:49 a.m.—so it looks more spontaneous. It's not necessary, but it gives the impression that you're not writing tweets and scheduling them in advance. However, conversational content should never be scheduled. It's more reactionary and lives in the moment. How you post your tweets really depends on the content. Figure 10.1 shows an informational tweet, while the tweet in Figure 10.2 is conversational.

Kyle Lacy
@kyleplacy

Following ⌄

I'm pretty pumped to be hosting the Agile Marketing Meetup at the @Lessonly offices on June 28th > Join me! >

Agile Marketing Indy: June Meetup at Lessonly
Join Agile Marketing Indy for its first downtown meetup on Wednesday, June 28! Whether you're already using Agile on your marketing team or just want to learn more about Agile
eventbrite.com

8:49 AM - 16 Jun 2017

2 Retweets 6 Likes

♡   ♺ 2   ♡ 6   ✉

Figure 10.1 *This informational tweet was sent out to announce an event Kyle was hosting at his office. Tweets like these can be automated.*

Kyle Lacy
@kyleplacy

Following ⌄

It was awesome to see you!

Joel Book @joelbook
Great way to start my day! Breakfast with @kyleplacy and @jkrohrs! Two of the best digital marketing pros I know!

11:39 AM - 19 May 2017

♡   ♺   ♡   ✉

Figure 10.2 *Don't automate conversations like this. They need to be spontaneous and natural.*

Unique Ways to Launch Your Branding Campaign

Now you understand the specific steps to take to successfully promote your personal brand. Complete your daily tasks and add some fun ways to make your day more enjoyable. The more fun you have launching and promoting your brand, the better the results. Here are a few ideas:

- **Send a "Thank you for meeting with me" note:** Yes, mail a handwritten or even hand-typed note. Yes, we understand we are asking you to use a pen and handwrite a note, but the power behind the note is extremely beneficial to your personal brand.

  Individuals rarely write a note after meeting or talking to someone these days. It is extremely important to utilize the art of a non-electronic note.

  Erik even owns two working typewriters. He had some half-sheet letterhead made with his name on it, and he types a short note and mails it to people after meeting them. Getting a real typed note makes a big impression on people.

- **Use video:** Video is an extremely powerful tool to promote yourself because it establishes trust and a deeper connection with your network. You could create one short video per week in your office, studio, or garden to talk about your latest success, go over a tutorial, and so forth. Just remember to be professional.

- **Hire a dancer with a sign:** You know who we mean, right? The person who dances around with the pizza sign on the side of the road. The ability to dance for hours and not get hit by a car is an extremely valuable asset to a personal branding campaign. Okay, don't really do this. We just wanted to see if you were paying attention. But, stay creative and think outside the box a bit for this.

- **Write for smaller publications:** Smaller publications are easier to land a byline in because they have fewer writers. If you write well, you'll have an easier time getting published and promoting your brand. (See "Chapter 14, Getting Published: I'm an Author!")

- **Use an email newsletter to connect on a different level:** Email providers like MailChimp are great tools for email marketing, especially if there's a free version. You don't have to send a weekly email, just a monthly or even quarterly newsletter centered around a topic or theme that you share with important network connections (like potential employers).

- **Give something away for free:** People always love free stuff. Give away a special report or white paper to gain some traction for your personal brand. We've seen people give away books or other valuable gifts just for an email address, then, use those to start an email marketing campaign (with users' permission, of course).

- **Write guest blog posts:** This is an extremely powerful step to getting your personal brand in front of other people.

  We've both written for Jay Baer's "Convince and Convert" and Douglas Karr's "Marketing Tech" blogs. Erik also writes for Dave Delaney's "Networking for Nice People" and the Florida Writers Association blogs.

  When you share content, you receive backlinks (remember the importance of backlinks to build search authority) and gain new eyeballs for your own content. There are a few ways to guest post on other blogs: Email the writer of the blog, write a quick post for an online publication and send it to the editor, or ask the person to swap blog posts for publishing. We suggest writing two guest posts per month.

- **Hire a graphic designer to design a business card:** Most people go to a third-rate printer to get the same business card that 100,000 other people have already printed. Spend some money and hire a graphic designer to design a fashionable and memorable business card with a logo. Print 500 cards and pass them out to contacts at networking events. Hand out your business cards sparingly, don't deal them out like a blackjack dealer on speed. (See "Chapter 12, How to Network: Hello, My Name Is..." for the best ways to network with other people.)

- **Write an email signature:** Your email signature is shared and sent more often than any other form of marketing. Include your name, title, and social media links (Twitter, Facebook, LinkedIn, and your blog). Put your signature at the bottom of every email you send. Go to the "Settings" option of your email platform to create your own signature.

- **Get involved in your local community:** Join organizations such as the Chamber of Commerce or an economic development alliance. We've talked extensively about networking in your community, so join the Rotary Club, volunteer your time and expertise to a charitable organization, or coach your kid's sports team.

- **Always have a smile on your face:** Make sure you're smiling when you're networking. This makes you approachable and amps up your confidence. It keeps your energy high, and someone who is energetic, interested, and enthusiastic always stands out.

Maybe we went a little overboard with that last tip, but it's important to keep a positive attitude while promoting yourself and meeting others.

How Should Our Heroes Launch Their Brands?

- **Allen (influencer)** needs a more creative promotional strategy than the others. His industry is harder to make a splash in because everyone makes a splash in advertising. He needs to spend more time developing a different communication strategy, reaching out to influential people, and creating some great ideas and messages. He may create and send different ad campaigns to principals at advertising firms, then follow up with a phone call or tweet after the package is sent. He should connect on multiple channels to be sure people remember him.

- **Beth (climber)** needs to stay within the corporate structure of her company. Her tactics will be networking and community involvement. She'll spend time sharing and writing content on LinkedIn. She'll also frequent community events for her company. Anything she can do to rub elbows with the executive team would help. She should also start a personal blog to talk about her industry without representing her company, as a way to establish herself as an industry thought leader— and thought leaders tend to get better jobs within the walls of corporate America.

- **Carla (neophyte)** is going to be like Beth regarding networking. Because she is switching industries, she needs to focus on networking and start a personal blog about nonprofits. She can learn and write about the things that will make her successful, like the networking events and seminars she attends to meet nonprofit professionals.

- **Darrin (free agent)** is established in his industry, which means he doesn't need to build a campaign as much as develop his already-strong reputation. Darrin should record and distribute videos of his expertise and interviews of happy clients, as well as screencasts of tutorials or examples of his work. He can create video recordings of his computer screen with software like Camtasia. Video content should be a key marketing tool in the IT world. The more video content Darrin distributes, the more likely he'll be recognized by potential new employers.

Do's and Don'ts of Launching Your Personal Brand

Certain rules and regulations should guide your use of social media, networking, and other tools when launching your brand:

- **Do accomplish your campaign launch task sheet (daily and weekly):** Your daily campaign task sheet (or even a short to-do list) drives your promotional activities for your personal brand launch campaign. If you stick to it, your promotional efforts will become easier.

- **Do have conversations:** We talked about tweeting conversational content earlier in Chapter 3. Content that is live, real, and involves other people will grow your personal brand more than anything. Respond to other people and help them achieve their goals.

- **Do give more than you receive:** Sharing, retweeting, and forwarding content from others is one of the more important techniques for making your promotional campaign succeed. Many people send more content about themselves than anything else. But it's not all about you. It's about developing relationships online. Share and retweet more content from others than you share about yourself.

- **Do be aware of criticism; just ignore most of it:** You can become the top dog in your sphere of influence if you use the strategies we've shared. But be aware that you will face some criticism no matter what you do. Don't take it personally, and don't respond in kind. Simply be aware of the criticism, but ignore it when it gets personal and petty.

- **Do be consistent:** Think of your personal brand campaign as a relationship. If you're in a relationship and aren't consistent about spending time with the other person, the relationship won't last. Consistency of content and conversation help drive your overall online influence and the strength of your brand.

- **Don't be socially awkward:** Imagine having a conversation with someone who changes the subject every 30 seconds. After the third switch, it becomes highly annoying because you can't follow anything he's saying. The same applies to social media. Create a list of things you like to share and focus on those areas the most, but don't bounce around to every subject under the sun.

> **@kyleplacy:** This is what it's like talking to you when you've had too many lattes.
>
> **@edeckers:** I don't bounce around. I just have a lot to talk about.

- **Don't expect quick results:** The campaign launch is a process. Building a brand takes time and energy that over time will build a strong and healthy personal brand. Unless you have million-dollar sponsors or are featured on morning talk shows, your personal brand will take some time to build. If you expect quick results, you'll become frustrated and either quit or make bad decisions.

- **Don't use only one tool:** If you're building a workbench, do you use only a hammer? No. It takes a miter saw, a tape measure, and a drill. The same is true for your launch campaign. Don't use only Twitter or Facebook to build your personal brand.

- **Don't share unworthy content:** Sometimes you shouldn't send a tweet or share a picture on Facebook. You generally shouldn't send any type of message between 11:00 p.m. and 5:00 a.m., especially if alcohol is involved, but we'll leave that for you to decide.

  We all know what content is worthy and what is not. If you're job hunting, a spring break photo of you getting drunk is not the best photo to share. If you're trying to portray a professional image, tweets about what you had for lunch for three weeks are a bad idea.

- **Don't hard-sell people:** Don't ever do this while promoting your brand online. Imagine walking into a networking event and the first thing you hear from a person is about his product or service. We want to build relationships before being sold to. Start with a conversation first, then build a relationship before you ever try to close any deal.

Measuring Success: You Like Me, You Really Like Me!

So far we have dealt with building your personal brand and understanding the intricacies of telling your personal brand story through blogging and using Facebook, LinkedIn, Twitter, and a number of other tools. You're now building your personal brand online, taking advantage of everything these tools have to offer. But how do you know if it's working? You need to measure the overall effectiveness of your personal brand on consumers. This is called metrics, analytics and return on investment (ROI).

In short, you need to know the numbers.

The numbers define the success of a brand. In any company, the numbers drive strategy, creative thinking, marketing development, and goal orientation toward the company brand.

Think of numbers in any sporting event. A score defines the winner of the event. The score must be defined and measured to reach a given outcome. In sports, the winner is the one who scores the most points. The more you score, the better your chances of winning an event (unless you're a golfer). The same concepts apply to personal branding.

A score in a personal branding campaign can be defined as numbers, followers, Facebook friends, blog posts, engagement with fans, and so on. The more engagement you have with your followers and friends, the more success you will have with your personal brand strategy.

Everything in this part of your life needs to be measured, scrutinized, and changed to find that success. As people, we lean on the concept of change to define how and where to focus our energy. If we don't change or improve, it's difficult to make an impression to our industry and the public at large.

We don't want to go all "live your best life now" prosperity guru on you, but measuring your personal brand is crucial to its success. If you are involved in any type of business role, you understand the importance of measurement. You measure the sums on a balance sheet. You track the shipping routes of a transportation company to adjust timing and ship packages on time. You develop measurable systems to track your closing rate through the sales funnel.

Your personal branding campaign is another marketing campaign. The training, planning, and development lead to a set of results about the success of your campaign. The measurement system you use helps you identify whether you're winning or losing in the world of personal branding.

Why Should You Measure?

Say you have a huge week on your blog, Facebook, and Twitter pages. Your traffic is through the roof. Congratulations! Your follower and friend counts are growing, and people are congratulating you on your awesomeness.

@edeckers: People never congratulate me on being awesome.

@kyleplacy: Fine. Congratulations on being awesome.

You think, "They're right. I am awesome! My personal brand is going to be the deciding factor in my ability to accomplish my dreams."

Good for you. You deserve it. We definitely pat you on the back. But let's back up for a minute. Do you know what the trigger was for that growth? Do you know what you did to elicit those responses? If so, you want to repeat the action and get that boost again.

Finding that nugget of information or that one post that sparked your readers' interest can be tricky. When you understand what works and what doesn't, you can build on multiple measures of influence and promotion to supercharge your brand's growth.

What Should You Measure?

You should measure plenty of metrics in accordance with your personal blog, but the most important ones are reach and engagement.

Reach

Reach is the total number of your connections on every social network. A few hundred on LinkedIn, a few thousand on Twitter, and a few hundred on Facebook—that's a decent reach. Provided you've actually got some kind of relationship with these people, you actually have a decent reach.

Of course, you want to have solid relationships with the people in your networks. You want them to know you, like you, and trust you. That translates into success, because these are the people who want to support you. They want to buy your book, attend your show, read your article, help you find a job, and so on. You're better off with a small but caring audience than you are with a football stadium full of people who wouldn't recognize you from Adam. (Hint: Adam didn't have a belly button.)

Just don't cheat. We talked in Chapter 5 about yo-yo following, where people follow and then un-follow hundreds and thousands of people just to boost their numbers.

That is not what good reach is! That's cheating, and it does nothing to boost your personal brand, except to lie to people who don't actually know whether your numbers are good or not.

We've seen plenty of people with tens of thousands, if not hundreds of thousands, of followers, but they've only published a few hundred tweets. No one's tweets are that interesting. The only people who can attract that kind of attention are famous movie stars who go on talk shows and announce, "I just joined Twitter. I don't know how it works yet, but I'm on it and I'm having fun."

Those people have unusually high follower-to-tweet ratios. But if they're not famous, then they're cheating, and it doesn't actually do them any good. They're being followed by people who probably aren't even paying attention to them, which means any time they actually need something, their so-called fans are nowhere to be seen.

When your actual friends connect with you, click on your links, and share your work, that's called engagement.

Engagement

What happens when you send a tweet or post a Facebook update? Do people "like" it? Do they share it and retweet it with their own connections? That's engagement. Do they reply or leave comments? Do they click the links you post and read the work you share? That's engagement.

Engagement is the basic act of people interacting with one of your messages in some way. Rather than ignore it or let it slip by, they engage with it because they thought it was witty, insightful, or interesting.

The more people who engage with your social messages, the better job you're doing. For one thing, it means you're becoming more recognized and more interesting to the people in your networks.

How many new people have you discovered because a friend shared her work? How many new friends have you made because another friend introduced you?

Not only is that real networking, but it's also social media engagement, which means it's from real people who are really interested in what you have to say.

You can have a high reach with tens of thousands of followers, but if no one actually engages with what you're doing, then what's the point? You could have celebrity-level reach, but no one will react to what you're doing, so all of your effort and work has been in vain.

Erik has seen several authors who have yo-yo followed their way to hundreds of thousands of followers. He saw one recently who had 336,000 followers and was following nearly that same amount. If even one percent of those followers actually engaged with his tweets, that would have been impressive. But that's unlikely because there's no way this writer engaged with his own followers. In fact, a quick check of his Twitter stream revealed that he was not. He was just filling his stream with random tweet after random tweet, with no real conversations with anyone. Any books he would have sold would likely have been by accident, because we doubt his strategy was the least bit effective.

In a case like this, quality triumphs over quantity.

Quality versus Quantity

You might be skeptical of the whole "quality, not quantity" argument. However, it does make sense in this new relationship marketing world. The more connected people are to a brand, the more valuable the brand.

Yes, the quantity of your followers on your social profiles is important, but only if you have a high number of the best people. These are the people most likely to support you and your brand. They're the people in your tribe, in your niche of the world. They like what you like, and they like what you do. If you're in a 20-something trombone punk band, your audience will not be people your grandparents' age.

Now, you can build a giant network using yo-yo following (and Erik will spam-block you because he really gets upset by this), but you're never going to reach all those people.

But if you build an audience of the only 1,000 people in the country who love trombone punk music, you're going to do well for yourself selling new videos and albums of your concerts for $5 each month.

As Dan Schawbel, author of Me 2.0, said, "Quantity opens doors. Quality opens wallets."

Visibility

And what about your search engine ranking? Basically, this is your ranking on Google, Yahoo!, Bing, and any other search engine. It's where your website appears in the different search engine results when a keyword is searched. It's safe to say that if you're ranked high on Google (you appear on the first page), you're doing well!

Remember, your search engine rank varies based on the different topics on your blog. Erik may rank first for "humor blog Indiana" but rank thirteenth for "humor blog." Erik has to decide which keywords and topics best promote his personal brand story. Determining that involves using Google Analytics to measure how many people have visited certain search engines. But remember, bloggers are no longer measuring specific keywords, only topics. So pay attention to which pages people are visiting and forget trying to figure out the specific keywords.

@edeckers: Four years ago, my blog ranked #1 for "animal fart gene."

@kyleplacy: That sounds about right.

As you have probably already gathered, your visibility depends on your reach. It's safe to say that the better the quantity and quality of your network, the more visibility you'll have. Whether you write interesting blog articles or thoughtful tweets, visibility depends on your content and where you share it. The more reach and visibility your brand has, the greater the chances of your followers spreading your brand message.

Influence

Influence is a measure of your online power. How easily can you get someone else to take an action on your behalf?

This idea of influence has been circulating for years and has been debated over and over again. The notion of influence is nebulous and difficult to define. Because it's more than simply the number of followers and friends you have, you need to define your influence based on your objectives.

Measuring Influence

What does it mean to be influential? What does it mean to push your followers and friends to action in accordance with your personal brand plan? Brian Solis, a thought leader in the world of social currency, defines influence this way:

> "Influence is the ability to cause desirable and measurable actions and outcomes.[1]"

In Chapter 12, "How to Network: Hello, My Name Is...," we talk about promotion, but the idea of influence needs to be defined based on your objectives. At a basic level, influence is the percentage of people who act upon a specific call to action. Fundamentally, influence is the number of people who do what you ask of them.

Many would say that actor Ashton Kutcher (@aplusk) has more influence than Kyle in the world of social media based strictly on the sizes of their audiences. At the writing of this book, Kyle has 35,800 followers on Twitter, and Ashton has more than 18 million followers. (We rounded Ashton's number down so Kyle wouldn't feel bad about himself.) We're talking about an extreme gap, but who has more influence? It depends on the subject matter and the goal.

It's easy to assume that if Ashton tweets about entertainment or his latest show on Netflix, he is going to have more influence than Kyle. Ashton is going to get a larger number of people retweeting, sharing, and commenting on his thoughts because he's a celebrity, and that's his element. But if Kyle were to tweet something about the tech industry in Indianapolis, he would have more influence than Ashton. (However, Ashton is getting more involved in tech himself, investing in several companies, so he may give Kyle a run for his money.)

This is an important distinction: Influence is not just a raw measure of fame. Your influence is based on your ability to inspire your followers to take action—not anyone and everyone on Twitter, just your followers.

You create your personal brand story to increase your influence within your network. Whether you influence a room at a networking event or get multiple retweets from a blog post, the influence you have depends on where you focus your content and create change.

You can also measure your network's actions based on the number of visitors your blog receives: The more visitors, the more highly valued your content is. If one of the goals in your personal branding campaign is to increase traffic to your blog, you can measure progress and growth to see if you meet that goal. We discuss measuring yourself with Google Analytics later in this chapter, but it also helps to measure against your competitors. You can gauge what content is right, wrong, or indifferent for your followers and your competitor's followers.

---

1. www.briansolis.com/2010/09/exploring-and-defining-influence-a-new-study/.

How Should You Measure?

From Facebook to Twitter to your own blog, each networking site and tool provides opportunities to measure your effectiveness. Armed with this information, you can then measure your effectiveness—and possibly your influence—across the entire Internet.

Measuring Your Blogging Effectiveness

Remember, the blog is the central point of all content on the Internet. It is the hub of your social media branding strategy. It's the place where stories are told and your personal brand is built from the ground up. You need to know how to measure your effectiveness as a writer and content distributor. You must understand what posts are the most effective and what content your followers and network like and appreciate.

A blog is most effective when you monitor these four extremely important metrics that help measure your personal brand influence:

1. **Number of backlinks:** A backlink is a link that goes back to your site from an outside site. The more backlinks from trusted, high-value sites you have, the higher your site ranks on the search engines. Search engines like Google use backlinks as one way to measure a site's credibility. At their simplest, backlinks can come from other authors and readers writing about you on their own blogs and linking back to your own. Think of them as footnotes in a research paper. If Erik writes an article about something Kyle said, Erik links to Kyle's post to give him credit for the original.

> ✉ *Note*
>
> Backlinks used to be a significant tool of search engine optimization (SEO) for helping your blog rise to the top of the ranks. Because of Google's Panda update in 2011, backlinks are less easy to earn as they once were. Google only counts backlinks from other websites that have been proven trustworthy; shady backlinks on websites that were created just for link farming are often dropped or penalized in Google's ranking system.

2. **Number of posts:** No one agrees on the effectiveness of posting several times during a week. The Internet gods have not laid down the law on how often you should post, but the consensus is that more is often better. Once a week is the minimum, but unless you're part of a media company, several times a day is going to be counterproductive because you presumably have other work you could be doing.

3. **Number of comments:** This used to be important, but so many spammers have clogged up the comments, it's not really a factor anymore. We used to work with clients who strongly believed comments were crucial, but we've known several popular bloggers who just turned comments off because they not only did nothing, but they were getting clogged with spam.

4. **Number of visitors:** This is self-explanatory. If your blog has visitors, you have some influence and are compelling people to come and read your posts. Generally, the more visitors a blog has, the more influential it is.

The best way to measure and track all this data is with analytics software. We particularly like Google Analytics, (though it's not the only system available), which gives you information about things like:

- Which referring sites send you the best traffic?

- Which visitors are most likely to subscribe to your email list?

- Which pages have the highest number of visits?

- Which articles have the lowest bounce rate?

- Where are most of your readers coming from?

- How long are they spending on your site?

Using Google Analytics for Your Blog

Google Analytics can be an extremely powerful tool to increase the effectiveness of your personal brand. These features are easy for even the least tech-savvy blogger:

- **The Google price tag:** This is the best part. It's free!

- **Usability of the application:** Google Analytics is easy to use. Unlike other analytics platforms, Google Analytics is easy to implement, there's no need for development support, and you can immediately start to collect data that can help you. For more information, check out the Google Analytics Academy.

- **Unbelievable amount of data collection:** Google Analytics organizes gobs and gobs of data at your fingertips. The system is extremely comprehensive and lets you track all forms of information from visitors to bounce rates. You can create a custom dashboard to easily find the information that's most important to you.

- **Conversion tracking:** Conversion tracking helps you measure the effectiveness of your calls to action, which are the actions you want a visitor to take, like buying a product or signing up for a newsletter. You can track and cross-reference that information against other factors on your site. For example, a consultant can use conversion tracking to track visitors to her blog, the campaigns they follow, and how they happened upon the site. She can learn that visitors who find her through Google are twice as likely to sign up for a newsletter than those who come from Twitter. This means she should focus more energy into getting additional visitors from Google and cut back on the amount of time she spends bringing in people from Twitter.

There's only one reason to use Google Analytics to gather all this data: to tweak your site and your content to create a better user experience. No matter what tweaks are made to your site, you can see what happened based on the changes you made. If Kyle uploads new content and switches around his ads, he can instantly see whether the new positions are more or less effective. From there, he can decide whether to move them back or leave them in their new place.

Setting Up a Google Analytics Account

Before you can use Google Analytics, you need to set up your account.

When you go to the Google Analytics website (www.google.com/analytics), you are asked to access Google Analytics with a big blue button. Click on "Sign Up Now," located directly beneath the blue "Access" button. This takes you to a page where you can sign in with your Google account. (If you have not set up a Gmail or Google account, be sure to do this first. If you already have a Gmail, YouTube, or Google Drive account, sign in with that account.)

In the next window, provide Google with the URL of the site you want to analyze. As shown in Figure 11.1, fill out the remaining data, including country and time zone, and provide your contact information. After you provide the necessary information to Google, you are given a block of code. Copy the code, and then sign in to your blog. We'll tell you what to do with that code in a minute.

Figure 11.1 *Be sure you have the correct information on hand to fill out Google Analytics quickly and easily.*

Installing Google Analytics

Now you need to install the analytics code you just copied into your blog. By installing this code, you give Google Analytics permission to pull data from your site and organize it in the analytics dashboard.

Now that you're in your WordPress blog, click "Appearance" in the left sidebar, and then click "Editor." Next, go to the right sidebar and click "Theme Header." Finally, search for the line "</**head**>" and paste your code right above that. And that's that!

Most blogs have plug-ins or other easy ways to install Google Analytics. For example, WordPress has more than 250 different easy-to-install plug-ins for Google Analytics. Kyle prefers Google Analytics for WordPress, while Erik uses the Ultimate Google Analytics plugin on his professional site. By using a plug-in on your WordPress account, you can change the setting for the Google Analytics account in your WordPress dashboard. You can also just hand-install the analytics code in your site's CSS (Cascading Style Sheets) code, but the copy-and-paste method we just did is a little easier.

With the exception of a WordPress.com blog, most blog platforms have instructions on how to install Google Analytics code on your blog. (WordPress.com allows Google Analytics only in their Business package) Find those instructions on your blog platform, and follow them.

✉ *Note*

Remember the difference between WordPress.com and self-hosted WordPress from Chapter 3? Self-hosted WordPress is where you host the blog on your server. WordPress.com is where they host it on their server. You can't install Google Analytics on WordPress.com unless you have a Business account.

Getting an Overview of Your Website Performance

You are well on your way to data bliss. Your Google Analytics platform is ready to provide you with the information and data discussed earlier in this section, from bounce rates to conversion tracking. However, the service may take up to 24 hours to begin pulling data from your site.

You first need to pull information to give you a basic overview of your site's performance. When you log in to your Google Analytics account, you are presented with a dashboard that gives you a snapshot of your data from the last seven, 28, or 90 days or from a custom date range you specify.

At the top of the page is a line graph chart that represents the site traffic over the specified date range. It can compare traffic over a certain period or change the data to show page views. Immediately beneath the chart are further charts which give information on everything from user acquisition to page views. You can also click on the "Audience Overview" link to see additional data and metrics. For definitions of terms in the Google Analytics dashboard, refer to Table 11.1.

Table 11.1   Google Analytics Vocabulary Defined

Visits	How many visits there were to your page. A visit is defined as a page view when a particular user has viewed no other page on your site in the past 30 minutes.
Page views	How many times the pages on your site have been viewed.
Pages/visit	How many pages, on average, users view when they come to your site.
Bounce rate	What percentage of users left after viewing only one page on your site.
Average time on site	How long each user spent on your site
New visits	What percentage of your users have not visited your site before.

Below the "Site Usage" area is the "Visitors Overview" graph, which shows how many people have visited your site. The number is usually lower than the visits figure because many people will be repeat visitors.

You can tell from Figure 11.2—the dashboard from Erik's company page—that there is a ton of information to take in and analyze. On the left sidebar of the dashboard window (see Figure 11.3), you can click any of the links to read a more detailed report on the information at hand.

It is up to you to spend enough time to fully realize the potential of Google Analytics. Google made some big improvements to Google Analytics between the second and third editions of this book, so it's now even more useful and powerful for both personal branding and company branding.

Google Analytics also tracks users reaching your site from social networks, like Facebook, Twitter, and LinkedIn—that is, referring sites. These are links you shared on a social networking site (or someone shared it for you), that get clicked on by a new user. By improving your Twitter, Facebook, and LinkedIn use, you can increase your referring sites and create a system to further your personal brand.

Figure 11.2 *The Google Analytics dashboard has a tantalizing amount of information for you to read and measure. This is a custom dashboard where you can choose which widgets appear on your dashboard.*

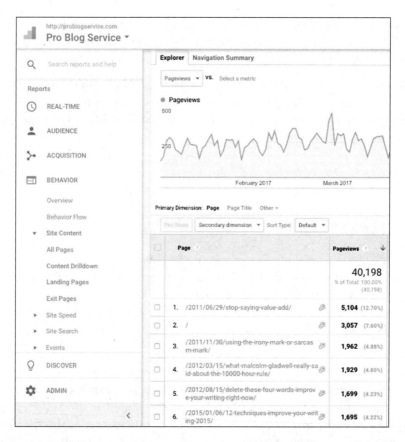

Figure 11.3 *The dashboard sidebar. This is where you can drill down to find different reports of your analytics, whether it's the country of origin, the browsers, the keywords, and so on.*

Measuring Your Twitter Effectiveness

Of the three major social networking sites, Twitter is the easiest one to measure for your personal brand effectiveness. Although the site has fewer data points to measure, Twitter has made sure to grant access to the most important ones: impressions and total engagement (which includes likes, retweets, link clicks, and replies, to name a few).

You can look at the statistics for all of your tweets for the past 28 days or any of the previous four months and the current month, as well as any custom date ranges. Figure 11.4 shows what the Twitter Analytics dashboard looks like.

Twitter also lets you see some valuable insights into your Twitter followers, including their primary languages, main interests, demographics, buying habits, and even wireless companies.

You can see what kinds of events people are talking about the most, and then develop campaigns—or at least blog content—around those interests. You can even spot some of the recurring trends getting hashtagged, like #TBT (throwback Thursday) and #FollowFriday.

```
@edeckers:  My favorite is #FealtyFriday.
@kyleplacy: Don't you mean #FollowFriday?
@edeckers:  It's kind of the same, but with more fanatical
            commitment.
```

Even though most of this information won't be important to your personal brand, it can be extremely valuable if you run a small company or are a professional marketer. It's also useful if you want to advertise or promote anything via Twitter—it will give you an idea of the kinds of people you want to reach and whether your product is part of a Twitter trend.

Bottom line: Focus on the basic Twitter analytics. Look closely at your impressions and total engagement data. This will not only tell you what kinds of tweets your audience prefers from you, but you can also measure the times and days that earn you the most traffic, letting you schedule your most important tweets (for example, "I have a new blog post for you to read!") at the best times, then schedule additional tweets for the other good times.

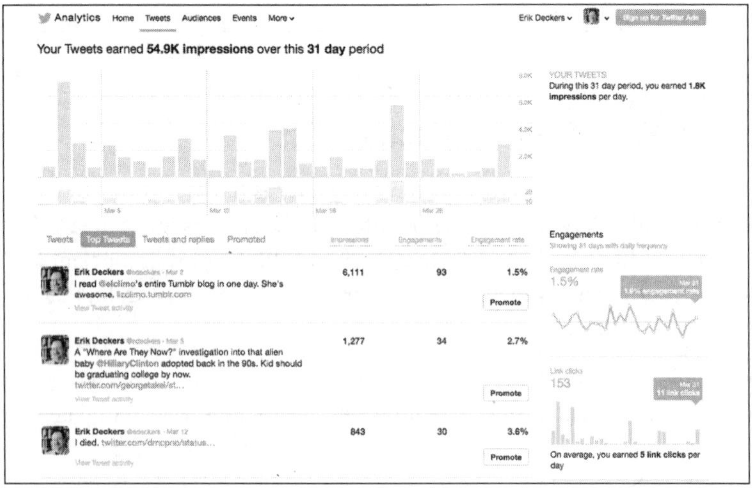

Figure 11.4 *These are some of Erik's most popular—that is, most engaged—tweets from March 2017.*

Measuring Your Facebook Effectiveness

Facebook has a long way to go toward helping individual users measure their marketing effectiveness. You simply can't measure effectiveness with personal profiles, apart from how many new friends you have.

But if you're a marketer, there are measurements galore! You can measure effectiveness with insights on your brand's page. (See "Chapter 6, Facebook: Developing a Community of Friends," for more information on when you might need a brand page.)

If you launch a brand page, you can check out its reach for the last seven to 28 days as well as today and yesterday. You can see which of your posts have had the biggest reach as well as what kind of engagements they had.

You can also measure the number of page views, followers, and likes for different posts. Remember, however, that Facebook has throttled a brand page's reach to roughly one percent of its total audience, or one out of every 100 people. So if you're not very active on Facebook with your page, or you don't pay to promote your posts, you're not going to see much activity here.

Measuring Your LinkedIn Effectiveness

LinkedIn gives you the fewest tools to measure your brand's success. Unlike Twitter, LinkedIn doesn't provide code to allow programmers to develop measurement applications. But you can measure your personal brand effectiveness on LinkedIn in a couple ways.

A small section within your LinkedIn profile is "Who's Viewed My Profile." Here, LinkedIn identifies how many visitors have viewed your profile in a certain number of days by name, title, or industry. If you are looking for a job, the number of profile views you receive should be extremely important to you. The more profile views, the better for your LinkedIn profile. You can see up to five of your profile visitors with the free version (although one or two of them always seem to be "Anonymous," which reduces the amount of effective information), or all of your visitors with the premium version. Occasionally, "free month" offers let you try the premium version, so you may want to wait for one before you commit to anything.

Next to the profile views section of your LinkedIn profile page is one that lists how many connections you have and how many new people have joined your network in a given number of days. You should pay attention to how many connections you have, because that's a sign of the strength of your overall network.

Kyle has 1,730 connections, which links him to 8,402,000 people. That means he's no more than three degrees separated from 8.4 million people, so he can, theoretically, reach that many people via introductions.

In the same area is a line that tells you how often you have shown up in searches over the past day, plus a few of the companies where the people who looked at your profile work, along with their job titles. Of course, you don't get to know who those people are, but if you've applied to some companies that show up on your search results, that can tell you who may be interested in your résumé. Similar to Twitter's analytics, LinkedIn provides information on the likes and shares of your status updates, as well as those of any articles that you write and publish. Figure 11.5 shows a recent article by Erik about the time he helped the Prancercise Lady with some SEO issues.

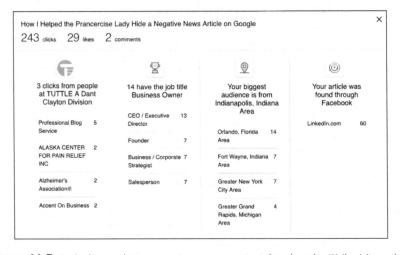

Figure 11.5 *LinkedIn analytics can give you some insights that the "Who Viewed My Profile?" section cannot.*

Measuring Your YouTube Effectiveness

YouTube has its own analytics tool, which lets you see not only how many views your videos have had, but who saw them—including their geography and demographics and the technology they used—as well as subscriber growth, likes and dislikes, and even traffic sources.

To get to your analytics, either:

- Go to your channel home. At the top of the screen is the number of subscribers and views you've had. Click the "Views" link.

- Go to your channel, select a video, and then click the "Analytics" button associated with that video (see Figure 11.6). You can do this if you followed the previous step, too.

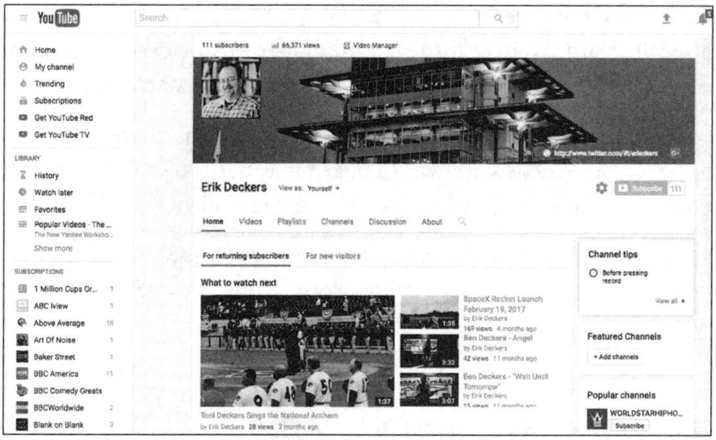

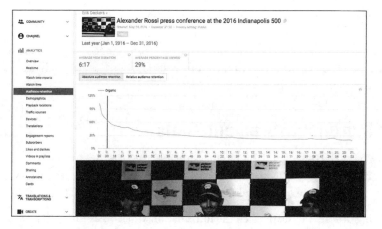

Figure 11.6 *The YouTube Video Channel screen. Click the "Analytics" button above the banner photo and avatar photo. You can see it there above Erik's head.*

By examining a particular video's reports, you can learn a few important factors about how people reacted to it. First, go to the "Audience Retention" section (under "Watch Time Reports") and watch your video with the audience retention graph. You can see where people have abandoned the video and stopped watching. If you see a spike of departures at a particular point in a video, you can either edit the video to remove the unsuccessful section, reshoot the video, or just know what not to do next time. Figure 11.7 shows the audience retention graph of a video Erik took at the 2016 Indianapolis 500 post-race press conference, after Alexander Rossi won for the first time.

Figure 11.7 *The Audience Retention screen on YouTube Analytics lets you watch your video and see when most people abandon the video. This view is for the entire 2016 year. (Video taken by Erik Deckers.)*

Also, check "Traffic Sources" to see where people are coming from. In Figure 11.8, you can see the traffic sources for Erik's Alexander Rossi video. YouTube-suggested videos are those that appear to the right of a video you're watching.

YouTube's traffic sources tell you where most people found a particular video. YouTube-suggested videos are always a big source, but YouTube search can tell you what people were looking for when they found your video.

YouTube search results are an important measurement, especially because YouTube is the second largest search engine in the world. Knowing what terms people used to find you can help you optimize future videos.

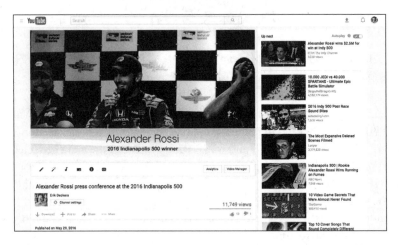

Figure 11.8 *Alexander Rossi won the 100th running of the Indianapolis 500, becoming the 10th rookie ever to win the race. Erik's video of the press conference appears to be the only full press conference video available on YouTube.*

If you want to reach people with videos, especially by embedding the videos on your blogs, you can get only so much information from Google Analytics. So pay close attention to YouTube Analytics as well.

Four More Measurement Tools

With so much content and data to measure and track in the world of social media, it's hard for anyone to keep track of it all. Getting a handle on all the data is made easier when you use tools in addition to those provided by social media sites.

By using different tools to track the information, it becomes easier to become successful in this world of instant communication. Some of this data is fairly accurate, some isn't very important, but it all sometimes adds a nice boost to your ego.

However, most third-party measurement tools charge subscription fees. We recommend only the tools that have a good free option:

1. **Website Grader:** This tool is brought to you by the same people who created Twitter Grader, HubSpot Marketing. Website Grader enables you to compare your website to a competitor; the report includes blog analysis, blog grade, recent blog articles, Google index pages, and readability level. It also helps you optimize your content from headings to images. It is a comprehensive and worthwhile report.

2. **Keyword Position Monitoring Report Service:** This tool is a way to check the rankings for a domain for a particular set of keywords or phrases. This is a suitable tool for tracking the progress and ranking for your particular keywords or phrases.

3. **HootSuite:** We've talked at length about this tool. HootSuite offers an analytics suite that helps you track links and create analytics for several different tools. The free version is very limited, only allowing you to connect to three social media networks. At the Professional level, you get full access to all their analytics data. However, you'll need to use HootSuite as your main posting portal, so you can take advantage of their Ow.ly link shortener.

4. **Klout:** This was one of the first serious tools designed to measure influence. It takes into consideration your true reach (your engaged audience), amplification, and network influence. Of course, Klout has its detractors because people tend to drop and rise over the slightest changes to their activity—if any of your social networks disconnect from your Klout account, your score will drop, and reconnecting it won't immediately solve the problem.

5. **Bitly:** This used to be one of the top link shortening tools available, and the free option was more than enough for any personal branding practitioner to keep track of past tweets, website URLs, and other shared links. But their latest tool only lets you search the last 30 days of your links, and doesn't share nearly as much information as it used to. If you use it, remember its 30-day limitations.

Effectively Measuring Your Personal Brand

We want to give you the necessary tools to empower you on the road to personal branding success. The tools may seem complicated or difficult to use, but they are designed to be used by regular people, and they can empower your personal brand story. Your main goal throughout this entire process is threefold:

- **Understand your social media engagement:** Twitter, Facebook, LinkedIn, and even YouTube let you measure your reach, readers, visitors, and connections.

- **Use Google Analytics:** Get to know Google Analytics if you have a blog or personal website. A ton of data is processed through this system, but you need to understand the implications it has on your personal brand. There are even videos you can watch to better understand how Google Analytics works.

- **Use one tool for each network:** You have an overall system in Google Analytics, but you need to use at least one tool for each social network. For Twitter, there's Twitter analytics, and Facebook has its Insights. We like Klout for a overview of trends, but look at each tool individually to be sure.

Overall, it's about the information you glean from the site and not the measurement tool you use. Data is the most important thing you can get because the numbers and metrics will tell you how influential your personal brand is (or is becoming). Check and track the data to make the most out of the time you have spent developing your personal brand story.

How Can Our Heroes Use Analytics and Measurement?

In the other chapters, our heroes have used our tools and ideas in different ways. However, for measurement and analytics, they each need to measure the same thing: how many people visit their different profiles on Facebook, LinkedIn, and blogs, as well as where they come from and what they look at.

One thing each of our heroes can do is promote their blog posts on their different networks using Google campaign codes. Posts can be promoted via LinkedIn, Twitter, and Facebook, but each time, our heroes should use different headlines or promote them at different times of the day as a way to see which are the most effective. Then, once they know how well a certain type of headline performs or the best time of day to promote a post, our heroes can improve on that.

They can also use individual Bitly or Ow.ly links to promote their posts to specific hiring managers or decision makers and then track whether those managers have opened those links.

Finally, they can use the map function on Google Analytics to see if people from their chosen cities—hiring managers and decisions makers—have visited their websites and blogs.

Do's and Don'ts for Analytics and Measurement

- **Do measure the metrics that give you actionable data:** Pay attention to the measurements around your social media activity, such as the posts that get the most click-throughs.

- **Do focus on metrics that help you determine your influence in your network**: Visits to your blog or the number of Twitter followers or LinkedIn connections are the most useful.

- **Do focus your blog's topics:** Track those that give you the best visibility through Internet search terms.

- **Don't use every measurement tool on the Internet**: Focus on just the ones that are easy to use and give you the results you need to improve your personal brand.

- **Don't measure every metric available to you:** Figure out what it is you need to know to determine your effectiveness and ignore the rest.

- **Don't obsess about your numbers:** Check only every couple of days. You don't need to focus on your numbers hour after hour. Remember, this is about trends, not actual figures. As Erik likes to say, "You want the little line to go up, not down. If it goes down, make it go up."

Analytics Tips in 140 Characters

- Don't take it too seriously. —@slicklaroo

- True influence is measured by the conversations you're having, not the # of followers, Klout score, etc. —@paigeworthy

- Use Klout's metrics, not its number. Make sure things trend upward. Pay attention to unfollows only if you follow them, too. —@allisonlcarter

- Even if you don't analyze the data now, make sure to set up the mechanisms to compile it. —@prebynski

- Drive traffic and check measurements on specific landing pages. —@lorraineball

- If you want to see how influential you are on social media, try helping someone else raise money for their cause. —@charlesbivona

- Klout can provide rough figures, but I don't worry about small score changes. There may be issues if your score seriously drops long term. —@joshhumble

- Be concerned more with people and productive, targeted engagement— not purely stats from machines. —@edeckers

- Keep current on your measuring tools' latest algorithmic changes and updates, and how they can impact your reported influence. —@edeckers

III

Promoting Your Brand in the Real World

12 How to Network: "Hello, My Name Is..." 249

13 Public Speaking: We Promise You Won't Die 283

14 Getting Published: I'm an Author! 311

15 Personal Branding: Using What You've Learned
to Land Your Dream Job 335

12

How to Network: "Hello, My Name Is..."

We've spent the previous eleven chapters talking about how wondering social media is. Most social media books stop right there: It's awesome and everyone should use it.

We agree, except it doesn't stop there. Social media is only the tip of the iceberg. You must also have personal, face-to-face interactions. It's the personal touch that truly makes networking, and thus personal branding, so valuable.

You're doing pretty well so far. You've set up a blog, started using Twitter, created a Facebook account (or at least took the inappropriate photos off your existing one; you know which ones), and are on your way to becoming a LinkedIn power user. Now you're going to leave the comfort of your computer and go out into the real world.

It's one thing to create your personal brand as an online persona. It's another to get yourself out into the real world and leverage the brand you've been creating online.

Meeting people in the real world—in the "meat space," as it's sometimes called—is so important that we're breaking the number one computer book rule and spending the last few chapters talking about real life. After all, your personal brand isn't worth anything if real people don't get to react to it in real life.

You're also going to invent or reinvent yourself into someone who speaks in public (Chapter 13, "Public Speaking: We Promise You Won't Die"), publishes articles in print publications (Chapter 14, "Getting Published: I'm an Author!"), and finds a new job (Chapter 15, "Personal Branding: Using What You've Learned to Land Your Dream Job"). But for you to do those things, you need to actually meet people face to face and deepen those relationships further.

Ultimately, the human connection is what's going to propel your personal brand to great success. Similarly, a lack of human connection will cause it to fail.

In "Chapter 1, Welcome to the Party," Erik created and grew his personal network not because of his online work. Rather, it grew because of his face-to-face meetings as he met people at networking events and conferences, sharing stories, knowledge, and experiences and getting to know people as people, not as avatars and handles. Erik had been networking for years before that, but this was his first time in a new city, in a new industry, and in a situation where he didn't know anyone who could be helpful to him.

Kyle has built his network the same way: by meeting people and learning from them directly, spending his days doing research for his employers and his evenings writing. He travels to other cities to network via conferences and talks, and he always tries to find time to meet with people from his online network as a way to add them to his real-world network.

Networking is not easy. It's hard, time-consuming work, but it's also a lot of fun. It's a great way to see your city, meet people, and develop the kinds of relationships that will lead to great opportunities.

Some of you may disagree, thinking it's enough to connect with people on the Big Three—LinkedIn, Facebook, and Twitter—but it truly isn't. Think about the people you know online and the people you know in real life. Which of them would you rather do business with? Which of them would you rather help when they asked? Chances are, it's your real-life connections and friends, not the people you have never met, who you prefer to help.

To build your personal brand, you need to network in person in a variety of situations and settings beyond the social networks.

Why Should I Bother Networking?

In Chapter 2, we discussed how to tell your personal story. But telling someone your story at a networking event doesn't mean you're now their best buddy and that you can call and ask them to do you a big favor. Far from it. They won't remember you within a few days because you were one of eight people they met, and you haven't done anything to stand out from the crowd.

That's why you need to meet people face to face and one on one, spending time together over coffee or a meal: so you can develop the deeper relationships that lead to new business opportunities, job openings, and even collaborative partnerships like writing a book together.

PERSONAL BRANDING CASE STUDY: STARLA WEST

Starla West is a corporate image coach with clients all over the United States. She has a great story about how long-term networking and relationship building have paid off for her, even after she left the industry where she built those relationships.

She's a great example of the saying, "Effective networking is all about farming, not hunting."

"The goal is to cultivate relationships and gain trust. If we network only when we have to, we're way behind the game, as the full benefits of networking are most often realized after solid relationships are developed and maintained over time," said Starla.

She explained that she "never fully understood this until I left the corporate world to pursue my entrepreneurial dreams." Prior to starting her own business, she was a consultant for various financial institutions throughout the United States. Her job was twofold: 1) help clients obtain more than their fair share of new customers (bank executives), and 2) help them keep these customers for as long as they possibly could.

To effectively assist her clients, it was crucial that West quickly gain (and maintain) the trust and support of her clients' executive teams. Day in and day out, she called upon her relationship building skills to win over these bank executives.

"Over time, these relationships eventually strengthened. At the end of my eight years as their consultant, these executives were more than just business acquaintances; they were now my friends," said Starla.

How did she know that? Well, late on a Thursday evening, she sent an email to her clients announcing she was leaving the company and starting her own business. After pressing "send", she closed her laptop, and within 30 seconds, her phone rang.

The senior vice president and director of marketing for a large client of hers in Florida was calling.

"I assumed he was calling to wish me good luck, but I couldn't have been more wrong. He was calling to share his marketing knowledge and advertising expertise with me," said Starla.

"He wanted to help catapult my business into full operation as quickly as possible by helping me develop a marketing plan. I couldn't believe it! This extremely busy man who is next to impossible to catch on the phone was graciously giving me two full hours of his time and expert advice, and I didn't even ask for it!"

Over the next 24 hours, West received phone call after phone call and email after email from clients who wanted to help her build her new business. This is when it really hit her: Networking is simply relationship building.

"If cultivated and nurtured correctly, these relationships develop into life-long friendships that include a healthy balance of giving and receiving that over time positively impact your professional growth and advancement," added Starla.

The Rules of Networking

If you understand a few basic rules and practices that guide networking, you'll always know how to behave when meeting new people. We have learned these rules over the years after being involved in various Chambers of Commerce, attending small networking groups, and being regular members of Rainmakers.[1]

It's Not About You

This may be the most important rule of networking: You're not networking to help you; you're networking to help the other person.

As counterintuitive as this may seem, this is the best way to succeed and ultimately add value to the people in your network.

This is what's known as "Giver's Gain," or the idea that by helping other people, they will want to help you in return. The philosophy was first espoused by Ivan Misner, the founder of Business Network International (BNI), a network that has grown to more than 7,915 chapters worldwide. (It was 5,400 when we published the second edition of this book in 2012.)

Basically, Giver's Gain means that if you give value to someone else, you gain goodwill. If you add enough value to other people's lives, your goodwill will be returned to you many times over. So you, as the giver, gain more goodwill by being helpful than if you were selfish and tried to keep all the opportunities to yourself.

---

1. Rainmakers (GoRainmakers.com) is a small-business networking group that started in Indianapolis in 2002. At one point, it grew to more than 1,800 people and 70 local chapters in Indiana, Kentucky, and Ohio.

In business networking terms, it means that if you focus on other people, other people will want to help you in return. (It's especially fun to watch two Giver's Gain proponents scramble to be the one to give first. Of course, this can lead to complications.)

```
@kyleplacy:  I think it's my turn to buy lunch.
@edeckers:   No, it's my turn.
@kyleplacy:  No, I insist. I want to buy lunch. I'd like to do
             something nice for you.
@edeckers:   Sounds good. I'm in the mood for a steak.
@kyleplacy:  Er, wait...
```

Let's be clear: Other people won't, or at least shouldn't, help you in exchange for your efforts. This is not a one-for-one exchange. Good networkers don't keep score; they don't tally up the number of times they have helped other people. They don't hold favors in reserve, refusing to help anyone or to even ask for small favors because they might need to "call in a favor" later. This is not a cop show where the tough-but-fair police captain "calls in a bunch of favors" to help the loose-cannon-but-gets-the-job-done cop solve a major crime.

This may sound a little odd to those who work in industries where secrets are held close to the vest, where favors are doled out like candy from a Pez dispenser, and where people keep score of the number of times they've helped someone else. To these people, the phrase "Thanks, I owe you one" is recorded in a mental notebook and kept track of.

We want you to stop thinking that way. Life is not a zero-sum game. You don't run out of opportunities to help or be helped. Believe it or not, there are enough opportunities and money to go around for everyone. But the people who fail to realize this fight and claw for every little advantage, every small sale, every victory they can claim. They end up being lonely and fall the farthest in their failures when they could have been helped by the people they used up instead. It's a sad and lonely life that would make even Ebenezer Scrooge say, "Wow, that's rough, dude."

```
@kyleplacy:  Jeez, that's depressing.
@edeckers:   Sorry, I was listening to The Cure.
```

It doesn't have to be that way. The whole point of this chapter is to tell you that your career—your whole life, in fact—can be successful without keeping score or hoarding favors. In fact, your career and your life will be more successful, enjoyable, and fulfilling if you embrace Giver's Gain.

Giver's Gain Is Not Quid Pro Quo

But this adding of value is not going to (it's not even supposed to) result in an immediate returning of the favor. It might, but don't expect it. Instead, when you provide value to other people, their goodwill can and will be returned to you in any number of ways, many of which you may not even hear about for years to come. But if you have been successful in your networking and business efforts (and thus have more influence and contacts), the favor you return is going to be even bigger than the one you were given.

Here's a hypothetical example. Let's say Erik is looking for a new speaking opportunity. He mentions this to Kyle, who just happens to know someone organizing a conference in another state. Kyle calls his friend Katherine the conference organizer, and he recommends she hire Erik for her next conference, which she does.

To some people, Erik's response is obvious: Return the favor. Find Kyle a similar speaking gig. Or give Kyle a finder's fee out of his speaking fee. But that's not how Giver's Gain works.

According to Giver's Gain, Erik's response can be anything that helps Katherine, Kyle, or another person:

- In talking to Katherine, Erik learns she is looking for a new job at a company he's familiar with. He puts her in touch with the appropriate person, and now she has an insider's edge into the company.

- He pays it forward when he meets someone at the conference who needs writing advice, so Erik spends some time answering his questions.

- Erik can bring the goodwill back around to Kyle when he meets someone who says she needs social media training for 50 customer service representatives; Erik can introduce her to Kyle, who has worked in email and social marketing. But it happens two years later.

Erik is willing to help others because he was helped. But let's take it a step further. Let's say Katherine gets the job, and in gratitude, she outsources a project to Erik, but it's one he's not really equipped to handle.

According to Giver's Gain, Katherine doesn't need to give the first project she gets back to Erik—a thank-you card or email is more than appropriate. If she does, Erik may suggest someone better suited to handle that project and introduces the two of them.

Similarly, Erik shouldn't expect an immediate favor in return for introducing a contact to Katherine. Rather, he should just go about his day and his life, knowing that someday the goodwill will be returned to him, even if it happens five years later when she recommends him to another conference organizer who needs to hire a keynote speaker at an event with a nice fat speaking fee.

In the years since we first published this book, we've seen this chain of events unfold many times, whether it was for us or for one of our friends. We've seen it unfold three, four, and five steps before the "gain" was returned to the original giver.

This is an ongoing circle of giving and receiving, and if you wait to be helped before you help someone, you'll be waiting for a long, long time. (It's like when our moms told us, "If you want to have a friend, you have to be a friend.") The best way to start practicing Giver's Gain is just to step into the circle and be the first one to give.

But, here's a twist on this: Your motivation can't even be that you're going to give so you will receive something in return. This isn't a cause-and-effect relationship. If you go to a networking event or enter into a new relationship thinking, "I'm going to really help this person because then I'll get all sorts of goodwill, and he'll do something valuable for me," you'll be disappointed.

Instead, you just help that person out because you want to add value to their life. You're a good person who understands that when others succeed with your help, you succeed as well. Here's an example.

A few years ago, Kyle met with Mark Wilkerson, vice president at a large insurance company, and gave him some tips on how to use social media to raise money for a charity run he was in charge of. This meeting turned into a relationship of breakfast meetings just to talk about "life, business, and the world of the Internet." Mark even attended one of Kyle's training sessions to learn more about how he could use social media for the charity run and his own career.

Then, without being asked, nor out of any sense of obligation, Mark introduced Kyle to a board member of a large financial services company. The board member ran a nonprofit as a sideline to his main business, and Kyle was given the opportunity to produce a social media strategy for that nonprofit, creating a long-term client in the process.

Why did this happen? It all started because Kyle was willing to meet with someone and give him some pointers about how to use social media as a charity fundraising tool. It could have ended there. Or Kyle could have refused to help. Or Mark could have paid Kyle for an hour of consulting, so he wouldn't be indebted to him.

Instead, Mark and Kyle got to know each other, talked about a lot of things that weren't related to business, and formed a connection. Kyle became someone Mark likes and trusts, and that's the key.

People buy from people they like and trust. That's an age-old adage that many salespeople are now embracing as they delve into relationship sales. But the corollary is that people will do favors for people they like and trust.

Be Honest Online and Offline

On the Internet, you can be anything you want. You can say you're a 6'4" model from Sweden even if you're really a 5'2" poster child for childhood baldness from Chicago.

But when you meet others face to face, they see who you really are. They realize you're not 6'4" and you have a decidedly non-Swedish accent. And that's when your reputation and your credibility go down the toilet. Today it's easy for people to find out your true identity. If you get caught in a lie, word will spread that you don't represent yourself truthfully.

If you want to enhance your personal brand, let your online persona be who you are in real life. If you want to kill it, lie about who you are or act like a jerk in one place, but be nice in the other.

Honesty is the key. You need to be honest about who you are, what you do, and what you think and believe. Don't try to be someone other people want you to be. Be who you really are. It sounds trite to say it; our parents said it all the time, and it sounded trite then.

But it's true: Let people accept and reject you for who you are. If others don't like you or want to connect with you, that's fine. (They don't know what they're missing; we think you're great.) But if people do like you and connect with you, you know it's because they truly like the real you.

```
@kyleplacy: Are you done, Mr. Rogers?
@edeckers:  Hey, Kyle, did you know you are special? There's no
            one in the world like you.
@kyleplacy: Cut it out.
@edeckers:  You make each day special, just by being you.
@kyleplacy: Seriously, if you start singing, I'm leaving.
```

The best way to develop your personal brand is by meeting your connections in person. Arrange a one-on-one meeting at a coffee house or over lunch and get to know each other. Remember, this is about forming relationships. Although you can form relationships online, they're rather fragile and unstable. A personal relationship can go much deeper in person, and that's where trust and liking really develop.

Tip

> We're not advocating that you hang out with anyone and everyone you meet
> online. We understand that some people aren't comfortable with this at all,
> and that women face additional challenges networking (check out Hazel
> Walker and Ivan Misner's book, *Business Networking and Sex: Not What You
> Think*). Bottom line: If you don't feel comfortable meeting someone, don't
> go. If you do meet someone you talked to online, meet in a busy public
> place, like at lunch or a coffee shop. Use common sense and be safe.

You're Just as Good as Everyone Else

You already got a dose of Mr. Rogers once, so hopefully that's still fresh in your mind
when we tell you not to be afraid to meet other people, even if you think they're
"above" you in status, popularity, or fame. You're just as good as they are. The only difference between you and them is that more people know who they are. And that's it.

There is nothing special about people you might hold in high esteem in your
industry. Sure, they may be "celebrities" in their field: They write a popular blog, are
industry experts in the media, give keynote speeches at conferences and then have
dozens of people who scramble to talk with them afterward, or they may even write
books and have book signings.

But that doesn't make them better than you. It just means they've been practicing
these personal branding techniques for a few years more than you. But now you
have this book. You know their secrets, and you can do it, too.

Think of it this way: Jay Baer is a thought leader of social media marketing. He's
written five books, one of them a *New York Times* bestseller. He gives keynote
speeches all over the country. He has more than 242,000 followers on Twitter, and
everyone talks about him like he's Elvis Presley.

But he's only Elvis to social media people. He's not actually a celebrity. When Jay walks
into Home Depot on a Saturday morning, people don't shriek, "OMG, it's Jay Baer!" No
one flocks for his autograph when he goes to his kids' baseball games. He doesn't have
screaming groupies following him around whenever his wife sends him out to buy eggs.

The people Jay meets outside the social media world couldn't care less who he is. To
them, he's just another do-it-yourselfer, proud parent, or grocery shopper, and he's
approachable inside or outside that world.

We asked Jay about this, and he said "I would rather be known in a micro-community
than in no communities. That said, it's easy (especially online) to think you're a much

bigger deal than you really are. I constantly remind myself that in the grand scheme of things, nobody cares what I do or what I've written. And anytime I forget, my friends remind me over beers!"

Avoid Selfish People

So what do you do if you help some people, but they do nothing for you? Plenty of people are selfish like that, unfortunately. As long as you can do something for them, they'll be your best buddy. But once you're done or you can't do any more, you don't hear a word from them. They don't answer your emails or return your phone calls. But when they want something from you, suddenly you're the most important person in the world to them again. How do you deal with people like that?

Short answer: Quit helping them. You might think that maybe it will be different this time. This time, they're going to connect you with that vice president of marketing you've wanted to meet or connect you to the decision maker at company X so you can pitch your idea. But they never do. And when you ask them for the favor (and ask again and again), you don't hear a word until they need your help a third time.

Just quit helping them. They're not going to change. They've gotten this far in the world without returning favors for people, so you probably won't be the one to change them. Just politely decline their requests. Don't even bother referring them to someone else who can help, because they'll just do it to the next person too.

Network with Your Competition

Some of your best referrals and connections may come from the people you consider your competition. You may work in the same general industry or even compete in the same area. But before you steer clear of that person and draw black eyes and devil horns on her photos, take a long look at what both of you do.

We learned from Tony Scelzo, the founder of Rainmakers, that two small businesses working in the same market can end up being bigger resources for each other if they focus on a specific niche, picking their niche based on the types of customers they work with.

Let's say two CPAs work with small businesses. On paper, they may compete with each other, but if they dig a little deeper, they may find they each have a particular type of customer they prefer and their own separate niches they prefer to practice in. CPA Tom likes working with professional practices, like doctors and lawyers. CPA Shauna likes working with retail businesses, like restaurants and small stores. If they discover this truth about each other, they can actually work together without ever bumping heads. In fact, they can start referring potential clients to each other.

This sounds crazy to a lot of "zero sum" thinkers who believe that Shauna and Tom should cling to every client who crosses their paths. But if they did that, Shauna and Tom would not enjoy working with all their clients and would spend too much time and energy on those clients. Ultimately, that could lose them money and even cause them to burn out. But if Shauna passes to Tom the kind of clients Tom prefers and vice versa, they each enjoy the work, and they can even make more money.

Another benefit from this matchup is that now each CPA has someone else selling for them. Not only is Shauna looking for restaurants and stores for her clients, Tom is looking on her behalf as well. Any time Tom gets a call from a restaurant or small retail shop, he says, "I'm sorry, I don't handle that kind of work, but let me tell you about my good friend, Shauna. She specializes in operations like yours and does a much better job."

That's not to say that Tom is out beating the bushes, trying to find clients for Shauna at the expense of his own business. But Tom is prepared to sing Shauna's praises to anyone who fits the description of Shauna's ideal client. Although this trade-off will not work for every situation, we know plenty of people who have adopted this strategy with great success.

Our friend Douglas Karr owns an Internet marketing agency, DK New Media, handling six-figure projects for large corporate clients. When he started his company, he was taking on every project he could find. Doug says he was working 16–20 hours a day trying to meet deadlines, and he was not always successful.

Doug decided he wasn't going to do certain kinds of projects anymore. He passed that work off to one of his competitors who actually liked doing the projects that Doug didn't, and Doug never asked anything in return. Now Doug works fewer hours per day, meets his deadlines easily, and is actually making more money because he can take on big projects and ignore the small, time-consuming ones.

Imagine if you had a small group of people, all in cooperative businesses—say, a wedding planner, a florist, a cake decorator, and a caterer—and all working for each other as referrals. Whenever the wedding planner gets a client, she knows exactly whom to recommend as a florist, a baker, and a caterer. Similarly, whenever the caterer gets a wedding client, he can recommend the planner, florist, and baker in his little group.

Now, if you work for a large corporation or a small business in a highly competitive industry, this approach may not be possible or even allowed. You need to make those decisions yourself and abide by your company's policies. But if you ever have the chance to share work and opportunities with your so-called "competition," try it and see what happens. At the worst, you won't get an opportunity that actually aligns with your goals and preferences. But ideally, you will get an ally in your field and an extra pair of eyes to help you find the opportunities you want.

Of course, to do anything we've talked about, you actually have to meet those people. So let's talk about how you do that.

PERSONAL BRANDING CASE STUDY:
HAZEL WALKER

When it comes to networking, we both owe a lot to our friend and mentor Hazel Walker. From the first time we met her and she told us not to wear blue jeans to give presentations, and that she hated using PowerPoint, we've listened closely to what she tells us. Even if we ignored her about the jeans.

Hazel is best known for her work with Business Network International (BNI), the organization responsible for "Giver's Gain." She started her own chapter in Indianapolis in 1991, and seven years later, became an assistant director and bought the Central Indiana BNI franchise. She ran and managed the different BNI meetings that happened throughout Central Indiana, provided training, and became one of the city's leading experts on business networking.

Today, Hazel is the National Training Director and Franchise Development Director for BNI Australia, living and working seven months each year in Perth; she spends the other five months in Indianapolis. She has also been published in more than a dozen books and is the author of *Business Networking and Sex: Not What You Think*.

"Networking has opened the world to me," said Hazel. "I grew up in a small town and never considered getting on a plane to travel anywhere."

But now, Hazel literally has a global network at her fingertips. "I have always been able to turn to my network anytime I need anything at all. I can post on Facebook for help or pick up the phone and call anyone."

Another key component of her networking has been social media. She started in the same place we did: the Smaller Indiana local network. It connected her to her local community, which let her build relationships with people in Indianapolis, both online and face to face at local events.

Ultimately, all her networking led to speaking events, which led to writing opportunities, more speaking events (she's spoken in 17 different countries), and to her current position in Australia.

"That's a big deal for a small town girl who never bothered to go to college," said Hazel.

Hazel prefers to do her networking face to face, because she likes meeting new people. She enjoys getting to know who they are in real life, while social media only lets her see a one-dimensional version of the person. However, she relies strongly on social media to keep up with her network, her family, and her friends. It helps her keep lines of communication open, as well as tells her what's going on in her own hometown and her country.

When she first started, LinkedIn and Twitter were her two biggest tools. But now she's primarily on Twitter and Facebook. She'll even conduct coaching and training sessions via Facebook Messenger. And she's an avid blogger, calling it one of the best tools to help her build her brand.

"I've gotten several of my best clients via interactions on Facebook and another dozen from my blogs," said Hazel. "I maintain two of them, HazelWalker.com and BlogBNI.com. I would be wealthy if I were consistent at my blogging!"

When asked about her one piece of advice for people starting out, she said, "Social media allows us to live a global life today. I can have conversations with my network all over the world; 20 years ago that was not the case."

"Technology has changed the way we connect and do business, so I get the opportunity to meet clients, prospects, and referral sources from all over the world. It's through this network that I have been able live in a distant country and get speaking engagements internationally," she added.

Not too bad for someone who never wears blue jeans during a presentation. Maybe we should start dressing up more.

Three Types of Networking

You should focus on three phases of networking as you grow your personal brand: 1) networking groups, 2) one-on-one networking, and 3) the follow-up. These three networking phases are not separate styles or techniques. Rather, they're all stages of the same process. Most likely, you will meet people in a group setting before moving on to the second and third stages of networking.

We've been talking about being a resource to your online contacts and how it's possible to form some good networking relationships with your LinkedIn connections and Twitter followers. This advice is not meant to contradict that. Instead, sometimes you'll need to develop deeper relationships with certain influencers in your network (or even to add new influencers).

Be sure you're still using the principles we told you about in the other chapters. But when you identify somebody you think would be especially valuable to know, follow these strategies:

Networking Groups

The most common form of networking for professionals is the group networking event. This may be a group strictly dedicated to networking, like Rainmakers or a Chamber of Commerce "Business After Hours" event or national organizations like the National Association for Women Business Owners (NAWBO) and Network After Work. Or you might attend an after-hours mixer at an industry conference or have a chance meeting at a trade show or expo.

Regardless of where group networking occurs, if you are at a place where a lot of people have gathered for the sole purpose of making business connections with the other people in the room, you need to be ready for it.

In many ways, this stage is the most stressful of all networking opportunities because you may not know many people in the group, and you're looking for a friendly face. But instead of sticking to the walls or talking with your friends, now is your chance to strike out on your own and meet someone new.

Meeting New People

This is the hardest part for a lot of people who consider themselves introverts and would rather be at home in front of the TV than out in public meeting a bunch of new people.

You may even feel that way yourself, but making new contacts is important to grow your personal brand. So let's test something: Hold this book in your left hand, and stick out your right hand. Say, "Hello, my name is _____," and then say your name.

Did that work? Were you able to do it without getting light-headed or throwing up? Great. You're all set.

We understand, group networking is stressful for many of you, especially if you're shy. You're probably too intimidated to walk up and just blurt out your name in a room packed with strangers. That's understandable. The fear of public speaking is the same fear as meeting new people in large group settings: it's fear of rejection, being laughed at, or judged.

But you need to suck it up, just for a little while. We promise nothing bad will happen. It's perfectly acceptable to walk up to someone you've never met, introduce yourself (use that handy phrase, "Hello, my name is _____," we just practiced), and just start a conversation.

Don't be a wallflower. Talk to the people you don't know, not those you do. Maybe you can start out the meeting talking with someone you know as a warm-up, but you'll need to move on to new people. Join a conversation already taking place between someone you know and someone you don't know. Get introduced to the new person, using your acquaintance as the warm-up to meeting someone new.

The Networking Dance

Here's typically what happens at a networking group—something Erik likes to call the networking dance. Let's say Kyle and Erik are talking to each other. A third person, Lorraine, walks up and introduces herself. She starts talking to them, and as it usually happens, she subtly, subconsciously, engages one of us—Kyle—a little more. You can actually see Kyle and Lorraine square off a little more, leaving Erik as an observer.

Next, Hazel walks up to the trio, notices Erik is not actually engaged in the conversation, and starts talking with him. Now we have two new conversations instead of one, like an amoeba splitting. There may even be some subtle distancing of the two pairs as they continue to talk.

After a few minutes, Doug walks up to Lorraine and Kyle and engages them in conversation. Lorraine and Doug eventually square off to face each other, leaving Kyle as the lonely onlooker, but he is soon rescued by Bruce.

This whole process continues for as long as the networking portion of the meeting goes. We've both been in situations like this where the networking dance will take us to the other side of the room within an hour.

What Should You Say?

Figuring out what to say can be difficult. The question, "So, what do you do?" is used over and over at business networking events, but it can get you only so far. You'll probably run out of things to say about your job, so ask these other questions, too:

- What do you do when you're not working?
- What made you get into this field?
- How long have you worked in your industry?
- Really? And you still have all your fingers?
- Where did you work before this job?
- What do you want to be doing in five years?
- Where did you grow up?
- What are you reading right now?
- Who are some of your business influencers?

After that, you need to listen. Don't talk, and don't answer your own question. Let the other person do most of the talking. And if you're one of our shy, introverted types, this is perfect for you! You just have to ask a few questions, then listen to the answers for several minutes.

If you want to make others feel appreciated and happy with the conversation, let them talk about themselves. If they feel appreciated, they're more likely to want to meet with you later.

A common problem you might have when meeting others is feeling like you need to carry the conversation. You might pour out everything about yourself, unloading as much as possible, hoping some of it will stick. And if you've done all the talking, you may come away feeling like you were heard, but the other people won't feel that way; and you may not get another chance to connect with them later. So let them talk more, and see if you find them interesting enough to do it again.

As you're talking about what you do, where you work, who you know in common, and what knowledge you want to share, you may decide this is someone you want to get to know better. Now is not the time to start to make this person your friend or form a strategic partnership. You only need to connect enough so they're willing to meet with you later for coffee or lunch.

Just say, "I've really enjoyed talking with you. Would you be willing to meet later so we can discuss this further?" If the other person says "yes," don't even propose a time (unless you can schedule it on your phones right there). Just offer to email or call later and set it up then. Make sure you get your new acquaintance's business card (or contact info) and email or call within 24 hours.

Finally, help your new contact meet other people. When that inevitable third person comes up to your little duo, introduce each other. To show that you have really been listening, explain what it is the first person does, and then ask the new arrival what they do. If it turns out the two work in businesses that have an obvious fit—one is a graphic designer, the other works at an advertising agency, or one person is an IT repair specialist, and the other is in charge of a school's computer lab—make sure they make the connection.

Continue talking to your two new friends for as long as you can all manage the conversation, but be prepared for the inevitable fourth person to complete the split. If the other two are making a great connection, take one for the team and connect with the new person yourself, leaving the other two to continue.

Networking Faux Pas

If you're introducing yourself, listening to others, and being pleasant, it's hard to make too many mistakes at a networking event. However, you should never do these three things, even though people do them over and over and they're never effective.

Don't Deal Your Own Cards

Some people think networking means passing out as many cards as they can. They whip their cards out like they're a Vegas blackjack dealer, equating the number of cards received with the number of contacts they have made. Some "card dealers" even count the number of cards they gave out, as if this is some score that will predict their success.

"I gave out 20 cards today," they boast. "And I got 18 in return." They repeat the process over and over, thinking they're making progress in their networking, before finally giving up on networking altogether, declaring it stupid and ineffective.

We have seen these people operate, and we can honestly say that we have never connected with any of them after a single event. We might find their cards a few weeks later and try to remember who they are or where we met them, but try as we might, their identity is a complete mystery. More often than not, their card just gets recycled.

The problem for card dealers is that if no one can remember who they are, no one will ever know if they need their services. If you ever need a computer repaired, you're not going to call the guy who shot you his card, then darted off in search of another hapless victim.

Don't Use Clever Elevator Pitches

It's a real pet peeve of ours to hear generic elevator pitches given by people who were trained by sales coaches who don't seem to understand personal branding and marketing.

"Your elevator pitch should get people to ask questions about what you do," they coach.

This flies in the face of everything we've talked about and everything we ever tell people about personal branding. Your brand, wherever people find it, should tell people immediately what you do, not make them guess or ask questions.

When we first met, we were at a small-business marketing seminar where we were broken up into small groups with another friend. She ran a custom embroidery business and had a machine that could embroider anything. We were told to come up with our opening statement of our elevator pitch, our "hook."

"We help make your company more memorable," said our friend.

"We all do. Even the guys who wave signs on sidewalks make companies more memorable," we said. This annoyed her.

"But it makes people ask questions."

"Maybe," we said, "but if you only have 30 seconds to talk to that person, do you want to waste time answering 'What does that mean?'"

"Fine, what would you say?!" she said. She was really annoyed.

"What's the weirdest thing you've ever embroidered?"

"Well, I embroidered on a roll of toilet paper once to show it could be done." Okay, that was pretty cool—now we're getting somewhere.

"Then you should say, 'I can embroider any design on any medium. I even embroidered on a roll of toilet paper once.'"

When we returned to the full class discussion and shared our opening statements, our friend's was so surprising that even the seminar leader stopped what she was doing to ask some questions.

Elevator pitches that are designed to be clever only waste time and lump you in with everyone else who "makes your company more memorable."

We're not actually telling you to drop your elevator pitch; just don't try to be clever. State up front what it is that you do. That way, any questions you're asked are follow-up questions, not clarification requests.

"We provide accounting services to doctors and lawyers" tells people a lot more than "We keep your company from seeing red."

(Our favorite vague elevator pitch was "We take the 'SH' out of IT." Anyone who has ever dealt with computers understood immediately what that person did.) So that means it sounds more clever than vague. Not sure this example totally serves your purpose. But it is awesome.

Figure out what it is that you do, what niche you serve, and figure out your hook. That way, when you're talking with people, your time is spent talking about how you can help the other person, not helping them decipher the super-secret cleverness of a 10-second mystery.

Don't Sign People Up for Your Newsletter

Email newsletters are supposed to be opt-in. That is, readers choose to subscribe to your newsletter, usually on your website. That grants you permission to send them your newsletter.

Handing you a business card does not grant you that permission. It grants you permission to contact that person in the future, say, for coffee or to ask a question. It does not mean he wants your weekly newsletter. That's overly presumptuous, and more than a little tacky.

After the Meeting

Follow up with people you've met within 24 hours. An email usually suffices, but give it a personal touch rather than sending a generic message. Mention something you talked about, send them any information you promised, and ask about meeting at a future date.

We can't count the number of emails we've received from people we aren't even sure we met, asking us to get in touch with them if we ever need whatever it is they do. Just like your networking goal is not to meet as many people as you can, your follow-up goal is not to email as many people as you can. Just email those you have actually talked to and connected with.

Follow-up is especially important if you have agreed to get together during the group event. Don't wait for others to follow up; take the first step. Propose a time and day that is convenient for you, and see if it's convenient for them too. After you settle on that time, you're ready for a one-on-one meeting.

One-on-One Networking

One-on-one, face-to-face, IRL (in real life), whatever you call them, these real-world meetings are where the actual networking and relationship building happen. You're not going to build a relationship at a networking event; you're going to do it sitting across from each other, over coffee or food. That's one of the great things about the increased popularity of coffee shops: they're nearly everywhere, and they give you a place to sit for a while, get to know each other, and then go on your way, all for the price of a latte.

And while we're on the subject, try to support your local coffee shops and restaurants whenever you can. Anywhere from 40–78 percent of the money you spend at a local establishment stays in your local economy; when you spend money at national merchants, only 14–30 percent stays local.[2]

How to Set Up the One-On-One Networking Meeting

Setting up one-on-one meetings with someone you recently met is pretty easy. Just send a note, including reminders of how you met, what you talked about, and why you want to meet, to ask to get together, like this:

> Erik,
>
> I enjoyed meeting you at the Chamber of Commerce Business After Hours event on Tuesday and talking about blogging. I was wondering if you would be free for coffee next week because I wanted to talk about blogging as a marketing tool. I have been blogging for my own personal enjoyment, but I wanted to meet with you to discuss some ideas I had for a possible

---

2. https://ilsr.org/key-studies-why-local-matters/

blog dedicated to reviews of hamburgers at independent restaurants. How does your schedule look over the next two weeks? Mornings before 10 are usually good for me.

Thanks,

Dick

The message can even work as a script for a phone call; just use the same ideas and main points when calling.

You can use a similar approach when trying to meet with someone you've only been referred to by someone else.

Kyle,

I was referred to you by Erik Deckers, who said you would be interested in learning about a bottled water service at your office. Erik mentioned that you moved to a new location a couple of months ago.

I am free to meet Monday, Wednesday, or Friday next week, any time between 1:00 and 4:30. I can meet at your office, or we can get coffee at the coffee house nearby. I'll call you in a couple of days to follow up.

Thanks,

Larry Smith

Again, this email has everything Kyle needs to know about whether to meet with Larry: how Larry knows about Kyle, what he wants to talk about, and when and where they could meet.

@kyleplacy: Yeah, I haven't forgotten about that guy either. I ended up with an 18-month plan before he left, and I don't even like bottled water.

@edeckers: Me?! You're the one who gave that vacuum salesman my name last fall. I had to buy one just to get him to leave.

What to Talk About

Social media can help with this part of relationship building. Think about what it's like when you meet people for the first time. You usually talk about where they live, what they do for a living, what their family is like, where they went to school, and so on.

With social media, you can find out this sort of thing without wasting valuable one-on-one time. Maybe you discover you went to the same university but never met on campus. Maybe you find out they grew up in a place where your dad worked when he was younger.

Social media lets you make these kinds of discoveries without spending time talking about them. That way when you get together, you can dig deeper into those topics rather than only finding them out for the first time during your one-on-one meeting, or worse yet, never finding them out at all. Several times we've found interesting connections about a new friend through Facebook, Twitter, or a blog.

Don't be afraid to talk about your personal life with others. We're blurring the lines between personal and professional lives all the time in our society. It's fairly safe to assume that the people you meet with in a business setting have a personal life as well. No one gets put back into a locker at 5 p.m. and pulled back out the next morning.

Remember, your goal in networking is to find connections you can trust and respect. How can you trust and respect others when you don't know anything about them?

We're not saying you have to be involved in every part of their lives, but we think it's okay to ask about their family, what they like to do for fun, and what their hobbies are. Get to know them on a personal level, and you can be a trusted resource for them, and they can be one for you in return. (Keep in mind, this advice is geared more toward a North American audience. Some cultures might view these questions as intrusive. So wherever you may be in the world, be sure to ask questions that are appropriate to your society and culture.)

When you and your acquaintances are talking, listen carefully to what they're saying. Ask them questions about how they're trying to achieve their goals, who they want to meet to make those happen, and if there is anything you can do to help them.

This last question is an important one; not only does it let others know you want to help them succeed, it helps you add value to their lives. Remember, adding value to others' lives will earn you goodwill that will eventually return to you in terms of new opportunities and new connections.

Finally, depending on how well you connected and the feeling you get from the meeting, you should try to get a commitment to do it again. All you really need at this point is a "Would it be all right if we met again?" kind of commitment, although if you can get more, go ahead. When you get the okay, follow up in a month or so and set up your next one-on-one meeting. Use that time to build on what you've already learned, and help your relationship go forward from there.

No One Wants a Sales Pitch

We talked earlier about not turning an entire conversation at a networking meeting into a sales pitch. The same is true for the one-on-one meeting. In fact, it's even more important. Both of us have sat through our share of one-on-one sales pitches for whatever product or service others were selling.

What is especially frustrating about these meetings is that not only do you not get to know the other person, you missed out on a chance to talk about yourself and your goals. And wasted an hour of your time to boot.

Although we have said it's more important to let others do most of the talking, you do need to have some time where you get to share a little about yourself. After all, we all like to feel heard and appreciated. And listening to a 60-minute pitch about life insurance or a multilevel marketing plan is not the place where you're likely to get that chance.

So be respectful of others' needs and goals for one-on-one meetings, and respect their time. Go beyond what's fair, and let them do most of the talking. Ask questions and listen to the answers. And if they don't leave time to share your story, you'll have to decide whether you want to try again later.

The "Pick-Your-Brain" Meeting

Oftentimes, as you network and learn more about your industry, you should ask others if you can pick their brain about their knowledge of a certain topic. As you grow in your expertise, you will find more people are asking if they can pick your brain.

We advise that you ask as often as you can, for a few reasons. When you're the "picker:"

- You get a lot of valuable information from experts. They have learned their lessons and the pitfalls, and found the best and worst ways to do things, usually the hard way. This helps you grow faster because you are learning which obstacles to avoid.

- Others will feel listened to, valued, and appreciated. This is a good way to form relationships and bonds.

- Others recommend other people you should meet. They may have access to people you would never meet otherwise because they don't go to networking events or move in the same circles you do.

- You may find a mentor to guide you, give you advice, and help you move up your career ladder.

- You should buy lunch or coffee because these people are giving you valuable information; you should show your appreciation by paying.

As you progress in your career, newbies and neophytes will ask if they can pick your brain. When that happens, agree to be the "pickee" because:

- Remember Giver's Gain? This is your chance to continue the cycle of adding value to people's lives, as homage to the people who added value to yours. You can especially be helpful if you can connect someone you're helping to someone who helped you.

- It will help grow your personal brand. The more people you can demonstrate your expertise to, the more people you'll have telling their friends and colleagues about what you know. Both of us have gotten clients and speaking opportunities from doing this.

- You never know where others you help will end up. They may be unfamiliar with your area of expertise, but that doesn't mean they're complete neophytes at everything. They may actually be VPs of companies you would like to work for or could become VPs shortly. They may be presidents of trade associations in a field you want to work in or whose conferences you want to speak at.

Remember Mark, Kyle's VP of a large insurance firm? He only wanted some social media pointers for a charity race he organized. Now, what if he had approached Kyle in that role—"I organize a charity race each year, and I wanted to pick your brain on how we can use social media to promote it"—and Kyle had turned him down, not knowing the man's day job or who else he knew? Kyle would have lost out on the opportunity to get to know someone who turned out to be a valuable resource.

The one problem with being asked over and over to "brain-picking meetings" is that you could spend all day, every day, doing it, drinking latte after latte, and never getting any work done.

As much as we don't like to admit it, plenty of people don't believe in Giver's Gain. After they've gotten your information and paid for your coffee, you won't hear from them again. Just let those people go.

You may also become so wildly successful that you don't have time to meet with people who are just starting out and run through basic how-to information for them. That's understandable, but remember where you were just a few years ago; think about the people you asked for help and advice.

Try to avoid getting such a big head that you refuse to ever meet with people. We've encountered people like this, and frankly, they come off as arrogant and cocky. They've forgotten what (and who) made them successful, and they think they're too important to help others.

However, we also understand that it's not always possible to meet with someone when you're pursuing your own goals. But that doesn't mean you're too important to help anyone. When you reach this stage in your career, you can do the following things:

- Limit your brain-picking meetings to one or two a week, early in the morning—6:30 a.m. is not out of the question if you can get yourself out of bed. Scheduling meetings this early will weed out the people who aren't serious about learning from you.

- Figure out what your time is worth per hour, and charge that as a consulting fee. Keep in mind that this is not appropriate in all cases, like if you work for a government agency. Also, keep in mind that people who approach you may be asking for personal advice, and there's something unseemly about charging for that. But it is entirely appropriate to charge a fee if a business wants advice. We've both struggled with this advice, and there's no easy answer. Ultimately it comes down to whatever you're comfortable with.

- Tell others you don't have time to meet with them for a few months but you would be happy to refer them to someone else who can help them. Then refer them to someone who isn't as far along in their career growth as you are. This adds value to the person who originally wanted the meeting, and the person you referred them to.

Under no circumstances should you ask what value the other person can offer you to determine whether they should meet with you. It's elitist and comes off as arrogant, as if you're not going to speak with anyone who can't help you immediately.

Erik once asked a former professional football player if he could meet for coffee. The player emailed back saying he wasn't sure he would meet unless Erik could show what sort of value he could bring to the player. Erik had already hired the player to speak at a networking event, and he knew other conference organizers who would have been interested in hiring the player to speak at their events. Erik was so put off, he never responded, and the player missed out on a number of possible paid speaking opportunities.

How to Make an Email Introduction

When it comes to meeting new people, there's a certain etiquette to the process. A warm introduction—that is, an introduction between you and another person to a third person—will always yield better results than you calling someone out of the blue and mentioning a random friend's name.

That is, "Erik, meet Sheryl" will always do better than "Hi Sheryl, Kyle said I should call you."

When you introduce two people at a networking event, you get to explain why you want two people to meet. You can describe what each of them does (if nothing else, that shows you've been paying attention), and why this is a good connection for them both. Then you can listen to their conversation and watch something cool unfold.

If you can't do that in person, you should do it via email. But like everything else, there's a right way and a wrong way to do it. The wrong way is this: "Sheryl, meet Erik. Erik, meet Sheryl. You two should chat." This does nothing to explain why Erik and Sheryl should meet.

A proper email introduction should look something like this, instead:

Introduce Person A to Person B, and explain who Person A is. Be sure to mention how you know her. Introduce Person B to Person A, and explain who Person B is. Mention how you know him, too. Then, give a bit of background. Why did you make this connection? Make a recommendation. What do you hope will happen out of this? Are there any miscellaneous connections or tidbits they should know about? Then, close it up.

Here's an example:

Tonia, meet Brad Fotheringay [pronounced "Fanshaw"]. Brad is a freelance graphic designer I've known for the past several years. I first met Brad when we were working on a team logo for the professional bass fishing team the Wawasee Whales, and we've worked on several projects since then.

Brad, meet Tonia Hebert. Tonia owns a French bakery downtown, Let's Go Croiss-ay, specializing in crepes and croissants. We met at a networking event a couple weeks ago, then had a chance to go out for coffee this morning.

When we were talking, Tonia mentioned she was looking for a new logo as part of a larger rebranding effort for her bakery. I immediately thought of you, Brad. Tonia, he's not only a graphic designer, but has led several rebranding efforts for other baked goods brands.

By the way, I think you were both at the digital marketing conference last month, but I don't know if you met each other. Both of you were at my keynote speech, but since it was a packed house with 3,000 people, I doubt you had a chance to meet, especially once that Prince cover band had me come on and sing "Purple Rain" with them.

Anyway, I'm hoping you two have a chance to meet for coffee in the next couple of weeks and talk about some ways you could help each other. Have a good weekend.

Erik

That's how a proper email introduction is done. If you can do that for people, it will go a long way to building relationships with people, especially if you've only met them once or twice. But if you can make these kinds of solid, beneficial connections, this is the sort of Giver's Gain karma we were discussing earlier.

The Follow-Up

The follow-up is where you make or break your networking efforts. You should come away from every meeting with some sort of action you need to take, even if it's a simple thank-you email or note to send.

Follow-up is necessary, whether it's someone you met one on one or someone you talked with at a networking event for any length of time. (Unless you still have the nasty habit of being a "card dealer" and whipping out as many cards as possible. Then, don't bother.)

Forwarding Articles and Links

Forwarding articles and links is one of the easiest, yet least used, ways of building a relationship with another person. Read blogs and online magazines about your industry and the industries of the people you're meeting.

Be on the lookout for areas of overlap where you may have something in common with another person. This is hopefully why you're trying to get together in the first place. If you find something new or interesting, forward your new friend the link to the website or blog post or send the entire article. Most online articles now have some sort of "Share" link you can use. Be sure to send a personal message, like: "This sounds a lot like what we were talking about a couple weeks ago over coffee."

If you're really on the ball, you can even keep track of the discussions and articles you send in your meeting notes or calendar and use it as part of your discussion the next time you meet.

If you run across a print article, take the time to clip it and mail it with a handwritten note. As uncommon as personal letters are these days, your efforts will stand out as memorable and thoughtful. It will also show the other person that you're truly interested in getting to know him better.

Or if you really want to make an impression, go old school! Erik owns two refurbished typewriters, and had some personalized half-page stationery printed. He'll type out notes that he mails to contacts for a truly memorable follow-up.

Sharing Opportunities

One of the things we both like to do for friends who are looking for jobs, grants, or RFPs (request for proposals) is forward the opportunities we find. Whether it's a job listing in a newsletter or a note from another friend looking to hire someone, we keep our eyes and ears open for any opportunities that we can pass on to people we know.

We're also proactive about recommending people to hiring companies before candidates even apply. An unsolicited letter of recommendation can put a potential candidate at the top of a pile of résumés, especially when the person we're writing to already trusts us. We've both helped people find jobs this way, which adds to our personal brand of being connectors, which can create new opportunities for us.

Making Connections

One of the best ways to help your friends is by introducing them to someone else. If you're in any kind of sales position, you know the pain and heartache of cold-calling potential customers. That's why salespeople always appreciate an introduction (also called a referral) to other people.

Let's say Kyle wants to meet Tom, and Tom is Erik's friend. In a proper referral, Erik can do as follows:

- Call Tom, tell him about Kyle, and ask him to expect Kyle's call.

- Arrange a meeting for the three of them so that Kyle and Tom can get to know each other.

- Make sure Kyle and Tom are at the same event, introduce the two of them, and explain why Tom should be interested in talking to Kyle.

But a referral is not simply saying, "You should give Tom a call. Here's his number."

A referral lends credibility to the person who needs it (Kyle) because it's coming from someone the other person trusts (Erik). In essence, Erik is counting on Tom's trust of him to carry some weight when he suggests that Tom should meet with Kyle.

You can email this introduction to both parties (we discussed how that should look earlier in this chapter), or you can call the other person (Tom) and let them know your friend (Kyle) is going to call.

But it would be a bad referral if Erik just gave Tom's number to Kyle and said, "You ought to call him." That's still a cold call, and it doesn't help. It doesn't help Kyle to say, "Erik said I ought to call you." Dropping Erik's name during a cold call might give him an advantage over not mentioning Erik's name at all, but not by much.

Other times, Tom might be suspicious and wonder whether Kyle was even telling the truth.

So if you have a chance to make a referral, do it. If someone offers you a referral, ask for an email introduction. Or ask them to call the other person first and then let you know when it's done.

But I Just Don't Want to Meet the Other Person

Sometimes you just don't have anything in common with someone who wants to connect with you. Or you know she just wants to sell you something and isn't actually interested in a real connection. There's nothing wrong with this person, but maybe she doesn't fit into your plans or goals, and you aren't interested in the connection. What should you do?

Be Honest

So how do you say no to someone like this without hurting feelings? Honesty is usually the best approach.

"I'm sorry. I'm not really interested in that at the moment," is usually the best thing to say. If they persist, be firm.

Sales training teaches people to be persistent, so don't be surprised if she calls you back again and again. If she does, you have a few options for making her stop such as

- Avoid her calls, never return her calls, and hope she goes away. (We don't recommend this, but it's a common practice for some people.)

- Tell her you'll never be interested and she can save time and energy by not calling. Try to be very gentle if you do this. The other person is still a human being with feelings.

- Meet with her anyway (make her buy the coffee), listen to her pitch, and say no again.

- Ask her for a return favor: You'd like a separate hour to tell her about your product or service.

- Ask her for a bigger favor, like introducing you to the decision maker in her organization so you can sell your product or service.

Some of these suggestions may seem a little silly or flippant, but sometimes they're the best options to avoid wasting time on a connection you're not interested in making.

What if the Other Person Isn't Honest?

What if the other person lied about wanting to meet you? Erik was once asked by a sales associate for a well-known insurance company if he would like to meet so they could "get to know each other better." Erik had met with different associates on several other occasions and usually spent more than three-quarters of the time listening to the sales pitch every time.

"All right, I'll meet with you," said Erik, "but I've been pitched at least four other times by people from your company, and I'm not interested. But if you would like to meet just to get to know each other, that's fine."

The other person agreed, and the two met for coffee. That's when the other person pulled out a questionnaire and began to ask Erik the questions on it, so he could "put together a quote on a life insurance plan for you."

Erik was rather annoyed by the presumption. If he had been a more direct person, he would have reminded the other guy he had specifically said he wasn't interested in the product and left. But Erik also didn't want to make the other person feel bad—the guy was still new to networking and may not have known the protocol. So Erik did the only thing he felt he could: he lied about his answers.

@kyleplacy: Are you serious? That's pretty passive-aggressive of you.

@edeckers: You think so? I could give the guy your number and you could meet to discuss it with him.

@kyleplacy: No, that's okay.

This won't happen very often, and there's no one right way to respond to someone like this. Should you storm out in a fit of righteous indignation because the guy lied? Should you sit quietly and secretly fantasize about the other's demise? Should you say you were under the impression that you weren't going to get a sales pitch and attempt a real conversation instead?

Although we lean more toward the last option, your reaction is up to you. Just remember: Even reactions in situations like this can have an effect on your personal brand. If you're rude, word will get around that you're the kind of person who yells at people you meet with. Justified or not, this would become part of your reputation and something people may have in the backs of their minds when you ask to meet with them.

PERSONAL BRANDING CASE STUDY:
DAVE DELANEY

Dave Delaney loves talking with people. And he loves social media, because it lets him talk to people from all over the world, which has led to some amazing new opportunities. In fact, he loves connecting with people so much, he's made it his full-time job.

Whether it's as a keynote speaker, a digital marketing consultant, or as the founder of "Networking For Nice People," an online community and an email newsletter, Dave is known throughout North America as a master networker, and all-around nice guy—he's a Canadian living in Nashville. He's also the author of *New Business Networking*.

Dave spends most of his social media time on LinkedIn, but prefers in-person networking.

"Nothing beats hugs, handshakes, and high-fives," he said.

Still, he uses LinkedIn to boost his in-person networking because it makes researching people and companies so much easier, as well as helping him to make stronger connections with people.

"The connections feature is amazing, because you can find people you know who know the people you want to meet," said Dave. "They can provide you with the introduction you need to get through the door."

As part of his work, Dave provides companies with in-person training on how best to use LinkedIn to close deals with existing clients and to find new clients. He also works with individuals on how to use LinkedIn in a job search or even for their sales efforts.

Dave said the biggest mistake people make is thinking LinkedIn is only an online résumé, when there's so much more value in the network than that. But many managers believe this and think LinkedIn updates mean their staff is jumping ship.

"They should reward their sales staff for being smart about how they're networking their way to new business," said Dave.

More recently, Dave built Networking For Nice People. He said it's for anyone who "wishes to improve their business and jumpstart their career using networking, nicely."

When asked about his one piece of advice for you, our reader, Dave said, "treat others how you wish to be treated. Provide value to the people you meet and the rewards will come. Never help people expecting something in return."

Network While You Still Have a Job

As the saying goes, the best time to start looking for your next job is when you still have one. Even if you plan to be at your current job for several years, you need build a network that can bail you out if you're suddenly and unexpectedly looking for a job.

You should attend professional development groups and events, and attend networking functions, to meet people in allied industries and around your city. If you're meeting with the right people, it will help you to do your job better, anyway. But it's also laying the groundwork for a large network of influential people who are connected to other influential people.

So network with people outside your company as much as you can. Nothing is worse than starting a new job search by looking at your network and realizing the only people you know are at your old company. (That was Erik's problem in the opening story of Chapter 1.)

Don't Discount Serendipity

One thing we've both learned through networking and being open to meeting so many people is the power of serendipity, the occurrence of seemingly random events that happen in a beneficial way.

For example, Erik was working at a packed coffee shop when a man and a woman were looking for a place to sit. Erik invited them to sit at his table and said he would ignore them so they could have their conversation. Instead, the three of them talked about personal finance and writing—their respective fields—for an hour.

Several weeks later, Erik and the other guy met for lunch. While they were talking, the guy mentioned a client he had just finished meeting with, so he texted him and asked him to join them for lunch. The third man owned a company that developed an artificial intelligence tool for online marketing. They spoke briefly, and Erik and the AI developer met for coffee a couple weeks later.

Erik introduced the AI developer to John Wall, one half of the Marketing Over Coffee podcast (one of the case studies in "Chapter 8: Other Social Networking Tools."). He suggested John invite the developer onto his podcast as a possible interview guest.

All of that happened because Erik invited a couple of strangers to join him at his table in a coffee shop one afternoon.

And that's the power of serendipity. You never know which conversation or connection is going to lead to a long chain of events that ends up in something interesting or amazing happening for you or someone else.

It's never going to happen if you don't network, though. The more people you talk to, the more connections you make with people, the more relationships you develop, the more likely some of these amazing connections are going to happen in your own life.

Do's and Don'ts of Networking

The Twitterverse shared with us their best networking advice. What's cool about this list is that, with a couple of exceptions, we have met with all of these people face to face and one on one. The fact that the list turned out this way makes us think that our extra time spent with them helped them want to answer the questions.

Do

- Listen and ask questions. And say the person's name three times in your head so you remember them next time. —@courtenayrogers

- If you forget someone's name, admit it. —@jaybaer

- Design biz cards to include on back: It was a pleasure meeting you! Event___ Date___ It helps people to remember who they met, and it helps me to keep track, too! —@CourtneySampson

- Put your face on your blog/biz card so that people remember who you were later. Had someone in Paris say they knew me from my pic online. —@DouglasKarr

- Do give a firm, assertive handshake when meeting people. And yes, this goes for females, too. Pet peeve: Weak handshakes. —@BeckyAPR

- How about social media tool "Meetup" in terms of how it gets people face to face based on interests etc.? It's tech & old school synergy! —@NRWHenning

- Put down the gadget. —@JasonFalls

- Always phrase your work in terms of a solution for your client. Find their pain points and brand yourself as a problem solver. —@y0mbo

- When you're planning a face-to-face meet, find a nonthreatening locale (coffee shop, bookstore, etc.) that facilitates open conversation. —@joeystrawn

- Ask more than you answer. —@JasonFalls

- Network while still employed! One of the more common regrets I hear. —RosserJobs

- Breakfast networking beats cocktails networking—you'll remember more. —@jaybaer

- Follow-up if you say you will. —@NickiLaycoax
- Tactical tip. If meeting goes well, schedule your next meeting before leaving. Always write a personal thank-you note. —@TrustHomeSense
- Always buy the drinks. —@jaybaer
- Maintain eye contact. Nothing conveys confidence and sincerity like eye contact. —@TeeMonster
- Small groups are always better than big groups. —@jaybaer

Don't

- Don't be a name dropper or look around like the person you are talking to isn't important. —@courtenayrogers
- Don't offer your card before asked or before getting theirs. —@LotusDev
- You don't have to give a card to everyone you meet. —@NickiLaycoax
- Don't assume. A person you network with may not be the connection you need, but they may know the person you want to talk to. —@ChrisAyar

How Would Our Heroes Network?

- **Allen (influencer)** was an account manager for a marketing and advertising agency for 14 years but is looking for a new job. Allen's best bet is to start attending meetings of his local American Marketing Association and Public Relations Society of America chapters. As he meets other account managers and higher-level account managers, he should try to connect with them one on one as often as possible. When Allen strikes up a friendly relationship with them, he should nurture it as much as he can. They will tell him about job openings around town, and they may influence the hiring process at their own agencies. Allen should also use his downtime to take a leadership role for one of these associations to make himself more visible and become the person others want to meet to pick his brain.

- **Beth (climber)** is a marketing manager for a large insurance company. She has been with them for 10 years, but this is her second insurance company. Assuming there are no policies against it, either written or unwritten, Beth should meet other marketing managers and chief marketing officers in other insurance companies.

Although they may not mentor her directly, if she can provide value to them—job openings, notices about conferences, but nothing that might give a "competitive" benefit, which Beth's supervisors may frown upon—they'll likely remember her later, if she ever looks for a new job at another company.

Beth should also consider getting more involved with the Chamber of Commerce, which often has programs aimed at corporate executives. This will make her supervisors notice her involvement in the local business community, which is what every corporation wants to do but sometimes lacks the time or resources for.

- **Carla (neophyte)** is a former pharmaceutical sales rep who was laid off after eight years. She wants to work for a nonprofit as a program director or a fund-raising specialist. Her best bet is to have informational meetings with executive directors, board of directors members, and other program directors of the kinds of nonprofits she wants to work for. She should ask questions like, "What kinds of qualities does a successful program director or fund-raiser have?" and "Do you know anyone else I should talk to so I can learn more?" And of course, "Do you have any openings coming up in your organization, or do you know of any in other nonprofits?"

Carla can add value to the people she meets by forwarding articles, arranging introductions with influential people, and volunteering for an organization or two while she's job hunting.

- **Darrin (free agent)** is an IT professional who leaves his job every two or three years in pursuit of more money. Because of the nature of Darrin's job, he is unlikely to need to attend Chamber of Commerce and business networking groups. However, larger cities often have IT-related professional groups and even social groups that meet after work hours. Darrin should attend as many of these as he can and then meet his contacts for lunch or breakfast. Just like our other three heroes, Darrin can hear about any kinds of opportunities, as well as pass them along to the people he meets with.

13

Public Speaking: We Promise You Won't Die

Maybe it's because we both have an obsessive need to be the center of attention, but we live for speaking in public.

This admission gets a lot of weird looks and comments from our friends because most people hate public speaking. Hate, hate, hate it with a fiery hot passion reserved only for snakes and tobacco executives. (Our apologies to any snakes who may be reading this book.)

We speak in public for three reasons. First, public speaking is essential to building our brand and establishing our credibility. If we want companies and colleagues to realize we're experts in our field, we need to find ways to share that expertise with others. When we are seen as experts in our field, bigger clients are more willing to hire us for larger fees.

Second, we enjoy sharing knowledge with large groups of people. A big focus for Kyle's employer is helping companies create online lessons and courses. Erik taught public speaking to college students for three years, and he nearly went into education. So, we both share a teacher's heart. (Kyle keeps it in a jar under his bed.)

Third, we like public speaking because people pay speakers to share their wisdom and knowledge. We were staggered to learn that organizations pay someone anywhere from a few hundred to several thousand dollars to come in and talk about stuff they do for a living. It could be giving a keynote speech at a conference or a motivational talk at a national sales meeting or leading a day-long seminar, but professional public speakers are paid well to teach their skills to other people.

Think about what you do right now. Whether you're a purchasing agent, a marketing coordinator, a chef, or a license branch manager, you've probably found several shortcuts that help you do your job better, or you have some thoughts on the direction your particular industry should go. Now imagine if someone gave you a $2,000 check to talk for an hour to a group of colleagues about your ideas.

Staggering

You've probably thought about a number of ways you can do your job better. You likely think that if you had a chance to share this knowledge, your job, your company, or your industry would be a better and happier place. The fact that you bought this book is proof of that: You want to learn how to share knowledge, thus creating or growing your personal brand. This is where public speaking is going to help.

Should You Speak in Public?

Depends. Do you like money and being a minor celebrity in your field? Next question.

No, Seriously

Yes. Because if you're looking to move to the next level in your career, gain a national reputation in your industry, share knowledge and information, and even earn more money—in general, growing your brand—becoming a public speaker is one of the most effective ways to do this.

But You Hate Speaking in Public

It's okay if you hate speaking in public. Public speaking is not for everybody. We don't expect everyone to become a public speaker. Not everyone can be an expert; not everyone wants to speak to large crowds. You can still have an outstanding career and can create a great personal brand without doing it. But note: most leaders and rock stars in their industry are asked to speak in public.

If you don't like public speaking because you're afraid, don't worry. We already promised you wouldn't die, so what's the worst that could happen?

A lot of people are afraid of public speaking. They're afraid of being judged. They're afraid people won't like them or will find out they're frauds. They're afraid of making mistakes and looking foolish.

One year Erik was a volunteer speechwriter for a woman running for U.S. Congress. She was scheduled to debate the incumbent at a local TV station, but she was so nervous that, before she could even give her opening statement, she tore off her headphones and walked off.

Someone from the station calmed her down and encouraged her to try it one more time. She put her headphones on, got through her opening statement, and then lost it. "I can't do this, I just can't do this," she cried.

She then ran out of the door, got into her car, and drove away. Unfortunately, that was the news clip that made national news, which Erik watched while he was at a conference ten hours away.

The candidate's explanation later was that she got stage fright and let it get the best of her. She had been giving speeches around the district for a few months, but came unglued when there were TV cameras involved.

You need to remember two important points, which Erik's candidate forgot, when you give a speech, make a presentation, or even just toast the bride and groom at a wedding:

1. Everyone wants you to do a good job. Nobody is hoping you screw up so they can leap to their feet, point their finger, and shout "See? See, I told you she was a phony!"

2. Everyone in the room is just as nervous as you are when giving a talk, so no one's going to be unsympathetic or judgmental about your efforts. When Erik's candidate left her debate, even her opponent told the local news that he understood her nervousness.

Overcoming Your Fear of Public Speaking

If you're afraid to speak in public, or you want to but just don't have the experience, you're not alone. There are organizations and opportunities to help you overcome your fear or gain valuable experience.

Toastmasters

The most popular, most useful organization for learning to speak in public is Toastmasters. You'll learn how to speak in front of groups, organize your speeches, give impromptu talks, and even learn how to recognize what makes a good speech.

Depending on where you live, there may be one, two, or even dozens of Toastmasters clubs that meet weekly, every other week, or even once a month for 60 minutes. Each meeting has a set, regular agenda the group follows. Members give speeches to earn credit toward certifications, including the Certified Toastmaster and Advanced Toastmaster. Also, they learn to give feedback on others' speeches, which they present like a regular speech and even have the opportunity to compete in local and regional contests.

You can find out more information by visiting the Toastmasters' website at Toastmasters.org. Click the "Find a Club" button to, well, find a club in your area. Keep in mind that some clubs have membership requirements, like working for the company where the meeting is held. The downside to Toastmasters is that it can be a big time commitment. The upside is that the clubs are filled with people who want to learn how to speak in public. You'll be surrounded by friendly people who want to see you succeed.

Classes at Your Local College or University

Taking college classes is another option for improving your public speaking ability. Although Toastmasters is an ongoing effort, you can give yourself a deadline by taking a course. You can take basic public speaking and even move into advanced public speaking, if you want. The downside is that a college class can be pricey compared to Toastmasters. The upside is that you can cram everything you want to learn into a single class that meets once a week, or even a few times a week, for four months, and then you're done.

Seminars and Courses

Several organizations help people learn more effective communication skills. Whether it's leadership training, team management, or even public speaking and storytelling, you can take one-, two-, or even three-day courses on these techniques. The upside is that you get everything you need in less than three days. The downside is that they're often more expensive than a college course, and you don't get the same amount of time for practice and feedback that you do in either Toastmasters or college classes.

These seminars are great for refreshers or crash courses, but they're not enough to build an entire speaking career. Thousands of courses and seminars are available from national groups, including National Seminars or Dale Carnegie and local ones organized by nearby groups and instructors.

Speakers Associations

There are several organizations for professional speakers, like the National Speakers Association, the American Professional Speakers Association, the World Speakers Association, and the Advanced Writers and Speakers Association. These are geared toward the advanced or professional speaker, and some may have an income-from-speaking requirement for applicants.

Many of these organizations have meetings in larger cities, where members meet and learn how to become better speakers, how to get more speaking engagements, and how to promote their speaking events.

Private or Executive Coaches

We even know a few people who provide one-on-one coaching for public speaking. These coaches not only teach you how to speak in public, they also help you reshape your image, dress for success, learn how to deal with new situations, and give you individually tailored, no-punches-pulled feedback on where you need to improve. The downside is that they can cost a few thousand dollars. The upside is that you get specific feedback, and you learn how to fix your issues from a professional.

We don't recommend this option until you're ready to take your speaking career to a professional level. Start with the easy, less expensive options first, and get some speeches under your belt before you look at a private coach.

PERSONAL BRANDING CASE STUDY: LORRAINE BALL

Lorraine Ball was a major influence on both of us when we were first starting out as networkers and professionals. Kyle actually began as a part-time employee at her PR agency, Roundpeg, in 2007. Erik began attending Rainmakers networking events (see "Chapter 12, Networking: Hello, My Name Is...") thanks to Lorraine's encouragement. She has been a major figure in Indiana social media, PR, and public speaking, and someone we have both looked to for advice and guidance.

Lorraine started Roundpeg after spending more than two decades in the corporate world when she got tired of the bureaucracy, glass ceilings, and bad coffee. She started her own company as a way to create the kind of work she wanted to do, serving clients she wanted to work within an environment that attracted creative and interesting individuals. One of the ways she has built her business is through public speaking.

Lorraine started speaking in her role as a corporate PR pro, so it only seemed natural to continue doing workshops and seminars as a part of her business with Roundpeg. She usually speaks on digital marketing, creative thinking, and business management, primarily to business owners. She's also an adjunct faculty member at the University of Indianapolis, teaching courses on content strategy and social CRM (customer relationship management).

She holds 20 to 30 speaking gigs per year, but she tries to stay as local as possible, often bringing people into her conference room at Roundpeg world headquarters.

"I spent 11 years on the road when I was in the corporate world, and I didn't want a business that would put me on the road week in and week out," Lorraine said.

However, she travels on occasion, especially when she can combine business and fun. She's accepted speaking gigs in Hawaii, St. Thomas, New Orleans, and Washington, D.C. in the last few years. She is often invited to speak by people who have seen her speak in other locations. Other times, she submits an application to be a speaker at some bigger conferences.

Lorraine does most of her speaking by offering free seminars to people in Central Indiana on a variety of things, whether it's email marketing, using Twitter to find business leads, or even corporate blogging. She gives away her information and processes for free, which demonstrates her experience and abilities to the people who might want to hire her.

And rather than educating people to do her job without her, those people actually realize that they can't do what she does as well as she does it. They often end up hiring her instead.

Public speaking has been a great business development tool for Lorraine, because her free seminars are often a split between prospects and clients.

"My clients will often promote me to the prospects in the room," said Lorraine.

Social media has also been an important part in growing her personal brand. "I'm able to reach a much wider audience, by sharing videos, podcasts, and blog posts to establish my credibility," she said. "It also lets me reconnect with people who knew me from my previous roles."

When we asked her what she would recommend to someone starting to build their personal brand, she said, "Figure out who you want to be; serious, silly, sarcastic or sensible. Then make sure every part of your brand, from the photos you select for your web page and social media avatars to the words you choose in bios and social profiles, support that brand. Think about how you will describe yourself in 200 words and 140 characters, and make sure you sound like the same person."

Finding Your Speaking Niche

You need to discover your speaking niche. What are you good at? What is your industry or field of interest? If you've been following along in this book, you've already figured this out. If you turned straight to this chapter, just be aware that this is something you need to do. We'll show you how.

First, this needs to be something you're not only good at, but have some expertise in. If you just started your first job as a copywriter at a marketing agency two months ago, chances are you don't have the knowledge to speak to a room full of other copywriters about "10 Advanced Copywriting Secrets."

So if you want to become a speaker, you need to pick something you've done for a few years. That's how you'll be able to find your niche.

Finding your niche is critical to establish your speaking career. You can't just select "everything" as your subject matter, any more than you can select "everyone" as your potential audience.

Even business motivational speakers only want to reach a certain group or type of people—businesspeople, salespeople, people who want to make more money, and so on. Their audience is not the general population or non-salespeople.

Start with the general picture, then drill down further. Even a specialized field may have areas of sub-specialty.

Let's say you're a cost reduction consultant. You help companies improve their bottom line by reducing their costs. That's even your elevator speech when you explain what it is you do: "I help companies improve their bottom line by reducing their costs." (We'll ignore that this is a boring introduction to what you do.) Believe it or not, that's not your potential audience when you're trying to find speaking gigs. Dig deeper.

"I help small businesses—companies with fewer than 100 employees—reduce their costs."

Better, but that's still a lot of businesses. According to the Small Business Administration, there are 27.9 million small businesses in the United States. Get more specific.[1]

"I help small manufacturing companies reduce their costs."

That's pretty good. We can live with that. We can actually go deeper into our specialty (think: small tool-and-die manufacturers or small tool-and-die manufacturers who work in the automotive industry), but that might be a niche to pursue for a business route, not your speaking field.

Keep in mind that you don't have to live exclusively in your niche. You just have to focus on that one particular field, finding different conferences and trade shows

---

1. https://www.sba.gov/business-guide/manage/manage-your-finances-business-credit

to speak at. Then, when you're comfortable there, you can branch out to a second niche. By focusing on one niche, like reducing costs for small manufacturing companies, you can successfully choose a second one—say, one- and two-partner law firms—that rarely overlaps with the first. This way, you can specialize in more than one niche without causing any conflicts of interest.

You can also have a small niche that fits within a large field. For example, we're both social media consultants and users with deeper specialties. Kyle focuses on online lessons and courses for companies, and Erik frequently speaks on content marketing and writing (see Figure 13.1). These can easily cross into other industries. Whether it's social media training or online marketing, companies from every industry can use our services.

Figure 13.1 *Erik often speaks about content marketing and writing to PR and marketing groups, as well as humor writing and personal branding at writing conferences.*

You can create your own specific niche that crosses borders, too. Whether it's transportation safety, identity theft protection insurance, Generation Y image consulting, or executive travel coordination, you can choose such a narrow niche that you can then focus on a wide market of ideal companies, like companies that are a specific size or based in a certain region.

Again, drill down. For example, don't just pick "small business consulting" as your niche. Even "marketing for small businesses" is too big. "International sales and marketing for small businesses" is a decent speaker's niche. A good number of businesses do business overseas, and you can tap into all kinds of government programs, sales organizations, and even specific industries to find speaking opportunities.

After you identify your niche, you're ready to start speaking.

How to Launch Your Speaking Career

Do this: Go to your bathroom mirror, look confidently at yourself, raise your arms over your head and shout, "I am a public speaker!"

And now you are one.

@kyleplacy: Is that seriously how you got started?

@edeckers: Well, I didn't have a big mirror, but I...no, not really.

@kyleplacy: We need to write more than that. We have a page count we have to meet.

If you want to get started as a speaker, identify your goal as a speaker. Is it to make $5,000 in your first year as a speaker? To be a keynote speaker at your industry association's national conference? To speak to more than 500 people at once? Some goals can be met right away; others may take a few years, with smaller goals serving as milestones along the way.

For the purposes of this chapter, we assume you want to get paid as a speaker, whether you're giving talks as part of your regular job and you receive an honorarium or you want to become a professional speaker whose full-time job is to travel around and give talks. These other steps we just mentioned will be milestones along the way.

Here's the problem: Most of your speaking gigs are going to be for free, especially in the first year. That's because you don't have credibility as a speaker, even if you just finished your third year in Toastmasters. You're still an untried, unknown quantity, and you're not going to get the same respect as the industry experts who have been doing it for several years. (And if you've spent three years in Toastmasters without speaking outside, you need to move out of your safety zone.)

Don't get hung up that you're speaking for free; learn to appreciate the opportunities. Think about all the stage time you're getting. You're honing your skills, developing your stage presence, and learning what works for you. This will help you achieve the speaking goals you have set for yourself.

Plus, speaking for free can sometimes produce the same results as speaking for money—getting more business, getting other speaking gigs, generating traffic for your blog, and finding a new job.

Stand-up comics work like this when they start out, building stage time, trying to get as much as they can, as often as they can. They work up just five minutes of material and perform it over and over—for free—at open mic nights. Then they move up to showcases, expanding their set into seven minutes, and then ten minutes. They hone that ten minutes until it's perfect, and they keep performing it as many times as they can, usually for free.

A lot of these new comics drive for two hours just for the chance to do seven minutes onstage. Any successful comic talks about how he just did the same short set over and over, for free or little pay, until he started making it to bigger venues.

That's because one club owner will see that perfect ten minutes and offer the comic a chance to do an industry showcase for $50. Then, all the other club owners assume that if the comic did an industry showcase, he's good enough to do their industry showcases for $50. Then, the comic is good enough to do another showcase, after which another owner asks the comic to open for a headliner in her club, and *bada-bing, bada-boom!* One day, the comic is a headliner. And it's all because he was willing to drive two hours to do a free ten-minute set a few years earlier.

But the comics who do only two sets and then give up because they don't get a paying gig will be unknown, out-of-work comics who slowly grind their way to anonymous retirement at their data analyst's job in their tiny cubicle that's slowly killing them. (Oh, but we're sure it's different for you. Seriously, that won't happen to you.)

The lesson is the same for speaking. You need to speak for free for a while. That's the way these things work. But you won't always do that. Because in the meantime, you're still blogging about your industry, you're still growing your network, and you're communicating to your network about all the talks you're giving, which is helping grow your personal brand.

As you give more talks, more people will see you. Specifically, more people who make decisions about getting speakers will see you. There are almost always decision makers or influencers at conferences. And they'll assume that if you are good enough to speak at this conference, you're good enough to speak at their conference.

We can't count the number of speaking opportunities we've had because someone saw one or both of us speak at an event, only to be invited to their event a few months later. So while we're both out of the speaking-for-free part of our careers, we recognize that it was an important part of our growth.

Identify Speaking Opportunities

You'll start your speaking career by giving basic talks about your niche. They'll be to small audiences, local, and most likely free. That's because you're going to talk to local business groups, local fraternal organizations, and even small seminars for your local Chamber of Commerce; plan to give them a basic overview of what you know.

You need to be greedy about these small, free opportunities. Get your name and your face in front of as many people as you can by calling business groups, attending their meetings, and asking for speaking opportunities.

As you become involved with the business groups and Chambers of Commerce, you're bound to catch someone's attention in an area, like a member of the board of a trade group or industry association, nonprofit or a conference organizer.

When you meet this person, pursue your own opportunities; don't wait for them to come to you. Ask the organizers and board members if they have any speaking opportunities—you can find a lot of speaking gigs this way.

Many of these people need to find speakers for their upcoming events. They may need someone to talk about your particular topic, or they may just need a speaker to fill a slot in three months. But they know that they are going to need to fill that spot, and that means asking their friends and colleagues for recommendations, putting the word out to group members, and working their contact list until they find the right speaker.

And then here you come, charging in on your white horse, shouting, "I'll save the day! I'll be your speaker for your next event."

@kyleplacy: What is it with you and shouting today?
@edeckers: WHY, DOES IT BOTHER YOU?!

By offering to fill the speaking slot, you're helping the organizer solve a big problem. Also, you'll both get the speaking slot and make a memorable impression on the organizer. When the organizer is asked by her contacts if she knows any good speakers, she'll recommend you, because you bailed her out of a jam several months ago by approaching her first.

Industry Groups

Industry groups provide great speaking opportunities because you can focus your niche to laser-like specificity. We have been to conferences in which the presentations and sessions have been so esoteric, so far out, we were surprised people even came up with the ideas, let alone found a roomful of people interested enough to sit through it for an hour. But, that's the great thing about social media and the Internet: You can find a group or community that interests you and then find other like-minded people.

Whether it's a trade association, a collection of professionals, or even a group of companies that focus on a particular issue, some industry groups are national, while many others are local. Figure out your chosen specialty area and see if a group in your area focuses on it. It could be technical writers, visual artists, corporate travel planners, heating and cooling contractors, or left-handed actuarial scientists.

Your goal in speaking to these local groups is twofold: 1) To find new clients. Remember, if you show people how smart you are, they'll hire you to work for them. 2) To find new, bigger speaking engagements. Small speaking gigs lead to larger ones, so speak to industry groups on a local level because they can lead to national speaking opportunities down the road.

After you make your name on the local scene in your specialty, take the leap into the national scene. Go for a speaking slot at the national conference. Check out the conference's website, find the "Call For Speakers" section, and submit a proposal.

You don't have to limit yourself to just speaking to your own industry groups. If your topic fits other industry trends, go for it. Just make sure your chosen subject will somehow fit within what that group is already thinking about, even if it's a cross-over topic.

Actually, a cross-over topic can sometimes be a bigger draw than the traditional topics you usually find at an industry conference. For example, HR professionals are probably sick to death of hearing about the latest equal opportunity hiring requirements, but would love to hear a seminar on how to use Facebook for recruiting and hiring.

Table 13.1 lists a few cross-over ideas:

Table 13.1 Possible Cross-Over Groups and Topics

Your Specialty	Cross-Over Industry Group	Cross-Over Topic
Tax law	Chamber of Commerce	Doing taxes for small businesses
Trade show displays	American Marketing Association	Doing pre-trade show promotion
Technical writing	Startup companies	Documentation software properly
Web design	High school teachers	Creating a class website
Marketing	Visual artists	Marketing artwork
Direct mail	Nonprofits	Saving money on fundraising
Financial planning	High school business teachers	Financial planning for teens
Cost reduction analysis	Office managers	Cutting office expenditures
Health insurance	Human resources pros	Saving employee benefit costs

If there's not a particular industry group in your area, find one that's within driving distance and make the trip.

Remember, if stand-up comics are willing to drive two hours just for a five-minute set, you should be willing to drive at least three hours to deliver a one-hour talk. Although it's good to get paid, don't expect to make big money when you're starting out. But it doesn't hurt to ask for travel expenses for those multi-hour trips.

Civic Groups

If you think of industry groups as a B2B (business-to-business) audience, civic groups are a B2C (business-to-consumer) audience. You're not going to get as in depth with a topic with civic groups as you would with industry groups. For example, instead of talking about tax law for small businesses, you may end up talking to a group of Shriners about the personal tax implications of using those little cars and scooters for parades. Or instead of talking about financial planning for young professionals, you may end up talking to a fraternity's national conference about how to pay off college debt in five years.

The best place to find civic groups are online. Do a Google search for the civic groups you're interested in talking to or just do a generic search for "civic groups" in your area, then check their website to see if they have any lunches or special events where you can address the members. Send them an introductory email and see what happens.

Conferences, Trade Shows, and Expos

This is where both of us got our start on the speaking circuit. We scoured conference websites for the industries we want to be known in and checked for speaking opportunities. We also began subscribing to newsletters that have different speaking opportunity lists, like SpeakerHub.com.

You can find different trade shows and conferences with a little detective work and your favorite search engine. First, check for trade associations or groups for your chosen industry or profession. Many trade associations have a national conference, and you can usually find that information on their website. Some will even have regional conferences or local chapters, and you might find opportunities there, too. If you live in a city with a big conference center, look at their calendar for the conferences coming to your city and check out the conference websites.

Submit speaking proposals during the posted application period. Next, look for the conferences of any allied, related, or even competing trade associations. Finally, blog about the issues the association members are facing in case they check out your website. Then make sure the conference organizers are in your social networks, especially Twitter and LinkedIn, and that they receive notifications about your blog posts.

When you find a trade show or conference that looks interesting, visit the submission page to see what kinds of speakers they're looking for. You could make one of four main types of presentations:

- **Poster session:** You usually find these at educational conferences. A poster session is a series of 6-foot folding tables with pop-up displays and pages of your latest research taped to them. You stand around and hope that people ask you questions, but they don't. They're only there for the free hors d'oeuvres used to lure disinterested attendees into the poster session. (Not that we're bitter or anything.)

  Maybe we're biased, but we don't consider these real speaking sessions. Don't waste your time with them. In many cases, poster presenters won't even get a discounted admission to the conference, which tells you how highly they're regarded. (Hint: They're not.)

- **Round table:** Imagine putting 75 people in one room with seven different tables, and presenters sit at each, talking about a different topic. The attendees split up and sit at different tables. Talks may take 15 minutes or an hour.

  You may not get the same benefit as speaking to your own room, but at least it's not a poster session. Sometimes this may be your foot in the door for a future speaking slot at the next year's conference. When you've been a speaker for a while, avoid doing round tables unless you also get to do a breakout session. You don't get enough time to get into the meat of your topic, and the room is often too loud to be heard properly. You'll get to make personal connections though, which can be important later on. (Reread "Chapter 12, How to Network: 'Hello, My Name Is. . . '")

- **Breakout speaking session:** These are the standard speaking sessions. Most breakout sessions are scheduled as one of several going on during an hour, and the attendees have to choose which one they want to go to. You speak at your session for an hour and don't need to worry about competing tables, posters, or people showing up for free hors d'oeuvres.

  Sometimes you may be asked to give your session more than once because there aren't enough speakers. Other times, there are so many submissions, the conference can only accept a fraction of them. There is a varying degree of skill and energy among the speakers, so this is a great way to stand out from the others. If you can do a great job compared to the other speakers, you look like a brilliant orator. Sometimes these are paid slots, but most often they're not. Speakers often get free admission to the conference.

- **Keynote address:** This is the granddaddy of all speaking sessions. While a breakout session only lets a speaker reach a fraction of conference attendees, the keynote speaker not only addresses all the attendees at once, he or she often kicks off the entire conference. Some conferences will even have one keynote speaker per day, which means there's more than one opportunity for you. Plus, this is usually a paid speaking opportunity. Never agree to give a keynote session for free!

Introducing Yourself

After you identify the groups you want to speak to, write an email that explains what you want to talk about, your area of expertise, how long you've been doing it, and where you've done it in the past. Make sure that your grammar, spelling, and punctuation are perfect. Write each email as an individual pitch to that group. Explain why you and your session would be a good fit for their audiences. Direct the groups to your blog. (You do have a blog, right? Check out Chapter 3, "Blogging: Telling Your Story," if you don't.)

> Dear Ms. Havisham,
>
> I am interested in speaking to an upcoming luncheon of the Wedding Planning Professionals of Orlando. I am a direct mail planner and would like to speak to your members about how using direct mail postcards can help brides and their families save money on invitation costs.
>
> I have been in direct mail sales for 10 years and have been speaking to wedding planning professionals and other party planners for three years. I recently gave a talk at the National Wedding Planning Professionals Association conference about this same topic. It was well received, ranking as one of the top five sessions of the entire conference.
>
> You can read more about me at my blog, http://BobScrumrunner.blogspot.com, as well as see some videos of my past talks. My usual speaking fee is $500, plus travel expenses. I will follow up with you via phone in five days. Thank you.
>
> Sincerely,
> Philip Pirrip

Follow up your emails with phone calls a few days later as you promised, to see if the groups received your email and if they have any opportunities for you.

(And give yourself 10 bonus cool points if you said, "Hey, that's *Great Expectations*!" when you read the letter.)

Promoting Your Talk

You've got your first speaking session arranged. Now you need to make sure people actually show up. You can always hope the organizer is going to do some promotion, but much of it should fall on your shoulders. After all, you have access to people that your organizers may not: your blog readers and your Twitter and LinkedIn networks. Not only will you invite people from your network to your own talk, but you may end up introducing those people to the entire event, which is an added bonus for the organizer, and makes you look like a star. (Some conferences even offer affiliate payments if you bring in attendees.)

What are the best ways to invite people to your talk? In this section, we're going to help you:

- Learn five ways to attract an audience to your presentation

- Discover three secrets every professional speaker uses to increase audience participation.

Do you see what we did there? Your brain probably fired a few extra neurons, and your metaphorical ears perked up a little bit. We attracted your attention by promising a finite number of ways to attract attention and three secrets that the real pros use.

This is a common technique used by professional copywriters to get people to read their sales material and to buy their products. If these techniques work in a sales letter, then you should use them too.

Something about a numbered list in a headline or copy makes people take notice. It's like brain candy for humans, because our minds see that information and say, "Hey, that's something I can easily understand. I want to read that!" Umberto Eco even told German news magazine, *Der Spiegel*, in 1999 that people like lists because they establish order out of chaos.[2]

So take advantage of that little psychological quirk and use it to promote your talks. You can also do this when writing a blog article or email.

First, write captivating copy. (Don't write the headline first. The headline is going to come from the copy.) Use a numbered list and come up with three big ideas the audience is going to learn. But then give each of those items its own list. For example:

1. Learn five ways to attract an audience to your presentation.

2. Discover three secrets every professional speaker uses to boost attendance.

3. Learn the five free social media tools you can use to promote your next talk.

---

2. www.spiegel.de/international/zeitgeist/0,1518,659577,00.html.

Once you have written all the text, write the headline. Create a headline that covers one of the big issues your audience wants to hear about. You can find this out by asking the event organizer what hot-button issues their members are facing. Then, design your presentation and write the headline based on that.

For example, if Facebook is a big issue among human resources professionals, write a headline like "Five Ways to Use Facebook to Streamline Your Recruiting."

With this headline, we have hit three hotspots for HR professionals:

1. We have a finite numbered list. It's more than just how they can use Facebook, but an actual number of items they can use.

2. Facebook has become an important recruiting tool for a lot of hiring managers.

3. In 2015, 98 percent of recruiters used Facebook and LinkedIn to find job candidates.[3] (Mostly LinkedIn, but 55 percent also use Facebook.)

4. We're trying to make their jobs easier. Everyone has things they don't like about their jobs. Recruiting is one of those things for HR professionals, so by offering to help streamline recruiting, you're telling them you can help simplify that part of their job.

Email the description of your talk to the show organizer, who will put it in the conference directory. Then post an article on your blog to promote that blog post via Twitter, Facebook, LinkedIn, and any other social networks you belong to. Seek out and connect with people who will attend the conference (search for the conference hashtag on Twitter).

Promote your talk frequently, about two to four times per week. Don't just send a notice out once and hope people show up. It's going to take several different messages on your various networks and blog to get people to notice that you're going to speak somewhere, and then a few more to get them interested in coming.

When you're at a conference, don't be afraid to invite people to your session. We know, we know: You don't want to feel needy, but you're speaking in public because you crave the attention, so that ship has already sailed. Swallow the last of your pride and start inviting people.

Several years ago, Erik was attending BarCamp Nashville, a social media "unconference." He was already on the schedule to speak, so he started connecting with other Nashville area social media pros who were attending. He would tweet them and say things like "I'm speaking at #BCN10 in a couple weeks. Stop by and

---

3. https://www.eremedia.com/ere/how-to-recruit-on-facebook/

say hi." With more than 200 people in attendance that year, Erik had more than two-thirds of them at his session.

Remember, the fuller your rooms are, the more you can spread your personal brand and earn new opportunities or gain new clients. Visit other sessions during the day and invite people to your session afterward, especially if the two topics are related. You can also invite the other speakers, and as a form of professional courtesy, give them some love during your talk. (That's what the cool kids say for "mention them.")

Your goal is to get as many people in your session as you can, which unfortunately means other speakers may have fewer attendees at their session. Don't feel bad; it just means they should have promoted their talk better. Buy them a copy of this book.

PERSONAL BRANDING CASE STUDY: CRYSTAL WASHINGTON

Crystal Washington is a professional speaker and technology strategist with her own speaking and training business, CWM Enterprises. She teaches everyone from Generation Y to Baby Boomers about using social media. She has worked with entrepreneurs and small-business owners, and she's helped companies like Google, Microsoft, GE, and British Airways in the U.S., Europe, and Africa improve their social media strategies.

She's also the author of two books, *The Social Media Why* and *One Tech Action*, and has been published in *The Huffington Post, Entrepreneur Magazine, Bloomberg,* and *Business Week.*

Crystal originally started her own marketing firm in 2006 and was getting great results for her clients when larger companies like Google, British Airways, and Microsoft started hiring her. They asked her to speak at their events, which she started doing as favors. She eventually got so many requests (to speak for free) that she had to turn some of them down.

"Then one organization said, 'We'll pay you,' and I said 'Oh!' And that was the beginning of my professional speaking," said Crystal.

Social media hasn't just been a big part of her growth as a speaker, it's been a major part of it. Crystal is a futurist and speaks about myriad technologies, including social media, apps, email marketing, web searches, and devices. But when it comes to personal branding, she's relied almost solely on social media.

"That's how I got my name out there, posting things on Facebook and LinkedIn," said Crystal. "I even got one speaking engagement because of something I posted on Twitter."

Video has been a big part of Crystal's marketing strategy as a professional speaker. Because Google owns YouTube, Crystal figured placing well on YouTube search results would improve her Google ranking. So she worked on having very well-thought out and polished videos with all the right keywords. She landed her first two international speaking engagements because of those YouTube videos.

Professional speaking has opened up a lot of doors for Crystal, and it's allowed her to travel around the world. She's especially proud to have hosted one of the first ever social media bootcamps in the Bahamas, and she once spoke to an auditorium full of women in Accra, Ghana.

And her one piece of advice for people trying to build their personal brands? "Figure out what your one word is, if you can distill it down to a single word. Think about what you want people to see when they see you. All of your imagery, colors, and keywords should revolve around that one thing."

Giving Your Talk

When it comes to giving speeches, you can read many books, newsletters, and blogs, as well as take classes. We assume you know how to take the steps to prepare for your talk, like outlining your presentation beforehand, rehearsing, dressing appropriately, and using language effectively. But we offer these seven ideas for organizing your talk:

- **Write brief copy:** Our preference is to put no more than five words on a single slide in 144-point size or bigger. Use photos and graphics instead. This way, you can speed up or slow down your talk as needed. You can skip slides, spend only a few seconds on them, or even tell a five-minute story about that particular slide. And people in the back won't burst a blood vessel trying to read the tiny print on the screen.

- **Show up early:** Scope out the room. If you can go a few days early to check it out, do it. You want to get a feel for the room, see where the projector is, how the room is laid out, how much room you have to walk around, and generally get comfortable.

  But if you're speaking at a conference, you may not have that chance. Then you have to assume the conference organizers know what they're doing and be fairly flexible on your requirements and adaptability. Still, it doesn't hurt to plan for the worst, in case the organizers aren't too adept at managing technology. (See the section titled "Important Technology Tips for Presenters.")

- **Make sure the lighting is appropriate:** Under no circumstances should you allow the lights to be turned down low so people can see the screen better. They are there to see you, not your images. You can give your presentation without PowerPoint/Keynote; your slide deck can't do squat without you. Lights need to stay up at a normal level. Let the people see your smiling, beautiful face.

- **Treat talks like theater:** You're not relaying information; you're acting! You should consider yourself a performer, and it's okay to act like one. Actors often use the phrase "playing to the back row." This means their gestures are meant to be bigger so they're seen by the back row (it helps if you're on a stage, like Kyle in Figure 13.2). Although you don't have to bellow and make large sweeping gestures, don't have conversations with the front row. Make eye contact with the people in the back, so they feel included. Also, new speakers often have a tendency to speak faster than they think they do. Make sure you speak at a normal rate of speed.

Figure 13.2 *Kyle has given over 200 talks since 2012 in different parts of the globe. He's learned how to speak to even the largest crowds and connect with them.*

- **Mention other people, especially other speakers, during your talk:** This gives you more credibility, plus you come off as gracious, sharing, and noncompetitive. Speakers who do this tend to be recognized and appreciated when it comes to future, more lucrative opportunities. (At which point, you can totally crush those other speakers and grind their noses into the dirt.)

@kyleplacy: Man, that's pretty dark.

@edeckers: They made fun of my Hello Kitty backpack!

- **Have a soundtrack you sing to yourself as you're being introduced and walk on stage:** If you have time beforehand, listen to music that puts you in a good mood and leaves you feeling confident. One public speaking trainer once suggested humming the opening bars of the *Rocky* theme song to ourselves as we walked across the stage to begin our talks.

- **Record your talks and study them afterward:** You will be your own harshest critic, so watch and listen to recordings of yourself speaking. Take notes on what you need to fix, then fix them. Stand-up comics record themselves and then listen to the audio playback to see what parts of their set need to be fixed. You can do that too.

Important Technology Tips for Presenters

We both love using our computers for our talks, and we're particular about what we use. We're both rabid Apple fans and use our MacBooks for everything. We love Apple Keynote because it's stable and not prone to crashing. However, we recognize that PowerPoint is widely used, and it's easier to transfer a slide deck to someone else's computer. (Keynote can also export slide decks to the PowerPoint format.)

Both systems have their pros and cons, but regardless of who's right (us—we're right), you should know these several technology tips before giving a talk:

- **Make sure your computer is focused:** Shut down every program, hide all the files on your desktop in another folder, and clear out your browser history and disk cache. We've all heard stories about presenters who clicked the wrong button on their computer and had some embarrassing photos pop up on the screen for everyone to see. While the safest bet is to never look at those kind of not-safe-for-work things to begin with, at least make sure they're not easily accessible or accidentally switched on. So clear your history and cache, hide any personal photos and documents in a safe place, and make sure all programs except your presentation software are off. You should even turn off your wifi unless you need it for your presentation.

- **Use big photos and (almost) no text:** PowerPoint and Keynote can be used effectively if they're used correctly. When we do slide decks, we get Creative Commons photos for slide images and put no more than five words on a slide.

Remember, you are the focus of the room, not the slides. The slides are there for visual support and perhaps a little comedy. They should not contain the important information; you should.

Tip

Creative Commons licenses are copyright licenses from the creator of a work (photo, graphic, or text) that allow others the right to reuse the copyrighted work—without changes, and at no charge—in things like presentations or in blog posts. If you use photos from a photo-sharing site, such as Flickr, Pixabay, or Wikimedia Commons, you need to make sure they are Creative Commons photos and not "All Rights Reserved" photos (which is legalese for "Do not reuse!"). There are different kinds of Creative Commons licenses, so make sure you research before you start publishing someone else's content.

If you do use text, make the point size at least 144 (two inches), so people in the back of the room can see it. If they're straining to see from the back, your projector isn't big enough.

Hopefully you scoped out the room ahead of time, saw how huge it is, and noticed that the projector was about as effective as holding up slides and a flashlight.

But if you don't get that chance, always assume the worst when it comes to available technology. If you stick with photos and huge text, you'll be fine. If you only use photos to support your points, you're not lost if the projector fails or is too small, or your presentation software crashes. You can still speak without these props.

- **Use your computer for presentations:** A lot of well-meaning people will offer you the chance to use their computers for your presentations, but that is sometimes more trouble than it's worth. They may have an older version of PowerPoint, Keynote won't run on a PC, or the right monitor cable for their laptop is missing. You've already tweaked your computer to perform the way you want it to, and it's hard to learn someone else's setup, especially if you're preparing your presentation five minutes before you start.

If you use someone else's system, you're at their mercy. Rather than putting yourself in a situation in which your entire presentation hinges on the quality of someone else's system, insist that you use your own computer. If you can't, be gracious about it, find a way to make it work, and hope it goes well. (If it doesn't, don't apologize to your audience for not having a slide deck. There's no point in embarrassing the organizers; that will get you blackballed from speaking at future events. Instead, use your computer as personal cue cards, and speak without a deck. That's why the point about using big photos and almost no text is so important.)

- **Get a separate presentation computer, preferably a MacBook:** If you want to make a living giving presentations, you need a computer that's not prone to virus attacks, crashes, and glitches that can pop up in the middle of a presentation.

  For stability, ease of use, and graphics capability, you can't go wrong with a MacBook. And yes, there's Windows 10, which is much easier to use and more stable than all the other versions that came before it, and yes, Macs aren't immune to viruses. But a Mac is less likely to suffer these things and is less likely to crash in the middle of a presentation. And if you have the budget, get a decent LCD projector. Don't cheap out and get the smallest, least expensive one you can find. Get a good one that can brightly fill up a screen from 25 feet away.

- **Upload your slide deck to SlideShare.net before you give your presentation:** We've been in rooms where everything was hard-wired and bolted in place, including the computer, and we were forced to use their system instead of our own. Although it's possible to export a Keynote deck to a PowerPoint version, this really screws up the formatting and fonts, and it looks bad. There's nothing worse than seeing weird fonts and screwed-up slides as you're giving your talk and having no possible way to fix it.

✉ Note

SlideShare.net is a presentation slide deck sharing site. Just like YouTube lets you share movies and Instagram lets you share photos, SlideShare lets you, well, share slides.

Instead, upload your deck to SlideShare the day before your presentation (see Figure 13.3). Then, before your talk, log on to SlideShare and pull up the deck in full presentation mode. It may mean you have to stand next to the keyboard to change the slides instead of using a remote (which is wicked cool and makes you feel like a big shot). But at least you don't have to mess around with putting your presentation on a thumb drive and hoping your presentation software isn't newer than theirs, or exporting your deck to their software and hoping the formatting isn't messed up. We've done all these things, and they can really mess up a presentation.

We also recommend paying for the premium membership for Slide-Share. It's worth it.

Figure 13.3 *One of Erik's presentations that's available on SlideShare, which is now owned by LinkedIn, which is owned by Microsoft. Note the clever use of a numbered list in the presentation title.*

Finally, by having the SlideShare URL, you can give people the link to your deck rather than printing 50 copies of handouts and giving them out to the 20 people who showed up.

You can also shorten the URL at a shortening service like bit.ly. A bit.ly-shortened URL is 20 characters, so it's easier for audience members to write down. You can also ask people to email you so you can send them the URL. This helps you add to your list of contacts as well, and you can communicate with them in the future, like when you're speaking again or have a book for sale.

- **Always carry a monitor cord and extension cord:** Most places already have a projector available, but they don't always have a monitor cord. Carry a monitor cord (and a Mac-to-RGB adapter if you took our earlier advice and got a MacBook) to be safe. Also, get a 12-foot 3-to-1 extension cord. Then you can plug in a laptop and the projector and reach the plug across the room. You may even find it helpful to carry a presenter's bag with the cords, colored markers, notepads, index cards, duct tape for cords, and any props you may use in your talks. Leave it in the trunk of your car when you're not using it, so you don't forget it if you drive to your presentations.

- **Create screen shots of websites you want to use:** It's nice to pull up a live website and show it off to a room full of people. But too often, you don't have access to the conference's private wifi, or the wifi is public wifi and everyone is on it, so it's slower than a turtle with a limp. Don't depend on having wifi access. Create screen shots of every website you need and keep them handy. Better yet, incorporate the screen shots into your slide deck, so you don't have to jump between applications.

If you do have wifi access, open all the websites you're going to need ahead of time. Consider using a browser like Firefox or Google Chrome for additional stability and speed.

How Does Public Speaking Apply to Our Four Heroes?

Although people generally speak for the same reasons—they desperately crave attention and want to make some money at the same time (Don't lie! We all know the truth!)—the path they take to get there may be a little different. So how will our four heroes use public speaking to advance in their career path or find a new job?

- **Allen (influencer)** spent 14 years as an account manager and has a lot of expertise in account management, marketing campaigns, ad creation, and the like. He would be a valuable resource to new marketing managers and coordinators, so speaking about a niche within marketing management would be a good one to pursue.

Topics like marketing analytics and ROI measurement would be good subjects to present to his local chapter of the American Marketing Association. Not only can he share his knowledge, he might make good connections with potential employers there.

- **Beth (climber)** wants to move up the career ladder to a chief marketing officer position in the insurance industry, so she could pursue a speaking plan in one of two directions: she can either speak to marketing people, or she can speak to insurance people.

She can even do it with the same presentation: "Marketing Tactics in a Heavily Regulated Industry." The talk can be geared toward any regulated industry, like finance, health care, or pharmacy. Or she can gear it back toward her own industry and retitle it "Proven Marketing Tactics in the Insurance Industry."

- **Carla (neophyte)** wants to change careers from pharmaceutical sales to nonprofits, so she is better off focusing on nonprofit issues rather than pharmaceutical ones. Although it would be easy to focus on a pharmaceutical audience, those aren't the people she wants to work for. Because a lot of nonprofit professionals don't think of themselves as businesspeople, business topics geared toward nonprofits tend to gather big audiences.

  Carla should focus on speaking to nonprofit professional organizations, such as the Kentucky Fundraising Professionals Organization or Planned Giving Professionals of Ohio, and teaching people how to take a sales approach to fundraising. This will not only show her business expertise, it will put her in front of people who either hire fundraisers or know about fund-raising positions.

- **Darrin (free agent)** is a commodity as an IT professional because he "fixes computers." (Sorry, IT folks, that's the way we non-IT folks see it.) Darrin wants to start public speaking to enhance his career and job growth possibilities, so he has two choices. He can try to impress the IT hiring managers by giving presentations about a particular growing field, like "Walking the Fine Line Between Network Security and Social Media." Or he can do basic presentations to reach C-level (CEO, COO, CIO, and so on) hiring managers, like "Basic Computer Security for Office Staff."

  Either way, Darrin's talks should be geared specifically toward the right audience. Because Darrin usually only transfers laterally based on salary, giving the right kind of talk to the right kind of audience might also get him a bump up the career ladder.

Speaking Tips in 140 Characters

- You're on the minute you walk into the building. The person you're gruff or abrupt with could be the person who gives your introduction. —@edeckers

- "Winging it" disrespects the audience. If you couldn't bother to take the time to prepare, why should they bother to pay attention? —@LisaBraithwaite

- At a conference, be friendly and helpful to everyone before/after your session. They'll remember that as much as they remember your talk. —@edeckers

- Ask people to email you for a copy of the slide deck. It's a great way to track the number of people interested in your topic. —@kyleplacy

- Asking people for their email is also a great way to gather names for your newsletter. Just be sure you ask if you can send it first. —@kyleplacy

- Practice vocal variety by reading aloud. Children's books, newspapers, poetry, and comedy dialogue help you work on pitch, pace, tone, and volume. —@LisaBraithwaite

- Have a central idea to come back to if you get on a tangent. It should be something to make it seamless while you find your thoughts. —@that_girl_lola

- Start fast, especially online (e.g., webinar). Attention spans are shorter than ever. —@1080group

- Don't give a speech. Talk to your audience and add at least some element of discussion to it. —@GloriaBell

- We all have butterflies before we speak. Train yours to fly in formation, so the energy expends with purpose. —@IkePigott

- Before you start, drink something that gives you something in your stomach. —@CoxyMoney

- Make a friend (or four) in the audience by using them as repeated points of eye contact. Smile within the first 30 seconds. —@GrindTheMusical

- Keep your visual aids as free of words as possible. Use blank slides between photo slides often, so they're looking at you, not the screen. —@GrindTheMusical

- All the books, blogs, and trainings in the world don't mean a thing if you don't apply your learning. Make opportunities—get out and speak! —@LisaBraithwaite

- Q&A your ass off. —@CoxyMoney

- Put your closing after the Q&A. The last thing the audience will hear is your final message, not a random or irrelevant question from the crowd. —@LisaBraithwaite

14

Getting Published: "I'm an Author!"

There's nothing like getting published with real ink and paper: Seeing a physical manifestation of something you created with your name on it and knowing that you put something out into the world, for other people to read, experience, and react to, is amazing.

The minute the ink hits the paper and your work is distributed to dozens, hundreds, or even thousands of people, you're a published author. And for a writer, there's no feeling like it in all the world. It's a historical record, an artifact, and a validation of your thoughts and ideas.

```
@kyleplacy: What about digital publishing and online publish-
            ing? Aren't you going to talk about that?

@edeckers:  Seriously? You're going to interrupt my flow *right
            now*? I was just getting warmed up.

@kyleplacy: I just think you need to mention digital
            publishing.

@edeckers:  Sure, it's important! There were over 485 million
            ebooks sold in 2016. Happy?

@kyleplacy: You don't need to get cranky.

@edeckers:  This is the introduction where we create imagery
            and set the mood, not where we "well, actually" the
            opening theme.
```

It's the same feeling we had when we published our first-ever articles, and it's continued for the subsequent ones and even this book. In fact, by the time you read this, we will have eagerly grabbed the first copies of this book out of their boxes, gripped them tightly, giggled a little—a little more than normal for two grown men—and positively beamed at our names on the cover. Erik may have even wiped away a tear or two.

Nothing can beat that sense of accomplishment, the feeling that you've somehow made history. All writers who have ever published a book, magazine article, newspaper column, or letter to the editor know that joy; they're on top of the world for days and weeks at a time.

This feeling is nothing like that you get from blogging. Don't get us wrong; blogging is great. It's the future of publishing and marketing. But there's a permanence to printed words. Books are sacred, magazines are interesting, and newspapers carry a sense of tradition and gravitas (even as the print newspaper slowly dies). Blogs are just, well, blogs. You'll forget all about your blog the first time you see your words and byline in a print publication.

As much as we both love blogs, we realize that anyone can write them. But being published in a newspaper, magazine, or book requires established knowledge and expertise. That's why there's a certain respectability that comes from being published. An editor thought highly enough of your work that she wanted to take the effort and spend the money to put ink on paper; a publisher trusted you enough to share your ideas with his readers.

It's an awesome feeling.

Kyle was once asked to write an article called "Developing a Policy for Your Company and Social Media" for the *Hamilton County Business Magazine*, which he geared toward the non-social media community. For him, it was exciting not only to be asked—to be recognized as an authority in his chosen field—but to see his work published in a high-gloss magazine. And although that publication didn't garner him immediate recognition, future articles on the subject did.

We're not disparaging bloggers. In fact, we think blogging is vital to today's business world. Erik owns a content marketing and blogging agency, and Kyle started his career teaching people how to blog, so we understand its importance. But right now, we want to look at writing beyond your blog and getting your work published in other venues.

Being published will boost your personal brand immensely. It shows that not only do you have a command of the language and the ability to form cohesive ideas, you have mastery of your topic (or at least the ability to completely BS an editor into thinking you know what you're talking about).

In this chapter, we're going to discuss print writing. Whether you're talking about newspapers, magazines, trade journals, or even newsletters, writing for print is a lot different than writing for a blog.

With a blog, you are your own editor, and you can pick any topic you want. In a print publication, you have to write to others' standards and follow their editorial calendar. In a blog, you can make your own errors and correct them, form your own ideas, and change your mind. In a print publication, everything has to be perfect, and your thoughts need to align with the overall mission and philosophies of the publication. Conversely, in a blog, you won't get paid for writing your own articles. In print publishing, you can get paid for what you do. (It may not be much, but there are some publications that pay their writers.)

Print writing will add so much more credibility to your personal brand if you're published in someone else's print publication.

Why Should I Become a Published Writer?

There are very few reasons you should not try to get published. Actually, we can't think of any. So, you know, just...do it. Just because.

@kyleplacy: I think they want a better explanation than that,
                Mr. I-Write-For-a-Living.

@edeckers: Fine, whatever.

There are two main reasons to start thinking of yourself as a writer, or at least not think "I hate writing, I hate writing" every time you write anything longer than a five-word email.

First, look at any job description. They always ask for "effective oral and written communication skills." Despite the fact that companies never say what "effective oral and written communication skills" actually are, it's safe to assume that you're going to be seen as "an effective written communicator" if you actually have some publishing credits to your name and maybe even a few ink stains on your fingers.

@edeckers: I meant metaphorical ink stains, not actual ink
               stains.

@kyleplacy: I wish you had said that earlier. This stuff is hard
                to wash off.

Second, you're always going to need to be a skilled communicator, whether you want to build your résumé or expand your personal brand. Whether you're writing a blog post or communicating an idea to your co-workers, you need to get your ideas across quickly, easily, effectively, and persuasively. The people who succeed in the workplace are often the people who can convey their ideas better than anyone else.

Consider becoming a published writer for these reasons:

- **It builds your personal brand:** Not only will more people learn who you are, but you will be seen as an expert on your published topic.

- **You can share your knowledge, which helps you be seen as an expert in your field:** Your articles will be read by people in your industry or in a market you want to be known in.

- **You can find new sales or job opportunities:** Just as we said blogging can help find new opportunities, (see Chapter 5, "Twitter: Sharing in the Conversation"), writing for print can get your ideas and name in front of someone who needs your expertise. That can turn into a sale of your product, a speaking engagement, or even a job opportunity.

- **You can make some extra money:** Many print publications pay their writers, whereas blogs and online publications typically don't.

- **Plenty of people still read print publications, whether newspapers, magazines, or books:** Although it may seem like the whole world is going digital, print still has a large audience.

PERSONAL BRANDING CASE STUDY: JACKIE BLEDSOE

Jackie Bledsoe is a noted author and speaker about family and marriage issues. But he wasn't always that. In fact, when we first met him, this was the furthest thing from his mind.

We first met Jackie at our 2010 launch of *Branding Yourself*. It was in December, and Jackie was there with his wife Stephana. They had stuck around to the end to meet us, and we found out later that they were out for Jackie's birthday celebration. The thing he wanted to do for his birthday was come to our book launch.

Jackie had recently lost his job, and his family was homeless, living in some friends' home, using his hotel points, and eventually in a week-by-week furnished apartment. He had tried starting an online business, which he said had failed miserably.

"I spent more time planning and getting the business started than I actually spent in business," said Jackie.

"One person who I looked up to in the online space actually told me, 'You're a nobody.' He didn't mean to be negative, but he meant that I knew nobody, and nobody knew me."

That's when he came to our book launch. Jackie and Erik began to spend time together, and Erik began mentoring Jackie in his brand new writing career. He was doing so well, Erik even hired Jackie to do some freelance writing for his business.

"Getting paid to write wasn't something I knew existed, really," said Jackie. "But that first freelance writing opportunity, coupled with my blog, opened the door to other freelance writing opportunities."

Before he knew it, Jackie was freelancing for some of the web's largest blogs and websites, and he was getting paid for it—AllProDad.com, Disney's Babble.com, USAFootball.com, GoodMenProject.com, CoachUp.com, and BlackandMarriedWithKids.com. He's been interviewed on NBC, CBN, Moody Radio, Huffington Post Live, and Yahoo about his different writing projects.

He was writing constantly, creating an average of 50 new blog posts and articles every month. He was eventually able to replace the income from his previous job, and his family was living in a new house. He did it by following his "three basic steps: 1) Start a blog; 2) build a following; 3) write a book."

His writing led to other opportunities as well, such as creating a series of articles that turned into a book, *The 7 Rings of Marriage*. That turned into a publishing deal in 2015 with LifeWay Publishing, a Christian publishing company, as well as an 8-part DVD-based Bible study and book, all published in 2016.

This has all turned into new opportunities for Jackie and Stephana as well.

"My blog, my book, and my online platform opened the door for regular speaking opportunities for both of us," said Jackie. "I currently receive requests to speak on a monthly basis."

The two travel the country monthly (something they'd always wanted to do, but never could), teaching classes and seminars for various church groups. They're also organizing additional online events.

What's funny about this all is that Jackie never envisioned himself as a writer. He said that his least favorite school subjects were writing and speaking. But writing became a way of expressing himself and dealing with what he calls some of the toughest times of his life.

"Expressing my thoughts and my feelings in my writing helped me to deal with the failure and grow from it, while also helping other men who had similar experiences," said Jackie.

"I've gone from being broke to having a blog, to writing a book, and to running a business in which we create digital products such as online courses, webinars, membership sites, and online events to help married couples grow together."

But Jackie said the coolest thing about it was when his three kids learned that "daddy is a writer. Soon after that, they all began writing their own stories. My kids have written short stories, books, and comic book series."

When we asked him for one piece of advice for you, the reader, he said, "Do what I did when I started. Read *Branding Yourself*. I would have been totally lost if I had not read it. I still practice much of what I learned today."

Give us a minute, we're a little misty-eyed.

Finding Publishing Opportunities

While this book is primarily about social media and blogging, a writer can be (should be) more widely published than just his or her own blog. There are a lot of opportunities for people to be published, with literally thousands upon thousands of print publications. You can get your foot in the publishing door in several ways, starting with writing a query letter. You also need to know what rights you should offer (or will be offered to you) and how to get paid.

It's much harder to be a print writer than a blogger because you're trying to meet others' standards, follow their editorial calendar and writing style, and fulfill their readers' wants and needs.

Understand that getting published is competitive and difficult. A magazine typically publishes 12 times a year and accepts only a set number of articles from freelancers. A newspaper can publish anywhere from once a week to every day, and again, it has limited space. So although our advice may sound like "Write a story; submit it; collect $200," it's not that easy. You're competing with other writers who also want to see their name in print.

Our goal with this chapter is to show you the basics of where to publish, how to submit ideas or articles for publication, what you can expect, and tie it all back to your personal brand. All kinds of websites, books, and magazines exist about the writing life that discuss these topics further.

🔍 *Tip*

Get the book *Writer's Market,* published by *Writer's Digest* magazine.
This is the writer's bible for learning about publication rights, how to write
a cover and pitch letter, what rates to charge, and best of all, contact
and submission information for nearly every publishing house and periodical
in the United States and Canada. If you're looking for the best place to
submit an article, you need the latest copy of this book.

Local Newspapers

You can write any number of articles for local newspaper, whether it's a guest
editorial, an op-ed piece, a weekly column, or even a freelance news article. If you
live in a big city or your paper is owned by a media conglomerate, you may have a
tougher time getting a piece in there. But smaller towns and weekly newspapers are
always looking for well-written content. If you have a business-to-consumer (B2C)
business, for example, apply to publish how-to and advice columns in your local
newspaper.

Let's say you run a personal finance business in a city of 30,000 people. You can
spend a lot of money on Yellow Pages ads, newspaper ads, etc. and spend a lot of
time going to networking events. Or, you can write a personal finance column in
the paper, giving general (not specific) advice on saving money, investing in stocks
and bonds, paying taxes, and so on. The upside is that the newspaper will get some
well-written, informed content, and you'll be seen as more of an expert by your
potential clients (people in your city) because you're in the paper.

Of course, these are like a normal job, just like any freelancing work. You have
to apply for them or contact the editor. Send a query letter to the editor of your
local paper, or if your city has a large newspaper, submit the letter to the editor
who manages your chosen section. Pitch the idea of the column to the editor, and
include a couple of sample columns you have written. Make sure you understand
the paper's style and tone.

If you have an idea for a single article, pitch it to the editor first, especially if you're
not an established freelance writer. Then you'll know whether to devote the time
and energy to writing the article, rather than hoping your hard work gets accepted.
(This is why a lot of writers get into blogging in the first place. They publish the
work that didn't get accepted for print, but they still want it to be read.)

If you aren't having much luck with one newspaper, look for others in your
area, both smaller and larger. What about the next city or town over? How about
weekly newspapers? Or smaller dailies? After you start building a reputation as
a decent newspaper writer in other cities, your local newspaper is more likely to
consider working with you.

Business Newspapers

In addition to dailies, some regions have dedicated business newspapers, which is great for people in business-to-business...uh, businesses. These are filled with news for the various businesspeople and industries in the city they serve. Articles analyze the economic progress of the city, real estate, business growth, and development. They discuss who's joining what company, which companies are merging or expanding, and the political issues that affect local businesses. Often, the papers include how-to articles, trend analyses, and introductions to new technology, which are ideal for emerging writers who are knowledgeable about their field.

If you work in a B2B business, you want to get your information in front of the executives who read these publications. Getting published in a business paper is a great step toward becoming an established writer.

Our friend, Bruce Hetrick, owns Powerful Appeals Inc. and is a professor of public relations at the Indiana University School of Journalism. In a rare bridging of the PR/journalism chasm, Bruce also doubled as a columnist for the *Indianapolis Business Journal*, the local business newspaper, for many years. But rather than writing only about PR/marketing or even client-category subject matter, Bruce tackled bigger issues, from the environmental benefits of living downtown instead of the suburbs, to how BP mishandled its crisis communication during the Gulf of Mexico oil spill , the importance of nonsmoking initiatives in the state, and even lessons he learned driving his sons to college one fall.

By publishing his column twice a month, Bruce has earned a citywide reputation for being a business thought leader. He is often asked to serve on nonprofit boards, to pilot nonsmoking initiatives, and to participate in citywide corporate events.

The biggest benefit? Some of Bruce's past and current clients are the biggest in the community, all of whom trust him because he writes thoughtful commentary in the city's most respected business news publication.

(Let's circle back to our opening section for a second to make this point: Did Bruce do anything special to earn these business leaders' trust? Did he change his ideas or behave differently to earn it? No, he kept doing what he was doing, but he had a printed platform in which to share his ideas.)

Finding a column- or article-writing opportunity in business papers works just like it does in dailies. Read the publication to get a sense of the tone and style, send a query letter pitching your idea, and include some spec samples.

Specialty Magazines and Newspapers

A step down from the journals, in terms of rigor and formality, are industry trade newspapers and magazines.

When Erik worked in the poultry industry, he used to receive stacks of magazines and specialty newspapers each month about production, processing, equipment, overseas issues, and regional issues in that industry. There were magazines from Illinois and Arkansas, England and The Netherlands. Several of these trade magazines published content from people in the field, including companies that sold poultry production products because they were the experts.

The only caveat was that the articles couldn't be commercial—writers couldn't promote their own products or services. Sure, the articles could answer questions about problems that only their products could solve, but they had to be advisory or educational in nature, not commercial. So Erik wrote a couple of articles about problems that his product just happened to solve. From that, he generated some sales and trade show recognition from them. ("Hey, weren't you in that poultry magazine?")

Subscribe to your industry's trade journals (many are free), even if they seem tangential to the work you do. Figure out if you can contribute articles. Some of these journals or magazines hire their writers, while others accept contributor articles (that is, articles from other readers). Because they're usually on the lookout for content, they'll consider just about anything if it's well written and on topic. But there are rigorous standards and editorial guidelines you have to follow.

Our development editor for this book, Leslie O'Neill, often writes trade journal articles, and she told us, "Nothing that gets submitted will be published as is. There is always a review process, which can suck, and even contributed articles must adhere to editorial standards. They will be edited mercilessly. It won't feel good. It will hurt their egos. They will feel like bad people and terrible writers; they're not."

If you work in an industry closely allied with other industries, your content might fit in their publications, and if you want to give it a try, Table 14.1 has some allied industry suggestions to get your mind thinking in that direction.

Table 14.1 Article Ideas for Crossing into Allied Industries

Your Industry	Allied Industries	Article Ideas
Direct mail	Nonprofits, magazines, banking, restaurants	How to reduce direct mail costs; how to personalize variable data; how to increase holiday donations
Business banking	Small businesses	How to apply for credit lines; how to use alternative data sources for lending decisions; explanation of the tax implications of business credit

Your Industry	Allied Industries	Article Ideas
Recycling	Construction, city governments	Challenges facing city recycling programs; how to implement construction recycling programs
Personal insurance	Small business owners, entrepreneurs, and farmers	Explanation of the importance of insurance for entrepreneurs; how to help farmers cut insurance costs

By crossing over into these allied industries, you accomplish two things:

1. **You find a new niche audience who may need your product or service:** By establishing yourself as the expert in your field as it relates to their field (as opposed to trying to be an expert in their field), you become much more useful and trusted.

2. **You stop preaching to the choir:** It's a common desire to want to be seen as the expert among experts in your own field. We do it, too. Some of the content we create is designed to outdo other social media experts and professionals, so we can show off and prove how awesome we are...

   @edeckers: But I *am* better than you.
   @kyleplacy: Older doesn't always mean better.

   ...or to see if we can write about a topic first and get everyone else to jump on the bandwagon.

   However, we're not going to be hired by other social media consultants. And you're never going to get work from other direct mail firms, business bankers, recycling plants, or insurance agents. (Well, almost never. See Chapter 12 on networking.) So, don't worry so much about trying to impress them, except at national conferences.

Hobby Publications

Small hobby publications, such as magazines about crafting, cooking, and collecting, are a good place to pursue writing about your personal passion or hobby—and there is one for even the most esoteric personal interest. They let you practice writing for publication, you can learn more about your particular passion, and, if nothing else, they give you another notch on your writing belt.

Some hobby publications are less stringent than other types of publications. That's not to say they're lax and willing to accept any schlock you throw at them, but they're a little more willing to accept contributions from new writers. They're a great way to build your writing portfolio as you go for bigger and better-paying writing gigs. However, some premier hobby magazines publish articles from the leading practitioners, so you're going to have a tougher time breaking into those.

Submitting to hobby publications is just like submitting to other publications: Submit a query letter and pitch an idea. If you're blogging already, be sure to tell the editor about your blog. Although this is a good strategy for any writing you're doing (except maybe for the scientific journals), it may be more helpful for hobby publications because you're already demonstrating your expertise and authority in that field.

Major Mainstream Magazines

This is the pinnacle of magazine publishing. If you can make it in general interest magazines—*Time, Newsweek, Better Homes & Gardens, Sports Illustrated, BusinessWeek, Wired*—that's really saying something. The articles in these magazines are of the highest caliber, the writers are the best in their field, and the pay is some of the highest in the industry.

But the competition is intense, and some of these publications don't even accept freelance submissions; check out the writers' guidelines before you pitch anything. You also want to make sure you have some serious writing skills and publishing credits in other publications before you submit to the major magazines.

One way to get your foot in the door here: Some of the big business magazines, such as *Entrepreneur, Inc.* and *Forbes,* accept blog articles from outside contributors. We know several writers who contribute these blog articles and have seen some incredible opportunities as a result. Of course, you're doing this for free, and there are dozens of new articles appearing each week, so it's hard to stand out. But if you write the right article at the right time, it could be a career changer for you.

Go Horizontal Instead of Vertical

Still other publications are geared toward people who work in a particular segment that can be covered horizontally, rather than vertically. For example, there are trade magazines for people in the retail industry, such as lumber yards, grocery stores, electronics stores, and liquor stores. There are trade magazines for people in all levels of IT, people in different facets of marketing, and people in different positions in the restaurant industry. An article such as "How to Save Money on Credit Card Processing" would work for any magazine in the retail industry. "Direct Mail Still Improves ROI" could fit in any marketing trade magazine.

> ✉ *Note*
>
> A "vertical" refers to a particular industry or market, like a "publishing vertical" or "automotive vertical." If you sold software used only by book publishers, you would sell to the "publishing vertical." Going "horizontally" means you have a product or expertise that spans all verticals, like marketing or accounting.

The nice thing about these types of magazines is that you can easily tailor one article to each niche and have it run several times without being read by the same people. Your article about lowering credit card fees for restaurants can be recycled as an article about lowering credit card fees for lumber yards, grocery stores, and liquor stores. This is also a favorite trick of freelance writers: Build one story from scratch, rewrite it for a different publication (use the same ideas, but different language and structure), and generate some additional revenue out of it. We discuss ownership rights later, so be sure you haven't signed over all rights to an article. Read the magazine's contract for mention of intellectual property rights and republication rights.

> 🔍 *Tip*
>
> Many magazine editors hate simultaneous submissions. They don't want you to publish identical articles in different magazines. They don't even want you to submit the same article to different magazines. Also keep in mind that some magazines don't like reprints, although most will accept them. Check out the "Publication Rights" section later in this chapter to see what kinds of conditions you can and should sell your articles under.

Build Your Personal Brand with Your Writing

One problem associated with writing B2B articles is you can sometimes be overshadowed by your own employer. Your company gets all the credit for your work, your expertise, and your knowledge while you get the byline.

Getting the byline is important, but sometimes you may end up giving away the credit that should build your brand. We've talked to people who have written extensively for trade publications, but they later realized they have not reaped any of the benefit. Sure, they get an item to put on their résumé, an article to include in their personnel file, or a story that led to more writing opportunities. But when it came to building their personal brand, they missed out on a significant opportunity.

Our friend and owner of DK New Media, Doug Karr, who we've mentioned in other chapters, said that when he worked for a newspaper publisher as a database marketer, he wrote extensively for trade publications about database marketing in the newspaper industry. The problem was, said Doug, he always wrote about the great things his employer was doing, even though he was the one doing all the work. He wrote the articles about the company's efforts, without alluding to any of the work he had done.

Doug said that when the time came for a job search and he wanted to tell people about all the great stuff he had been doing, all of his articles—his "proof"—showed that it was a company effort. He found that although other people in his industry knew about the database marketing his old employer had been doing, no one realized that he had been the one actually doing it. As such, he didn't get the benefit by taking more ownership of what he had written, and he may have missed out on several job opportunities because no one in the industry knew his accomplishments like he had hoped. He now thinks he would've made it clear in the articles that the efforts described were actually his work, if he had known how his contribution would be overlooked.

This may be a tough line to walk—how do you talk about "my" efforts versus "my team's" efforts without sounding like a glory hound? Still, you need to take some ownership of your knowledge and experience in your articles, whether you're writing the article in first person, using personal anecdotes, or even including your title in the byline. Remember, this isn't just about adding a single line to your résumé; it's about building your personal brand within your field.

If the magazine publishes a bio section, you will get a chance to talk about your accomplishments. You can at least take credit there by saying you led the efforts, worked on the project, or managed the team that did everything you described in the article.

Continue to promote accomplishments like this to your network. Tweet messages and post Facebook updates like "So excited to see my latest article in 'Marble Collectors Digest' yesterday!" with a link to the online article. Then, assuming your network includes a bunch of marble collectors, others will see the article and associate you with it.

Promoting your published articles this way, especially if you can link to an online version, is no different from promoting your blog posts and other accomplishments (see Chapter 3, "Blogging: Telling Your Story"). Treat them the same way, but point out they're also available in print. As long as the people in your network see them, you can get more benefit than if you limit your publication accomplishments to just your résumé.

Finally, don't forget to publish your Twitter handle or your main website in your bio. Make sure you write a tight bio on your website, in your Twitter profile, and in your article.

Publication Rights

We need to discuss publication rights briefly here, although you'll want to do further research. You may be offered several basic types of rights:

- **First North American serial rights (FNASR):** These allow a publication in North America to publish your piece for the first time. These rights tell the publisher that you've never published this piece anywhere else. The publisher cannot reprint in another publication or outside of North America. Often (but not always), FNASR now includes electronic rights.

- **First rights:** These say a publication has first use of the piece, but isn't limited to print. Electronic publications use first rights, and they're usually global since it can be accessed from anywhere.

- **Second rights or reprint rights:** Second rights are those you can give to any other publisher after you have sold FNASRs, but you can publish the piece simultaneously.

- **One-time rights:** These let a publication use your work once, but not first and sometimes simultaneously. They're similar to second rights. They're also called ONASR (one-time North American serial rights.)

- **Electronic rights:** Many writers try to avoid electronic rights because this makes no distinction among the media where your work is published (database, website, blog, and article site). Sometimes the article becomes exclusive to the publisher, so you can never republish it anywhere else.

- **All rights:** This means a publisher buys every instance where your piece could be published—electronic, print, you name it. Writers should avoid these rights whenever possible, but if you can't escape it, figure out how much you realistically could get paid for the piece over several years, and charge that much.

In general, publishers have their own contracts they require writers to sign before they accept your material, and many magazines do not negotiate on the publication rights they give the writers. They also have set fees they will pay, and they're often not open to negotiation. So when a publisher accepts a piece for publication, you need to consider whether you're willing to live with their terms and their pay rate, especially when being asked for electronic rights or all rights.

Create Your Own Articles' Niche

In Chapter 3, we talked about creating a narrow writing niche so you could be known for, and an expert in, that particular topic.

 Note

> Remember, a general topic might be cooking, a narrow topic might be Italian cooking, but a niche is something like "gluten-free Italian cooking."

When you blog, you can just write whatever you want, and your readers will follow you and love you. But the readers of a print publication want all kinds of things and might abandon a publication if they're not getting what they want. Also, bloggers have a personality and voice that readers respond to. All print publications have their own voice, and don't want their writers to deviate from their standard. When choosing where to submit articles, consider if your voice fits with the magazine's voice.

The point we're trying to make is that it's not always necessary, or even a good idea, to focus on a single niche all the time. If you're that gluten-free Italian cooking writer, you're going to find few opportunities to write about gluten-free Italian cooking for print publications.

Despite all of the industry health magazines, local parenting newspapers, and even national cooking magazines that may allow you to reprint your articles, there are only so many publications that are looking for your particular niche.

In this case, it may be more important to widen your niche a little bit. Don't focus so narrowly on a single type or country of origin of food. Rather, stick with gluten-free cooking, and you can talk about a variety of topics. For example, you could publish these articles in different newspapers or general interest magazines to fit the editorial calendar, or even the same publication:

- Gluten-free cooking for new Celiac sufferers (general)
- Gluten-free cookies for the holidays (holiday season)
- Gluten-free tailgating ideas (football season)
- Gluten-free romantic dinner ideas (Valentine's Day)
- Gluten-free cookout ideas (summer)

Without once talking about Italian food, we came up with five ideas for different publications without over-limiting ourselves.

The additional benefit of doing this is that you're establishing a more impressive reputation as a gluten-free writer, not just a gluten-free Italian cooking writer. If you ever pursue speaking opportunities, book opportunities, or the chance to appear on the various news and cooking shows, you'll be the "gluten-free writer who loves Italian cooking."

Getting Started

Being published is just like getting a job. (Skip ahead to Chapter 15, "Personal Branding: Using What You've Learned to Land Your Dream Job," if you don't believe us.) You have to find a possible opening, send in your résumé (your query letter), have an interview (your completion of the writing project), and be paid. (And in some cases, you may actually be asked to send in a real résumé and do a real interview.) Follow these basic steps to start getting published:

- **Do research first:** After you figure out which kinds of publications to write for, don't just submit an article. Maybe they don't publish that particular topic, or they just published a similar one last month. Get back issues of the publication to see what kinds of stories they publish and whether anyone has written about yours before.

- **Get the writers' guidelines:** Each magazine has writers' guidelines, usually online. When you get the guidelines, follow them exactly! If they say to submit a query letter but no article, then submit a query letter without an article. Deviating from the guidelines will mean a certain literary death.

  Editors can be cranky and finicky...

  @edeckers: Not ours, of course.
  @kyleplacy: Absolutely, not ours.

  ...and if editors see you deviating from their guidelines, they'll toss your submission into the trash can without the slightest twinge of remorse. Editors are often asked what their biggest pet peeve is. Almost all of them say getting queries and articles that don't follow the writers' guidelines.

  @edeckers: It's death, I tell you! Death!
  @kyleplacy: Settle down.

- **Write a solid query letter:** This is the "résumé" we referred to earlier. There are certain pieces of information you need to include in a query letter.

✉ *Note*

Include a cover letter with an article submission. A query letter, on the other hand, asks if you can write or submit an article.

Include a paragraph about the article you plan to write and what it will be about. Next, cite your experience as an expert on the topic. Third, cite your experience as a writer on this topic. (This is where personal branding comes in handy.)

Several websites, magazine articles, and books discuss the best way to write a query letter. Refer to them for the particulars of the language and information to include or exclude.

- **Do the work you're supposed to:** This is your "interview." Not only does the editor want to see if you can write, she wants to see if you can follow instructions. If you write a good article, you'll get the byline and the paycheck. If you don't follow instructions, your story may not even get published, and you won't get paid. Which brings us to our next point...

- **Invoice immediately:** You're a professional now, so act like one. Don't wait for a publisher to pay you; send an invoice. Send it with the work if you can. Although some magazines already have a well-established system in place, don't wait for them to show you whether they do or don't.

  If you are not paid within 30 days, send another invoice. If the magazine fails to pay, don't accept any more work from that magazine until you see your money. Treasure the relationships you have with the ones that pay immediately and drop the ones that don't.

- **Once you establish your reliability, you may be able to pitch other ideas to the editor:** It's important to feel out the editor first, though. Make a couple of basic suggestions for new ideas via query email. See if the editor is receptive to them. If she is, and you can continue to provide solid ideas and follow the editorial calendar, you become a valuable, reliable resource.

- **Continue to network with the editor and staff:** Don't be a pest, but don't be a stranger either. Keep in touch with these people via LinkedIn and Twitter, if they use them. When they leave for another publication (or corporate communications job), keep in touch. If they loved you for their old publication, they'll love you for their new one, too. At the same time, you'll need to start over with the new editor at square one. Although your old editor thought you were a valuable resource, the new editor has his or her own vision, and you may not fit it. Don't take it personally if you don't.

Getting Paid

Writers are paid. They write for money, not for exposure, for contributor copies, or for the promise of more money at a later date. And despite what sites like Clients-FromHell.net (see Figure 14.1) may make you think, most editors are a good and fair bunch of people who want to see their writers fairly compensated.

@kyleplacy:	Absolutely. So good they're fattening! And very fair!
@edeckers:	And good looking, too. In fact, the best looking of any editor there ever was.
@YourDamnEditor:	Guys, forget it. You already signed the contract.

Figure 14.1 *People who offer you a chance to write for exposure sometimes have more grandiose expectations of what you're going to get.*

 Note

Contributor copies are free copies of the magazine your article is published in, presumably so you can give them to all your friends and family.

However, there are two things you need to know about writing professionally. First, writing for print is a tough way to make a living. The pay is not lucrative, and you're going to work harder doing this than you would with a regular 9-to-5 day job. However, from a personal branding standpoint, writing professionally is worth the time and effort.

Second, you're not going to make much money in the beginning. You're going to have to establish yourself and prove that you're a great writer and that you can turn out high-quality material on the deadlines.

Paying Your Dues

You have to pay your dues for a while. That's a given. It may suck, and you may think you're above it, but you're going to have to put up with it. However, depending on how good you are—don't make this assessment yourself; ask one of your brutally honest friends—your dues-paying period can be shorter or longer.

There are a few reasons why all new writers have to pay dues:

- **Every writer and editor before you did it:** They didn't get to exact revenge on those older writers and editors, so they have to take it out on the newbies. That's you.

- **No one knows you:** They don't know if you suck or if you're awesome. You need to prove your worth by being easy to work with, turning your work in on time, giving editors exactly what they want, and being a good writer.

- **You'll be paid what you're worth:** As you prove that you're better than the others, you'll get more money. As you prove that you're more reliable than the others, you'll get even more money. And as you prove that you're better at this and know more about the subject matter than anyone else, you'll get even more money than that. (Of course, most publications have a set rate, and the only way you'll get more money is if you write for them more often. They generally don't increase their rates for just one writer.)

This is personal branding in a nutshell. You need to prove that you're as awesome as you—and we—think you are. The only way to do that is by doing what it takes to succeed in this or any other business. Do that, and you'll start reaping your rewards.

The Myth of Exposure

Having said all that, you will reach the point where you should not only ask for money, but expect it. You will reach the point where you should be writing only for money. You've proven yourself and made a name for yourself, so money should be the only form of payment you receive.

This means you should turn down those who say they'll give you exposure instead of money.[1]

They say, "We can't pay you, but you'll get great exposure," or "You'll get a great article for your portfolio."

Turn these people down. If you're getting paid decent money for your articles, you are beyond the need for the benefits that exposure offers. If you're getting top dollar for your articles, you've probably stopped clipping articles for your portfolio months ago.

Erik has had exchanges like this with editors of small publications before, and they all usually end the same way:

Erik: How much do you pay for publication?

Editor: Well, we give you five free copies of our magazine.

Erik: And...?

Editor: Uh, and you get some great exposure for your writing.

Erik: Sorry, my supermarket doesn't let me pay for groceries with exposure.

Editor: But more people will hear about you, and you can secure paying gigs in the future.

Erik: Or I could secure paying gigs right now.

We don't advocate writing for exposure after you have several published articles under your belt. Exposure is fine and all, but it doesn't pay the rent, and you can't eat it. We've been offered exposure by magazines with print runs that are measured in the hundreds. We have to wonder just how good that exposure could actually be. (Most of them fold a few months later—they're not paying you because they don't have the money to.)

Having said this, we mentioned earlier the large business publications that allow people to contribute blog articles for their online publication. It's quite a boost to your brand if you can say "I'm a blogger for *Forbes*."

The Do's and Don'ts of Writing for Publication

There are a few do's and don'ts to writing for publication, just like for anything you want to pursue. These are rules handed down from writer to writer, article to article, book to book, website to website.

---

1. Okay, there may be a few times you don't want to turn them down, like when the people asking are your friends, or it's a startup publication that you want to see do well, or it's a nonprofit you support. Or *The New York Times*. At the least you should get lunch out of it. Just remind them that you're beyond exposure, so you can feel like a big shot.

@edeckers: There, I worked in something about digital publishing. Happy?

@kyleplacy: Deliriously.

We have found that while most professionals are sticklers about the rules in their industry, publishers and editors are adamant about these. Ignore these rules at your peril:

- **Do read the writers' guidelines:** That's the best indication as to what the magazine or newspaper will accept from writers. These publications know what they need from their writers to please their readers and support their editorial mission.

- **Do proofread everything:** This is especially important when you're submitting your first query letter. Remember, you're submitting a story idea to a professional wordsmith. Editors take language and spelling seriously and will not look favorably upon a submission with even a single misspelling. That's not to say they'll toss the article they agreed to purchase for a single typo, but even so, avoid them.

- **Do read your submitted pieces out loud, including your initial query letter:** This will help you spot any errors or double words, like "the the."

- **Do meet all deadlines:** Nothing makes an editor go crazy like a writer who can't meet his deadlines. If you have a problem with time management and can't even meet the simplest deadlines at work, you may want to reconsider whether you should go into writing. At the very least, find a time management system and get better about meeting deadlines.

- **Don't get creative, wacky, or funny with your submissions, because it won't make you stand out in a positive way:** Just print your letters and your articles on plain white paper. There are websites that detail horror story after horror story of weird submissions to publishers and editors. Many publications have begun using Submittable.com, so get used to that and don't try to deviate from it to stand out.

- **Don't get married to your words:** Don't think of them as your babies. Don't refuse to be edited. Even the best writers in the world are edited. If anything, an editor makes your writing better.

- **Don't plagiarize:** We shouldn't have to say this, but you would be surprised at the number of people who lift entire articles from other sources, thinking they won't get caught.

```
@kyleplacy:  It was the best of times, it was the worst
             of times.
@edeckers:   No! That's been done before.
```

Over the years, Erik has caught three newspaper professionals—an assistant editor, a columnist, and a publisher/owner; two from Canada, one from the U.S.—who lifted several of his newspaper humor columns. He caught the first one by doing a basic Google search on a unique phrase in that particular column, and this was before Google and search engines were so extensively used. Erik told the guy's publisher about it, and then pleaded for leniency on behalf of the offending writer. The offending editor wasn't fired, but he lost his newspaper column and was suspended without pay for two months.

While we were working on the second edition of this book, Erik learned he was plagiarized twice, once by a newspaper editor in Minnesota and once by a publisher in Canada, both of whom had made a long-running habit of stealing from other humor writers. Both men resigned in disgrace after the stories of their serial theft made national and journalism industry news. So, in terms of stealing Erik's stuff, Canada leads the U.S., 2–1, but we're hoping the U.S. can make a comeback before the next edition.

```
@edeckers:   Actually, no we don't. That was an awful
             experience.
@kyleplacy:  Seriously. Haven't you people ever heard of
             Google?
```

- **Don't stray from the writers' guidelines:** We know we already said it, but we can't say it enough. Nothing will get your article thrown in the trash faster than straying from the writers' guidelines.

How Can Our Heroes Turn to Writing for Publication?

- **Allen (influencer)** spent 14 years working for a marketing agency and is considered a veteran of the industry. He has a good idea of what works and what doesn't and could write articles for various marketing magazines, which are usually read by other marketers. Another possibility is to publish basic how-to articles for small-business magazines and Chamber of Commerce publications—things that the do-it-yourself marketer would benefit from. These may also help Allen catch the eye of agency owners and business owners.

- **Beth (climber)** has a plan to become the chief marketing officer of an insurance company. One way to prove that she knows her stuff is to publish marketing articles—especially case studies of her company's own marketing efforts—for trade publications.

  Beth will actually get two things out of this. First, she can bolster her reputation among other marketers, some of whom may want to recruit her as she climbs her way to the CMO job. Second, she can be noticed by other C-level executives in her company who hire their new CMO. Her case studies will let her show off her past work in a public setting. If she uses these articles and her social networks, she can get her name in front of those C-level executives on an ongoing basis.

- **Carla (neophyte)** is a former pharmaceutical sales rep who is out of work but trying to find a fundraising or program director position at a nonprofit. Publishing in trade journals may not help her much, but she should still consider it. Blogging may be a better and more effective outlet for showing how well she understands the nonprofit field. However, she could write career advice pieces aimed at college students who want to go into sales, especially in the pharmaceutical industry. She can also write sales advice columns for business magazines.

- **Darrin (free agent)** is an IT professional who leaves his job every two or three years in pursuit of more money. Darrin has a few industry options, like publications geared toward chief information officers and IT networking professionals. These tend to be more newsy than how-to focused and often rely on reviews of products. So, Darrin can create the "product reviewer" as part of his personal brand by reviewing new products and services.

  This will do two things: 1) set him up as someone who is always forward-looking and willing to try new ideas and products, and 2) plug him into beta releases of software and hardware. He'll know what's coming down the pike months before the general IT community will. So when he's not writing reviews for print, he can write them for his blog and get a boost to this part of his brand. The upshot is that for less than double the amount of effort, he gets twice the benefit.

15

Personal Branding: Using What You've Learned to Land Your Dream Job

Let's say this up front: If you start looking for your new job on the day you were let go from your last job, you're already behind.

If you're out of work, looking for work, and trying to create your personal brand to help you, you should have done this during your previous job. But it's not too late, not by a long shot. You're just going to have to develop your network much more quickly.

If you're currently employed, you need to start putting the lessons in this book into practice right now, today. Lay the groundwork for your next job while you still have an income, not while the pressure of taking care of yourself and your family is looming over your head, stressing you out.

Whether you're happy in your job or searching for your next gig, you need to plant the seeds now for a professional network that can reach potential employers and colleagues who will give you solid job referrals. Building this type of network takes time, and you want it in place before you actually need it.

We have both received calls from people looking for work, wondering if we can help them, know of any openings in their field, and introduce them to other people they should talk to. We're always willing to help as much as we can, but it can sometimes be difficult to be helpful on short notice.

Erik once received a call from a friend a few days after the friend—we'll call him Bob—was laid off from his old position.

"I'm reaching out to the people in my network to find a new job," said Bob.

"Who does that involve?" asked Erik.

"The people I used to work with," said Bob. The problem was he came from a fairly closed company—no outside networking, no outside meetings. In short, the only people Bob knew were just as professionally isolated as he was. And the only job opening they knew of was Bob's old one.

But if you don't have a job at this moment, you still have time to network. (We were just trying to scare the hell out of the people who already have a job and are wasting time watching reality TV night after night.) Building your network to find potential employers and job referrals can take a few months, and if you're wondering about your next paycheck, this can be an especially scary time.

So you need to start building your network because 1) you might get lucky and find something right away and 2) you want to have the network in place so when you're looking for another job, you don't have a long and expensive ramp-up time.

If we haven't said it enough, we'll say it again: Building your personal brand is all about building relationships. You need to build and maintain those relationships over weeks, months, and years, both online and offline. Use social media to build your brand and expand your network to help with your job search when the time comes.

Our friend Jack[1] has benefitted from having a strong social media presence and landed a couple of jobs that way. The director of global Internet marketing at a Fortune 100 corporation once hired him for a social media position after reading his blog. He wrote regularly about how social media humanizes a brand and builds community with its customers. The corporation just happened to be launching a social media initiative at the same time, and the director liked what Jack wrote.

---

1. Also not his real name, but he's really our friend. No, really, we have friends!

During the job interview, the director told Jack that he was impressed with his blog and thought Jack had the knowledge to help him launch the company's global social media initiative.

Jack's blog basically positioned him as the thought leader for leading the corporation's new initiative. He got the interview because someone within the company had been reading his blog and passed the information to the global Internet marketing director.

The only time he presented a résumé was during the interview, when he and the director discussed other points of his professional background. Jack got the job and worked there for over a year.

This is what the previous 14 chapters have led up to. This is where your personal branding efforts will ultimately pay off. Using these tools, you will have a better chance of finding and landing the job you want in the industry you enjoy.

This is why you need to treat social media as a networking tool, not just a way to play Words with Friends on your phone or organize pub crawls with your college buddies. You need to be your own marketer and create your own buzz. If you can create enough buzz about yourself, employers will start to imagine what you can do for them.

Using Your Network to Find a Job

Jack's story about being contacted by a marketing director is not that unusual. In Jack's case, the two were connected on a few different social networks for more than a year. They were well aware of each other, had followed each other's progress, and kept up with each other before the job opened up. Jack first connected with the marketing communications director before he landed at the Internet marketing company.

Even though Jack didn't get the job, the fact that he made it that far into the company's hiring process says a lot about the online connections he made. It wasn't a position he sought; rather, he just happened to be connected to the right person at the right time.

Since we wrote the first edition of this book, this has become much more commonplace. We've heard more and more stories from our readers about how they made that first job-related connection on social media, rather than on the major job boards or by sending a résumé. They followed the steps in these pages, and landed an interview, a contract, or even a full-time job.

We've talked before about the serendipity of social media: the idea that you will meet the right person with the right opportunity at the right time. Of course, this doesn't just magically happen. You must be present and participate for a long time before that right person with the right opportunity comes along. Just like the athlete who spends countless hours practicing her sport, you need to spend countless hours developing your personal brand. Those hours will eventually pay off by connecting with, not the first person, not the tenth person, not even the hundredth person, but with the person who is your thousandth connection.

And you can't rush these things. So, no cheating.

Twitter: Connections in 140 Characters

This is when it's okay to talk about yourself more than a little. (See Chapter 5, "Twitter: Sharing in the Conversation.") If you're job hunting, feel free to tell your Twitter friends. In fact, tell your entire network on social media. Ask them to keep an eye open for any position that matches your skills and experience. Direct them to your LinkedIn profile, your blog, and your online portfolio (if you have one). A lot of friends and industry colleagues will know about job openings that may not hit the job boards or even be widely known within the hiring company yet.

Tweet a variation of this message more than once or twice a week, and ask people to send you a direct message if they have anything. Ask them to retweet your request.

⚠ *Warning*

Do not tweet, post Facebook updates, make LinkedIn updates, or otherwise publicly tell your social network you are looking for a new job while you are still employed. Erik knows someone who did this. Her employer helpfully gave her an additional 40 hours a week to focus on her job search.

LinkedIn: Professional Connections

While we were working on the new edition of this book, Erik was asked by a freelance writer to introduce her through LinkedIn to a hiring manager at a publishing house. Interestingly, Erik didn't even know the person he was supposed to introduce the writer to. But he did know someone who knew the hiring manager.

By reviewing Erik's connections, the freelancer had seen that he was connected to the hiring manager by two degrees. In other words, there was one person between Erik and the hiring manager.

So, she sent Erik a "Get Introduced" request, which not only had a message to the hiring manager, but a message to Erik asking him to make the connection. He forwarded that on to the person he was connected with, who then forwarded it on to the hiring manager. The connection was made, and the writer sent her résumé. The freelancer worked the system in the best way possible: by leveraging her existing network.

One of the great things about LinkedIn is that you can see who knows whom, who is connected, and what they do for their employer. You can make the decision about who to connect with.

The Art of the LinkedIn Connection

Making a connection on LinkedIn is an important part of the job search process. For one thing, you don't want to constantly pepper your entire network about whether they know of any job openings. It's okay to ask every week or two, but bugging them day after day is bad form and will get you unconnected and ignored as fast as any spammer. (See Chapter 4, "LinkedIn: Networking on Steroids" to learn more about how LinkedIn connections are formed.) Figure 15.1 shows how many connections you have on your LinkedIn page.

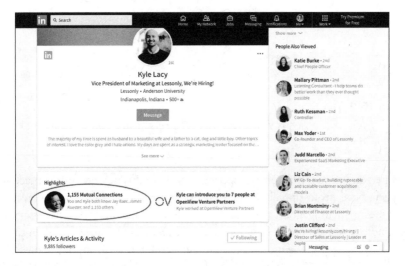

Figure 15.1 *LinkedIn shows you how you're connected to someone else in your network. This is Kyle's profile, as seen through Erik's account. We have 1,143 connections in common. The second degree connections on the right are the people who are connected to Kyle, but not to Erik.*

@edeckers: Man, we sure know a lot of people.

@kyleplacy: Tell me about it. Do you know how many Christmas cards I sent out last year?

@edeckers: One less than you think you did. I never got one.

@kyleplacy: What? I can't hear you! I'm going through a tunnel. <**signal dropped**>

@edeckers: Nice try. We're on Twitter.

Asking your networking contacts for a connection is a tricky process. For one thing, you may ask your best friend to connect you with one of his contacts (someone you don't actually know), but addressing him like you would in any other email may not be appropriate. Figure 15.2 is a good example of what not to say to your friend in an introduction request.

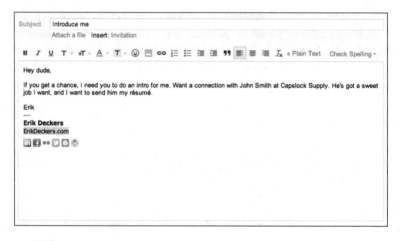

Figure 15.2 *This is an example of what not to write in an introductory email. It doesn't matter if your connection is your best friend. The person you want to connect to is not your friend.*

The person you're ultimately connecting to will see this note to your contact, so it needs to be as professionally written as your cover note to your final connection. This means spelling, grammar, and punctuation must be perfect. If necessary, write your note in a word processing document, edit it a couple times, and then sit on it for 24 hours. Edit it one more time, and then send it. Do this for both notes.

Your friend may have a few errors in his note to your connection, but you can't afford that luxury.

If you need to, send a separate email to your contact telling him what you're about to do. See if he can recommend any strategies for dealing with your final connection.

Should You Connect Directly or Ask for a Connection?

Isn't it easier to contact someone directly rather than ask someone to ask someone to connect you? Sure it is. But it's not always more effective.

It's one thing to connect with someone because you're both in the same LinkedIn group, belong to the same social network, or even are part of the same trade association. You can always send a personal note that tells the other person how you're connected.

Tip

Don't just use the default note that comes with your LinkedIn connection request. Write a note about how you know the other person or why you want to connect. Leaving the default note shows laziness and may cause the other person to click "I Don't Know This Person," which gets you in trouble with LinkedIn. If this happens, your account could be temporarily suspended until you read and sign an online form that says you promise not to try to connect with people who don't know you.

But what if that other person has no idea who you are? It's not always a great idea to try to connect with someone you have absolutely no connection with. It may be perceived as annoying, intrusive, or some cheap way to connect because you're trying to look for a job. (Sure, that's what you are doing, but you just don't want it to look that blatant.)

This is why asking someone for that introduction is a better step to take; you're asking a trusted acquaintance to vouch for you. By forwarding a connection request, an acquaintance is, in essence, saying, "I know this person. This is someone I think you should get to know, because it will be a mutually beneficial connection." (Reread the section on making an email introduction in Chapter 12, "How to Network: Hello, My Name Is...")

Use LinkedIn and Facebook to Get Inside Info

The best way to understand a company's culture is to talk to current and former employees. Search for a company name on LinkedIn, and look for people who work or used to work at that company. Try to pick the ones who are closest to you in terms of degrees of connectedness.

Connect directly through the usual process by asking for introductions or by joining an industry group and then connecting that way (again, see Chapter 4, "LinkedIn: Networking on Steroids"), and explain that you're looking for insight into that employer. After you connect, ask some basic questions about life at the company, their areas of responsibility, the sorts of issues they regularly face at work, and a typical day at the company.

This strategy can be a bit risky if you do it the wrong way or ask the wrong questions. Make it clear that you're not looking for gossip or secrets, but you want to know some day-in-the-life type information. Ask things like what you can expect if you work there, what the work climate is like, and what the hot button issues are that you might mention during an interview.

Don't try to find out insider information or dig up dirt on your potential boss. Your new contact may have a long-standing friendship with this person, and your nosiness can get back to them in a few seconds.

Of course, if your contact happens to drop a little gossip about the person who might ultimately be your boss, or why they left, don't ignore it. Everyone has a bad boss now and again, and if your information gathering reveals the person you're trying to work for is a tyrannical egomaniac who could reduce Genghis Khan to tears, it's better you find out now than two weeks into your new job.

Creating a Résumé

Your résumé is basically a synopsis of your career, your best qualities, and your successes. It's evidence of your overall awesomeness, and it gives companies a reason to bring you in for an interview.

That's worth repeating: A résumé is not supposed to get you a job; it's supposed to get you an interview.

We'd love to say that you could have Jack's luck and connect with people online...

@edeckers:	Actually, we are saying that. That's the point of the whole book.
@kyleplacy:	I know. I just didn't want the legal department jumping all over us with their disclaimers.
@LegalBeagle:	Whereas many, but not all, of your claims might possibly be taken as guarantees of performance, we have concerns that some, but not all, rec— ***CHARACTER LIMIT REACHED***

...but that doesn't happen to everybody. It happens often enough that this is a strategy worth pursuing, but it needs to be one part of a job search campaign, not the entire campaign. You need a résumé.

Should I Write a Paper Résumé?

Short answer: "Well. . ."

Longer answer: "Yes, but...."

Best answer: "If you have to."

Our friend and social media guru Doug Karr says he hasn't used a paper résumé in years. He steers potential clients toward his LinkedIn profile, and if they don't know how to use it or still insist on a paper résumé because "that's the way we've always done it," he doesn't want to work with them.

Of course, Doug is in the rather enviable position of being "kind of a big deal." He co-wrote *Corporate Blogging for Dummies*, he's a highly sought-after speaker on blogging and marketing technology, and has become one of the leading marketing technology voices in the industry.

Doug's attitude may be a little unusual because much of the corporate world is still locked into using electronic résumés that can be easily uploaded into a company's candidate management software. But when will LinkedIn become the standard operating procedure for more and more companies? How long will it be before companies start allowing resume websites like about.me?

We're longing for the day this will happen—that corporate America will join the rest of us here in the 21st century and find a new, better, more efficient way to screen candidates. Until then, right or wrong, like it or not, you should develop a traditional résumé and be prepared to give it to anyone who asks. At least until you become a big shot and can afford to refuse to work for anyone who doesn't want to check your LinkedIn profile.

How Does Social Media Fit in Your Résumé?

Everyone uses social media so much these days that people now ask whether they should include it among their skills, at least for nonsocial media positions. Another, more important question is if you have skills, knowledge, and experience in social media that can be demonstrated.

It comes down to this: If you know enough about social media to teach an entire day-long seminar on the subject, you can list it. If you spent an entire day creating a Double Rainbow/Over the Rainbow mashup video, keep that to yourself. Table 15.1 shows some other do's and don'ts for mentioning social media on your résumé.

Table 15.1 When to Include Social Media Skills on Your Résumé

Do Include	Don't Include	Exception
You spend several hours a week creating a video reality series.	You post videos of your dog dancing to Ray Charles songs.	Your dancing dog videos have 2 million hits a month and you're in negotiations for a TV series.
You blog about Facebook marketing.	You made $1 billion in gold coins playing *Pirate Clan* on Facebook.	You made $1 billion in real coins creating *Pirate Clan* for Facebook.
You helped a restaurant create a Swarm marketing campaign.	You're the mayor of your favorite coffee shop, and you get a free muffin every Monday.	Your army of Swarm followers has increased revenue for your favorite coffee shop by 200 percent.

Six Tips for Listing Social Media on Your Résumé

Social media is part of daily life now, so it's often okay to include a couple of networks, especially LinkedIn and your blog:

1. **Make sure you can demonstrate your success on past campaigns:** Use analytics to show the results of past social media campaigns. Mention your best ones on the résumé, but come to interviews prepared to discuss numbers. Have printouts of results and summaries. Use tools like Google Analytics and a spreadsheet to show your successes.

2. **Only list the social networks that you use in a professional manner:** "Started the Cougar Moms Who Love *Twilight* Facebook Page" is probably not suitable for a résumé. Keep things like Facebook and Snapchat off yours, unless you have a professional business page with a design portfolio or hundreds of thousands of Snapchat connections. Keep your Facebook profile free of incriminating photos and content, even if it's not on your résumé. (Hiring managers will probably search for it to learn more about you, so be prepared.)

3. **Make sure your personal networks are clean and devoid of any inappropriate photos or comments:** Don't worry too much about what your friends have done or said; employers won't hold that against you. Just make sure your own house is in order. You can also delete negative comments if you think it's necessary.

4. **Stick with three or four social networks:** Don't list every network you belong to, but use the ones that you think a hiring manager might be part of. Twitter and LinkedIn are the two big ones, but if you belong to an industry network, list it. Avoid esoteric networks if they're not related to the job or industry you're applying for.

5. **Shorten URLs using ow.ly or another URL shortener, if you have long URLs:** Use URLs whenever appropriate to point hiring managers to important information. This can include blogs, articles, galleries and portfolios, and LinkedIn URLs.

6. **Claim your personalized URL on Facebook and LinkedIn:** Although you won't necessarily post your Facebook URL on your résumé, you should at least try to own it. Do post your LinkedIn URL on your résumé. Personalized URLs generally look like http://www.facebook.com/erikdeckers or http://www.linkedin.com/in/kylelacy.

PERSONAL BRANDING CASE STUDY:
JASON FALLS

Louisville's own Jason Falls is one of the most widely read and respected voices in digital marketing and social media marketing. He was one of the first practitioners of the art and science of having online conversations, and he was fortunate enough to turn what people thought were just a bunch of "teenagers talking on FaceSpace" into a significant portion of a company's marketing budget and time.

He currently runs the Conversation Research Institute, but has been a VP of digital marketing and social media marketing for several marketing agencies, as well as CafePress, the print-on-demand tee-shirt and promotional products company.

But it all started when he first started in sports broadcasting and PR, and then wrote a newspaper humor column for his hometown newspaper in Pikeville, KY.

"I've been in communications, which requires storytelling, since my high school days as a radio disc jockey," said Jason. "Everything I do is some extension of storytelling. My family is full of communicators, writers, broadcasters and the like. It's always been there."

One of the first things Jason got to do on social media is still one of the coolest. He sat in the crew chief's tower at a NASCAR race, running social media for a Baja 1000 off-road team for NASCAR driver Robby Gordon.

They didn't have cell phone access in that part of the country, so Jason worked with a satellite phone and laptop, and he tweeted updates about the race every few minutes. Back then, there weren't many Twitter users, but those who were watching were fascinated, especially since they couldn't even see the race on TV.

Thanks to opportunities like this that have helped him build his personal brand as a digital marketing expert, Jason has been in the rather enviable position of being recruited or sought out for certain positions.

"If it weren't for my reputation, I never would have been noticed by CafePress. My role as VP for digital strategy was 100 percent the result of having a personal brand and a reputation as a thought leader in the digital marketing space," said Jason.

"Now, my personal brand and reputation is probably about 90 percent of the reason I get clients. Very seldom are my clients the result of anything other than, 'I've heard you are the man to see about this kind of thing.'"

Jason uses his blog and social media engagement to show prospective clients that he's on the leading edge of what companies are doing in digital marketing. He shows that he knows how to tell a story, manage a narrative, and can handle himself, even in sticky conversations online.

(Never mind that he put himself in those sticky conversations. Hey, you don't know him like we do! I remember one time when he—)

@jasonfalls: Are you really telling embarrassing stories about me in the middle of my own case study?

@edeckers: How the hell did you even get in here?

@kyleplacy: Yeah, seriously. No one gets to do the tweet gag except us.

From there, employers only have to watch his online activity for a while to know he can help their team.

"I'm also starting to drive paid social, CRM, and social sales tactics to be able to say, 'I can show you how I landed you as a client, which will help you land more yourself.' It's fun when that works out," said Jason.

When it comes to personal branding, he said, there are three types of people who are using social media for their efforts: 1) those who don't use it at all, 2) those who want to be a recognizable voice in their industry, and 3) those who want to be famous for being famous.

The third group are the people "who want to write books, speak, and be interviewed about how to write books, speak and be interviewed. Sometimes they have a core skill they're known for—marketing, public relations, social media—but more often than not, they're just hyping themselves as people who can help you hype yourself."

So what piece of advice does Jason have to offer you for your personal brand?

"Focus on illustrating that you're good at delivering business value, that you know something like marketing, sales, accounting, law or whatever your specialty area is," said Jason.

"Don't focus on showing people you know how to talk about you all the time. Be a brand about something businesses need, not just promoting yourself as a famous talking head. Personal brands focused on personal branding are annoying. I mean, I'm shocked I'm still Erik Deckers' friend. Heh."

Yeah, so are we.

Do's and Don'ts of Résumé Building

Writing a résumé is both an art and a science. There are people who devote their professional lives to résumé writing. If you can afford to work with one of them, it could be well worth it. You can also read books and blogs on résumé writing. In the meantime, here are a few do's and don'ts for you to consider:

- **Don't lie:** You'd think we wouldn't have to say this, but you'd be surprised at the number of people who act like they've never heard this at least once in their lives. Do not lie on your résumé! It's as simple as that. If you lie, you will be caught. Maybe not during the job search; maybe not even during your first year. But you will be caught. And when you are, things will most certainly hit the fan.

  In 2001, football coach George O'Leary left his job at Georgia Tech University to become the head football coach for the University of Notre Dame. His tenure there lasted all of 120 hours because he lied about having a Master's degree and lettering three times in college football; he never played a single game. Five days after he was hired, O'Leary was asked to resign—he was humiliated and derided across the country.

  Lucky for O'Leary, he was hired by the Minnesota Vikings the next year. He stayed in football until 2015, when he became a college athletic director. But you won't be so lucky. Your reputation will be ruined, and you'll be forced to take a job you hate in a field you detest, all because you lied on your résumé.

- **Don't pad your résumé:** Padding is the same thing as lying. If you earned a certification, don't say you earned a degree. If you were a cashier, don't make yourself sound like an accountant. If you unloaded trucks, don't say you were in charge of shipping.

- **Don't worry about fancy paper:** Back in the early 1990s, Erik bought an entire ream (500 sheets) of fancy résumé paper, and he printed dozens of résumés and sent them out. Not only did the fancy paper not help him find a job, but he only used 100 sheets and ended up recycling the remaining paper five years later.

  @kyleplacy: I was only 6 years old back then.
  @edeckers: Shut up. Stupid punk kid.

  White paper is more than adequate for your résumé. Still, don't use the cheapest copier paper you can find. Get something with some heft, like 24-pound or 28-pound bright white paper. You only need a few copies to take to your in-person interviews.

  Don't misspell anything: This is probably one of the most important pieces of résumé writing advice, although the fact that your résumé will be tossed because of a single typo also strikes us as one of the dumbest reasons to reject a candidate. Forget the years of hard work you've put in at other jobs, the Harvard MBA, the Medal of Honor, or the time you saved the president's dog from choking on a chicken bone. None of it matters because you accidentally missed the third "s" in "antidisestablishmentarianism."

Hard as it is to believe, some people are petty and small-minded enough to throw out an application—maybe even from the best person ever for the job—just because of a single typo. (Not that we're bitter or anything.) Don't give people that chance. Make sure your résumé is perfect and free of errors. Have a couple friends or even a résumé writing professional look over your résumé to ensure there's nothing that even the most officious bureaucrat could find wrong with it.

Having said all that, typos and mistakes make you look careless and not that smart. Even one typo can make you look like you don't care enough to carefully proofread your résumé.

- **Do keep it short:** Your résumé should be one page. Not two, not three, not five. One. Hiring managers spend an average of six seconds looking at your résumé, regardless of length.[2] They're most likely not going to look at a second page, and they certainly won't look at a third. So, it doesn't do any good to have a five-page résumé that details all your work accomplishments, including the time you were assistant substitute cashier at the Pick-N-Pay.

Remember, your résumé is supposed to get you an interview. The interview is where you will win the job. Use bullet points to highlight accomplishments, use complete sentences that start with "I," and avoid listing all your job responsibilities.

List your accomplishments instead. If you've been in your field for 20 years, including your internship is not as helpful as explaining how you led a company-wide initiative that saved $5 million.

Of course, if you're going for a position that requires an eight-page résumé (for example, a college president or corporate CEO), it means you're looking for the kind of position for which you will deal directly with an executive head hunter or search committee. If that's the case, your résumé is going to be long because of your accomplishments over the past 15–20 years; still, you shouldn't include your internship. You definitely need to work with a recruiter and résumé professional in this situation. (And if you get the job, can you hire us?)

- **Do show your accomplishments:** A six-item bullet list of your job responsibilities at each position is not nearly as impressive as an

---

2. http://business.time.com/2012/04/13/how-to-make-your-resume-last-longer-than-6-seconds/

explanation of how you solved a particular problem, managed a crisis, or helped your company save or make money. A bullet list of your responsibilities is not at all impressive; most people know what that kind of job entails. The goal of your résumé is to show how outstanding you are, not that you can come to work each day and perform your job description.

- **Do tailor your résumé for each position:** Remember, the résumé should be about how you can solve the company's problems, not get your own needs filled. Figure out what the company wants to accomplish by filling the position (that is, what "pain point" are you going to solve for them?), and then figure out what qualities the perfect candidate would have to solve that pain.

Tip

Most large companies now use electronic résumés and candidate software for their search processes. One of the functions of this software is to look for specific keywords in a candidate's résumé. If yours has them, you make the first electronic cut. If it doesn't, you're cast out immediately, never to be seen by human eyes. Check out the job description, figure out what keywords are going to hit the hiring manager's hot buttons, and use them. Make each version of your résumé fit the job description.

- **Do use action words and active voice:** Action words are things like "organized," "launched," or "managed." Phrases like "was responsible for" are weak and real yawners. Writing with authority and commitment shows drive and energy. Similarly, use the active voice, rather than the passive voice. Not only is the passive voice too wordy, it's boring.

Tip

Active voice is where the subject does something with the object: "I launched the campaign." Passive voice is where the object gets promoted to the subject position in the sentence: "The campaign was launched by me." If you can add "with zombies" to the end of your sentence and it makes sense, it's passive voice. Stick with active voice.

- **Do get creative, when appropriate:** If you're in the creative field, a creative résumé is expected. If you're in a conservative field, like banking or insurance, too much creativity is frowned upon. Feel free to let the creative juices flow if you think it will go over well. If you think it will cost you an interview, don't risk it.

Don't Rely on the Job Boards

If you're searching for a job, don't put all of your faith, time, and energy into the job boards, like CareerBuilder.com, Monster.com, and Indeed.com. Instead, you should spend most of your time following the steps we've discussed in the previous 14 chapters, as well as on informational interviews.

At the beginning of 2017, 6 million jobs—blue collar, white collar, manufacturing, technical, governmental, and so forth—were waiting to be filled,[3] the highest since the U.S. Bureau of Labor Statistics began tracking this information in 2000.

Although the numbers seem to vary depending on who you talk to, job boards can hold anywhere from just five percent to 25 percent of all new jobs. No one seems to have a definitive answer.

On the other hand, we've read that 70 percent[4] to 80[5] or 85[6] percent of all new jobs are landed through networking. One in 16 candidates hired come through referrals, while just one in 152 candidates hired come from a company's job postings or the other big job boards.[7]

We've heard from people who were laid off who said, "My new job is to look for a job." In essence, they're going to spend eight hours a day cruising all the big job boards, applying to every job they qualify for (and even some they're not), and they're going to do that until they're successful.

This is such a dreary way to search for a job, and it's going to push you into depression within a few weeks or push you out of the job search. Even though one in 152 company jobs get filled on job boards, that doesn't mean your odds are one in 152.

Instead, you're going to face hundreds of rejections, going weeks and weeks without hearing anything back, and eventually get so discouraged, you start watching daytime television and get emotionally invested in some of the worst shows ever. You also get so desperate for any kind of job, your anxiety will blare through so loud and clear during your first phone interview that you'll never get a second interview.

---

3. https://www.fastcompany.com/3066700/how-youll-search-for-a-job-in-2017

4. https://money.usnews.com/money/blogs/outside-voices-careers/2014/09/17/dont-believe-these-8-job-search-myths

5. http://www.recruitingblogs.com/profiles/blogs/80-of-today-s-jobs-are-landed-through-networking

6. https://www.linkedin.com/pulse/new-survey-reveals-85-all-jobs-filled-via-networking-lou-adler

7. http://www.globenewswire.com/news-release/2016/10/05/877340/0/en/New-Research-Shows-Only-One-in-100-Candidates-is-Hired-Referred-Candidates-Nearly-10-Times-as-Likely-to-be-Hired-as-Applicants.html?parent=877341

Back in 2005, Erik spent months and months cruising the job boards and applied to at least 300 different jobs. He finally lucked out and found one an hour from his house, but only after nine months of searching. And he experienced a lot of feelings of rejection and anxiety.

We're not saying you should ignore the big job boards completely. Just don't spend more than five percent of your time on them. Many companies post job vacancies just in the hopes of gathering a lot of candidate information, but they never fill the job. Others will automatically reject your résumé if you don't have the right number of keywords. Many of them are rigged to discriminate against older job seekers.[8] Go read the section on starting your own company in a few pages instead.

Otherwise, if you're going to spend eight hours a day on anything, spend it going to networking events and having one-on-one meetings with people (re-read Chapter 12, "How to Network: Hello, My Name Is..."), or starting your own company and focusing on that. Anything beats eight hours of rejections. If you do have to do an online job search, check out the careers sections of the companies you want to work for.

Try the Company Job Boards

For every job posted, an HR department can receive a couple hundred applications through the job boards. Remember, the average time spent perusing a résumé is six seconds, so yours isn't going to get much of a look. If 200–300 résumés come in through a job board for a single opening, and many of them aren't even remotely qualified, it's easy to see why applicant tracking software is popular.

Career sections of a website are a good idea for a company because they keep HR from being flooded with not-quite-qualified candidates. Companies are more likely to get applicants who are truly interested in the company through their Career links. After all, if you take the time to fill out an application, you should have more interest than the average job seeker who clicks "Apply to This Job" buttons like a telegraph operator.

If you want to keep track of what your target companies offer, you can try these steps:

- **Use Indeed.com**, a Google-like job board search engine, to save searches into an RSS feed.

- **Follow people in your industry** who are connected and will tell everyone about the openings in their industry or community. Create a

---

8. https://www.forbes.com/sites/nextavenue/2017/04/10/the-problem-with-job-boards-for-older-job-seekers/#5104d8d72075

private list for them on Twitter and keep track of them on TweetDeck. Some Twitterers do nothing but post jobs in their community, so it's a good idea to follow them.

- **Follow job opening blogs.** We've known people who had blogs about different job openings in the various agencies, firms, and large companies around their hometown. One such blogger featured people looking for jobs, listing their skills, experiences, and a brief explanation of why they should be hired.

- **Don't forget your own industry newsletter.** For example, several marketing newsletters and websites—Mashable.com, AMA.org (American Marketing Association), and MarketingProfs.com—aggregate marketing jobs around North America. Again, these are jobs that don't always appear on the big job boards, so you can be sure that not everyone is going to be finding and submitting an application.

Use LinkedIn to Bypass Job Boards

Although we've said not to rely on the job boards to find openings, the corporate boards are useful for discovering jobs that will never make it to the big boards. Even if you don't apply for those corporate jobs, they can still help guide your job search campaign.

One strategy is just to do a basic job search on the boards, see which companies are hiring, and then make connections on LinkedIn and Twitter with the hiring managers. Follow the strategy of connecting with them on LinkedIn and other platforms and demonstrating how you are a valuable resource. Have Twitter conversations with them, share blog posts and articles about their industry, and arrange an informational interview if they're in your city.

Another strategy is to find the companies you want to work for in advance and start connecting with them now, before they're hiring. Use the job boards, as well as their company's LinkedIn profile, to find out more about those companies as well as see their employees. Then connect with the people who are most likely to work in the department you want to work for. Make yourself a valuable resource to them. That way, they'll be more receptive to receiving your résumé and more interested in making sure they include you in their candidate pool.

Skip HR Altogether—Work Your Network

Of course, you can skip HR altogether. Going through standard HR channels can be extremely frustrating. It often seems like HR's only function is to say "no"; to find the best people for the position and then toss their résumés out; or to completely miss the point of what the hiring manager is actually looking for. It's not actually that bad, but sometimes the best way to land a new job is by talking directly to the hiring manager. This is where your network comes in handy.

Back in the 1980s and 1990s, Erik's father-in-law Carmon was the VP of a large multi-national corporation. He was in charge of all the sales staff for the entire company. He said that whenever he asked the HR department for sales candidates, they made sure every candidate met the minimum HR requirements: they could type 45 words per minute and had a college degree. Of course, none of them could sell or spoke a second language.

But because he was also the VP of the company, Carmon could add his own candidates to the process. Although these candidates couldn't always type and may never have gone to college, they spoke two or three languages, had sold multimillion dollar projects, and usually already had their own extensive network in their territories.

Guess which candidates Carmon hired. Every time.

Our point is, HR doesn't always get it right, so it's a good idea to have someone on the inside evangelizing for you. You don't need to connect with an executive to get that introduction to the company. It can be anyone. But the more people you know within an organization, the better your chances.

Another strategy—one that will help you avoid the masses who are still slogging it out on the job boards and in HR departments—is to follow your chosen companies in the news. Create a Google News Alert and keep an eye out for any mentions of expansion, new programs, new funding, or rounds of venture capital. Also watch out for promotions and departures by the people in the departments you want to work in. (You know they're going because you connected with them on LinkedIn.)

As you hear about these promotions and departures, start asking your contacts at those companies if they are making plans to add new positions. Make sure you're already communicating with them, so this isn't the first they're hearing from you. Just make it part of your regular conversation.

Also, be sure to blog about the news as you hear it. Retweet articles and give a shout out to your contacts who work for that company so they know you're talking about them.

Tell Your Friends

Most importantly—and we can't stress this enough—tell your network that you're looking for a job. That's what it's there for. If you've followed along with us through all 15 chapters, or if you skipped straight to this chapter because you're already using social media, you should already have an outstanding social network filled with people who would love to help you.

So tell them, "Hey everyone! I'm looking for a new job! I've been a _____ for the last few years and want to stay in that field." Be sure to mention that you're currently freelancing or started a business, if applicable, and that new clients are helpful, but you're also in the market for a full-time position.

Put it on Twitter, put it on Facebook, change your LinkedIn bio, and post your news anywhere else you need to make sure people see it. This is what your social networks are for! You've been building relationships with these people for months and years so you can help them and they can help you!

This is not the time for shame or false modesty. You need a job, you need to pay your rent or mortgage, you need to take care of your family. So tell people what you need. If you have a strong network, you'll be amazed at the number of people who will offer some sort of help, information, introduction, assistance, or just straight up hire you because you told your online friends, "I need a job!"

But it's not going to happen if you haven't been building your networks and forming relationships with people. So if you did skip straight here, go back to Chapter 1 and do everything we told you.

The Informational Interview

Okay, this is the big one! This section right here is worth the price of this book alone. It's one of the biggest but most productive secrets we've seen in action over and over, both in our own lives and the lives of our friends and readers. If you do this, you greatly increase your chance of finding a new job.

Erik had been living in Indianapolis for a year, working as the crisis communication director for the state health department, when he realized he didn't know anyone in the city other than his co-workers. He wanted to break into the marketing world, but also knew better than to try to beat his head against the fortress walls that seemed to surround it.

He didn't know anyone to ask for help, so he did something audacious: He emailed the CEO of the city's largest PR firm. In addition to being the CEO, Bruce Hetrick was also a columnist in Erik's local business newspaper, and they shared a lot of the same ideas and habits as fellow writers.

Erik introduced himself and asked if Bruce would be available to talk so he could learn about the industry and his new hometown. Erik was surprised to receive a reply a couple of hours later inviting him to Bruce's office. As they talked, Bruce told Erik how he got his start and what ultimately led him to open his own firm. He mentioned people Erik should talk to, traps to avoid, and what kinds of things he should be looking for and asking about.

Bruce said he was happy to meet with Erik because this was exactly how he got his own start when he moved to Indianapolis nearly 15 years before. He did informational interview after informational interview, always asking the same questions. After three months, Bruce had three job offers and enough freelance work to keep him busy 40 hours a week, all without applying for a single job.

He ended up running the PR department for a local hospital, which led to him starting his own agency a few years later. Because of what his own informational interviews led to, he always agreed to meet with people who asked for the same thing.

Bruce has since become a good friend to both of us, and we still meet on occasion to discuss writing, PR, and social media. But that initial meeting taught Erik all about the importance of informational interviews and what it can do for networking and personal branding.

If you go on informational interviews, here are five tactics to use.

- **Ask how the other person got started:** Many people forget this. Dozens of people ask us for the same interviews, but only a few have asked about how we got our starts. We learn through stories, so ask people to tell you theirs. You'll gain some valuable lessons about what to do and not do. Most people's lives can serve as morality plays to our own, so learn from them.

- **Take careful notes:** If nothing else, you look like you're paying attention. But more importantly, the people you talk to will interrupt their story to say "you need to speak to so-and-so." Write that name down and anything else they tell you about that person.

- **Never mention open positions at their company:** Otherwise, that sounds like the only thing you're looking for, and they'll feel like you took advantage of them. It may be tempting. You may even be the ideal fit for that position. But don't do it. If they mention it, just say, "I saw that on your website, but I didn't want to mention it because I didn't want you to think that's why I was here. My goal was to meet with you, not ask for a job."

- **Always ask "Who else should I talk to?"** This is the chance to tap into the expert's network. Ask her for an introduction to another person, as that will make your reaching out to him easier, and he's more likely to respond to you.

- **Stay in touch:** Some of these people, just by virtue of being influencers in their fields and the communities, could be powerful mentors and allies. Keep in touch with them, let them know what you're doing, and get together every few months. If the relationship progresses, make it a monthly thing. Ask them to be a mentor and learn as much as possible from them.

Information interviews work for one simple reason: People love to talk about themselves. If you're job hunting, and you call someone to talk about opportunities, there's a very good chance they won't want to talk to you.

If you're a freelancer, and you call someone about freelancing for them, they might want to talk to you. Fifty-fifty chance, tops.

But if you call someone and ask them to talk about themselves for an hour, they're going to all but leap at the chance.

So if you're looking for a job, try this before you spend much time on the job boards. And share your results with us on Twitter or an email to tell us how you did!

Start Your Own Company

This is the other big secret we like to share. If you ever find yourself laid off, the very first thing to do is start your own company, or declare yourself to be a freelancer, in the very field or role you want to be working in.

If you used to be a marketing copywriter, now you have a copywriting agency or are a freelance copywriter.

If you used to work in HR, you're now an HR consultant who helps fast-growing companies troubleshoot their hiring practices and creates processes that will help them manage their rapid growth.

If you used to be a corporate accountant, you are now a CPA and bookkeeper helping small businesses or serving as a part-time CFO for slightly larger businesses.

Erik was once asked by an out-of-work CFO for some career advice. Erik suggested he start a CFO practice while he was job searching, and the guy landed four clients in six weeks. Now he owns his own roving CFO business and makes more money than he ever did with his former full-time job.

Even if you never actually land a single client, you need to create this company or list this freelance position. Don't forget to change your social media bios, especially LinkedIn, to reflect this new role.

Unfortunately, especially during the recession of 2008–2011, plenty of hiring managers looked down their noses at people who couldn't find jobs. Never mind that there were hiring freezes throughout the country and unemployment was nearing ten percent in some industries.

These people assumed that something must be wrong with a job candidate who hadn't worked in six months. If that candidate lived in a city of 200,000 people and only a handful of companies ever hired for that person's particular role, and none of them had any openings, that wasn't a reflection on that candidate. It was a reflection of the economic climate. But that made no difference to the hiring managers who had forgotten their own good fortune.

Even though such hiring managers could have made a big difference in the life of that out-of-work candidate, and possibly saved him from bankruptcy, they would have rather hired the candidate who already had a job. Many still feel that way.

Even if it was just a freelance job, the working candidate was assumed to be somehow better than the out-of-work candidate, because they were keeping their skills and knowledge fresh.

So, if nothing else, start your own company and put it on your résumé so it appears as if you've been working during your layoff period. Set up a free website on WordPress.com and get some business cards printed.

However, with this new business, you have an "in" to companies that others don't. Remember when we said, "If you're a freelancer and you call someone about freelancing for them, they might want to talk to you"? Your odds may not be great, but with some cold calling and regular networking, you could find yourself sitting down with the manager who hires freelancers and contractors.

If you're lucky, you'll get some freelance work, and that can keep you afloat until you find a full-time job again. But if you're really lucky, the hiring manager will say, "You know what? It's too complicated to keep hiring you for freelance projects. Just come work for us." (We've known a couple people that happened to, so it's possible.)

But best of all, you may find that you're actually good at freelancing and can build a successful business out of the work.

When your freelance business turns into a real company and you're hiring people for open positions, that hiring manager who looked down her nose at you is going to show up, hat in hand, looking for a job, hoping you can toss her a lifeline. You're going to sit down and tell her the story about how you got to be where you are and why. And then you're going to toss her a lifeline, offer her a job, and help her provide for her family, because you're a good person.

How Can Our Heroes Find a Job Through Networking?

- **Allen (influencer)** spent 14 years working for an ad agency, amassed a large network with contacts in that world, and is a member of a professional advertising association. Because his aim is to stay in the industry, he needs to spend time cultivating and deepening his online relationships with people he is already connected to and making new contacts with other industry people.

If he's willing to move, Allen should also expand his network to the cities he would like to move to. Allen needs to connect with people in those cities on LinkedIn and Twitter, and start developing online relationships with them.

- **Beth (climber)** plans to become the chief marketing officer of an insurance company, but she prefers the one she is in. Still, this doesn't mean she is guaranteed to stay, especially because she's willing to switch jobs to move up the career ladder. Beth should focus on connecting with people who are one and two steps above her, as well as industry colleagues outside her company. The people a step above may eventually move up their own ranks or leave the company. If she knows early on about her colleagues leaving (they would tell her before the opening ever hits the internal job listings), she's in a good position to get her résumé into the hands of that person's manager, who is two steps above her current position. The same is true with connections in other companies.

- **Carla (neophyte)** is a former pharmaceutical sales rep who is out of work but trying to find a fundraising or program director position at a nonprofit. Not only should she connect with people who work for nonprofits, she should connect with their board members. These people often know about open positions before they are made public, and Carla can ask them for a direct referral. Although Carla may be a neophyte in terms of industry connections, she has a head start because many corporate pharmaceutical executives sit on boards of nonprofits.

- **Darrin (free agent)** is an IT professional who leaves his job every two or three years in pursuit of more money. He should communicate with IT workers in other companies via email and Twitter direct messages. These people often know about new positions opening before HR does and can alert Darrin to the fact, as well as pass his résumé on to their managers. The logical thing to do is to work LinkedIn and any industry discussion boards to tell people he's interested, but this could be a problem if Darrin's current manager is connected to him as well.

Job Searching Tips in 140 Characters

We asked our Twitter friends for some job searching advice, and these are some of the gems they shared with us.

Don't wait until you're thirsty to dig a well. —@CynthiaSchames

@ChrisBrogan is fond of saying, "You live or die by your database." —@edeckers

Follow companies in the industries where you would like to work. Then engage! Comment, reply, and retweet their posts. —@jlisak

Create a private Twitter list of businesses and influential people. Make intelligent connections with this group. Be subtle. —@LeilanMcNally

For recruiters, you are what you tweet. —@MaryBiever

Audit your social media footprint before a job recruiter does. —@MaryBiever

Learn about the company's culture by following the company and the staff, if possible, on Twitter. Decide if you fit or not. —@MaryBiever

Let your mail/UPS/FedEx person know you're job hunting. They may know of unadvertised opportunities. —@PamelaReilly1

Follow hashtags on twitter to find opportunities not advertised on job boards. —@sandrulee

Get active with network groups and set up meetings w/influencers in field of your choosing. —@IndyBethG

Be professional; a feed full of racist/sexist comments isn't a good thing to show a potential employer. —@McMullen_Greg

Your résumé is your first impression. You have 10 seconds to stand out from the crowd. Be sure the good stuff rises to the top. —@AprilLynneScott

Index

A

accomplishments, prioritizing, 23–24
active voice, 349
add-ons, 52
advertising via Facebook, 131–132
Akismet, 57
all rights, 324
Allen. *See* Influencer (Allen)
allied industries, writing articles for, 319–320
alternative text, 73
analytics. *See also* measurement
  Facebook Insights, 132–134
  Google Analytics
    benefits of, 232–233
    installing, 234
    setting up, 233–234
    terminology, 235
    viewing website performance, 235–237
  rules of, 245
  tips for, 245–246

anchor text, 70–71, 189
Anderson, Chris, 61, 70
anecdotal value, 33–34
Anglotopia.com case study, 49–51
anonymously Googling yourself, 185
applications with Twitter, 107–108
  BufferApp.com, 110
  choosing, 110–111
  Hootsuite, 109–110
  TweetDeck, 108–109
articles
  forwarding, 274
  writing
    for business newspapers, 318
    for hobby publications, 320–321
    for industry trade journals, 319–320
    for local newspapers, 317
    for mainstream magazines, 321
    for trade segment magazines, 321–322

authority posts, 64
authors, need for self-promotion, 17. *See also* publishing writings
automation stage (personal brand campaigns), 217–218
avatar/photo (LinkedIn profile), 79
average time on site, 235

B

backlinks, 71, 189, 231
Baer, Jay, 257–258
Ball, Lorraine (public speaking case study), 287–288
Beth. *See* Climber (Beth)
Bing searches, 199–200
biographies. *See* personal brand stories
Bitly, 243
Bledsoe, Jackie (writing case study), 314–316
Blogger. *See* Blogspot

blogging
  Anglotopia.com case study, 49–51
  benefits of, 43–44
  Climber (Beth), 71
  defined, 44
  domain names, buying/ hosting, 58–59
  effectiveness, measuring, 231–237
  Free Agent (Darrin), 71
  frequency of posts, 66–67
  Influencer (Allen), 72
  inspiration for, 59
  length of posts, 67–69
  Neophyte (Carla), 72
  photos, embedding, 158–161
  platforms for, 46
    Blogspot, 51–52
    choosing, 56–57
    Medium, 55–56
    Tumblr, 54–55
    WordPress, 52–54
  reasons for, 47–49
  rules of, 72–74
  search engine optimization (SEO), 64–66, 69–71
  setting up blog, 56–57
  subject matter, finding, 62
  terminology, 46–47
  topic focus, choosing, 59–62
  types of posts, 62–64
  videos, embedding, 161–162
Blogspot, 51–52
body copy, 71, 188–189
boldness, 12–14
bounce rate, 190, 193, 235
bragging, self-promotion versus, 12–14
brands, 6
BrandYourself.com, 201–202
breakout speaking sessions, 296
Brogan, Chris, 21
Brown, Sheryl (personal brand campaigns case study), 212–214

BufferApp.com, 110
business cards, handing out, 264–265
business newspapers, writing for, 318
buying domain names, 58–59

C

cameras, shooting videos with, 148–149
Carla. See Neophyte (Carla)
case studies
  Anglotopia.com, 49–51
  Anthony Juliano, 91
  Crystal Washington, 300–301
  Dave Delaney, 278
  Grammar Girl, 8–11
  @HaggardHawks, 99–103
  Hazel Walker, 260–261
  Jackie Bledsoe, 314–316
  Jason Falls, 345–346
  Lorraine Ball, 287–288
  Lynn Ferguson & Mark Tweddle, 149–151
  "Marketing Over Coffee" podcast, 179–180
  @MuslimIQ, 113–115
  Park Howell, 29–31
  Sheryl Brown, 212–214
  Starla West, 251–252
choosing
  blogging platforms, 56–57
  niche
    for public speaking, 289–290
    for published writing, 325–326
  themes for blogs, 57
  topic focus for blogs, 59–62
  Twitter applications, 110–111
  URLs for blogs, 57
civic groups, public speaking opportunities with, 295
classmates, connecting via Facebook, 122
click-through rate, 190

Climber (Beth), 19
  blogging, 71
  Facebook Causes, 123
  job seeking, 358
  launching personal brand campaign, 221
  LinkedIn recommendations, 88
  networking, 281–282
  P&T statements, 209
  personal brand stories, 27–28
  public speaking, 307
  publishing writings, 333
  social networking, 181
  Twitter usage, 118
coaches for public speaking, 287
college classes on public speaking, 286
comments on blogs, 232
company, starting own, 356–357
company information, finding while job seeking, 341–342
company job boards, 351–352
company profiles (LinkedIn), 352
competition, networking with, 258–259
conferences, public speaking opportunities at, 295–297
connections
  contacts versus, 87–88
  on Facebook, 122
  on LinkedIn, job seeking via, 338–342
  quality versus quantity, 228–229
contacts
  connections versus, 87–88
  inviting to connect on LinkedIn, 84–86
content marketing, storytelling in, 22
contributor copies, 328
conversion tracking, 233

copyright
  Creative Commons
    licenses, 156–158, 304
  publication rights, 324

co-workers, connecting via
  Facebook, 122

Creative Commons licenses,
  156–158, 304

cross-over topics in public
  speaking, 294

Crush It! (Vaynerchuk), 11

customized URLs on
  Facebook, 130

D

Darrin. *See* Free Agent
  (Darrin)

degrees of connectedness
  (LinkedIn), 77

Delaney, Dave (networking
  case study), 278

design of website, 192

development stage (personal
  brand campaigns), 214–215

digital cameras, shooting
  videos, 148–149

discovering
  niche
    *for public speaking,
      289–290*
    *for published writing,
      325–326*
  passion, 11–12

dishonesty, dealing with, 277

domain names, buying/
  hosting, 58–59

dues-paying, as writer, 329

E

education section (LinkedIn
  profile), 79–80

effectiveness, measuring
  blogging, 231–237
  Facebook, 239
  LinkedIn, 239–240

personal branding,
  243–244
  Twitter, 237–238
  YouTube, 240–242

ego surfing. *See* reputation
  management

electronic rights, 324

elevator pitches, 265–266

email contacts, inviting to
  connect on LinkedIn, 83–85

email introductions, 272–274,
  297, 338–341

email newsletters, 175–176, 266

embedding
  photos in blogs, 158–161
  videos in blogs, 161–162

employment, finding. *See* job
  seekers

employment section (LinkedIn
  profile), 78–79

encryption, 190

engagement, 227–228

entrepreneurs, need for
  self-promotion, 18

exposure, myth of, 329–330

F

Facebook
  advertising via, 131–132
  benefits of, 120–123
  Bing searches, 199–200
  Climber (Beth), 123
  effectiveness, measuring,
    239
  Free Agent (Darrin), 123
  Influencer (Allen), 122
  Neophyte (Carla), 123
  photo sharing on, 156
  professional pages
    analytics, 132–134
    benefits of, 131–133
    creating, 134–135
    profiles versus, 124–125
    types of, 122–123
  profiles
    creating, 126–127
    customized URLs, 130

  linking on LinkedIn, 83
  pages versus, 124–125
  privacy settings, 127–129
  rules of, 136–139
  terminology, 124
  tips for, 135–136, 139
  usage statistics, 119–120

Facebook Causes, 123

Facebook Insights, 132–134

Facebook Live, 147–148

face-to-face networking. *See*
  networking

Falls, Jason, 74, 345–346

fear of public speaking
  overcoming, 285–287
    college classes, 286
    private coaches, 287
    seminars, 286
    *speakers associations,
      287*
    Toastmasters, 285–287
  prevalence of, 284–285

Ferguson, Lynn, 149–151

finding
  company information
    while job seeking,
    341–342
  employment. *See* job seekers
  followers (Twitter),
    104–105
  local events via Facebook,
    123
  niche
    *for public speaking,
      289–290*
    *for published writing,
      325–326*
  subject matter for blogs, 62

First North American serial
  rights (FNASR), 324

first rights, 324

Fishkin, Rand, 151

Flash, 194

Flickr, 152–153

Fogarty, Mignon
  Grammar Girl case study,
    8–11
  podcasts, 177

followers (Twitter)
finding, 104–105
quality versus quantity,
228–229

follow-up, 274–276
forwarding articles/links,
274
of group networking
events, 266–267
referrals, 275–276
sharing opportunities, 275

forwarding
articles/links, 274
opportunities, 275

Free Agent (Darrin), 20
blogging, 71
job seeking, 358
launching personal brand
campaign, 221
LinkedIn recommenda-
tions, 90
networking, 282
P&T statements, 210
personal brand stories, 29
professional branding on
Facebook, 123
public speaking, 308
publishing writings, 333
social networking, 181
Twitter usage, 118

*Free: The Future of a Radical
Price* (Anderson), 61

freelancing, 356–357

freemium services, 201

Frei, Terry, 36

G

Giver's Gain, 252–255

Gmail accounts, 85

Google
search engine optimization
(SEO), 64–66, 69–71, 187
video usage statistics,
142–143

Google Alerts, 198

Google Analytics
benefits of, 232–233
installing, 234

setting up, 233–234
terminology, 235
viewing website perfor-
mance, 235–237

Google Chrome, 108

Google Dashboard, 201–202

Google Image Search, 199

Google Photos, 153

Google Picasa, 152–153

Google+, 170–171

Googling yourself, 183–185.
See also reputation
management; search engine
optimization (SEO)
anonymously, 185
Google Alerts, 198
Google Image Search, 199
social media footprint,
185–187
TalkWalker.com, 198–199

Grammar Girl case study, 8–11

group networking events. *See*
networking groups

H

<h1>, <h2> tags, 190

@HaggardHawks case study,
99–103

headlines, 70

Hetrick, Bruce, 318, 354–355

hobby publications, writing
for, 320–321

honesty
dealing with dishonesty,
277
importance in networking,
256
when avoiding meetings,
276

hooks in personal brand
stories, 24–27

Hootsuite, 109–110, 243

horizontal segments, vertical
segments versus, 321–322

hosting domain names,
58–59

Howell, Park
podcasts, 176
storytelling case study,
29–31

how-to posts, 64

HR department, avoiding,
352–353

I

implementation stage
(personal brand campaigns),
215–217

industry celebrities,
networking with, 257–258

industry groups, public
speaking opportunities with,
293–295

industry trade journals,
writing for, 319–320

influence, 229–230

Influencer (Allen), 19
blogging, 72
connecting via Facebook,
122
job seeking, 357
launching personal brand
campaign, 221
LinkedIn recommenda-
tions, 88
networking, 281
P&T statements, 208–209
personal brand stories, 27
public speaking, 307
publishing writings,
332–333
social networking, 180–181
Twitter usage, 117–118

informational interviews,
354–356

inspiration for blogging, 59

Instagram, 152, 154

installing Google Analytics,
234

interviews, informational,
354–356

introductions (email),
272–274, 297, 338–341

J

Javascript, 193
job boards
    avoiding, 350–351
    company boards, 351–352
job seekers
    job boards
        avoiding, 350–351
        company boards,
            351–352
    need for self-promotion,
        18–19
    networking
        asking for work, 353–354
        avoiding HR
            department, 352–353
        Climber (Beth), 358
        Free Agent (Darrin), 358
        freelancing/starting own
            company, 356–357
        importance of, 335–338
        Influencer (Allen), 357
        informational interviews,
            354–356
        LinkedIn company
            profiles, 352
        LinkedIn connections,
            338–342
        Neophyte (Carla), 358
        Twitter, 338
        warning about, 338
    résumés
        rules of, 346–349
        social media skills on,
            343–344
        writing, 342–343
    tips for, 358–359
Juliano, Anthony (LinkedIn
    case study), 91

K

Karr, Doug, 323, 342–343
keynote addresses, 297
Keynote presentations,
    technology tips for, 303–307
Keyword Position Monitoring
    Report Service, 243

keywords, 70, 188, 349
Klout, 243

L

launching
    personal brand campaigns
        automation stage,
            217–218
        Climber (Beth), 221
        development stage,
            214–215
        Free Agent (Darrin), 221
        implementation stage,
            215–217
        importance of, 211
        Influencer (Allen), 221
        Neophyte (Carla), 221
        rules of, 221–223
        unique ideas for,
            218–220
    public speaking career,
        291–292
Law of Anecdotal Value, 33–34
LinkedIn, 75–76
    Bing searches, 199–200
    case studies, Anthony
        Juliano, 91
    Climber (Beth), 88
    contacts
        connections versus,
            87–88
        inviting to connect,
            84–86
    degrees of connectedness,
        77
    effectiveness, measuring,
        239–240
    Free Agent (Darrin), 90
    Influencer (Allen), 88
    job seeking via
        company profiles, 352
        connections, 338–342
    Neophyte (Carla), 90
    personal branding features,
        83–84
    profiles
        education section, 79–80
        employment section,
            78–79

        photo/avatar, 79
        summary section, 79–81
        websites section, 80–83
    recommendations on,
        87–90
    rules of, 92–94
links, forwarding, 274
LION (LinkedIn Online
    Networker), 87, 90, 92–93
list posts, 63
listening to podcasts, 176
listing qualities for personal
    brand, 7–8
live streaming. See videos
local events, finding via
    Facebook, 123
local newspapers, writing for,
    317
The Long Tail (Anderson), 70
long-tail searches, 69–70

M

magazines
    contributor copies, 328
    simultaneous submissions,
        322
    writing for
        mainstream magazines,
            321
        trade segment
            magazines, 321–322
MailChimp, 175
mainstream magazines,
    writing for, 321
Mansfield, Heather, 61
"Marketing Over Coffee"
    podcast, 179–180
McGeogh, Dewey, 146
measurement. See also
    analytics
    of effectiveness
        blogging, 231–237
        Facebook, 239
        LinkedIn, 239–240
        personal branding,
            243–244

Twitter, 237–238
YouTube, 240–242
importance of, 225–226
rules of, 245
tips for, 245–246
tools
Bitly, 243
Google Analytics,
232–237
Hootsuite, 243
Keyword Position
Monitoring Report
Service, 243
Klout, 243
Website Grader, 243
what to measure
engagement, 227–228
influence, 229–230
quality versus quantity,
228–229
reach, 227
visibility, 229
Medium, 55–56
meeting new people, 262
meetings
avoiding, 276–277
setting up, 267–268
Meetup.com, 173–174
Microsoft Word, blogging
with, 73–74
Misner, Ivan, 252
mobile-first usability, 189–190
Monty, Scott, 178
musicians, need for
self-promotion, 17
@MuslimIQ case study,
113–115

N

name confusion, 196–198
navigation ease of website,
192–194
Neophyte (Carla), 20
blogging, 72
finding local events via
Facebook, 123
job seeking, 358

launching personal brand
campaign, 221
LinkedIn recommenda-
tions, 90
networking, 282
P&T statements, 209–210
personal brand stories,
28–29
public speaking, 308
publishing writings, 333
social networking, 181
Twitter usage, 118
networking. See also social
networking
avoiding meetings, 276–277
case studies
Dave Delaney, 278
Hazel Walker, 260–261
Starla West, 251–252
Climber (Beth), 281–282
Free Agent (Darrin), 282
importance of, 249–251
Influencer (Allen), 281
for job seeking
asking for work,
353–354
avoiding HR depart-
ment, 352–353
Climber (Beth), 358
Free Agent (Darrin), 358
freelancing/starting own
company, 356–357
importance of, 335–338
Influencer (Allen), 357
informational
interviews, 354–356
LinkedIn company
profiles, 352
LinkedIn connections,
338–342
Neophyte (Carla), 358
Twitter, 338
warning about, 338
Neophyte (Carla), 282
phases of, 261
follow-up, 274–276
networking groups,
261–267
one-on-one networking,
267–274
rules of
avoid selfish people, 258

competition networking,
258–259
Giver's Gain, 252–255
honesty, 256
industry celebrities,
257–258
safety tips, 257
serendipity, 279–280
tips for, 280–281
while employed, 279
networking dance, 262–263
networking groups, 261–267
faux pas to avoid, 264–266
follow-up, 266–267
meeting new people, 262
networking dance, 262–263
what to say, 263–264
new people, meeting, 262
new visits, 235
news article responses, 63
newsletters (email), 175–176,
266
newspapers, writing for
business newspapers, 318
hobby publications,
320–321
industry trade journals,
319–320
local newspapers, 317
niche
for blogs, choosing, 59–62
for public speaking,
finding, 289–290
for published writing,
creating, 325–326
Niece, Larry, 178
Nonprofit Tech For Good blog,
61

O

Obama presidential campaign
(2008), 205–206
objectives of personal
branding
boldness, 12–14
discovering passion, 11–12
relationships, 15–16

storytelling, 14–15
taking action, 16–17
O'Neill, Leslie, 319
one-on-one networking,
 267–274
  email introductions,
   272–274
  pick-your-brain meetings,
   270–272
  sales pitches, avoiding, 270
  setting up meeting, 267–268
  what to talk about, 268–269
one-time rights, 324
opportunities
  forwarding, 275
  for public speaking,
   292–293
    civic groups, 295
    conferences/trade shows,
     295–297
    industry groups, 293–295
  for publishing, 316–317
    business newspapers,
     318
    hobby publications,
     320–321
    industry trade journals,
     319–320
    local newspapers, 317
    mainstream magazines,
     321
    trade segment magazines,
     321–322

P

P&T statements
  Climber (Beth), 209
  creating, 207–208
  Free Agent (Darrin), 210
  Influencer (Allen), 208–209
  Neophyte (Carla), 209–210
page load speed, 190, 193–194
page views, 235
pages
  blogs, 52, 53
  Facebook
    analytics, 132–134
    benefits of, 131–133
    creating, 134–135

profiles versus, 124–125
  types of, 122–123
pages/visit, 235
passion, discovering, 11–12
passionate people, surrounding with, 34
passive voice, 349
payment for published writing,
 328–329
Periscope, 146–147
personal brand campaigns
  defined, 206–207
  launching
    automation stage,
     217–218
    Climber (Beth), 221
    development stage,
     214–215
    Free Agent (Darrin),
     221
    implementation stage,
     215–217
    importance of, 211–212
    Influencer (Allen), 221
    Neophyte (Carla), 221
    rules of, 221–223
    unique ideas for,
     218–220
  Obama presidential
   campaign (2008),
   205–206
  P&T statements
    Climber (Beth), 209
    creating, 207–208
    Free Agent (Darrin), 210
    Influencer (Allen),
     208–209
    Neophyte (Carla),
     209–210
personal brand stories. See also
 storytelling
  Climber (Beth), 27–28
  Free Agent (Darrin), 29
  Influencer (Allen), 27
  Neophyte (Carla), 28–29
  writing, 23–36
    hooks in, 24–27
    information in, 31–33
    Law of Anecdotal Value,
     33–34

prioritizing
  accomplishments,
   23–24
  rules of, 35–39
  surrounding with
   passionate people, 34
  what to share, 34–35
personal branding
  case studies
    Anglotopia.com, 49–51
    Crystal Washington,
     300–301
    Grammar Girl, 8–11
    @HaggardHawks,
     99–103
    Jackie Bledsoe, 314–316
    Jason Falls, 345–346
    Lorraine Ball, 287–288
    Lynn Ferguson & Mark
     Tweddle, 149–151
    "Marketing Over Coffee"
     podcast, 179–180
    @MuslimIQ, 113–115
    Park Howell, 29–31
    Sheryl Brown, 212–214
  defined, 6–7
  effectiveness, measuring,
   243–244
  email newsletters, 175–176
  via Facebook
    analytics, 132–134
    benefits of, 120–123
    benefits of professional
     pages, 131–133
    creating professional
     pages, 134–135
    creating profile, 126–127
    customized URLs, 130
    privacy settings,
     127–129
    profiles versus pages,
     124–125
  for job seeking
    importance of, 335–338
    LinkedIn connections,
     338–342
    Twitter, 338
    warning about, 338
  LinkedIn features for,
   83–84
  networking. See networking
  objectives of

boldness, 12–14
discovering passion,
11–12
relationships, 15–16
storytelling, 14–15
taking action, 16–17
podcasts
benefits of, 176–177
content of, 177–178
defined, 176
listening to, 176
producing, 178–179
requirements for, 177
in published writings,
322–324
qualities, listing, 7–8
personal posts (blogs),
professional posts versus, 63
philanthropy via Facebook, 123
Photobucket, 152–154
photos
benefits of, 152
Creative Commons
licenses, 156–158
embedding in blogs,
158–161
for Facebook profile, 127
Google Image Search, 199
for LinkedIn profile, 79
low-resolution, 193
search engine optimization
(SEO), 164–165
sharing sites, 152–153
Facebook, 156
Google Photos, 153
Instagram, 154
Photobucket, 153–154
Snapchat, 155–156
tips for, 168
traffic statistics, 141–142
Picasa, 152–153
pick-your-brain meetings,
270–272
plug-ins
defined, 52
page load speed, 193
podcasts
benefits of, 176–177
content of, 177–178
defined, 176

listening to, 176
"Marketing Over Coffee"
podcast, 179–180
producing, 178–179
requirements for, 177
positioning, 206–207. See also
P&T statements
poster sessions, 296
posts (blogs)
defined, 53
frequency of, 66–67, 231
length of, 67–69
types of, 62–64
PowerPoint presentations,
technology tips for, 303–307
presentations
technology tips, 303–307
types of, 296–297
presidential campaign (2008),
205–206
prioritizing accomplishments,
23–24
privacy settings for Facebook
profile, 127–129
private coaches for public
speaking, 287
product reviews, 64
professional pages (Facebook).
See pages, Facebook
professional posts (blogs),
personal posts versus, 63
profiles
Facebook
creating, 126–127
customized URLs, 130
linking on LinkedIn, 83
pages versus, 124–125
privacy settings, 127–129
LinkedIn
education section, 79–80
employment section,
78–79
photo/avatar, 79
summary section, 79–81
websites section, 80–83
Twitter, creating, 103–104
promoting speeches, 298–300
public speaking

benefits of, 283–284
case studies
Crystal Washington,
300–301
Lorraine Ball, 287–288
Climber (Beth), 307
email introductions, 297
fear of, 284–285
overcoming, 285–287
Free Agent (Darrin), 308
Influencer (Allen), 307
launching career, 291–292
need for self-promotion, 18
Neophyte (Carla), 308
niche, finding, 289–290
opportunities
civic groups, 295
conferences/trade shows,
295–297
identifying, 292–293
industry groups, 293–295
organizations for learning
college classes, 286
private coaches, 287
seminars, 286
speakers associations, 287
Toastmasters, 285–286
promoting speeches,
298–300
technology tips, 303–307
tips for, 301–303, 308–309
publication rights, 324
publishing writings
benefits of, 311–314
case studies, Jackie Bledsoe,
314–316
Climber (Beth), 333
dues-paying in, 329
exposure, myth of, 329–330
Free Agent (Darrin), 333
getting started, tips for,
326–327
Influencer (Allen), 332–333
Neophyte (Carla), 333
niche, creating, 325–326
opportunities
business newspapers, 318
hobby publications,
320–321
identifying, 316–317
industry trade journals,
319–320

local newspapers, 317
mainstream magazines,
  321
trade segment
  magazines, 321–322
payment for, 328–329
personal branding in,
  322–324
publication rights, 324
rules of, 330–332
simultaneous submissions,
  322

Q

qualities for personal brand,
  listing, 7–8
quality content, 189, 191–192
quality of followers, 228–229
quantity of followers, 228–229
Quora, 171–172

R

reach, 227
recommendations on
  LinkedIn, 87–90
recording. *See* shooting videos
referrals, 275–276
relationships, creating, 15–16
reprint rights, 324
reputation management. *See
also* search engine optimization (SEO)
  Bing searches, 199–200
  BrandYourself.com,
    201–202
  Google Alerts, 198
  Google Dashboard,
    201–202
  Google Image Search, 199
  Googling yourself, 183–185
  name confusion, 196–198
  reverse SEO, 195–196
  social media footprint,
    185–187
  TalkWalker.com, 198–199
  tips for, 203
  Yahoo! searches, 200

requirements for search engine
  optimization (SEO)
  current requirements,
    189–191
  previous requirements,
    187–189
résumés, writing, 342–343
  rules of, 346–349
  social media skills on,
    343–344
retweeting, 106–107
reverse search engine optimization, 195–196
round table discussions, 296
RSS feeds, 58
rules
  of analytics, 245
  of blogging, 72–74
  of Facebook, 136–139
  of LinkedIn, 92–94
  of measurement, 245
  of networking
    avoid selfish people, 258
    competition networking,
      258–259
    Giver's Gain, 252–255
    honesty, 256
    industry celebrities,
      257–258
  of personal brand
    campaigns, 221–223
  of personal brand stories,
    35–39
  of publishing writings,
    330–332
  of Twitter, 115–116
  of writing résumés,
    346–349

S

safety tips when networking,
  257
Sagal, Peter, 33
sales pitches, avoiding, 270
salespeople, need for self-
  promotion, 18
Salzwedel, Jack, 213
Scelzo, Tony, 258

screen capture videos, 149
search engine optimization
  (SEO), 64–66, 69–71. *See also*
  reputation management
  backlinks, 231
  Bing searches, 199–200
  current requirements,
    189–191
  Google Alerts, 198
  Google Image Search, 199
  Google secrecy, 187
  Googling yourself, 183–185
  influencing, 191–195
    quality content, 191–192
    with videos, 194–195
    website design, 192
    website navigation,
      192–194
  name confusion, 196–198
  for photos, 164–165
  previous requirements,
    187–189
  reverse SEO, 195–196
  TalkWalker.com, 198–199
  for videos, 162–163,
    194–195
  visibility, 229
  Yahoo! searches, 200
second rights, 324
second-degree contacts
  (LinkedIn), 86
selecting. *See* choosing
selfish people, avoiding, 258
self-promotion
  benefits of, 5–6
  bragging versus, 12–14
  defined, 4–5
  importance of, 5
  what it is not, 5
  who needs it, 17–19
seminars on public speaking,
  286
sending tweets, 105–106
SEO (search engine
  optimization). *See* search
  engine optimization (SEO)
serendipity, 279–280
setting up
  blogs, 56–57
  Google Analytics, 233–234

one-on-one networking meeting, 267–268

sharing
articles/links, 274
opportunities, 275
stories, 34–35

sharing sites
for photos, 152–153
Facebook, 156
Google Photos, 153
Instagram, 154
Photobucket, 153–154
Snapchat, 155–156
for videos, 144, 193
Facebook Live, 147–148
Periscope, 146–147
Vimeo, 145–146
YouTube, 144–145

shooting videos
with digital cameras, 148–149
screen capture videos, 149

simultaneous submissions, 322

Slideshare.net, 305

Snapchat, 152, 155–156

social media footprint on search engines, 185–187

social networking
case studies, Jason Falls, 345–346
Climber (Beth), 181
Facebook. See Facebook
Free Agent (Darrin), 181
Google+, 170–171
Influencer (Allen), 180–181
for job seeking
social media skills on résumés, 343–344
warning about, 338
LinkedIn. See LinkedIn
Meetup.com, 173–174
Neophyte (Carla), 181
Quora, 171–172
Twitter. See Twitter

Solis, Brian, 230

speakers associations, 287

speeches. See public speaking

starting own company, 356–357

storyteller's promise, 21–22

storytelling, 14–15. See also personal brand stories
blogging. See blogging
in content marketing, 22
Park Howell case study, 29–31

streaming videos. See videos

subject matter for blogs, finding, 62

summary section (LinkedIn profile), 79–81

T

TalkWalker.com, 198–199

technology tips for public speaking, 303–307

themes, choosing for blogs, 57

third-degree contacts (LinkedIn), 85

Thomas, Jonathan, 49–51

time on site, 190

titles, 188

Toastmasters, 285–287

Toon, Kate, 177

topic focus for blogs, choosing, 59–62

trade segment magazines, writing for, 321–322

trade shows, public speaking opportunities at, 295–297

transactions, 207. See also P&T statements

Tumblr, 54–55

Tweddle, Mark, 149–151

TweetDeck, 108–109

tweets
retweeting, 106–107
sending, 105–106
what to share, 111–113

Twitter, 95–96

applications with, 107–108
BufferApp.com, 110
choosing, 110–111
Hootsuite, 109–110
TweetDeck, 108–109
benefits of, 97–98
Climber (Beth), 118
effectiveness, measuring, 237–238
followers, finding, 104–105
Free Agent (Darrin), 118
@HaggardHawks case study, 99–103
Influencer (Allen), 117–118
job seeking via, 338
@MuslimIQ case study, 113–115
Neophyte (Carla), 118
profiles, creating, 103–104
rules of, 115–116
tips for, 116–117
tweets
retweeting, 106–107
sending, 105–106
what to share, 111–113
usage statistics, 96–97

U

URLs
choosing for blogs, 57
customizing on Facebook, 130

V

Vaynerchuk, Gary, 11, 151, 213

vertical segments, horizontal segments versus, 321–322

video résumés, 165–167

videos
benefits of, 142–143
content of, 151–152
Creative Commons licenses, 156–158
embedding in blogs, 161–162

Lynn Ferguson & Mark Tweddle case study, 149–151
search engine optimization (SEO), 162–163, 194–195
sharing sites, 144, 193
Facebook Live, 147–148
Periscope, 146–147
Vimeo, 145–146
YouTube, 144–145
shooting
with digital cameras, 148–149
screen capture videos, 149
tips for, 168
traffic statistics, 141–143
Vimeo, 145–146
visibility, 229
visitors to blogs, 232
visits, 235

W

Walker, Hazel (networking case study), 260–261
Wall, John J. ("Marketing Over Coffee" podcast case study), 179–180
Washington, Crystal (public speaking case study), 300–301

Weaver, Belinda, 177
Website Grader, 243
websites
design quality, 192
navigation ease, 192–194
viewing performance, 235–237
websites section (LinkedIn profile), 80–83
West, Starla (networking case study), 251–252
Wilholt, Marty, 178
Wilkerson, Mark, 255, 271
Wolder, Burt, 178
Word, blogging with, 73–74
WordPress, 52–54, 234–235
WordPress.com, 53
WordPress.org, 52
Writer's Market, 317
writing. See also publishing
writings
blogs. See blogging
for business newspapers, 318
for exposure, myth of, 329–330
for hobby publications, 320–321
for industry trade journals, 319–320

for local newspapers, 317
for mainstream magazines, 321
personal brand stories, 23–36
hooks in, 24–27
information in, 31–33
Law of Anecdotal Value, 33–34
prioritizing accomplishments, 23–24
rules of, 35–39
surrounding with passionate people, 34
what to share, 34–35
résumés, 342–343
rules of, 346–349
social media skills on, 343–344
for trade segment magazines, 321–322

Y

Yahoo! searches, 200
YouTube
effectiveness, measuring, 240–242
search engine optimization (SEO), 162–163, 194–195
video sharing on, 144–145
video usage statistics, 142–143